DATE DUE

SEP 19 1985

OCT 17 1985

NOV 9 1985

A View of 20th Century Fads

Follies and Foibles

A View of 20th Century Fads

**Andrew Marum and
Frank Parise**

Facts On File, Inc.
New York, New York ● Bicester, England

A View of 20th Century Fads

Copyright © 1984 by Facts On File, Inc.

Library of Congress Cataloging in Publication Data

Marum, Andrew.
  Follies and Foibles

  Bibliography: p.
  Includes index.
    1. United States—Social life and customs—20th century.
  2. United States—Popular culture.   I. Parise, Frank   II. Title.
  E169.M393   303.4'84   82-2355
  ISBN 0-87196-316-7
        0-87196-820-7(pbk)

Printed in the United States of America

10 9 8 7 6 5 4 3 2 1

To Little Maria, Andrew and Emily

O, the times! O, the customs!
                              -Cicero

——

ACKNOWLEDGMENTS

We are indebted to the following people, without whose help this book would not have been possible:

To Merle Thomason of Fairchild Publications in New York City, who made available files on an extraordinary number of clothing items—from the Eugenie Hat to the thong. She was unstinting in her help and could be counted on to clear up many an ambiguous point.

To Gordon Stone of the Metropolitan Museum of Art, who answered numerous questions on fashion. And to the staff of that museum's Costume Institute who made it possible to look at a wide range of harem skirts, hobble skirts, cloches and New Look gowns, to name but a few.

To the staff of the New York Public Library who were most helpful at all these divisions: the Microfilm Room, the Newspaper Collection, the Theatre Collection, the Dance Collection, the Picture Collection and the research librarians in Room 315. We would also like to thank the librarians at the Library of Congress, the Boston Public Library, the New York Historical Society, Columbia University, and the National Archives.

To Leah (Ping) Neuberger, ping pong historian, who made available an account of the early years of ping pong.

To Rod Faber and Ron Plotkin of the *Village Voice*, who allowed us to use the files of that newspaper which, since its inception in the 1950's, has provided a valuable source information on American social life.

To Franklin Mitchell, who did a most enlightening series of drawings.

To Richard and Kathy Lorr, who extended their hospitality in Washington, D.C., so we could examine pictures at the Library of Congress.

And, to all the people whose memories and minds we picked for their recollections. Among them were Damon Rosbach, Kevin Mullen, Glenn Blake, Carol Rayside, Dan Reed, Sandra Kidd; also, Carolyn Francis, Susan Cowan, Tim Dyer, Rhonda Sekur, Jessie Moss, Dolores Monaco, Jack and Dorothy Frost, Patricia Harris, Joseph and Susan Rella, Jerry Consolvi, Jory Marino, Chuck Proper, Jeff Golden, Al Minelli, Fran Weizman, Robin Smith, Larry and Jan Lorimer, Gordon Hayes, Allan Mendelsohn, Fr. Howard Stowe, Clark Judge, John Rofheart, Beverly Payne, Pete Tinnin, Mary Polyn, David Allen, Brenda Royster, Glenn Gumpert, Nancy DiBartolemo, Phoebe Fleitman, Devin Mahony, Lillian Dixon, Eleanor Muir, Frank Fenlon, Laura Mastrangelo, Veronica Bermudez, Carl Schuster, Dolores, Christian, Bethany Budde, Chip Stans, Eddie Holmes, Donna Valadisous, Tony Sepia, Kate MacEnulty, Susan Baldwin, Ed Gilbert, Richard Besant, Alice Katz, Brendon, Edmond, and Pat Plunkett, Kathleen and Richard Sheehan, Martha and Marriot Bates, Marijo Fox, Dick Krathwohl and Carole De Vito.

We are also most grateful to the following individuals for their photo research: Michelle Bagdis of the M.I.T. Museum and Historical Collections, George Bailey of Modesto Junior College Public Information office, Joel Berger of the University of Michigan University Relations Office, William E. Bomgardner of the Antique Auto Club of America, F.X. Blouin of the Bentley Historical Library, University of Michigan, Thomas G. Brennan of the Newport Historical Society, Mary Dunkle of the Penn State Public Information Office, Gerald Fischer of Steiff Plush Animals, Glenda Galt of the Brooklyn Museum Public Information Office, Nancy Hamilton of the University of Texas at El Paso News Service, Lisa Hirsh of the Massachusetts

Institute of Technology News Office, Lois Holman of the International Rose O'Neill Club, Donna Howard of the Wisconsin State Journal, Betty James of James Industries, Hugh Jenkins of the Lincoln (Nebraska) *Journal-Star*, Tom Larson of the *Daily Cardinal* (University of Wisconsin), Judith Linn, Jim Lubitsky of Oberlin College Public Information Office, Eleanor MacKey, Yvonne Marshall, and Linda Moot; C.J. Orlean of Gilley's, Dan Roddick of Wham-O Inc., Beth Smith of the University of Colorado Public Information Office, Baird Still of the New York University Libraries, and Dave Umberger; also, Dave Vandell of the *Capital Times* (Madison, Wisconsin), Bill Volpe of Arthur Murray International, Deborah Warrington of Memphis State University, Media Relations Office, Elliot Caplin of the Al Capp Estate and Emily Whelan.

We have wanted to mention all the people who have helped us, but there have been so many that we may have overlooked some. Any omission is unintentional.

Above all, we would like to thank Susan Cohan for a remarkable reading of the work, for her comments and suggestions, and for her just plain common sense wisdom in pointing out where sentences and thoughts were unclear. And, we are most indebted to our editor, Eleanora Shoenebaum, who encouraged us throughout this work at every stage, from inception onward.

Our wives Lisa and Linda were constantly there to help on any matter, at any time. Their constancy is more fixed than even the longest lasting of fads.

Needless to say, while the help was all these people's any shortcomings and errors in the text are the authors'.

Andrew Marum
New York City, 1983

Frank Parise
Brooklyn, 1983

PHOTO CREDITS

Contents

FOREWORD

Davy Crockett fur hats, hula hooping, goldfish swallowing, streaking, mah-jongg—all in their time attained faddish fame. But this narrative about fads in America since 1890 will also cover many a fad that didn't reach such legendary proportions: G-R-O-N-K-I-N-G, bed tucking, op talking, coughing ashtrays and ankle bracelets. Included here are dances like the turkey trot and the twist; toys and dolls like slinky and the kewpie and Barbie dolls; items of clothing like the hobble skirt and the Eugenie hat; stunts like peanut pushing and flagpole sitting; college students' fancies like pie killing and piano hacking; cartoon-inspired fads like the crazes for Betty Boop and Batman; fads sparked by magnetic personalities, like the Milton Berle makeup kits and the "urban cowboy" obsession that followed John Travolta's appearance in the movie of that name; as well as just plain unclassifiable fads like commemorative historic spoons and pet rocks.

What, then, might a fad be? Essentially it is a short-lived activity, item of dress, toy or whatever that gives pleasure. For giving pleasure is definitely the primary excuse for a fad's existence. Engaging in a fad is in no way necessary for survival. You don't need a fad like you need to eat, sleep or work. You manifest this or that fad merely for the fun of it. You don a Eugenie hat when that striking chapeau is the newest thing, or you gyrate lithely in your hula hoop when that is the latest activity, or you doff your clothes and streak when a dash in the buff to catch people's fancy (or their outrage) is the pleasurable new craze of the moment.

A fad, then, is the newest thing, and it is precisely this novelty that accounts for much of its popularity—for much of the collective imitation so indispensible for faddom. The animal dances were new around 1910, as were crossword puzzles in the 1920s, the Eugenie hat in the 1930s, zoot suits in the 1940s, frisbee throwing in the 1950s, skateboarding in the 1960s, mood rings in the 1970s and Rubik's Cube in the 1980s. And those are only a few of the best-known examples. Every faddish manifestation in this book—and there are more than 240—was once considered intriguingly new, and hence ripe for the excited imitation of great numbers of always-receptive Americans.

This has proved true even when the fad is not new at all. Some "new" fads turn out to be just old fads that time had forgotten reappearing in a slightly altered form or even in the same guise. King Tut paraphernalia, bicycling, roller skating and ping-pong all enjoyed more than one moment in the faddish sun. Even among nonidentical fads that recur, very extraordinary similarities can sometimes be spotted. Coming immediately to mind are the wild dances of 1911–13 and the equally uninhibited steps of the 1960s. The first, known as animal dances, featured steps like the turkey trot, the grizzly bear and the rabbit wrastle; while five decades later there was the twist, together with its many later variants like the shaggy dog, the jerk and the fish. Both were done by the young, repudiating the slow rhythms of the old (or should we say "the older"?). The deely bobbers of the 1980s echo the crazy beach hats of the 1950s, and yesterday's kewpie doll is today's smurf.

And although it is by no means the typical case, it also happens at times that fads become "institutionalized," reaching the point of being so commonplace that people no longer think of them as passing pleasurable fancies. This has happened with crossword puzzles, which—after provoking feverish faddism in 1925—are now just a humdrum staple of the daily newspaper. It has happened, too, with the tango and the Charleston; while no longer the stylish steps they were in 1914 and 1925, respectively, yet they are not at all unknown on today's dance floors. The same fate has befallen frisbee throwing, scrabble and ping-pong. These "institutionalized" fads will also be included in this account, but the description will focus on the period of their most overwhelming obsession—the time when they were truly fads.

Yet there are certain manifestations often considered somewhat faddish in nature that this book will not cover. It will not include diet fads, for instance, because this is a book about things that have given us pleasure, not about types of abstinence. Nor, following a similar rationale, will it include the various rages for substances supposedly having medicinal properties, like Hadacol or chlorophyll. The ancient Oriental medical practice, acupuncture, which flourished in the 1970's will, however, be considered because it attained a most extraordinary celebrity status.

Also, since this book is about things and activities, not about ideas, it will not cover any religious, quasi-religious or inspirational fancies or brief movements. Thus, Coueism of the 1920s will not be discussed, nor est, Hare Krishna or transcendental meditation. Nor will it discuss other briefly experienced phenomena—encounter groups, open marriage, primal scream theories—that have more to do with ideas than with tangible objects and activities engaged in purely for pleasure's sake. In short, these are matters both serious and beyond this book's ken.

But fads are serious business, too, even if they sometimes appear entirely frivolous. Although it is admittedly difficult to regard deely bobbers or beach hats with donkeys on them as weighty matters, fads *have* added a zesty tang to American life while evoking great controversy and damning harangues—and what could be more serious than that? Fads may not mirror American society in quite the same sense as our national elections, but they do unmistakably reflect it.

How so? Here are a few ways. In the 1890s men's interest in such passing fancies as hootchy-kootchy ties and bright lavender gloves demonstrated society's approval of men's being as colorful and as exotically dressed as women—something that wouldn't be seen again until the late 1960s, when the unisex trend revealed a similar national state of mind. Miniature golf caught on big in the 1930s. In a time of Depression, it was a really amusing activity that didn't cost very much. The courses, consisting of the craziest obstacles to go around and through, also allowed Americans to laugh at the genteel country club way of life (which few could then participate in). It was, all in all, a very fine release from tension. Or consider the early 1980s rage to look like a "preppie"—to don weejuns, madras jackets, shetland sweaters and anything else that could give the impression of money, tradition and good breeding. While hilarious from a certain perspective, from another perspective it was hardly funny at all, given its elitist connotations. Such a trend might have been understandable in the late 19th or early 20th century, when there was a lot more rigidity in American life, but in the early 1980s? The implications merit serious consideration.

And this is not all. Consider the extent to which the really big fads have created controversy. Many a citizen has always equated squelching a fad with saving the nation—so pronounced, apparently, is Americans' puritanical streak. Bicyclists were strongly condemned in the 1890s on the grounds that their activity did everything from threatening free enterprise to demonstrating that the Devil had been making inroads. Two decades later, when the animal dances came along, couples doing any of these steps in a dance hall were subject to every rebuke short of arrest, while young ladies performing the dances on their lunch hours were summarily fired. Then the tango (which, as a step, had almost nothing in common with the animal dances) excited the same kind of hostility, as did the Charleston in the 1920s. Indeed, when a Boston dance hall collapsed on an exuberant crowd of Charlestoners, killing many (a tragedy attributed to the stresses placed on the building's structure by such uninhibited physical activity), it was seen as proof positive that this dance had to go, not that a building was flimsily constructed.

Nor has this intensely negative reaction been evoked only by dance fads. People have also truly despised skateboarding, Bermuda shorts for men, bobbed hair, harem skirts, hobble skirts, mah-jongg, Pac-Man, ping-pong and streaking. Here were things purported to endanger health and morals, threaten relations between the sexes and undermine parents' authority over children.

Which may well account for fads' amazing vitality. It is stimulating every once in a while to tweak the solemn nose of established tradition and authority. This does, of course, beg the question—why should established tradition and authority be concerned with such matters as video games and hairstyles? Such concern, though, has always been abundantly evident.

This is not to say, however, that participation in a fad always connotes a flouting of authority. Sometimes the reverse is true. Authority sanctions the fad or looks on it benevolently, thereby increasing its fame. When the Big Apple became the rage in the 1930s, its popularity was multiplied after it was danced during a wedding reception in the White House. And some twenty years later the biggest sensation of one particular afternoon of presidential interrogation came when Dwight Eisenhower was presented at a news conference with a Davy Crockett fur hat.

More often, it is the unacknowledged authority figures like noted dancers and movie and television actors and actresses who create fads. This was true even in the 1890s, when concert pianist Jan Paderewski was so celebrated and so strikingly handsome as to provoke crazes for clipping off locks of his thick, blond hair or purchasing toy mementos of him. That sort of thing was to happen many times in the coming decades. The theatrical *Florodora* sextette created a rage, followed by the dancer Irene Castle, then the silent movie vampire Theda Bara, the tyke Shirley Temple, "Uncle Miltie" Berle, Elvis Presley, the Fonz, and on and on.

In almost every case magazines, newspapers, radio and television all helped to hype the newest obsession. The prominent figures participating in the fad first sparked the national imagination; publicity then fanned the initial interest into a full-blown faddish blaze.

Yet the origin of American fads goes beyond the styles of celebrated stars of stage and screen. Rather, fads since 1890 reflect greatly varied sources. Ping-pong, Oxford bags and piano hacking all came from England. Hula hooping can ultimately be traced to Australia. Bed pushing originated in Canada, canasta in Uruguay; and South Africa can probably take credit for telephone booth stuffing.

Even the home-grown American fads originated in a variety of ways. An engineer tinkering around in his basement came up with slinky, little suspecting what a merchandising bonanza it would become after World War II. Rather similarly, Walt Disney never expected that his Davy Crockett television series—much less Davy's famous fur hat—would take off (he was planning to make his profits by releasing the installments in Europe).

Goldfish swallowing got started because a Harvard University undergraduate wanted to show he had what it takes to beat his friends' dare and thereby win a crazy bet. But not all actions that ultimately produced a fad had such an explicit purpose. Dancer Irene Castle hadn't a thought in the world about creating any impression when she got her hair bobbed; she was simply recovering from an appendectomy and didn't want to be bothered with long tresses. Little did she realize that bobbed hair—a style she was the first to adopt, and so innocently—would become a flapper emblem of the Roaring Twenties.

Now, a word about the popularity of fads. It is sometimes maintained that fads are associated with the life-style of college students. This is a misconception. Fads affect every stratum of the population, even though a number of the best-known ones (goldfish swallowing, telephone booth stuffing, streaking, panty raids) flourished on university campuses. When you think of mah-jongg, however, you picture everybody playing it in the 1920s. And when you think back only a couple of years to Rubik's Cube, you don't picture a handful of scientific types coolly and rationally trying to solve the puzzle—you picture everyone from toddlers to senior citizens struggling with the darned thing, their attitudes ranging from eager curiosity to heated frustration.

Still, as popular as some fads have been, one does not get the impression that people were pressured into participating in order to conform. There have been so many fads that people could more or less pick and choose among them, participating in the ones that most closely suited their temperament. In 1965, for instance, one individual might have been doggedly collecting all kinds of Batman paraphernalia, while another might have been content just to iron her hair. In 1953 there may have been some people obsessed with Scrabble and others obsessed with 3-D movies; there may even have been a few flexible souls obsessed with both!

While a fad often appears out of nowhere, like slinky or the puka shell necklaces, the occurrence of some fads is not at all arbitrary. There could have been no hula hoops had it not been for the frisbee of the previous year. The enticing frivolity of the mood ring in 1975 paved the way for the improbable success of bottled money in 1976. The short-lived faddish game called pin-the-pillbox-hat would not have been possible without the success of the pillbox hat itself in the early 1960s. In the 1920s and 1930s, marathon flagpole sitting led directly into marathon tree sitting.

It also happens that a successful fad spawns an immediate variant, but the people participating in the spin-off don't regard it as a variant (that would be too dull) but rather as an entirely new fad. This happened, for instance, with the animal dances of 1911–13. The turkey trot gave way to the grizzly bear, the buzzard lope, the rabbit wrastle and the chicken scratch. As dance steps, they didn't differ all that much. Yet to the couples who could get away with doing them (for strict vigilance was usually exercised to prevent the dancing of such wildly immoral steps), each of the versions was the latest thing; the others were passé.

So it appears that this matter of fads can be complex, indeed. It is therefore surprising that the authors got one nearly uniform response when they questioned people about fads: "Well, I'm just not the type who's interested in fads." The implication was that taking part in fads made you less of a person. Fads are regarded negatively, the word *fads* itself sometimes being considered synonymous with frivolity. Fads are not thought to be on a par with having political opinions, advocating a certain sophisticated psychological school of thought or even discussing the most interesting places to visit abroad. Fads are seen as . . . well . . . demeaning.

But they aren't demeaning at all. Fads are something that we all participate in or that, at the very least, we all observe as fascinated spectators. Nor can the authors make any claim to a holier than thou posture with regard to fads. While once there was a time when Marum denied taking part in fads, this book made him realize the extent to which fads had crept unheralded into the very fabric of his life: the frisbee he tossed about in 1957, the Nehru jacket hanging in his closet in 1968, the mood ring he sported in 1975—to name only those that come most immediately to mind (but there were many, many others). As for Parise, he sloshed around on a waterbed, proudly showed his friends his collection of pet rocks, and played THUMPER.

In developing a narrative about these and countless other fads that have affected the lives of so many Americans during the 20th century, the authors selected the year 1890 as the book's starting point. This choice was based partly on the fact that the 1890s are the prelude to the 20th century and partly on the fact that during that period magazine and newspaper indexes often began to be compiled, thus enabling the researchers to observe what caught the nation's fancy.

While deely bobbers, video games and smurfs may soon follow Trilby's foot, the pickle and bed racing into faddish oblivion, this book will strive to recreate all the hoopla and frenzy surrounding the crazes of the last 93 years. Its aim will be to capture the eager acceptance, the bemused interest, the haughty disdain and the outraged alarm that greeted such phenomena. Most of all, this narrative about our fleeting obsessions and our reactions to them will be a glimpse at our national psyche in its more unguarded moments: revealing, appalling, puzzling, nostalgic—always amusing.

INTRODUCTION

When we enter American life in the 1890s, it is a time very much different from our own—so much so that it seems exotic.

As a typical example, consider electricity then and now. Flipping on a light switch today is about the most mundane of events. Not in 1890, though, when electricity was something extraordinary—a feat hailed by pageantry. Consider one celebration of electric power held at the Brookings, South Dakota Merchants' Carnival in 1890 before many an onlooker. Mrs. E.E. Gaylord, wife of the Brookings Electric Light Company's manager, appeared wearing a dress of incandescent lamps, complemented by a matching crown, also of incandescent lamps. These were connected to wires at the heels of her shoes, so that when she stepped on two small copper plates on the stage floor, the 21 lamps atop her head flashed on—an event so exciting that it was featured in *Scientific American*.

Of course, the 1890s largely predated the time of the automobile, with most Americans traveling by foot, some getting around with horses and a few using the most elaborate carriages. Then there appeared the "safety" bicycle—pretty much the same bike we know today (though lacking 10 speeds). This became the rage and generated extraordinary controversy. Although it seems hard to believe now, clergymen denounced the cyclists from the pulpit, declaring that they risked eternal damnation. Nor was that all. Proprietors of an amazing assortment of commercial ventures (ice cream makers, hatters, barbers, theater owners) joined in the critical clamor, protesting against this obsessive interest in cycling that was cutting into their business.

The 1890s were also the time of the great expositions, which drew countless families, some to see the most recent inventions and the reconstructions of old palaces built to scale and others just to say that they had attended the latest exposition. Many regarded it as their most interesting journey of the year. In the 1893 Chicago World's Fair, the massive Main Exhibition Building alone had 27 restaurants and 115 dining rooms to cater to the crowds of novelty seekers.

For those who sought their adventure a bit closer to home, there were the stereopticon viewcards, which brought Yellowstone's geysers, Jerusalem's gypsies, Germany's castles and the wonders of many another exotic land right into American living rooms. In a similar vein, people gathered to view magic lantern shows, consisting of transparencies projected onto blank surfaces. The device's manufacturer even marketed it as a money-making venture, proposing that crowds of paying customers would eagerly flock to view scenes of Paris, London, Rome or even the Chicago stock-

yards. But something more tangible than a quick glimpse of faraway places was also available. Historic spoons commemorating notable events in various American regions became big in the early 1890s, providing collectors with mementos of everything from Paul Revere's ride to the Salem witch trials.

Idealized women accounted for a goodly share of the 1890s fad activity. First and foremost, there was the Gibson Girl—a raven-haired embodiment of every man's dream. This striking lovely, first seen on the pages of Charles Dana Gibson's cartoons, soon graced such diverse items as soup bowls, corsets and wallpaper. In contrast to the proper and genteel Gibson Girl, there was the heroine of George DuMaurier's novel *Trilby*, a saucy beauty whose "lovely and slender" foot sparked a brief craze. A brand of sausages was reportedly made in the shape of Trilby's foot, as were ice cream cones. The interest in these fictitious females had a real-life counterpart in the rage for music hall skirt dancers— naughty girl performers who kicked up their heels exuberantly, swishing their skirts to tantalizing heights.

Despite the tendency to place idealized women on a faddish pedestal, during this decade many average American women ceased wanting to be primarily fashion plates. Although long, long skirts continued to be worn, they were clearly on the way out for reasons of both comfort and health. Health? More and more voices were being raised against these skirts, citing how unhealthy they were because they dragged along city streets, picking up dust and—even worse—horse manure. Long skirts, as a result, got the nickname of "septic skirts."

Yet the 1890s were not a time of social revolution in attitudes regarding sex roles (or, for that matter, in attitudes regarding any grave question). Little girls were conditioned to have "feminine" interests, and little boys were conditioned to have "masculine" interests. According to the *Art of Entertaining* (1892), by Mrs. M.E.W. Sherwood, dolls should be used to teach little girls that their role was to care for families. When a little girl asked her mother what her doll should wear, Mother was supposed to answer, "You must decide; you know Dolly best." And on the masculine side, according to advice in an 1899 issue of *Ladies Home Journal*, birthday parties for boys had to be painstakingly planned, even down to the correct ice cream, in order to convey the proper image. The ice cream cake should be sculpted in the form of a fort, displaying cannons and guns and decorated with flags. The social revolution, it seemed, would have to wait.

In spite of these stereotypically traditional standards for the upbringing of boys, contrasting sentiments could be seen to stir among grown men at mid-decade. Lavender gloves made their appearance, together with the madly striped hootchy-kootchy tie.

3

Yet the fad represented only a brief fling at sartorial elegance, with men's attire quickly subsiding once again into the more somber and sedate styles.

Even in the 1890s, though, the modern world was inevitably encroaching upon the American way of life. The office typewriter was perfected during that decade, as was the industrial time clock—symbolic of a future way of life governed by the punching of a time card. The adventure of the remote American wilderness ended with the closing of the frontier, and the romantic beasts that formed so large a part of this country's heritage were being wiped out. A *Scientific American* editorial of 1890 bemoaned the wholesale slaughter of the bull moose, the caribou, the Rocky Mountain goat, the mountain sheep, the elk and the antelope—a consideration that led Theodore Roosevelt to set aside millions of acres for national parks in the early 1900s. (The exploits of Roosevelt were, in the coming decade, to inspire a fad for a cuddly stuffed animal then called the Roosevelt bear—now more generally known as the teddy bear.)

The automobile, too, first came upon the American scene toward the close of the decade. But while today's car conjures up images of air pollution, crowded freeways and purposeful haste, the car of the 1890s (then known as the mobe, the tomo, the mocle and the motorig) spawned a couple of leisurely and strikingly purposeless practices. Banned from the public roads, the autos were left to negotiate intricate obstacle courses as a form of entertainment on estate grounds of the very rich. The vehicles—like majestic horses not much earlier—were then adorned with wreaths of flowers and paraded before fascinated spectators.

Thus, while the modern world was beginning to rear its ugly head, even the most technologically advanced of the 1890s fads still retained their quaint and special flavor—as did life itself.

Automobiles were to be put to more practical uses as America moved into the first decade of the new century, but fads of a fairly exotic character still prevailed. The appeal of stereopticon viewcards and magic lantern shows continued into the early 20th century, and the Gibson Girl was not to lose her charm until 1910.

The Gibson Girl was, in fact, soon to be joined in Americans' fancy by a sextette of prim and pretty lovelies from the sensational musical *Florodora*. While the public's interest centered upon the actresses in the musical itself, the fad also spread to items of clothing and even to *Florodora* cigars.

While some women of the period emulated the slightly provocative yet traditionally garbed *Florodora* girls, others' tastes turned to more bizarre adornments. The snake look slithered briefly across the fashion scene in the opening year of the century, with hairstyles, hair ornaments, dresses and rings all taking on a serpentine tone.

What bicycling had been in the 1890s, ping-pong was in the very early 1900s—the participation sports fad of the era. The frenzied interest in the pastime was quickly termed "ping-pongitis." The craze prompted many a lively competition and spawned a spate of doggerel ping-pong verse in newspapers of the day. A new medical ailment—"ping-pong ankle"—was even attributed to the activity by its more diehard detractors. What they might have been really objecting to was the passing of the pre-eminence of luxurious lawn tennis, and maybe of high society, too

The popular interest in glimpsing distant places through the stereopticon viewers and magic lantern projections or in recalling them by collecting commemorative historic spoons took still another turn in the first decade of the 20th century with the advent of the picture postcard. The picture postcard—now a commonplace staple near any scenic attraction—is one of many fads that later became "institutionalized." But in their initial years, the lavishly colored cards were a truly torrid craze, with some aficionados amassing collections numbering in the tens of thousands. What's more, it was easy to do, which showed another characteristic of the new century, things would be easier to do. There would be no bumbling around in trying to fit a stereoscopic view in a holder in just the right way. Technology was moving ahead.

One especially quaint pursuit in vogue during the period was pyrography—the craft of sketching designs on nearly anything and everything with a heated platinum needle. Playing card cases, magazine stands, bread plates, pin boxes, hand mirrors, pen wipers—all could be painstakingly and elaborately adorned by an artist of steady hand and patient temperament. Yet, the fact that pyrography passed so completely by 1905 indicated that people just weren't interested in taking part in such old-fashioned active handiwork. They'd rather get themselves down to the most modern "Picture Palace," where they passively could watch some sexy or exciting scenes.

The close of the first decade of the 20th century was marked by a waning of the 19th-century influence upon American life and fads. The country was poised at a turning point. The tone of the time was about to shift toward the lively and carefree; the prim and proper fashions, the sedate pastimes were about to take a decidedly uninhibited turn.

STEREOPTICON VIEWS AND VIEWHOLDERS, HAND-HELD (1850–1910)

Stereopticon viewcards were not new to the America of the 1890s, as for instance, the fashionable drawings of the Gibson Girl (see GIBSON GIRL) or the safety bicycle (see BICYCLING) were. Yet these unusual picture cards—which you never see anymore except on a visit to a museum or a library—were still very popular then, a popularity that only finally died around 1910. Moreover, to understand life at the beginning of the 20th century, you cannot ignore the stereopticon.

Stereopticon views and the stereopticon viewholder, which were essential items for diversion in the parlor of 1905, made for many a lively afternoon or evening and were also a source of both instruction and pleasure. Their object was to pull the viewer into the picture, just like the 3-D movies of the 1950s, which were a further step in the sophistication of these stereoscopic principles (see 3-D). Just as the 1950s moviegoer felt himself or herself shot at by arrows, burning in hot oil or bitten by rattlesnakes, a man or woman of the late 19th or early 20th century could feel part of the horror of the San Francisco earthquake (1906)—the advertisements for these viewcards dramatized "Ruined Palaces on Knob Hill," "Views Along the Devastated Waterfront" and "The Remains of Magnificent Houses"—or think he or she was being lulled by a lazy boat ride under tall tropical trees in the Everglades.

Take "Gypsies Outside the Walls of Jerusalem,"

one of the very popular Holy Land Series. The viewcard itself is dual: In both the left and right frames, you would see gypsies tending a fire, entering a tent and standing. But when you put it into the stereopticon viewholder and adjusted the focus, you would eventually see a single, almost lifelike image, with a sense of both depth and distance, lacking in the conventional photographs of that time. When the photograph was originally taken, a double camera was needed to create this effect, just as in the 3-D movies of the 1950s two projectors were needed to give depth and to pull the viewer into the picture.

The stereopticon was invented in 1832 in England and had been in use in America since 1850. Stereoscopic cameras were used to photograph the American Civil War. You could get a stereopticon viewholder for as little as 12 cents in 1900. As for the viewcards themselves, you could get 100 viewcards for 85 cents. These cards were generally 7 inches long and 3½ inches high and were available by the thousands.

New in the 1890s was the introduction of comic pictures, which happened about the same time as the introduction of the first Sunday funnies (1896). This seemed to intrigue nearly everybody, with people eager to buy the adventures of the Master and the French Cook, the high jinks taking place when the wife was away. But there were also popular cards entitled "The Horrid Mouse," "Eavesdroppers Eavesdropped" and "One Stick of Gum for Two."

This was the amusing side of stereopticon views, but stereopticon pictures could also be used for instruction, about foreign places and natural attractions, and also to keep people up on contemporary news. There were thus stereopticon views of the geysers of

A stereopticon and a stereroscopic card.

A stereoscopic view of a ballroom scene at the turn of the century

Yellowstone Park, whaling expeditions, the turf cottages of Ireland and castles in Germany. When the Russo-Japanese War came along in 1905, there were views of soldiers on the march and in the trenches.

There were also stereopticon cards of the many novelties and interests of the day: of Robert Peary's expeditions to the Arctic, of people riding the new safety bicycles or even those "electric cars," or "mobes," which were coming along about that time (see ARCTIC FLEAS, BICYCLING, AUTOMOBILE OBSTACLE COURSES).

Stereopticon viewcards were big business, with their own company towns. In 1905 the printers, cutters and pasters of Littleton, New Hampshire worked on over 100,000 stereopticon views—all for Kilburn Brothers. When comic stereopticon cards were produced, they required indoor sets with painted backdrops, which necessitated more specialized work.

The first decade of the 20th century saw the final years of the stereopticon and its viewcards. The cards themselves were often used as "giveaways." It was possible to collect a "library of World Tours of Original Views" just out of cereal packages.

It has been maintained that some of these free cards were shabbily made and thus contributed to the decline of the stereopticon and the stereopticon viewcard. At the same time, the stereopticon had to contend with newer novelties like the Kodak "brownie" (1900), which allowed people to create their own pictures instead of being limited to the laborious, somewhat artificial procedure of buying ready-made slides and putting them into the stereopticon. Moreover, picture postcards became voguish in the early 1900's (see PICTURE POSTCARDS). Also new were the "picture palaces," where people could spend an exciting time watching movies. Not to mention the "horseless carriages," which might actually be able to take them to those distant places that they had known only from viewcards.

Also contributing to the viewcards' decline was a mechanized stereopticon, in which the views were turned into transparencies and could be projected—sometimes greatly enlarged—onto any blank screen. This was known as the magic lantern (see MAGIC LANTERN), and it was very popular. Nothing like stereoscopy would come back in a big way until 3-D came along in 1952, and people were transported to wildest Africa while watching the movie *Bwana Devil*.

In any event, by 1911 stereoscopic viewcards were really a thing of the past. Also the picture postcard, which needed no special viewer to show the glories of a scene, came along to replace the dual stereoscopic perspective (see PICTURE POSTCARDS).

GIBSON GIRL
(1890s [Heyday]–1910)

Before there was a *Florodora* girl, a musical comedy beauty who flourished in 1900 (see FLORODORA FANCIES), there was the raven-haired, pompadoured Gibson Girl of magazine cartoons. Before there were movies, before the nationally known attractions of the long-haired vampire Theda Bara (see VAMPIRE THEDA), before the "It" girl with the sensual red hair, Clara Bow, before the pin-up girls of World War II, and before Marilyn Monroe, there was the Gibson Girl. Cartoonist Charles Dana Gibson had created a beauty, whose face was familiar for over two decades and who almost became a model for American culture through her influence on all the beauties who followed her.

Indeed no one can say that Charles Dana Gibson, the cartoonist, was forgotten in his own lifetime. In one dinner engagement he attended, he had the satisfaction of eating the soup course out of a Gibson Girl bowl with a Gibson Girl spoon.

The Gibson Girl was nearly every man's dream of a dancing partner and a golfing and rowing companion. The trouble was that this black-haired beauty existed only on paper on Charles Dana Gibson's drawing board.

It has usually been maintained that Gibson used two models for the Gibson Girl: his sister Josephine Gibson Knowlton and his wife Irene Langhorn Gibson. In fact, Mrs. Knowlton later characterized her brother's idealization of the Gibson Girl as follows: "She was utterly American . . . was a little ahead of her time, definitely athletic, certainly did not drink or smoke."

The Gibson Girl first ran as a serialized cartoon in *Life* magazine in 1890, when Gibson was beginning to lose hope that anyone would ever be interested in his creation. *Interested?* By 1900 the typical home was filled with Gibson Girl china plates, saucers, souvenir spoons, tablecloths, pillows, ashtrays, matchboxes, fans and umbrella stands. And in keeping with a well-known Gibson cartoon, bachelors decorated their rooms with Gibson Girl wallpaper.

With her pompadoured look and her long gowns, the Gibson Girl typified the Gay Nineties in almost the same way that the "flapper" cartoons of young women with bobs and short skirts by cartoonist John Held Jr. typified the 1920s. The author Sinclair Lewis would call her "The Helen of Troy and Cleopatra of her day."

People were just riveted by the carefully drawn pen-and-ink Gibson Girl, and the cartoon captions were witty, as well. For instance, there was the cartoon of the Gibson Girl and her father, who was jealous of young suitors' interest in her. He therefore hung a sign around her: "Disinherited, Selfish, Bad-Tempered, and Unreasonable," which was designed to ward them off (the Gibson Girl, of course, was none of those things). Then there was the one of the Gibson Girl reading to a young man in a stopped rowboat; the caption read: "Advice to students. Be read to. It saves the eyes for better things." Or the one in which the Gibson Girl and a young man, attended by a caddy, are on the golf course. The caption read: "Is a Caddy Always Necessary?" There were also cartoons of the Gibson Girl on ocean cruises, at society dances, at the opera, etc. A Gibson Girl fan could not only see the cartoon in *Life* magazine, but there were also a number of books of cartoons about the Gibson Girl, among them *Pictures of People* (1896), *Sketches and Cartoons* (1898), *The Social Ladder* (1902) and *A Widow and Her Friends* (1904).

The Gibson Girl definitely set the fashion. She was shown wearing a sailor suit at the beach, so sailor suits became the rage. There were Gibson Girl corsets, shirtwaists, skirts, shorts and hats. The Gibson Girl was also seen cycling on one of those new safety bicycles, which also showed that she was attuned to the newest vogue (see BICYCLING). However, there were more pictures of the Gibson Girl on a bike than climbing on the seat of a new electric auto; indeed, since the Gibson Girl wasn't terribly interested in the "horseless carriage," some automobile manufacturers even came up with a female whom they called the "Automobile Girl," but whose image never caught on like the Gibson Girl.

In the hit musical of 1900, *Florodora*, there was even a song about the Gibson Girl. One of the members of the Florodora sextette, who is dressed to look like the Gibson Girl, is asked, "Oh, tell me, pretty maiden, are there any girls in life like you?" She answers, "Kind sirs, there are a few." As late as 1906 songs about the Gibson Girl were still heard.

The fancy for the Gibson Girl lasted well into the first decade of the 20th century. For a very short time in the 1890s, there was a passing interest in Trilby, the heroine of a novel by George DuMaurier (see TRILBY'S FOOT), because she had a most provocative way of displaying herself. Of particular interest was Trilby's foot, whose shape was copied by shoemakers, ice cream makers and sausage makers. The craze for Trilby, however, was really brief. The Gibson Girl remained preeminent.

When the Gibson Girl faded in importance around 1910, it was perhaps because a figure like the very comely but very proper Gibson Girl seemed somewhat irrelevant. Women were taking part, for instance, in really sensual dances like the turkey trot and the grizzly bear, which were unheard of in the 1890s (see TURKEY TROT AND OTHER ANIMAL DANCES). The Gibson Girl would never have dreamed of doing such things.

And finally, when Theda Bara came along in silent movies in 1915 in the sexy film *A Fool There Was*, a whole new conception of beauty had arrived to take the Gibson Girl's place. She was vampire Theda, who was not prim at all but continually suggestive; and unlike the Gibson Girl, who lived in a world of family, friends and social engagements and had to be very proper, this siren was wild, from her long tresses on down. The Gibson Girl had lasted a long time, but her time had now passed.

Charles Dana Gibson also came up with a Gibson Man, but he was never to match the great popularity of his female counterpart.

believed that witches used to roam before the famous trials in the late 17th century.

When the spoons' popularity became obvious, spoon manufacturers openly competed with each other to come up with designs that tourists might like. For instance, Portland, Maine not only had its Hiawatha spoon but also a Miles Standish spoon, a Priscilla Alden spoon and a Henry Wadsworth Longfellow spoon. Washington, D.C. had a spoon depicting the White House and the Washington Monument.

There were many others besides. Most, however, were New England spoons. Though this nation was becoming much more populous, and the frontier was closing, it took a long time for the cities of the West to really gain such recognition as was typically commemorated on the historic spoons.

Although commemorative historic spoons continued into the 20th century (there was, of course, a teddy bear spoon when teddy bears were the rage; see TEDDY BEARS), historic spoons' big moment was the 1890s.

COMMEMORATIVE HISTORIC SPOONS (Early 1890s)

The *Scientific American* of May 23, 1891 called it "the latest fad." From Maine to Oregon babies could now be born not only with silver spoons in their mouths but with ones that recorded something important about the city in which they were born. Or the historic spoons could be used for stirring a drink or eating soup. They could also just be kept in a case by historic spoon collectors, which is what happened most of the time.

During an era when people amused themselves by looking through a stereopticon, taking a ride in a carriage (perhaps they even owned one of those new safety bicycles; see BICYCLING) or going to the latest glorious civic exposition, commemorative historic spoons were something new and exciting. By traveling coast to coast yourself, you could get enough spoons to set an entire banquet table. Or someone might bring you back one as a present.

From New Orleans you could get a spoon depicting cane stalks, a crane and a cotton bale. From Portland, Maine you could get a Hiawatha spoon. From Boston you could get a spoon commemorating Paul Revere's ride, and from Lynn, an industrial town near Boston, a spoon showing Molly Pitcher and her black cat. From Pittsburgh, you could get a spoon with a picture of an oil derrick and a gas well. And those were only a few of the many spoons of the year.

The first late 19th-century historic spoon was said to be one made for Salem, Massachusetts, where many

Commemorative spoons of George Washington, the Liberty Bell, and Hiawatha

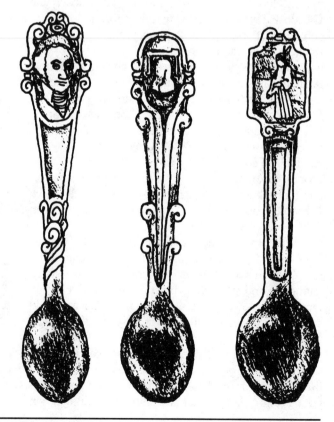

BICYCLING
(1890s; Revival, 1970s)

The watchmakers and jewelers say they are nearly ruined: that all pin money which the young people saved formerly with which to buy watches and jewelry now goes for bicycles . . . the tailor, the hatter, the bookseller, the shoemaker, the horsedealer, and the riding master all tell similar tales of woe. The tailor says that so many men go about half the time in cheap bicycle suits that they do not wear out their good clothes half as rapidly as formerly . . . the bookseller says people who are rushing about on wheels, days, nights, and Sundays, no longer read anything, and his business has become practically worthless.

—Contemporary newspaper article,
cited in *Scientific American* (1896)

A cyclist and his velocipede in the 1880s

It is hard to think of bicycling as a fad; bicycles are as familiar to us as the food we eat. Yet in the 1890s bicycles were a great conversation piece; to have a bicycle and to talk about bicycling was to be in fashion and to experience the greatest of pleasures. Mothers complained that their daughters wanted to get a bicycle for their birthdays or for Christmas rather than fashionable clothes or fancy furnishings for their rooms; many a newly wedded couple wanted a bicycle among its first gifts.

Nor were bicycles inexpensive. They cost between $50 and $150—not that much different from the cost today. But they were something people definitely wanted to own. To have an opportunity to take a relaxing trip from town to town, from city to city or through the countryside was nice, but bicycles were also very practical. Doctors used them to make housecalls; teachers and students used them to get to school; salesmen used them; house painters used them; mechanics used them. A bicycle was less expensive than buying a horse, keeping it fed and sheltered, and maintaining an elaborate carriage. What's more, it often happened that a gardener could make better time on his bike than a "millionaire in his costly equipage."

Far from a brand new invention, the bicycle's prototype went back to a Paris exhibition of April 1818. But the bicycle of the 1890s—which was known as a "safety bicycle," with its pneumatic tires and medium-sized wheels of equal diameter—was relatively new (it went back to the 1880s). It was comfortable and easy to ride. Until the "safety bicycle" came along, cyclists had ridden velocipedes, which had a large front wheel and a very small back wheel; the wheels were made of iron, too, which caused the rider to be jarred on his seat when the bike went over a surface that was even

slightly broken. For this reason, these bikes were known as "bonebreakers"; also for this reason it was really hard to ride them (women, for instance, almost never did). Another type of bike that was sometimes ridden was a tricycle; it worked on the same principle as the tricycle of today, familiar to all tots. The tricycle of the late 19th century, however, was a very large and unwieldy contraption.

The safety bicycle—which looked almost exactly like today's bicycle, except it had only one gear (multiple gears were invented about 1905)—changed all this. The bicycle—or the "wheel," as it was very often known—became really popular. Not only was it continually talked about, it was also sung about, in songs like The Cycle Man, The Maid of Ixion, The Scorcher and the most famous, A Bicycle Built for Two. Some people looked askance at all the cyclists—and in no uncertain terms. One Connecticut clergyman made it the topic of his sermon, declaring that all the bike riders were causing themselves to "roll down a hill" to "a place where there is no mud on the streets because of its high temperature." The vice of bicycling, that is—particularly on Sunday—led to hell.

The bicycle was the rage of the day. And people were interested not only in the safety bicycle; they wanted to devise their own variations, and any number of them wrote in to *Scientific American* to describe the "wheels" they came up with. In Louisiana, Evarto Fernandez, of 1819 Dumain Street, New Orleans (people not only signed their names to their letters but also gave the street on which they lived—it was a much more intimate world then), came up with an amphib-

A race between two velocipedes and a "safety bicycle" in Minnesota.

ious vehicle, which used a rubber rear tire when on land and lateral blades when on water and ice. In Chicago, T.J. Olson, of 427 West Madison Street, a hunter and fisherman, designed a "cycling and boating machine," made up of two boats and moved by a connected tricycle; he reported that he used it successfully on hunting and fishing expeditions in 1892. There was also something called the "Eiffel Tower bicycle" (named after the Paris structure built only recently, in 1887–89), which stood 10 feet above the ground and needed to be held by many people as it tried to go uphill. At political rallies in New England, a giant tricycle, nicknamed "Jumbo"—which was 17 feet long, weighed a ton and a half, and needed eight men to drive it—was seen. And these were only four examples of many.

The bicycle in the 1890s made people both happy and proud. A 94-year-old man from Unadilla, New York, named Amos Holmes, wrote in to *Scientific American* in 1895 to say that he must be the oldest cyclist in the Uited States.

Women were also comfortable on the safety bicycle, and cycling became something women really liked to do. Because of cycling, fashion began to change. There were special bicycle stockings, bicycle blouses and bicycle skirts; what's more, since there was no comfortable way that a woman could wear a long skirt and ride a bicycle, many women began to wear shirtwaists, which were still long dresses but much more comfortable ones.

All these things continued to prompt much disapproval of cycling; in other words, they kept it a big topic of conversation. Stories abounded—many of which may have been true—of how such people as horse and carriage lovers put tacks in the road to cause bicycle tire flats (the same trick supposedly was later used to deflate tires on the first horseless carriages). Religious leaders claimed that biking kept people from going to church. Entertainment figures claimed that biking kept people from going to shows. Candy makers claimed that biking kept people from buying sweets.

Barbers claimed that biking kept people from cutting their hair. Hatters claimed that biking kept people from buying hats. And the hatters must have had quite a lobby. A congressman introduced the proposal that each bike rider had to buy two felt hats a year! Due to the popularity of biking, which caused the relative unpopularity of all other diversions, merchandisers lost $117 million in one year in the 1890s, according to the *New York Journal of Commerce*.

Still, many continued to regard bicycling as a passing fancy. It was said to be "a toy of which people will grow weary"; the time would soon come when the horse would "resume his place in the interest and affections" of men and women. It was predicted that something would take the bike's place "in the popular fancy." Which was true enough, but that something was also entirely undreamt of when the prediction was written, and it made the horse even more obsolete: namely, the horseless carriage.

Bicycling was an obsession in the 1890s that had absolutely nothing to do with trying to imitate the rich. Safety bicycles were admired and acquired by people who had a decent amount of money but were by no means extraordinarily affluent. The rich families continued to prefer their horses and carriages. Even when bicycling did catch on among them in 1895, it was less because they were attuned to this new American cycling fashion than because they were desirous of imitating the French rich, who were riding bikes in the parks of Paris. However, when the horseless carriage came along, this was something that could only be enjoyed by the very rich, at least right at the beginning. Throughout the first decade of the 20th century, many more people had bikes than cars, a situation that would only begin to change with Henry Ford's Model T. Of course, millions upon millions of other people had neither car nor bike. They had to travel on foot.

With the coming of the automobile, however, in the late 1890s, the obsession with the bicycle passed. For over 70 years the bicycle lost a lot of its glamour.

Since the early 1970s there has been a biking revival. People took to bikes because of the energy crisis, or sometimes because they wanted a change from their cars. It has become a great diversion to take a ride on a bike rather than go for a ride in a car. Bikes have become much more sophisticated, too, with their 5 speeds, 10 speeds or more. This also adds to the great attraction of bikes today.

But compared to the passionate 1890s romance with bicycling, today's affection still appears rather lukewarm.

SKIRT DANCE (1890–95)

The more abandon they introduce in the swishing of garments, the higher salaries they draw.
—Report on skirt dancers in one American newspaper

The skirt dance was an entertainment in the music halls of the 1890s, and a most popular one. In this titillating little event, a girl performer would kick up her heels while swishing around her skirt with so much intensity that from time to time the garb would rise significantly. In 1890 it was said to be the "rage of the hour."

Reports had it that the skirt dance dated back to the late 1880s, when it was done in London, but in America the skirt was going higher and higher. And in America also, there was another twist to the skirt dance—one of a most daring sort. During the time of its vogue, a girl skirt-danced on a ledge at a peak known as Glacier Point in the Yosemite Valley in California. In one picture the athletic young woman (Kittie Tatsch by name) could be seen lying full-length on the rock, and in another she was swirling her skirt as her foot extended out into the "abyss." This was the kind of stunt that the well-known and well-paid skirt dancers like Sylvia Grey and Letty Lind never did. They stayed inside.

Miss Grey, however, teased people in another way; she would wear a very demure skirt as she went into her act, kind of looking like the Mary who had the little lamb. In her right hand, she held a cute market basket, which may have had fruits or flowers in it, and which also swirled as she swirled her skirt.

The dance was, of course, a little naughty back then. But it really wasn't all that naughty—not so naughty as the can-can in France a couple of decades before, which was featured in Jacques Offenbach's operas.

It was naughty more in the way that Trilby from George DuMaurier's novel *Trilby*, the sexy heroine of the early 1890s, was. Now little Trilby had about the most lovely foot that you could imagine, which caused people to go wild (see TRILBY'S FOOT). Among other things, sausages were created in the shape of Trilby's foot and even ice cream was sold in that shape. Trilby also had a live-for-the-day attitude, which was exciting, and the swirling skirt dance showed the same attitude.

The seductive skirt dance flourished for a while, but by 1895 people were demanding variations on it. Skirt dancers by then had become less explicitly sensual and more artistic. They had begun to dance in coordination with a complex of colored lights, and the effect of the dance was to present one single image: of movement, light and all. Skirt dancers of 1895—the most prominent of whom was perhaps Loie Fuller—showed that people were now in a phase of wanting many of their senses stirred, not just their erotic sense.

It is common to call the 1890s the "Gay Nineties," which expression tells only a partial story. Both the skirt dance and Trilby's foot were part of the "Gay Nineties," yet a person who by night might be fascinated with the skirt dance also might by day be fascinated by mechanics and engineering. He might be working on the invention of a bicycle-boat or a bicycle with a foot pedal that would activate a shower mechanism (see BICYCLING). This period was also the "scientific nineties."

Or any of these skirt dancers might have been a "modern" woman (or "new" woman, as they were known). They might have been turning down rides in carriages to get to town on a bicycle or giving up long dresses with trailers to wear something called a shirt-waist, which was a blouse to be worn with a simple skirt. Not a few people got "their hackles up" because of these innovations.

It is quite likely that the skirt dance belonged to the erotic ways of the past, while the skirt dancers themselves belonged to the modern ways of the future.

Four very elegant cakewalkers of the early 1890s

very first appearance, in the 5-cent *Tip Top Weekly* on April 18, 1896 (and later collected in Frank Merriwell novels), and the first words of that installment, "Get out," the kids just wanted to know about Frank Merriwell and what was going to happen to him next.

The Frank Merriwell stories were not properly a fad. They were a popular series of books for children (principally, but hardly exclusively, for boys). Yet they were such a favorite in their own very late 19th-century and early 20th-century times that they deserve a significant mention. Remember, marketing was nowhere near as sophisticated as it is now (marketing brings about fads to a great extent); there were no television heroes, because there was no television; and there was only very little in the way of movies. So popular books could become overwhelming attractions, and this was the case with the Frank Merriwell series.

The name *Frank Merriwell* was a combination of *Frank* (on the level) and *Merriwell* (jolly and healthy). According to the writer of the Frank Merriwell books, Maine-born Gilbert Patten, who wrote under the pen name of Burt L. Standish, Frank Merriwell was "the sort of fellow that the majority of American lads would like to be and a boy as all worthy parents would wish their sons to become." Most of his adventures took place at Yale University, where he was an outstanding star in all sports. He could also solve crimes and stick up for people against bullies. But Merriwell was no dour straight arrow and chose commonplace American youths as his companions, refusing to associate with "snobs, prigs, or sissies."

In any event, Frank Merriwell was the most popular series at a time when a young guy or gal could read about Frank Reade, Phil Rushington, Tom Wright, Bob Brooks, Diamond Dick or Fred Fearnot, whose deeds were featured in other series. He appeared in the magazine *Tip Top Weekly*, and judging from the letters written in, there was real concern about Merriwell and his gang at Yale University. One reader wrote, "Somehow, I just can't make friends with Bart Hodge and Jack Diamond"; while another reader, looking to the future, commented: "I would like to see Frank marry Inza. She has proved to be a good mascot of the crew." And a third reader wanted to make sure that one of the gang wasn't left out: "I think Barney Mulloy ought to play left field for Frank Merriwell's team."

A fan could find out what was happening with Frank Merriwell by paying just 5 cents, the cost of each issue of *Tip Top Weekly*. Though no reliable figures are available, it appears that many a young reader did exactly that. Or a reader could pay 15 cents for a bound book of three Frank Merriwell stories.

The Frank Merriwell series first appeared on April 18, 1896 and ran for 968 episodes, ending on November 14, 1914. During that time, Frank Merriwell was joined by a half-brother, Dick, who first appeared in 1901, and who originally did not want to join Frank's gang. Among the many Merriwell adventures during those years were *Frank Merriwell's Fame*, *Frank Merriwell's Fortune*, *Frank Merriwell's Sports Afield*, *Dick Merriwell's Test* and *Dick Merriwell's Day*, all of which first appeared in magazine installments and later were collected together in book form.

In the last few years in which episodes appeared, they were losing steam. To revive flagging reader interest, Patten introduced new characters like Frank Merriwell Jr. and Owen Clancy, who was not in the gang at all. This did not work.

Gilbert Patten said in his memoirs, which he wrote many years afterward, that the reason for the decline of interest in the stories was that kids could now go to 5- and 10-cent movies. But perhaps young kids had just become tired of Frank Merriwell. After all nearly a generation had passed since he had first appeared on the scene.

Incidentally, Gilbert Patten's mother had wanted him to become a preacher. But he would never have found himself a congregation big enough to accommodate all the Frank Merriwell readers that his narrative developed.

All in all, it is really hard to understand why the name *Frank Merriwell* is so little known today.

AUTOMOBILE OBSTACLE COURSES AND FLORAL PARADES (1898–1900)

Running obstacle courses and having floral parades were two things that the very rich—maybe the very, very rich—liked to do with their mobes, tomos, mocles and motorigs. Mobes, tomos, mocles and motorigs—what were they? Not vegetables or eyeglasses, but some of the things that "horseless carriages" were called before settling down under the plain old name of *auto*. If you were an Astor, Vanderbilt, Belmont or Fish, you would likely be spending a lot of your time putting the old mobe through an obstacle course or adorning it with flowers. After all, you couldn't do much else with it. Mobes were prohibited on public roads and were only allowed in the parks in some cities at greatly restricted hours. This was the way things were at the turn of the century. The mobe, being rather unfamiliar, was much distrusted. This was the time when motorists faced the well-known mocking cry "get a horse."

So negotiating automobile obstacle courses and

CAKEWALK (1890s–1909; High Point, 1898–1904)

The cakewalk—a dance originally done by blacks, which featured backward sways, prancing struts and shuffling feet—was a real favorite in the years around the turn of the century, although its origins went back a number of decades. The dance got its name because it was first done in cakewalking contests, in which performers who did it best traditionally won a cake. Nor was that necessarily all. Sometimes, a winner might find a diamond ring in the cake. And some of the other prize—such as grand pianos, gold and silver watches, or gold-headed canes—were not to be sneered at either. Many of these competitions were held in the 1890s.

The origins of the cakewalk went back to the pre–Civil War era, when blacks were slaves on plantations. The dance is said to be a satirical takeoff on the grand march of the whites, done at important balls in the big plantation houses.

By the 1890s, though, the cakewalk was performed by blacks and whites alike. This was a real opportunity for people to dress up, and men cakewalkers strutted their stuff in long-tailed coats, while women cakewalkers wore sleek white gowns. There were songbooks for the cakewalk, featuring tunes like Cakewalkers, Cakewalk Patrol, Jasper's Cakewalk and Rastus Johnson's Cakewalk. Or it was done to rags, like the Maple Leaf Rag or the Harlem Rag. Or you could watch it being done in brief features like "Ballyhoo Cake Walk" or "A Cakewalk on the Beach at Coney Island" for about a nickel at the picture palaces.

There were, of course, entertainers known for the grand style with which they did the cakewalk. Among them were Ida Forsyne, who was known as the queen of the cakewalk, and Bert Williams and George Walker, whose show in 1898 made the cakewalk a sensation in New York City. Forsyne, Williams and Walker were all black entertainers.

The cakewalk also became big in the early 20th century in both England and France. In fact, in England and France, as in America, if you didn't know how to cakewalk, you were certainly behind the times.

Interest in the cakewalk really declined around 1910, because its steps were much more complicated than the intimate dances—known as animal dances—that followed it. The best-known of these was the turkey trot (SEE TURKEY TROT AND OTHER ANIMAL DANCES). People wanted a step that was easier and at the same time very provocative.

JAN PADEREWSKI AND HIS HAIR (1893)

On December 22, 1892, in an issue of the *Brooklyn Daily Eagle*, there was an item about the steamship SS *Teutonic*, which had to go through a terrible gale while crossing the Atlantic from Europe; on the same page there was a news report about a socialite gentleman who was accusing his separated socialite wife of hypnotizing their daughter in order to take her away from him. The latter item showed that people cared about the machinations of the rich and the complexities of their lives; the former item was really about the man of the hour, Polish pianist Jan Paderewski, who was on that boat along with 420 other cabin passengers and 252 steerage passengers.

Paderewski was a man who had set Europe ablaze with his virtuosity and with his shaggy golden hair (or was it his shaggy golden hair and his virtuosity?). Before there was a John Lennon, Paul McCartney, Ringo Starr or George Harrison, there was a Jan Paderewski; before there was an Elvis Presley, there was a Jan Paderewski; before there was a James Dean, there was a Jan Paderewski. Having a snip of Jan Paderewski's hair in that time of all-night saloons in America, that time of long dresses, that time of the pompadoured Gibson Girl (see GIBSON GIRL) and that time when many a crazy bicycle was invented (see BICYCLING) was like having a lock of a rock star's hair or a movie actor's hair was many years later.

Jan Paderewski was 32 when he arrived in the United States for an American tour in December 1892. He had already been a sensation in Europe for many years. And again, in America, it was Paderewski, Paderewski, Paderewski. A merchandiser said of the traffic in his photograph that they sold "like crazy," adding to a reporter: "Sell! I should think they did sell! We can't import them fast enough, they sell like that." Like what? Like that: BIG *THAT*—as in when your arms are outstretched to show the magnitude, which is exactly what the merchandising man was doing.

And that was only the photographic likeness of the charismatic pianist with the classical repertoire from Frederic Chopin's country. A candy company came out with a stick that sold very well because it looked like Jan Paderewski; a soap company came up with a Jan Paderewski bar; and a toy company came up with a wind-up toy likeness of Jan Paderewski at the piano. When the toy was all wound up and ready to roll, the mechanical Paderewski would bang the keyboard while his shaggy hair flowed. This was very much like the cartoon on the front cover of the American magazine *Puck* (not the famous British *Puck*), which showed

Jan Paderewski

Paderewski, with wild unkempt hair, playing six pianos at one time.

It was faddish hysteria that not all the reporters and music critics appreciated. One cartoonist made fun of the bushy-haired star—for Paderewski was nothing if not a star—by showing him at his piano in a cage, on whose bars a sign read, "RECITAL CAGE OF THE FEMALE KISS-FENDER" and next to him, but outside the cage for easy plucking, a box full of cuttings bearing the instructions, "MY HAIR. HELP YOURSELVES." This was a comment on Paderewski himself, and on all the women who came to his concerts carrying small scissors in their gloves so they would be able to "snip off bits of his golden hair," as one newspaper account had it. Yet another cartoon made fun of Paderewski by showing him sitting at the piano doing nothing but grooming his hair. This cartoon said, "In his leisure time, he has acquired a very considerable knowledge of piano playing."

Stop for a moment and consider the enormity of this. This was 1893, not anytime from the fifth to the eighth decade of the 20th century, when automobiles have made it easy for people to get to see their music idols, when extraordinary musical amplification can get them into an even greater frenzy and when behavior has loosened up so that little or no comment is made when people do what they please. Yet back when Paderewski played in very proper concert halls, fans had to arrive by foot or by horse and carriage; the women had to wear long dresses with trailers; and everyone had to sit very calmly and never do anything like scream in the presence of that beautiful man and his music. All this to wait for just the right moment to quickly go snip, snip with the scissors.

This continued as long as Paderewski was on that particular tour in 1893. In Chicago the pianist gave up the tour, tired from the playing and weary, too, from the carping criticism.

Although Paderewski remained a celebrated pianist until his death in 1941, he was to become more than a maestro of the keyboard. In his later years he became prominent in Polish national affairs, serving as president of the nation.

TRILBY'S FOOT (1894–95)

Way back in the 1890s, there was a novel (which is still somewhat known) with a heroine named Trilby O'Ferrall. She was an Irish gal who went to seek her fortune in Paris. There she was hypnotized by a strange character named Svengali—hypnotism that resulted in her being able to sing beautifully.

In America people avidly followed the fortunes of Trilby, but what really became faddish were items created in the shape of Trilby's foot. For in its time *Trilby* by George DuMaurier was a racy novel, and one of the first racy things was its graphic description of Trilby's foot, said to be just plain "lovely and slender." Trilby herself said immodestly of her foot: "Ah, that's my foot . . . it's the handsomest foot in all Paris." Trilby also had a tendency "to kick off her slippers," which was most suggestive at a time when women wore long, long gowns.

So there came to be something of a Trilby foot fetish. A New York City ice cream store made ice cream cones in the shape of Trilby's foot. There was a shoe called the Trilby; it sold for $3, which was not exactly a small amount then, and thus may have been an item of high fashion. A Philadelphia company sold a sausage, said to be in the shape of Trilby's foot.

DuMaurier's novel, which was originally published in England and then serialized in America in *Harper's Monthly*, was big in 1894 and 1895. After the great interest in the novel wore off, so did interest in Trilby and her foot.

Yet for a short time, Trilby was as popular as the carefully coiffured, dark-haired Gibson Girl (see GIBSON GIRL). It may have been because she was as easygoing as the Gibson Girl really was proper. Trilby was said to have "had affairs with a half dozen men without knowing it was wrong." Now *that* was hot stuff.

In fact, it was so hot that a cosmopolitan girl like Trilby would never fall for just anybody. A fellow had to be cognizant of the choicest items of the time, like wearing hootchy-kootchy ties and lavender gloves, to romance a girl like her (see HOOTCHY-KOOTCHY TIE AND LAVENDER GLOVES).

But neither Trilby nor her foot really lasted a very long time as an American craze. In a sense, she was a one-night stand. No one like Trilby came along again for a couple of decades; and then in 1915 long-haired, sinuous vampire Theda Bara appeared (see VAMPIRE THEDA) in the silent movie *A Fool There Was*. Vampire Theda was to Trilby's foot what a typhoon is to a spring shower.

HOOTCHY-KOOTCHY TIE AND LAVENDER GLOVES (Mid-1890s)

Two items that the well-dressed man found voguish in 1893 were the hootchy-kootchy tie and lavender gloves. The hootchy-kootchy tie, which was introduced at Chicago's big fair, the Columbian Exposition in 1893, was really exotic, as it was two-tiered, consisting of two distinct patterns of mad stripes. This was an intriguing item, which perhaps could fascinate many a Gibson Girl, the fashion plate of the period (see GIBSON GIRL), not to mention a Trilby-type.

Even the name *hootchy-kootchy*, which means a type of dancer in Oriental apparel who performed provocative dances at carnivals and fairs, shows that the tie was supposed to have an exotic effect. Later, *hootchy-kootchy* carried the implication of being somewhat illicit. (In the 1920s, during Prohibition, any liquor you could get from a hip flask or in "speakeasies" might be called "hooch," a derivation of hootchy-kootchy.)

Lavender dress gloves for men were also big in the middle 1890s. During this century, people have gotten used to seeing men in not-so-striking colors, like black or brown gloves, and even in the 1890s exotic costumery in gloves was on its way out. Lavender gloves as a chic covering for men's fingers were something of a last faddish hurrah for sartorial flamboyance.

FRANK MERRIWELL STORY INSTALLMENTS (1896–Early 1900s)

In the mid-1890s young boys and girls, just like their elders of all ages, often wanted something intriguing to read. They really couldn't be expected to get much of that popular story to come out of England about the Irish girl with the beautiful foot who got charmed in Paris—the novel *Trilby* (see TRILBY'S FOOT). And by this time they had become tired of the always successful Horatio Alger.

What could be better for the young kids than a hero who was a crack pitcher on a baseball team, a crack explorer and a crack solver of crimes—a guy still in his teens who could do all things? What could be better than Frank Merriwell, in other words? From his

A gaily "beflowered" auto about to tour Main Street

having automobile floral parades became a great sport among the rich. If you looked at the ladies (it was considered very fashionable if they drove), most of them would probably be wearing red, because that was the favorite color for riding in these new mobes.

The obstacle courses were Parisian in inspiration, having originally been run on le rue de Magdeburg (Magdeburg Street) to train drivers. In the summer of 1898, however, they appeared in Newport, Rhode Island—the summer colony of the very rich—for the first time on Mrs. August Belmont's estate, Belcourt. The mobes had to negotiate between wooden horses, dummy figures of policemen and golf flags, rather like

the alpine skiing event known as the slalom. Whoever killed the fewest make-believe people was declared the winner. This was practice that one influential socialite, Mrs. Fish, needed very badly. When she was driving about in her tomo on a real road, she ran down the same person three times, because she didn't know how to go into reverse. The pedestrian was more or less unhurt, as the mobe didn't have a lot of power.

The obstacle course negotiating generally followed the horse show and the yachting festival at these gatherings of the very rich. With the obstacle course competitions, which usually lasted all afternoon, came the automobile floral parades, which also appeared for the first time in the summer of 1898. Autos were bedecked with wreaths of flowers—just as those majestic horses at the head of carriages used to be, perhaps just six months before—and then driven through the outskirts of Newport. This, too, led to much imitation. There were auto floral parades throughout the East in the next couple of years. These attracted many onlookers, who could also see other fascinating activities going on in the midst of the floral parade—like dummy pig sticking, hoops suspended in the air and a lavish display of parasols. You could sometimes catch a glimpse of August Belmont's car with its stuffed eagle insignia, too. Often these floral parades were held in the evening twilight, which made them appear even more romantic.

The obstacle courses and the floral parades came to an end when the automobile became a part of the general public consciousness in the early 1900s. No longer considered a toy of the rich, it was something within range of people with substantial, but not Scrooge McDuck, riches. This meant that there was now an Automobile Girl, modeled on the Gibson Girl (see GIBSON GIRL), that there were Broadway musicals about life on the highways, and that there were many news items about autos. There were also any number of automobile songs (the first was the Studebaker March in 1899), such as The Automobile March, The Automobile Waltz, The Automobile Polka, Love in an Automobile and The Auto Kiss; and also any number of Broadway shows with an automobile theme, such as *Automobile Honeymoon*, *The Great Automotive Mystery* and *The Vanderbilt Cup*. In 1904, to show the extent to which the automobile had become a regular consumer item, Saks and Company of New York published a 260-page catalog of various garments to be worn when out in the auto and other automobile appurtenances.

The rich by this time had probably lost interest in their obstacle courses and floral parades, anyway. The mobes were now allowed on the public roads as well as in the public parks. As for the great numbers of people who had become intrigued by the automobile but could not afford one, and who wanted to observe the rich as well as their autos, they could see them both in big automobile races, such as the Vanderbilt Cup.

The auto had come such a long way in just a few years that a lot of people probably didn't even remember the names *mobe*, *tomo*, *mocle* or *motorig*. To them, it was just plain *auto*. And within a few years there was yet another name—the *tin lizzie*.

MAGIC LANTERN (1898–1910)

Aladdin of *The One Thousand and One Nights* had his magic lamp, but many thousands of Americans had their magic lanterns, which were popular nationwide for maybe four thousand and one nights, or about 11 years. And what was the lantern's secret? Not a genie who would take you to faraway lands, but *how to make money*. Or as the Sears Roebuck catalog for 1901 put it, "Why work for $15–$25 a week, if you can make $50–$100 a week?" All you needed was a magic lantern. Just flick it on, and your friends and neighbors would enjoy the show and gladly pay for it.

Not everybody was commercially minded, though, and some people bought the magic lantern just for fun.

The magic lantern was a sophisticated adaptation of the hand-held stereopticon viewholder (see STEREOPTICON VIEWS AND VIEWHOLDERS, HAND-HELD), both seeking to achieve the effect of three-dimensional photography. But while the stereopticon view was only a flimsy paper plate, the magic lantern slide was a black-and-white or color transparency, which could be magnified up to six feet tall. All you needed was to set up a blank screen or white sheet on the wall, light the magic lantern at the wick with some kerosene, and the show was ready to go on. You could get any number of different series of 12 transparencies for about $4.50 per series—like The Chicago Stock Yards, Life Under a Circus Tent, Around the World in Eighty Minutes or The Passing of the Indian, to name just a few titles. Or views of London, Paris, Venice or Rome. Or transparencies showing the assassination of President William McKinley at the Buffalo World's Fair (1901).

For your magic lantern show, companies provided you with advertising posters, so that you could publicize the event, and also with tickets, which you could sell in advance or at the door. For $53—which was no small sum in the early 20th century—you would get the magic lantern, a white screen and instructions on how to use them, plus 1,000 advertising posters and 2,000 admission tickets.

However, if you didn't want to buy the whole assemblage and just wanted a magic lantern, you could get one for as little as 75 cents or as much as $8.00. The 75-cent model only gave a one-foot magnification, while the $8.00 model gave a six-foot magnification.

As the new century progressed, the magic lantern got more and more sophisticated. In 1909 the Sears Roebuck catalog advertised the Biopticon, which could screen animated slides. Soon thereafter, the "Modern Magic Lantern" came along, which could not only screen animated slides but also project onto a blank space magnified images of actual objects, not just transparencies you bought in the store.

Yet by 1911 all the magic lanterns were passing out of vogue. And the last of them could be had at a great bargain. Those usually going for $6.00 went for $2.49; those usually going for $7.00 went for $2.95; and those usually going for $8.00 went for $3.42.

The reasons for the decline of the magic lantern were probably several: People began to like going to the nickel movies at the "picture palace," or perhaps a more interesting diversion was just to take a spin in the "horseless carriage." The magic lantern was essentially a 19th-century device, too, and people were aware of living in a bright new century.

Yet magic lanterns hung around for a while. You could still see interesting geographical or historical transparencies. Or you could see comic ones, like Ten Nights in a Barroom, Joe Morgan with Delirium Tremens, Poor Donkey or Rip Van Winkle at Home. Chances are, however, that your neighbors would no longer be knocking your door down to join you.

FLORODORA FANCIES
(Early 1900s)

Florodora, a musical comedy, is one of those things that was once prominently on everybody's lips and has now passed into oblivion; it is roughly like people in the year 2040 looking astonished upon coming across mention of a musical called *A Chorus Line* ("*A Chorus Line*? What could that be?"). There is no one now who could really conceive of this happening, just as there was no one (who followed musicals) in America in 1900 who could conceive that *Florodora*—the great *Florodora*—could ever be forgotten.

Back then, people sang the *Florodora* songs continually; wondered about the fate of the *Florodora* players, particularly the actresses in the *Florodora* sextette; bought clothes based on *Florodora* costumery; and smoked *Florodora* cigars. Or as one article written in 1912 for the monied gentry relates nostalgically about *Florodora*: "At the breakfast table, your otherwise irreproachable and irreplaceable maid would be quietly humming, I've an Inkling." (I've an Inkling was one of the most popular *Florodora* songs.)

Florodora, by Owen Hall and Leslie Stuart, was named after a perfume (in the story) named Florodora, which was manufactured in the Philippines. There,

an intrigue involving Cyrus W. Gilfain, Captain Arthur Donegal, Frank Abercord, Tennyson Sims, Regindale Langdale, Lady Holyrood, Angela Gilfain, Anthony Tweedlepunch and others was played out, first in London, at the Lyric Theater, on November 11, 1899, and then in New York City, starting at the Royale, on November 10, 1900. From the opening lines, "Flowers a-bloomish so gay / Roses on every tree," there were cheers.

Audiences found the second act particularly impressive, when the chorus of Clerks and English Girls, known as the double sextettes, sang Tell Me Pretty Maiden, with the six young girls in their long gowns and the six young men on bended knee. The six young girls became so popular that even though they were only one of three groups of six who sang, these young girls became known as "the *Florodora* sextette." Young girls strived to be like a *Florodora* girl (one of the sextette), just as they had strived to be like the dark-haired Gibson Girl (see GIBSON GIRL), who had been around since the 1890s. Really the Gibson Girl and the *Florodora* girl weren't all that different: They were both pretty and prim, but just a little bit provocative, too.

To grasp the fascination with the *Florodora* girl, one has to realize it wasn't that easy to become a faddish sensation in 1900, and when you did, it really meant that people were most interested in you. There were no movies or television that could be beamed to the millions. There were no videocassetes to screen in your own home. The *Florodora* girl became a fad because people had to get themselves up and go to the theater or buy a newspaper and see a picture of her or see a music hall revue that featured the *Florodora* girl's act.

Interest in the *Florodora* girls became widespread; Britishers wanted to know what was happening to the original sextette in London (Edith Houseley, Jane May, Nora Moore, Beryl Somerset, Nellie Harcourt and Nina Sevening), and then people in America always wanted to know what was happening with the first American *Florodora* sextette (Marie Wilson, Vaughan Texsmith, Agnes Wayburn, Marjorie Relyea, Daisy Green and Margaret Walker). Most people learned what they had suspected all along—that the girls married a lot of stage door Johnnys around then, who also happened to be rich men looking for beautiful wives. Of the New York City sextette, one married a Virginia gentleman, one a stockbroker, one a silk manufacturer and one a wealthy native of Atlantic City, New Jersey. There must have been many a young lady aspiring to be a *Florodora* girl (or at least to be the *Florodora* girl of her hometown) who wanted the same thing to happen to her.

The *Florodora* girl, like the Gibson Girl, lasted a long time in the public's high estimation, and there were revivals of the show every year from 1901 to 1920. Thus, it is really rather surprising that the show has not been revived since, as so many other once-popular things have been. Or that a pop group has not come up with a variation on its songs, like Tell Me Pretty Maiden, I Want to Marry a Man, When You're a Millionaire or Under the Shade of the Palm. The authors heard the last sung by a deep baritone from early in the century, and it sounded very dated. America needs a new *Florodora*.

It was not until the Roaring Twenties that *Florodora* went out of fashion in the midst of a whole different conception of female beauty—defined by short skirts, cloches, cosmetics, imitation Egyptian finery and bobbed hair. A *Florodora* girl was many things, but one thing she was not was a flapper.

PING-PONG (Early 1900s; High Point, 1902)

It's ping-pong here and ping-pong there / They're playing ping-pong everywhere.
    —Anonymous verse, included in *A Little Book of Ping Pong Verse*, published in 1902

The first year of a century is always significant, whether it be 1700, 1800, 1900 or 2000. People are flushed with a new vitality, as the century is new; they want to try new things and be entertained by new things. In the case of 1900, the "horseless carriage" was beginning to replace the horse, and people were also flocking to the music halls to see a new type of beautiful girl, the Florodora girl (see FLORODORA FANCIES). And they were also really smitten with an entirely new sport, ping-pong, which had started a couple of decades earlier but didn't catch on until 1900. Next to ping-pong, lawn tennis (there were neither clay nor cement courts then) was stodgy and also demanded that you have a lot of money to build courts of your own or to be able to go to places where they had them.

How this ping-pong enthusiasm came about is a little exotic. Tradition has it that some of the first ping-pong paddles were made of cigar box lids and some of the first ping-pong balls were champagne corks. If this is true, it must have been some sight to see one man serving a champagne cork across an improvised ping-pong table to another man who was waiting to return it with a smart slam of a cigar box lid. In some accounts this is supposed to have happened in Eng-

land in the 1880s, when the game was first played by London gentlemen in their own special sporting clubs; in yet other accounts, the game was first played by English army officers in India sometime around 1890. By 1900, however, the players had given up their cigar box lids and champagne corks; ping-pong had become a worldwide craze—the first indoor sport fad of the new century.

In America ping-pong reached its most faddish hour in 1902, though sometimes it was known by any of a multitude of other names—among them, flim-flam, klik-klak and whiff-whaff. Of the ping-pong table, paddle and ball producers, it was said, "manufacturers are working day and night to supply demand."

You could see how popular the game had become here in America from all the poems about ping-pong that were featured in newspapers and magazines. To name just a few examples, ping-pong verse was featured in the *Chicago News*, the *San Francisco Examiner*, the *Spokane Chronicle*, the *Philadelphia Press* and the *Omaha World-Herald*. In the *Denver Post*: "The pinging of the ball against the racquet's hide / Is answered by the ponging when it hits the other side." From the *Boston Post*: "Where are you going, My Pretty Maid? / I am going a ping-ponging, sir, she said." Ping-pong was as important as bicycling and had almost as much popularity as that famous illustration the Gibson Girl (see GIBSON GIRL). Doctors talked about a "ping-pong ankle," caused by too much ping-pong, just as they talked about a "bicycle back," which resulted from too much biking. In London the ailment was called ping-pong tenosynonitis.

From 1890 on, the game, which was first known as indoor tennis, was becoming more and more popular in England. First, the clumsy champagne corks were dispatched, when one Mr. James Gibb—on a business trip to Chicago—saw a child playing with a celluloid ball and decided to use this substance for indoor tennis balls, as it had a lot more bounce than cork (india rubber was also sometimes used, but this, too, was replaced by celluloid). Tournaments became more and more common, and mere tyros at the game (what was the indoor tennis equivalent for duffer in golf, one wonders?) practiced on den and dining room tables. By 1900 ping-pong had become all the rage, as could be judged by the fact that in the hit musical of the year, *Florodora*, you could find a ping-pong equipment salesman as an up-to-date minor character.

Ping-pong? Yes, by 1899 the game had acquired its most unforgettable name. Why ping-pong? Because of the sound of the playing: The impact of the celluloid ball against the hollow racket made the sound "ping," and the impact of the ball on the table made the corresponding "pong."

In 1900 ping-pong was not only obsessively popular in England, it was obsessively popular in the United States, as well. People called the frenzied interest "ping-pongitis." By 1902 people were playing it all over, and many a tournament was also held. In one such typical tournament, the best two women players won a silk umbrella or a lace fan, and the best two men players won a tie clasp with a diamond in the center or a gold scarf pin. At men's sporting clubs in New York City alone, ping-pong was played at the Saint Nicholas Skating Club, the New York Athletic Club and the Democratic Club. In brokers' offices there were ping-pong tables where games were sometimes played for bets of up to $500. Ping-pong was also played on many an ocean liner, but winners of the tourneys there could collect only $5. Whatever its setting, ping-pong excited galleries of spectators.

Just as biking had an influence on women's fashions (see BICYCLING)—with the special cycling stockings and blouses and with shirtwaists—so did ping-pong. Women were told that a long skirt was not good to play ping-pong in—that they should wear loose garments that allowed freedom of movement; obviously, tight corseting would not help. They were told not to wear jewels around their necks, because they might get entangled with the paddles. All these were small enough things, but taken together and along with the apparel being introduced for biking and then for motoring, women's appearance was changing as they became more active.

Ping-pong was also attractive because it was relatively inexpensive. A set consisting of paddles and balls cost from $2 to $7; a ping-pong table went for $15 to $17; and you could get a dozen celluloid balls for 30 cents.

What's more, ping-pong had status. It had as much status as lawn tennis, but in order to play that, you had to belong to a private club—unless you were one of the very rich who had their own tennis courts made for them.

As a craze, ping-pong lasted only that one year, 1902. There are no clear reasons why this is true. Perhaps it had to do with the fact that ping-pong was enjoyed more as the thing to do than because of the

Socialite ping-pongers at the turn of the century

sport itself. In any event, it ceased being a national obsession.

It must have been attractive, though, because ping-pong is still a popular activity. In sports there is nothing quite like the sprightly ping of that celluloid ball bouncing off the paddle. Certainly, it beats the muffled thud of a champagne cork slammed with a cigar box lid.

And to show how fads return in different variations, the first popular video game, PONG (1972), was based on a ping-pong model.

Some more attention was also given to ping-pong about that time because of the interest in things Chinese resulting from President Nixon's recent trip to mainland China. (Ping-pong may have been started by the British, but the Chinese are now among the world's champs.) One would have to say, though, that compared to something like acupuncture (see ACUPUNCTURE), this interest was moderate. And certainly, there was nary a ping-pong poem in a daily newspaper—unlike 1902, when ping-pong verse was almost everywhere.

SNAKELIKE ORNAMENTS IN HAIR AND JEWELRY (January–February 1900)

The snake look was one of the very first fashions for women in the new 20th century. It started with a hairstyle, called the serpent because a section of hair was twisted in the shape of a snake and pinned back. Later, items of clothing and jewelry became every bit as serpentine. If you bought your lady a black lacy dress covered with snakes composed of solid black beads, it was thought smashing. Also, one, sometimes two, snakes twined themselves around milady's perfume bottles. Sometimes these snakes were of gold.

Snake ornaments were also added to the hair. If the girl were a redhead or a blonde, she could wear a black snake ornament, about as thick as one's finger, which looked as if it were ready to strike. If she had black hair, she could get herself a serpent the color of steel.

But in any event, the snakelike look could not be explicit—or as a fashion writer for the *Boston Herald* put it, not "so definite as to be repulsive."

And did the slithering look ever multiply! There were snake necklaces. There were snake rings for the fingers. Snakes, dragons and lizards were embroidered on robes and gowns. There were snake combs and hairpins.

The serpentine look came at a time when women still wore long dresses as well as long hair. There is no way of denying that even in spite of the suffragettes of the 1890s, women were still far from "liberated" (think, in contrast, of the "flappers" of the 1920s). They could not vote, could not smoke without derision. The serpentine look confirmed woman in her role of just being admired and covered with ornamentation. Also, she could not be provocative by raising the hemline of her dress. (Think, too, of the heavy two-piece sailor suits that women wore bathing.) To be suggestive, she needed something like the serpent look.

In any event, however, with the coming of spring, the snake fashion was abandoned.

PYROGRAPHY (1900–05)

Pyrography, an applied art that has almost disappeared, was anything but obscure in the early years of the 20th century, when it was about the most voguish thing there was. Meaning literally "fire writing," pyrography required an alcohol lamp, a bottle of benzene, a metal union stopper and, most important, a platinum needle with a point; after you gathered all these things, you would be able to design on wood or other materials, like leather. And this is what people liked to do and what they did.

On a wooden chest the pyrographer could craft a design of flowers, birds or dwarfs. If the pyrographer were interested in history, he or she could choose to create a design showing men in armor. All that was needed was a benzene burner (to heat the platinum point), which could be purchased for $4.35 to $12.00, and the platinum point itself, which went for $2.00 to $8.75, since there were many kinds, ranging from very sharp to a little bit blunt. Then the pyrographer was ready.

And was the marketplace ever ready for the pyrographer. In wood, prepared for designing with fire, he or she could get a playing card case for 75 cents, a bread plate for 36 cents, a box to keep pins for 50 cents, different kinds of panels for 12 cents to 50 cents or a lacquer bottle for 25 cents. Or perhaps the pyrographer's preference was for leather. Then, the artist could get a leather pen wiper, all ready for fire designing, for 35 cents; a novel cover for $1.00; a case for pins for $1.15. At the same time, the pyrographer was assured that he or she wasn't about to embark on any overwhelming task: "Do not imagine that it requires any special talent to do pyrography." On the other hand, it wasn't so simple as not to be worth the trouble: "You cannot learn it without some labor." And it was sort of prestigious, too, for it was a modern application of an ancient art. What's more, kids who were beginning to find drawing dull might like pyrography because it was "more interesting and provocative."

All this was described in a pyrographer's catalog created by the Rose Decorating Company of New York City. Yet the brochure went even further to note that there were profits to be made with the platinum needle, alcohol lamp and benzene bottle: "Many, who never learned to draw, are making money by pyrographic work." Just a few years back, when the magic lantern (see MAGIC LANTERN) came in as the newest type of photographic device, the Sears Roebuck catalog was advertising it as something to use to show slides to your friends and neighbors—and ask them a price at the door.

But to make money from pyrography, you had to be more original than to just take out a trusty gadget that could beam an image on a blank wall or a sheet. Here is how it was done.

In pyrography you drew with a platinum point, which was heated in the alcohol flame until it was reddened. Using a platinum point having a wide shape, you could become especially adept at broad lines or background effects. With a sharp platinum point, you could handle easy line work, but it wasn't possible to do any complex shaping. Some platinum points were good for designing flowers, while others were good for fire writing on chimney panels, for instance. But by about 1905 you could find pyrographic patterns on nearly everything: lampshades, fruit bowls, blotters; and you could find them taking off on nearly every imaginable theme: Japanese design, Egyptian design, Greek design, Gothic lettering. If you wanted to give someone a gift with a pyrographic pattern, you could choose among knives, hand mirrors, candleholders, magazine stands, hairbrushes and boxes, to name just a few. It was all rather quaint and lovely.

Pyrography had become popular in England in the late 1880s, when there was a great revival of interest in hand-crafted works. From there a vogue for pyrography spread both to Europe and to America. There were instruction books for pyrography written in German as well as in English. They all said the same thing: Do not press down too hard on the platinum point, and don't heat it too much; those were the cardinal rules of pyrography.

The best platinum came from near the Ural Mountains in Russia and from Peru. For heating purposes, platinum was better than even some of the finest gold.

After about 1905 the interest in pyrography seemed to die out. Perhaps the craft was just too hard, despite all the claims about its simplicity. And what with

picture palaces and automobiles, there was getting to be so much more to do.

There has been no noteworthy revival of pyrography in the 20th century, not even in the 1970s, when handcrafts once again became prominent.

PICTURE POSTCARDS (1900–12)

A sneering cynic said that "postcarditis caused faddy degeneration of the brain." A stage show actress built up what was said to be the largest collection of picture postcards in the world: 73,445. And picture postcard fanatics attacked post offices in America if they placed their cancellation stamps on the back of the postcards and not on the front. When postcards bore the mark of the distant place on the front, they were much more impressive. All in all, the postal card craze, which first appeared in Germany in the late 19th century, had become darn hot in the States—much more torrid than the collecting of commemorative historic spoons in the early 1890s (see COMMEMORATIVE HISTORIC SPOONS).

Picture postcards, both in their novelty and in their convenience, were a big step forward in contrast to the stereoscopic card (see STEREOPTICON VIEWS AND VIEWHOLDERS, HAND-HELD). You didn't need a special optical device to look at the picture postcard, and if you received one in the mail, you could appreciate its effect at once. Also, if you were buying a picture postcard, you didn't need to carry a special instrument around—the stereopticon viewer—to know what you were getting. No wonder postcard manufacturers immediately realized that "the postcard business is going to be a big thing."

Another great thing about postcards was that they were often in lavish color and really enticed the eye. An elaborate postcard collection at the New York Public Library shows this vividly.

Postcards first appeared in America at the World's Columbian Exposition in Chicago in 1893, at a time when expositions were really a big deal, extraordinarily elaborate, with an effect almost like Disneyland has today. It took about a decade, however, for the picture postcards to become the rage.

But when they became the rage, they really did. They were bought to show how much you loved cats, dogs or the favorite of the time—teddy bears (see TEDDY BEARS). Or the picture postcards could lend a sense of civic importance. A proud burgher of Cedar Rapids, Iowa sent out a picture of one of its great streets with the inscription, "The finest, widest, and longest paved street in Iowa."

Sometimes the pictures were dispensed with, as in the case of the young fellow who proposed marriage by postcard. In the first card he sent his lady love, he included only one letter, *W.* Then came an *I.* Then came an *L.* But he got tired of the prolonged procedure and sent a bunch of cards at once, so that together they spelled "WILL YOU MARRY ME?" He was accepted.

Picture postcards were voguish at a time when people were still genuinely surprised at how small the world was becoming. There was a joke that when travelers arrived in northern climes where Eskimos lived, the first thing they would find would be a stand at which picture postcards of igloos were being sold. And another joke had it that people would have to add an extra room to their houses—just to hold their picture postcards.

In 1907 a variation on picture postcards became very popular in its own right: leather postcard pillows (*see* LEATHER POSTCARD PILLOWS). And then there were teddy bear postcards during this stuffed animal's rage; and when that began to die out, there were Billy Possum postcards, emblematic of the new president, William Howard Taft.

Picture postcards continued to sell in great numbers, but they ceased to be a faddish item about 1912. Some claimed that the postcards just weren't what they used to be, that they had become too mass-produced. In any event, people began to look to other things to take the place of the picture postcard. One new item they found was the folded greeting card.

Picture postcards have, of course, lasted and lasted. You can find them at the corner drugstore or in any lovely European cathedral town. People just don't think twice about picture postcards. But back in the early 1900s, when the picture postcard was new, it was a whole different story. Here were scenes that really opened your eyes. Take them for granted? Never!

A typical, popular picture postcard, this one showing Saratoga Springs, New York

Relaxing on the veranda at the resort hotel—another frequent picture postcard sight

TEDDY BEARS (Roosevelt Bears) (1903–08)

In November 1902 President Theodore Roosevelt went on a bear hunt in the Mississippi swamp country. There, a peculiar thing probably occurred that changed the face of American popular folklore. Though an enthusiastic hunter, Roosevelt reportedly refused to shoot a defenseless cub. A cartoon drawn by Clifford Berryman depicting this event immediately ran in the *Wash-ington Star.* (The story was not confirmed in November issues of the *New York Times* or the *Washington Post.*) The sparing of the little bear caught the national imagination. And cuddly, sawdust-stuffed Roosevelt bears—only later did they generally become known as teddy bears—became the plaything that nearly every child desired. They may have been first sold by a Brooklyn, New York store.

Another story about the origin of the popularity of bears in America is not quite so mythic. It just happened that early in the 20th century, stuffed bears created by Steiff of Germany really began to catch on.

Stuffed bears abounded in magazines like *Cosmopolitan, Ladies Home Journal* and *St. Nicholas,* a respected monthly of the early 20th century. Here stories were told that would really please the children. In one, bears Ab, Ba, Peter, Little Scrub and Barbara go to a tea party with three little girls. In another, stuffed bears Bouncer and Gretchen are shut up in a box in a store before they are rescued. In yet others they go sledding or fishing.

The bears were sawdust-stuffed and had shoe buttons for eyes. You could get them for 89¢ to $2.59, and in sizes ranging from 10 inches to 16 inches high. As the years went by, the technique for making them got better and better. A child could get a stuffed bear with a "natural voice" or one whose head turned around. But teddy bears were more than stuffed animals. There were also teddy bear dolls, candies or pincushions. Or you could get a teddy bear spoon in 90 different variations, like one showing a bear on a swing.

This was a time when President Roosevelt was a real hero to Americans, and often the little bears were made to look and act like him. One particularly good example of this is the 1905 children's book by Seymour Eaton, *The Roosevelt Bears: Their Travels and Adventures.* There, two bears, Teddy G. and Teddy B. (perhaps after *girl* and *boy*), wore monocles and roughrider jackets. But they also taught children wherever they visited to "believe in fun and honest strife, and manly sport and strenuous life." This was definitely the kind of sentiment President Teddy himself often expressed.

This book became so popular that you could buy sets of dishes that featured the profiles of Teddy G. and Teddy B. The tale was indeed a most entertaining read. Written in chapters consisting exclusively of rhymed couplets, a child could read (or be read to) about bears on an automobile ride, bears going to the circus, bears teaching Harvard College students about

A family of teddy bears

President Theodore Roosevelt (Teddy) with a bear

life and bears being thrown off speeding trains. The book, which was published in serial form in 20 newspapers, was praised by Theodore Roosevelt himself, who said that his young children enjoyed it. There was also a sequel, in which Teddy G. and Teddy B. traveled beyond the continental United States.

The fad for the teddy bear, as for Teddy G. and Teddy B. books, began to pass when William Howard Taft was elected president in 1908. (Theodore Roosevelt had decided not to run for reelection.) Almost immediately the price for stuffed teddy bears began to drop. You could get them for 63¢ to $1.98. William Howard Taft even got to be symbolized by an animal, too. This was a possum, but it was only shown on a number of picture postcards and never reached the stuffed stage.

As for the teddy bear, it is still very much with us. But now it is just one of many playthings in the well-equipped nursery. Way back in the first decade of the 20th century, it may well have been the most important thing in it. While the adults were amusing themselves with visual gadgets like the stereopticon or magic lantern (see STEREOPTICON VIEWS AND VIEWHOLDERS, HAND-HELD and MAGIC LANTERN), or while older brother might be looking at pictures of the Gibson Girl, (see GIBSON GIRL), the younger kids could be having a great old time with the Roosevelt bears.

ARCTIC FLEAS, INK-KISSED KISSES, CIGAR BANDS, OLD LOCKS, PEWTER MUGS, BEER LABELS (Circa 1905)

There is many a fad to which only a passing reference exists, without description, such as arctic fleas, ink-kissed kisses, cigar bands, old locks, pewter mugs and beer labels. These are all referred to in an early 20th-century magazine article that was trying to figure out what was the big deal about picture postcards (see PICTURE POSTCARDS). It mentioned those other fads, implying that just as they had passed, so too, would picture postcards. No one needs to be told that picture postcards are still around, but those others—what were those other crazes that caught the public's fancy at the start of the century?

Arctic fleas? This was a time when Robert Peary and others were trying to traverse the North Pole, and people were really interested in the endeavor. They wanted some kind of memorabilia item commemorating it. But fleas? Yet there is no doubting that it was a fad.

Ink-kissed kisses? Now this was obviously a most romantic item. Maybe it was nothing more than girls covering their lips with ink and then pressing them on an envelope, to send to their beaux. But there were ink-kissed kisses—of that we can be sure.

People also collected certain things with a passion at that time, just as they do now. Back then they collected cigar bands. There were a lot more types of cigars than there are now, and they were considered really fine, rolled as they were by hand. Also the portraiture on the boxes and on the cigar bands was much more finely crafted.

Far different from the cigar label fad was the fascination with beer labels. People are still interested in them. And there was an interest in pewter mugs; that, too, is not much different from the 1950s, when college students almost had to have a whole lot of porcelain mugs.

And what's wrong with an interest in old locks? It just went to show that people have always been nostalgic—that a yearning for bygone, simpler times was no invention of the 1970s. In 1905 people might have wanted to collect a flyer for Lincoln's Gettysburg Address or a velocipede (particularly since progress was rushing onward, and everybody was now riding bikes, even if they didn't yet have autos).

LEATHER POSTCARD PILLOWS (Spring 1907)

In the heyday of the picture postcard (see PICTURE POSTCARDS), more than 150,000 different kinds were sold. You could get a view of a distant land, a postcard with just your first initials on it, one showing soap bubbles and a soap bubble pipe, a romantic one showing a young couple in the moonlight—and lots of others besides.

Leather postcard pillows were a spin-off from the postcard fad, and in the early spring of 1907 they were just the thing to recline your head on. The finely crafted leather pillows were divided into 16 sections, each of which looked like a postcard. The sections might show different places or be pictures depicting different sentiments. For instance, one leather pillow had a square in which two birds were chirping angrily at each other. The square carried the inscription "Don't scrap. What's the use?" Or you could get yourself a leather postcard pillow showing teddy bears or a heart. You could get one showing Santa Claus, flags or American Indians, too. There was also one in the shape of a bathtub.

Leather postcard pillows cost about $9 a dozen. They weren't things that everyone ran down to the store to buy, but they were definitely items that the romantically inclined found attractive.

The pillows had only one big year, 1907. They were just the right thing to give for Valentine's Day or a birthday that year. Perhaps after that spring season, they were found to be just too contrived.

INTRODUCTION

Lightheartedness was a theme of the 1910–30 period in America, but the quality of the lightheartedness was different in the 1920s from what it was prior to our entry into World War I (1917). The first decade has never won any nicknames, but it was characterized by a merry assault against the last vestiges of 19th-century Victorianism. The 1920s were, of course, known as the Roaring Twenties, and they were like a shooting star: but a star that flashed across modern—not Victorian—skies. It was a time of women in short hair and skirts, of "talkies," of stunting for publicity (flagpole sitting, dance marathons) as an everyday occurrence. In short, it was a time when you could do with ease nearly anything you wanted to—except get a drink. For this was the time of Prohibition, of "speakeasies," of "bootleg gin" and of "blind pigs," or suppliers of illegal liquor. You'd better believe that law enforcement officers were always hot on their trail.

Way back in 1911, the authorities were watchful, too. But the Argus-eyes of that period were standing guard not against that old devil whisky but against dancing. Wherever you looked, young people were doing steps called animal dances, which involved making like a turkey, chicken, buzzard, bear or rabbit on the dance floor. In desperation, the management of hotels and ballrooms assigned uniformed employees to try to maintain decorum by making the patrons confine themselves to a stately 19th-century waltz.

Then there was Annette Kellerman, a young swimmer and showwoman-fashion designer who came up with a bathing suit that enabled females to swim more comfortably. You can't imagine the magnitude of the hue and cry that arose because the daring new garment, which greatly resembled a leotard, was appreciably more revealing than the traditional cumbersome sailor suit. Actually being able to feel a splash of the Atlantic or Pacific (or even a splash of the local swimming hole) thus represented something of a milestone in women's liberation.

The 1910–20 decade saw the emergence of the first great sex goddess of the silver screen, Theda Bara, called the Vampire. Her seductiveness was thought to be a grave threat to public morality (yet she sold out all the movie theaters). Unlike Clara Bow, the bobbed-haired movie queen of the 1920s, there was something old-fashioned about Theda Bara. Although undeniably sexy in such roles as Cleopatra, Juliet Capulet or Salome, she brought no new cultural vitality into American life. Clara did, though. Known as the "It" girl, she was the ultimate "flapper," saying of her bedazzling Hollywood life-style as Paul Sann has recorded in *The Lawless Decade*: "We did as we pleased. We stayed up late. We dressed the way we wanted. I'd whiz down Sunset Boulevard in my open Kissel [a type of automobile] with seven red chow dogs to match my hair."

Now *that* was America! This self-loving American ebullience, however, was not always a healthy thing in the 1920s. Immediately after World War I, in 1919, despite President Wilson's exhausting battle to make America "international" in outlook, the United States refused to become a member of the League of Nations—the forerunner of the United Nations. There was no doubt that many an American of the period was xenophobic—really fearing foreigners and any kind of alien ways.

The isolationism of the 1920s nevertheless did not prevent Americans from seizing upon the Chinese game of mah-jongg with an obsessive interest. Nor did it prevent the lionization of the ancient Egyptian boy-pharaoh Tutankhamen—more familiarly known as "King Tut," as in King Tut jewelry or King Tut cigars. These Chinese and Egyptian influences were preceded by the Argentine influence of the tango, popularized around 1915 by dancers Irene and Vernon Castle.

Another pervasive influence in American life that made itself felt in these two decades was strictly home-grown—the influence of native American blacks. It was blacks who introduced the briskly moving turkey trot in San Francisco, just as it was blacks who first danced the Charleston in the American South (when the step first appeared in New York, it was part of showtime entertainment) and blacks who originated jazz.

By 1929 the carefree way of life had become ingrained in many Americans. Then the superstructure collapsed. Enter the Great Depression. This was to change everything—including our nation's favorite fancies.

HOBBLE SKIRT (1910)

It was rounded over the hips and tapered to the ankles narrowly, the hobble skirt was. It really was hard to walk around in—hence, the name—and did it ever cause a sense of outrage! They laughed at it in New York City and along Atlantic City's boardwalk. In Illinois the State Legislature banned its use. But in 1910 it was quite the rage among women who wanted to wear the most fashionable garments.

This was quite because it was really something novel, being different from the traditional very long and loose skirts of the period. Also, it was first worn by a heroic figure of the time, the aviatrix, and at that time many a typical fashionable lady wanted to look like an aviatrix. Never mind that the *New York Times* described the hobble skirt wearer as having to "hop like a bird from one spot to another." Consequently, it was also called the shackled skirt.

The most fashionable designer of the time, the Parisian Paul Poiret, made the hobble skirt even more of a high-fashion item by adding a garter and sash for it.

By December 1910, however, the hobble skirt fad was over. As was the usual case then, Paris got tired of it first. In its place came the harem skirt. Also designed by Paul Poiret, the harem skirt was a sort of half skirt, half pants (see HAREM SKIRT) and caused even more outrage.

All this showed that traditional long dresses, which had been in use since the 19th century and before, were passing out of fashion. Also, the hobble skirt did make one lasting contribution to female couture. This may have been a mad, mad garment, but it was the one in which slits were introduced.

It is interesting to note that 60 years later another fashion in feminine dress came along that made women feel both glamorous and awkward in their movements: the maxi coat (see MAXI).

HAREM SKIRT (1911)

In the America of 1911, harem skirts could only be considered outrageous. They had the sensuality of the Turkish concubine, but a modern woman could wear them to the office—they were that comfortable. Was it any wonder that they were called "frightful" and "horrible," or that it was proposed in the Illinois State Legislature to ban them? As one newspaper put it: "No one talks of art or literature or public affairs. All conversation is concerned on that detestable garment."

The detestable garment in question was the French designer Paul Poiret's interpretation of what was worn in Turkish pleasure palaces. The harem skirt was part skirt, part trousers, and it was the trousers part, that caused all the uproar. When the skirt with the pantaloon attachment was introduced in New York by a fashion publicist on February 28, after first being shown in London earlier in the month, the ladies who wore it were mobbed. Then the same thing happened a few days later on the boardwalk in Atlantic City. Meanwhile, in Des Moines police officers wanted to arrest a woman for wearing a harem skirt but could find no law on the books of which she was in violation. They let her go with a warning.

What a furor the harem skirt caused! Some said that it was indecent; others said that it was informal, free. There was talk of ending "woman's subjection" even in the early years of this century, and the harem skirt was better for her liberation than those heavy, long dresses. The president of the "Rainy Daisies," a prefeminist organization, said, "Women must be free; they have been bound too long." Hostility against the harem skirt was "male-dictated."

The harem skirt was so controversial, yet so much *the* significant item of fashion, that in February and March alone, it was featured in the *New York Times* on February 5, February 12, February 17, February 18, February 19, February 25, February 28, March 1, March 5, March 10 and March 12.

Not only was the harem skirt voguish, but there was along with it a vogue for turbans. It was all part of the fashionable Near Eastern look. People had become intrigued by this when they saw the exotic costumes of the Russian ballet, such as the very popular Oriental fantasy *Scheherazade*.

The harem skirt was the successor to the cumbersome hobble skirt (see HOBBLE SKIRT), also designed by Paul Poiret. It was much easier to walk around in than that 1910 garment, which had got the name *hobble* because of the difficulties in mobility it caused. In fact, the rage of 1911 and the rage of 1910 met head on at Auteuil, a racetrack outside of Paris, when angry women wearing the old fad, the hobble skirt, chased after women wearing the harem skirt. The hobble skirt wearers couldn't keep up, though.

The harem skirt—or Turkish trousers as the garment was also called—suddenly ceased being an item in the spring of 1911. It was no longer big in Paris, and American women, who took their fashion cues from the French, lost interest—just as the fickle old Turkish sultans had grown weary of their one-time favorite charmers.

The harem skirt was indeed a sensation, but still

it is necessary to keep things in perspective. It was a high-fashion sensation among women who not only knew about high fashion but also had the money to wear high-fashion garments, which were still much more handmade than mass-produced. Contrast this to the 1920s, when the voguish look—short skirts, bobbed hair and cloches—seemed to be sported by all American women (just look at any picture of a women's civic club or a college sorority). Beginning in the 1920s, fashion became much less the private preserve of the rich.

TURKEY TROT AND OTHER ANIMAL DANCES (1911–13)

Let no one out of the room . . . should there be any of you who have an inclination to dance the "grizzly bear" or the "turkey trot," the members of the committee will stop you.
—Incident at the Astor Hotel, New York City, reported in the *New York Times*, January 13, 1912

In the early 1900s the widely approved dance was the waltz, though when it first appeared on the scene in 19th-century Europe, it was considered vulgar. The waltz was appropriate for cotillions, private clubs and ballrooms. But by the time 1910 came along, the waltz was no longer thought anywhere near exciting enough. Also, the vogue for a dance known as the cakewalk (see CAKEWALK), which had any number of backward sways and prancing struts, was passing. The rage now was for something new and exciting: steps that came to be known as animal dances—like the turkey trot, the grizzly bear, the buzzard lope, the bunny hug, the chicken trot, the kangaroo dip, the monkey glide, the rabbit wrastle and many others.

Here were dances in which couples would get out on the floor and mimic animals. In the turkey trot they raised up and down on the balls of their feet, just like turkeys seem to do sometimes. In the chicken scratch the dancers scratched the floor with their toes. In the buzzard lope they made like buzzards diving in for carrion. At the same time there was a lot of sliding, dipping, side-stepping and back-stepping in these dances. And best of all, the dances allowed a lingering closeness. Or as one young girl said of the turkey trot, "The boys all seem to like it, and the best dancers hug you the most."

These dances were most stimulating, but perhaps another reason for their attraction was that here was a chance for young men or women to stand up for themselves. This is no exaggeration, because a lot of people tried to prohibit the animal dances. In Paterson, New Jersey a young girl got 50 days in jail for doing the turkey trot. A number of young girls who worked for a New York City publishing house got fired for doing the turkey trot during their lunch hour. The University of Wisconsin laid down the law that anyone doing the turkey trot would be thrown out of school. At high society dances men with "blue ribbons on their coats" watched the floor to make sure that no animal dances were being done. Informers were dispatched to debutante parties under cover of friendly invitations to see if there was any "outbreak" of turkey trotting. Nor did the influential National Association of Masters of Dance approve of the turkey trot. (In a few years it wouldn't approve of the tango, and in the 1920s it wouldn't approve of the Charleston, either.)

Yet the turkey trot and the other animal dances were a force that could not finally be resisted. In high society they trotted gleefully in resorts like Old Orchard Beach, Maine and Newport, Rhode Island, as well as in New York, Boston and Philadelphia. No matter that they called it a refined name, the "long Boston," it was the same sexy old trot. But if you didn't belong to the smart set, you could do it in a dance hall or a restaurant; in fact, it was sometimes said that the quality of the food in these restaurants was deteriorating because couples were more interested in trotting than in eating.

The popularity of the animal dances was nationwide. An observer described the craze this way for a Charlottesville, Virginia newspaper, *The Progress*:

Everybody turkeytrotted. They all caught hold of each other; it was catch as, catch can. First all the females tried to let their feet slip out behind, and the males brought them up . . . then the males tried to trip the females up, and the females retaliated . . . they turkeytrotted like anything . . . they danced the lingering drag and the Boston dip, and the kitchen sink [all animal dances in spite of their names] and the buzzard lope. They danced the bunny hug and the rabbit wrastle and the bear hug . . . they curved and swerved; they slipped and slid and slithered.

Another intimate animal dance was called the shivers, supposedly because it sent shivers down the spines of people who watched it. People also took offense if the animal dances, when watched, were mislabeled, which must have happened often. An usher at a supper club called up the *New York Times*, for instance, to correct a report that the patrons had been doing the turkey trot. It wasn't the turkey trot at all, he said, but the chicken trot.

Where the various animal dances came from is not always clear. The turkey trot, the first of them, probably came from San Francisco, where it might have been danced in a rough nightclub section known as the Barbary Coast. (Al Jolson, one of the big entertainers of the early 20th century, danced it there.) However, it became popular after it appeared in a musical revue in 1910, *Over the River*. The buzzard lope was said to have been done first in Georgia. The origin of the grizzly bear is uncertain, but by 1911 it was very popular, as can be seen in the song Everybody's Doin' It Now, by Irving Berlin. What were they doing? Why, the grizzly bear, of course. Other animal dances were probably made up as it became obvious that this kind of dancing was the thing to do. Moreover, the dances sometimes changed from week to week and from city to city. Frequently, things were confused by names. For instance, the turkey trot was also known as the slow rag, the lover's two-step and the walk back.

The animal dances emerged at a time when America really went dance-mad; the same kind of overwhelming, even obsessive, popularity would soon greet the tango and, in the 1920s, the Charleston. In a way, people's insistence on doing the animal dances—in spite of all kinds of hostility—showed how things were opening up in American society. Women, for instance, wore harem skirts and hobble skirts (see HAREM SKIRT and HOBBLE SKIRT), even though these garments were frowned upon. Fewer and fewer people felt bound by old traditions, although there certainly were still a lot of them. One physician said of the turkey trot that it was a good way to exercise, and who could argue with the morality of good health? He had no truck with those people who thought that the animal dances were "evil."

In late 1913 the turkey trot and the other animal dances began to lose popularity because a young professional dancing couple, Vernon and Irene Castle, became big in America, and they introduced the Castle walk and then the tango, both of which swept the nation. In earlier years the Castles themselves had performed the animal dances often, but now they pronounced them "ugly, ungraceful, out-of-fashion." But unlike the concerned social judges on the sidelines, the Castles were showing all the hoofers something new.

KEWPIES (1912–14)

I wish that every single child could have a kewpie of its own.

—Dotty Darling, a fictional little girl who lived in the house where all the kewpies were

Kewpie dolls are fat-cheeked, wide-eyed, and they are never without a topknot in the middle of their hair. They came along only a few years after the teddy bear—which was originally known as the Roosevelt bear (see TEDDY BEARS)—and proved to be every bit as popular as those sawdust-stuffed, button-eyed cuddlies. Right from the beginning, when kewpies first appeared in December 1909 in the *Women's Home Companion*, the "kewps" were a national hit. Who could resist them, any of them—the kewp in the military uniform, the kewp who looked very bookish, the kewp who was a gardener, the kewp who lolled in the hammock or the kewp who played the mandolin? People just liked having a kewpie around—if not a doll, still something kewpish. Maybe they would dip a pen in a kewpie inkwell. Or fix their features using a kewpie hand mirror. Or wipe their hands on a kewpie handkerchief. Or remember their engagements in a kewpie notebook. Or even eat a kewpie marshmallow or a chocolate kewpie.

It was somewhere around 1908 that Rose O'Neill, a professional writer and illustrator, got the idea of creating the kewpies. It may have been inspired by what her baby brother looked like, or it may have been suggested by an editor. Miss O'Neill called them kewpies because they looked like little Cupids. And every single kewpie did look like a little Cupid—the ones she called Careful of His Voice, The Chieftain, Kewpie Cook, Kewpie Army, Plain Kewpie or Always Wears His Overshoes. In any event, the first kewpies were round, and they were puckish. Or as Rose O'Neill wrote of them, in verse: "For tight-rope trips and backward flips / They are not built so well, you see / This leaves them for pranks and quips / And things which they excel, you see." With one exception, Katy O'Kewp (which Miss O'Neill created in the 1920s), the kewps were little male figures. And they always appeared to members of the Darling family, just like James Barrie's Peter Pan appeared to children of the British Darling family. This coincidence could not have escaped Miss O'Neill.

The popularity of the kewpies probably surpassed Miss O'Neill's wildest expectations. Originally, they were just fanciful illustrations (Miss O'Neill did the illustrating herself) for fanciful stories, which also often taught a little lesson. For instance, in one story the kewpies teach a little girl what a nasty thing it is to be a copycat by copying her every move till she can't

Rose O'Neill, creator of kewpie dolls

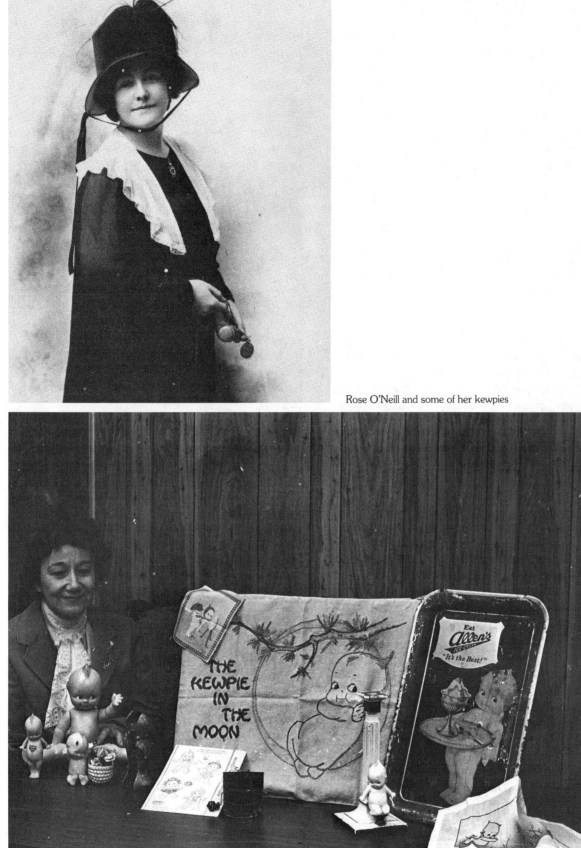

Rose O'Neill and some of her kewpies

stand it anymore. Also, although Kewpie Army wore a sword and a soldier's cap, he only fought against children's "crossness, crying and whining."

This was nice enough, but the American public must have wanted more. And in May 1912 Miss O'Neill wrote a poem for the *Women's Home Companion* in which the kewpies turned into dolls. From that time each issue would include instructions for a cutout of a paper kewpie doll. The first was a flying kewpie, which Miss O'Neill urged children to hang from a chandelier. But it wasn't from chandelier-hung paper dolls that kewpies would become the vogue. Rather, in 1913 bisque (unglazed ceremic) kewpie dolls burst on the scene. You could buy a kewpie from 2 to 14 inches high. You could get Kewpie Army, in his military uniform; or you could get tiny Kewpie Blunderboo, who was always falling backward; or you could get Instructive Kewpie, with his book; or you could even get two kewpies doing the tango, which was the fashionable dance then (see TANGO).

Nor was the kewpie found only in the nursery. There were also kewpie towels, kewpie ice cream trays, kewpie rattles, kewpie toy pianos, kewpie pillowcases, kewpie cups, kewpie saltshakers and kewpie perfume. You could wear kewpie earrings, kewpie bracelets or kewpie hatpins, too. You could even take a picture with a kewpie camera. And there were flannel kewpies that were used to clean pipes and could be found in cans of tobacco, as well as a kewpie magic lantern (see MAGIC LANTERN), which showed six kewpie magic lantern slides.

Kewpies were a worldwide craze in 1914, both in America, where people could still enjoy the benefits of peace, and in Europe, where World War I had broken out. One story has it that on one occasion, the English lifted their blockade against German ships (the kewpies were first produced in Germany) to let shipments of kewpie dolls into Britain. This may have happened because, in its early stages, World War I was still a gentlemen's war, following 19th-century chivalric codes; and what could be more chivalrous than making sure that children could play with their kewpies? Within a couple of years, of course, there was poison gas and fighting for inches of ground, which would wipe out about half the youth of England and Europe. There would be no safe passage for kewpies then.

After the First World War, in the early twenties, Rose O'Neill ceased writing about kewpies. But in 1925 Miss O'Neill brought them back. They were not the same old kewpies, though: no Kewpie Army, Careful of His Voice, Always Wears His Overshoes or a number of others; nor did the kewpies play among children in the old Darling household. Rather, the new kewpies lived in a place called Kewpieville, with stone walls, gates, marble fountains and turreted castles.

Somehow, these revamped kewpies never seemed to catch on.

In the 1930s kewpie dolls came back, but not as something that you would give to a child for his or her nursery. They came back as a prize that you could win at a carnival by throwing rings onto hooks or shooting mechanical ducks in a gallery or heaving a ball at a bunch of milk bottles, which would all fall down. Young men would give these kewpies to their dates, perhaps as a joke, perhaps as a token of affection. Kewpies continued as carnival prizes into the 1940s and even longer.

There might have been something romantic about all of this later kewpie activity but nothing like a national romance. In the early 20th century, however, kewpie dolls had been such a national romance, something to amuse children and adults alike and be instructive at the same time. Or as Rose O'Neill would write, "So while we're young and lively, chaps / take off our overshoes and caps / We'd like a kewpish time."

In this century kewpies were perhaps the most popular elfin-like dolls in America until the Belgian-inspired, mushroom-inhabiting Smurfs came along in the early 1980s (see SMURFS). There is still, however, a very active kewpie fan club, known as the International Rose O'Neill Club, for those who, to this day, treasure kewpies above all else.

TANGO (1914–16) AND DANCES OF IRENE AND VERNON CASTLE (1911–17)

One of the first things we learned in the dancing business was never to keep the same dance in vogue over a long period of time.

—Irene Castle, of the famous early 20th-century dancing Castles

The fascination with the animal dances—like the turkey trot (see TURKEY TROT AND OTHER ANIMAL DANCES), the grizzly bear, the buzzard lope, the bunny hug, the chicken trot, the kangaroo dip, the monkey glide and the rabbit wrastle—made it evident that in the early 20th century (starting around 1910), Americans wanted to spend a lot of time dancing. Until 1913 the animal dances, with their unusual barnyardlike movements, held the floor, as people raised up and down on the balls of their feet (the turkey trot) or scratched the floor with their toes (chicken scratch), but at that point there

Vernon and Irene Castle—those trendsetting tangoers—in 1913

Tango dancers

came along the great popularity of ballroom dancers Vernon and Irene Castle and also the great popularity of the tango.

Vernon Castle was a young British man, and Irene Castle was a young American girl; in 1911 the couple was in Paris, because that was a place where you could make a name for yourself. There, in a cabaret, they improvised a step to the song The Darktown Strutters' Ball. This included spinning, reversing and raising your toes and was called the Castle walk. This was just the beginning for the Castles. Within two years they were wildly popular, not only in America but also in Europe. Their dances were followed with great enthusiasm, but so were their mannerisms and the style of clothes they wore.

For instance, when Irene Castle got her hair bobbed—which she decided to do while recovering from an appendectomy, not wanting to bother caring for her long hair—women began to wear bobs (see BOBBED HAIR). When Irene wore white satin shoes, white satin shoes became the thing. When Irene started wearing a little Dutch bonnet, Dutch bonnets became

the thing. When Irene started wearing jodhpurs, jodhpurs became the thing. When Irene said that women should not wear dangling beads or heavy lace when they danced, dangling beads and heavy lace were immediately considered cumbersome.

Vernon Castle did not influence fashion in as many ways. But one way in which he was imitated has had a long-lasting effect. He wore a wristwatch; wearing a wristwatch then became the thing to do for men. Before Vernon Castle did it, the practice was considered effeminate.

It was the Castles' easy grace that made them so popular. It made people in the New York City area want to come into their dance studios, Castles-in-the-Air (in Manhattan) and Castles-by-the-Sea (in Long Beach, Long Island). It made them want to tango, which became the rage in America and Europe around 1914. Above all, the Castles tangoed. They did all kinds of tango steps, like the scissors, the Cortez, the eight-step, the media luna and the maxixe, so Americans also took up the scissors, the Cortez, the eight-step, the media luna and the maxixe.

35

Yet the tango was more than just a dance often done by Irene and Vernon Castle; its popularity was a worldwide phenomenon, and one that inspired intense hostility. Many were troubled by its provocativeness. It was forbidden in Boston. It was forbidden in Cleveland. Also, in Massachusetts it was proposed in the state Legislature (but never enacted into law) that doing any tango step be punishable by a $50 fine for the first offense and by six months in jail for the second. In Germany it was forbidden in Berlin to all, and it was forbidden to military officers at any time.

Moreover, to further discourage the tango, the newspapers ran scare stories like the one about the "tangoer" who collapsed after seven hours of dancing.

Yet nothing really stopped the tango. It was danced through the nation, and until World War I broke out in Europe in 1914, it was the rage there, too.

What attracted people to the tango was its elegant air, which was in obvious contrast to the crude movements of the animal dances. They looked as if they could be done on impulse, on the spur of the moment. Also, the tango was performed to a new beat, the Latin beat, or more precisely, the Argentine rhythm. After the Castles—who at an earlier time had done the animal dances themselves—pronounced them "ugly, ungraceful, out-of-fashion," the tango commanded all the attention.

For many a year, however, the tango remained, in the view of many, a naughty step. Didn't it end with the man falling back and making the woman lean close in his arms? The National Association of Dancing Masters, seeking to clean it up (as it had tried to clean up the animal dances a few years earlier), suggested 10 respectable variations for it: prince's hesitation, American grapevine, twinkle waltz, stroll hesitation, canter one-step, canter two-step, canter waltz, Exeter caprice, Sobey's hesitation and the Blue Danube waltz. (the Blue Danube waltz???)

The tango was popular in America until 1917, when the United States entered World War I. Then, dance really was not uppermost on anybody's mind. During the war Vernon Castle, an aviator, was killed in an accident at a training base in Texas.

After the war Irene Castle continued dancing and also continued her prominence. She was not quite the trend setter anymore, though.

As for the tango, it has continued until the present day. But it has never again become the national obsession that it was from 1914 to 1916.

In the 1920s Americans were ready for a new dance craze, the Charleston. With its much faster rhythm, its hands slapping knees and its southern American inspiration, this was an altogether different step.

VAMPIRE THEDA (1915–18)

I have set my heart on being what you are—queen of vampirism. . . . I am quite dark and have your drooping eyes to perfection.

—An Ohio girl's letter to actress Theda Bara

There was a time not even 70 years back when all eyes were focused on Theda Bara, the first sex goddess of the movie industry; the exotic siren who said, "Kiss me, my fool," and caused it to become a motto of 1915; and above all, the killer and vampire. Not a vampire in the Transylvanian sense of the word, like Count Dracula, but a vampire-woman—a raving, provocative beauty who seduces men and then destroys them. A vampire is more than a *femme fatale*, which is simply much too delicate and French; a vampire is without subtlety: She just goes right in there and steals. And this was Theda Bara, who was said to be an Arab damsel born on faraway Sahara sands but was really just a nice Jewish girl from Cincinnati named Theodosia Goodman.

But let the myth remain, and go with it. If Theda wore a slinky black dress in a movie, slinky black dresses would become the fashion. If Theda smoked while using a long, gold cigarette holder, long, gold cigarette holders would become the fashion. And everyone knew the picture of Miss Bara, the seducer of soft touch and fool John Schuyler in *A Fool There Was*, the actress's first film (1915) and her entry into the world of being known by all, in which she diabolically stares and fusses with her long, long hair. No wonder an Omaha, Nebraska women's association met in a blinding blizzard to try to ban her movies, and that she was the subject of Sunday sermons.

A Gibson Girl of the 1890s Theda Bara was not, nor was she a 1900 *Florodora* girl (see GIBSON GIRL, the cartoon figure who went out rowing and golfing demurely wearing a pompadour; see FLORODORA FANCIES, from the musical *Florodora*, whose girls in long dresses were called rare "pretty maidens" and who were often seen carrying a delicate light parasol). She was much wilder. Theda Bara lying sexily on a bearskin rug was a sight to behold. And this brought pleasure to more than a few; movies could attract far larger audiences than the stage. Hypothetically, thousands could be watching Theda Bara in movie houses throughout the nation, as opposed to a hundred watching the *Florodora* sextette at a theater.

Yet her performances were not in the realm of X-rated pornography, either; Miss Bara was a transitional figure. She knew that she was the symbol of sensuality but wasn't out for easy titillation, partly out of convic-

A somewhat more demure vampire Theda Bara

tion and partly because people were still ashamed of easy titillation—still ashamed to think that they wanted it. So Miss Bara said of her roles that they were really morally instructive: "I am going to continue doing vampires as long as people sin. For I believe that humanity needs the moral lesson." And so Theda went on in poses like giving ecstatic kisses, lying sexily on a divan holding a precious cat, or holding a jeweled snake around her. In this pose she was also being held by a man with a knife. This was a man who was not zonked out by her beauty; he had gathered together enough wits to be violent.

Vampire Theda—whose entire career was spent in silent films—was a magnet. In Baltimore, for instance, people lined up for hours to see her 1917 spectacle *Cleopatra* (she did not play one of the ladies-in-waiting), and many who could not get the tickets at the box office wound up getting them from a scalper, who charged them as much as 15 cents or 20 cents. Also, as for *Cleopatra*, if one goes through the scrapbooks on that event, one sees that this was a supercharged occurrence demanding front-page or feature treatment in almost every newspaper, and there were a lot more newspapers then. One newspaper even went so far as to present Miss Bara and Cleopatra as a "tale of the tape," or how the measurements of boxers are at the weigh-in. It looked like this for the struggle between Theda Bara, queen of vampires, and Cleopatra, vampire queen:

	Theda Bara	Cleopatra
Height	5'6"	5'5"
Waist	30.1"	29.3"
Hips	40.2"	39.6"

And so on.

Theda the vampire was irresistible, and at the time of *Cleopatra*, she said this of the blood-sucking woman: "My idea of this woman is that she is pantherish in her every pose and action as well as in mind . . . fascinating her victim as a cat fascinates her prey."

For three years Theda Bara—whose name is almost an anagram for "Arab death"—was an irresistible vampire-woman, and her gestures and clothes were affected by many an American female. Even when some reporters began to realize and write in 1915 that Theda was really only an American girl from Cincinnati named Theodosia Goodman, the vampire continued to be a haunting presence in American life. Time after time she parried any outrage by saying that the vampire was only a role and morally instructive. When the Omaha ladies in early 1918 compared her unfavorably to elegant women who wore fur coats, Theda's manager said that if Miss Bara lived in Omaha, she would be wearing a fur coat, too. And then he continued indignantly to them, asking these Nebraskans to look around and see "down the street women in short skirts; women with painted noses and darkened eyebrows; with tight clothes." Of course, he was talking about prostitutes—the real thing.

Yet by 1918 Miss Bara's popularity was fading. This happened for many reasons: America had gone to war in 1917, and people were less interested in movies. At the same time, when they went to see Miss Bara, they had also become tired of her lavish costume dramas (not only *Cleopatra*, but also *Carmen* and *Romeo and Juliet*), and the fact that these productions were just vehicles for her sensual movements. Or as one critic wrote of her 1918 movie *The Soul of Buddha*, all there was to it was "Bara making faces, Bara wriggling, Bara shoulders." People were getting tired of Miss Bara's vampire look, and in silent movies that's all there was. If Miss Bara had been ac-

tive in the time of "talkies," which began about a decade later, she might have had a chance.

By 1920, when Theda Bara starred in *The Blue Flame*, in which the audience saw her more as a ludicrous figure than as a vampire, the time for Miss Bara had passed. She acted blatantly, and people now wanted more inhibited performances. It was also the time of Prohibition, and *prohibition* means "preventing."

Theda Bara really was never to return, but little Theda Baras were—even within a year. When young girls teased in the 1920s, they saw themselves as "vamps" in their bobbed hair, short skirts, cloches and their liberal use of cosmetics, very new on the American scene. When they went around to do a little sexual toying, not like a panther but like a kitty, this was known as "vamping." The vampire was defanged of all its horror: Vamping was something to be done harmlessly in a salon or at a debutante ball. But it was still a coaxing feminine mannerism, and it was still carried out directly, as Theda had first done it. Vampire Theda had opened up the world of romantic pursuit. The Gibson Girl and the *Florodora* girl really lived in the 19th century, with its Victorian codes; vampire Theda lived in the 20th century, when all of this decorum was breaking down quickly.

Vampire Theda had yet another influence: She made it inevitable that when there was a sex queen on the silver screen, the effect would be so potent that the audience would do as she did. In 1927 women adopted a bob like Clara Bow, the "It" girl, had or dyed their hair with red henna. In the middle 1930s they became platinum blondes because idol Jean Harlow was a platinum blonde.

As for Theda Bara herself, she regarded the end of her vampire days calmly, saying at the time, "Five uninterrupted years of vamping have drawn my nerves taut."

She had made her contribution, and she could rest.

OUIJA (1917–18; 1966–67)

Ouija is a combination of the French and German words for yes (oui + ja). It was also the name of the "mystifying oracle," which could tell you anything: whether it would rain tomorrow, how much it would rain, if your girl friend or boyfriend would go walking with you in the rain, for instance. All you had to do was put the board on your knees, ask the seer the question by placing your fingers on Mr. Ouija (who was nothing more than a pointer) and wait to see how he moved to various letters or to numbers from one to nine or to the answers yes or no. One thing, though: The board had to be moistened first.

And in the mid-1960s, if you were a teen-ager, you probably would be directing questions to Mr. Ouija. Some remembered being scared by Ouija, and others remembered thinking it was "just plain silly." One sometime player of Ouija said that she heard that a Ouija board had once flown (just like the bed in *The Exorcist*) when it was asked a question. She did not like this one single bit.

But the 1960s were not the first time that the Ouija® board was the rage. During World War I, after the United States entered in 1917, people flocked to buy up Ouija boards (produced in Baltimore) and ask Mr. Ouija questions about the battles across the Atlantic, including such tragic questions as "Will my son survive the Battle of the Marne?" The American form of Ouija had been created by two brothers, William and Isaac Fuld, about the turn of the 20th century. But the origin of the Ouija boards predated the 20th century. In some form they existed in mid-19th-century Europe. In any case, Ouija boards (which cost $3 for plastic sets and $7 for wood sets in the 1960s) continued to linger in America through the 20th century. The Ouija board was even responsible for a celebrated murder case in Texas in 1934. A young girl concluded from Mr. Ouija's signals that she was supposed to kill her father so that her mother could marry a lover.

When Ouija came back in the mid-1960s, it did not have a concentrated public relations campaign. People learned about it by word of mouth, as there was very little advertisement. Still, it proved more popular than Monopoly® in 1966 and 1967.

People have always found, though, that the effect of Ouija was finally repetitious. In the 1960s teen-agers got tired of the game. It did, however, herald the great astrological obsession of the 1970s.

And to this day, Mr. Ouija can still answer your questions. Perhaps only he can foretell when he will come back as a fad again.

BOBBED HAIR (1920s)

That this hair, this wonderful hair of hers, was going— she would never again feel its long voluptuous pull as it hung in a dark brown glory down her back.
—F. Scott Fitzgerald, "Bernice Bobs Her Hair"

You could almost predict the coming of bobbed hair. Ever since the late 19th century, women had been altering their life-style so as to make things less cumbersome for themselves. Floor-length dresses with sweeping trains had disappeared. One-piece swimsuits had replaced the two-piece sailor suits of days of yore. Thus, it wasn't any wonder that long hair—called woman's "crowning glory"—would soon be on the block.

Irene Castle, the popular ballroom dancer (see TANGO AND DANCES OF IRENE AND VERNON CASTLE), had made bobbed hair a rage just before World War I, when she cut her long tresses only because she didn't want to take care of them while recuperating in a hospital from an appendectomy. American women hung on Irene Castle's every gesture, and, sure enough, what she did in sickness, they soon did in health. Nonetheless, the bobbed hair fad a la Irene Castle was quite short-lived at first; or maybe it was just that World War I intervened, and no one was paying much attention to fads in any case.

It was a different story in the Roaring Twenties, when young girls were known as "flappers." (The term is said to have originated when young girls wore their galoshes unbuckled, creating a flappiness when they walked.) They were also sometimes known as "vamps," after the vampire actress of the screen, Theda Bara, if they were going out on engagements where they were going to toy with men and tease them. When Theda did it, she destroyed men. (Of course, she was a "vampire," and they were only "vamps.") Then, for years bobbed hair was considered almost obligatory for the well-styled female. First appearing in 1922 among very young girls, bobbed hair quickly caught on. In the Fitzgerald story long-haired Bernice decided to bob her hair to be in vogue, and then, sitting in the barber's chair, continued to insist upon it (although she really didn't like the looks of it) because she didn't want to lose face with her friends.

Since the flapper was afraid of losing face with her friends by not having a bob, she would even ignore the warnings of her doctor. Some among the medical community held that bobbed hair caused an irritation of the scalp called "folliculitis" or, more simply, "flapper's rash." Didn't the good doc take into consideration what a nice time a young girl was having with her bob?

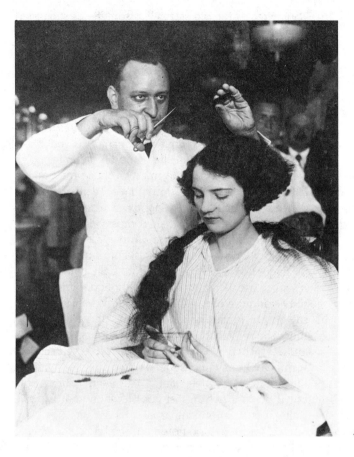

A young girl gets her hair bobbed, September 1920

But it was hardly necessary to look to short stories or medical articles to appreciate the extent of the bobbed hair conquest. In any fashion magazine of 1925, not only young girls but also middle-aged matrons wore bobbed hair, almost without exception. Due to the bobbed hair fashion, haircutting parlors had increased from 5,000 to 23,000 during the 1920s. Why? Well-known artist Mary Garden left no doubt. In an article, "Why Did I Bob My Hair?" she answered the title query by saying that the bob showed alertness and up-to-dateness. She just wanted to avoid those "long, entangling tresses." It can also be added that bobbed hair was thought to be convenient, but convenience was not necessarily its major attraction. It also had to look just right—"perfect," as the magazines put it.

It was also stylish if the gal wore the bob with a bell-shaped hat fashionable at that time, the cloche. The cloche was first introduced in France in 1921; American women at that time were wearing big floppy hats. Within a couple of years, however, all the floppy hats were off, and ask not for whom the cloche tolled—it tolled for all American women.

Bobbed hair also introduced yet another item to the American scene: the bobby pin. It kept bobbed hair in place, just as the tiara had kept long hair in place in times past.

Short, bobbed hair was yet another indication that women were changing their way of looking at themselves. Also in the 1920s came the short skirt and the introduction of cosmetics on a large scale. Elegant flappers also wore the fashions of Madeleine Vionnet when they were voguish—i.e., the Spanish shawl, the handkerchief dress and the velvet dress.

The bob established the young girl's (or flapper's) identity in the early 1920s, was in vogue a couple of years later and had become passe in 1927. In that year women tried to adopt the "It" look, after the sensual movie actress and "It" girl, Clara Bow. Clara had red hair, and she wore it long. The bobbed style continued into the 1930s, but no heads would turn to look at a bob as might have happened in the early twenties.

In any event, never was there a seer more totally off base than the one who wrote in a 1922 issue of the *American Hairdresser* that the bobbed hair craze wouldn't "last through the summer." It lasted through that summer, and the next summer, and the next summer, and . . . (not to mention winters).

41

FLAGPOLE SITTING (1920s)

I just went up for a breath of fresh air.
— Alvin "Shipwreck" Kelly,
on why he sat on a flagpole
in Curtiss Field, New York

It was Alvin Kelly, known as "Shipwreck," who made flagpole sitting a national fad in the 1920s. A professional stunt man, among other things in his early manhood, "Shipwreck" became the fellow to emulate in those heady days of the Roaring Twenties. Any flagpole would do if you wanted to show your stuff. One LeRoy Haines did 12½ days on a flagpole in Denver. H. V. Crouch did 17 days and 2 hours on a New Bedford, Massachusetts flagpole. And Bobby Mack lasted for 21 days on a Los Angeles flagpole. Hot stuff, eh? Well, "Shipwreck" Kelly took one look at that, hopped the first vehicular conveyance to Atlantic City, found himself a flagpole over the boardwalk and stayed aloft for 49 days.

And this doesn't even take into consideration all the schoolchildren who climbed real and improvised flagpoles because they were overwhelmed by "Shipwreck"'s feat and saw him as something of a role model. Among the younger set, the center of flagpole sitting, or more precisely a later variant, pole sitting, was Baltimore, Maryland. There their sitting was a deed that met with great accolades; both Baltimore Mayor William F. Bruening and the local newspaper, the *Sun*, cited the daring kids.

Sitting on a flagpole, as you might imagine, was by no means an easy task. To make sure he didn't fall asleep and topple off, "Shipwreck" Kelly had stirrups attached to the flagpole. "Shipwreck" was also likely to carry on a shouted conversation with you from his perch.

The first time that "Shipwreck" Kelly publicly flagpole-sat was in 1924 in Los Angeles. This initial effort was modest enough—only 13 hours and 13 minutes. Yet the act caught the national fancy, and quite soon flagpole sitting, like dance marathons (in which contestants danced continuously for weeks at a time; see DANCE MARATHONS), was a great attraction. When "Shipwreck" did it in Atlantic City, for instance, 20,000 people watched. On other occasions flagpole sitting caused such a storm that the police had to come and arrest the flagpole sitter. It was civic authority, for instance, that finally put a stop to Bobby Mack's valiant effort in Los Angeles.

There are a number of accounts about the origin of flagpole sitting in America, but the most convincing is that "Shipwreck" Kelly did it as a dare in 1924 after performing a similar stunt in a movie. However,

"Shipwreck," the old storyteller, sometimes suggested a different version of how it all began. He would claim that he got the idea when heavyweight champion Jack Dempsey—then in his prime—chased him up a tree in Florida in 1922. The champ always denied this, though.

There can be little doubt that flagpole sitting was outlandish. But it was also probably fun to watch. And sometimes, to multiply your enjoyment, you could take in a dance marathon at the same time, for flagpoles were often erected in the midst of those mad dance halls. What a sight this must have been! While the dancers marathoned, the flagpole sitters perched.

Flagpole sitting flourished most brightly in Baltimore. There, hardly a stone's throw from the nation's capitol, where the highest legislators sat (though not on flagpoles), the kids climbed to really high perches. It wasn't exactly flagpole sitting, though. Fifteen-year-old Avon Foreman, who started a related 1929 craze, sat on an ironing board mounted atop a pole. And there she remained for 10 days, 10 hours, 10 minutes and 10 seconds. Many another youth followed suit that summer. One even brought along a violin and fiddled the hours away while sitting. Not even "Shipwreck" could do that (which just goes to show that flagpole sitting was an improving art).

As for Miss Avon Foreman, she had something to tell her children and grandchildren (or anyone else, for that matter). In a declaration, Mayor Bruening of Baltimore had said of her:

The grit and stamina evidenced by your endurance from July 20th to 30th, a period of 10 days, 10 hours, 10 minutes, and 10 seconds atop of the 22-foot pole in the rear of your home shows that the old pioneer spirit of early America is being kept alive by the youth of today.

After 1929 flagpole sitting lost a great deal of its excitement, though it was still done by "Shipwreck" Kelly and others as an occasional stunt. The Depression came along, and people wanted to do things—such as play a round of miniature golf (see MINIATURE GOLF) or watch Mickey Mouse—and laugh.

The Depression was also a time of most unusual personal stunts, and flagpole sitting had a very definite and obvious effect on one of them: tree sitting. This fad—which spread from the East to the Midwest, at least in 1930—involved roosting for a long, long time in a tree, maybe on the back lawn, in a public square or wherever. Tree sitting didn't have the Hollywood flavor of flagpole sitting, however. Perhaps this was because of the lowered expectations of the people themselves, living in an era when things were no longer, shall we say, "roaring." The tree sitters, too, lacked a "Shipwreck" Kelly—they had no idol who had as-

"Shipwreck" Kelly sits aloft, shielded by an umbrella, in Atlantic City. He remained on the flagpole for 49 consecutive days.

cended a perch to gaze down upon the sparkling denizens of Los Angeles or the high rollers at Atlantic City; no one who even claimed to have had a run-in with a heavyweight also-ran, much less with the world champion himself.

Mah-Jongg (1922–25)

Mah-jongg, a Chinese word meaning sparrow of a hundred intelligences, was the Chinese board game that took America by storm in the 1920s. The newspapers ran special mah-jongg columns. Hotel manag-

ers had to open mah-jongg rooms. To make sure that all Americans who wanted to could put their mah-jongg tiles into their mah-jongg racks, small Chinese shops were turned into mah-jongg mass production lines. The *New York Times* cited the "present peril of mah-jongg."

Mah-jongg was both exotic to play and attractive to look at. Consisting of either 136 or 144 tiles—depending on the variation played—this ancient Chinese dice game started with the building of a wall made of tiles and ended when the winner went mah-jongg, or got rid of all his or her tiles. The tiles themselves represented winds, dragons, circles, bamboo, flowers and seasons. Even better, the pieces were made of ivory, at least at the very beginning of the fad. And Americans soon had nicknames for many of the tiles based on what the Chinese calligraphy looked like to them. For instance, the dish of blueberries, desperate char-

43

acters, the stilts, the dinner plate, Palmolive or the happy villagers.

When the sets first appeared in the United States, they were a luxury item, going for as much as $500, at a time when this was still a lot of money. Thus, they first became popular among members of Long Island society, who could easily afford these sets with their tiles of fine ivory. Soon, however, mah-jongg had become a nationwide obsession. A cool 1.5 million sets were imported from China in 1923, 10 times more than in 1922. In department stores in Milwaukee, Kansas City (Missouri), St. Paul, Des Moines and Chattanooga, itinerant players proficient in the art of mah-jongg gave demonstrations. It was probably as big a topic of discussion as where people could find a "speakeasy" to drink some illicit "hooch," those being the days of Prohibition. Mah-jongg was as much part of the Roaring Twenties as was the dramatic new hairstyle for women, the bob (see BOBBED HAIR).

While mah-jongg became popular among all classes of Americans, this had not always been the case in China, if some accounts of the game's history are to be believed. There, until the 19th century, it was played only by royalty. Then mah-jongg penetrated the Chinese gambling halls, and it was in a Shanghai gambling hall that Joseph C. Babcock, a representative of Standard Oil, who first introduced the tile game to America, discovered it.

With great difficulty, Babcock convinced Chinese craftsmen to hand-carve the game for Americans and to put numerals on the tiles so it would not seem so unfathomable, while preserving its Oriental mystery. Then he found Chinese manufacturers and had the game shipped to the States. And did Babcock ever strike gold!

But at the height of the craze, the mah-jongg makers began to run out of a most important item of raw material: the shinbones of cattle used to make the tiles. Fortunately, they could call upon another source: Chicago slaughterhouses sent their excess shinbones to the mysterious East where they were turned into these very popular mah-jongg tiles.

Not only did mah-jongg inspire a fad, it inspired any number of stimulating controversies. This resulted from the fact that there were many variations of the game, each with slightly different rules. In China this was an honored tradition, but in America people were always searching for the pure, right form and consequently looked disparagingly on competing mah-jongg versions. In truth, they had only themselves to blame. Babcock's game was so successful that other importers, working with their own Chinese manufacturers, came up with their own variants. Every city in the United States was said to be playing a different mah-jongg game. One man's mah-jongg was another man's ma

cheung and a third man's pung chow. The confusion got so bad that Congress had to step in to try to stop it! In 1924 it declared that all imported Chinese sets had to have the name *mah-jongg* stamped on them.

By the middle of 1924, the fad had ceased being at fever pitch. Though millions still played mah-jongg, it was no longer considered the "in" thing to do. The days of the $500.00 and $100.00 sets were long gone; you could get a set for $25.50, then for $10.00, then for $5.00 and finally for 10 cents at Woolworth's—not ivory, of course, just paper versions of all the tiles. And by 1925 the fad was over. One domestic manufacturer of mah-jongg equipment was in particularly serious straits. Forced to declare bankruptcy, he had to get rid of 25,000 mah-jongg tiles, 20,000 mah-jongg dice and 3,000 mah-jongg score counters.

In 1925 faddish interest passed to crossword puzzles (see CROSSWORD PUZZLES), which were appearing for the first time in book form. Crossword puzzles were really much easier than mah-jongg, could be carried around with you, demanded no special equipment and were written completely in English.

Though mah-jongg has continued to be played in America throughout this century, there has been no major mah-jongg revival. This is somewhat surprising, considering the cyclical nature of many fads—e.g., ouija, Howdy Doody, bicycling (see OUIJA, HOWDY DOODY, BICYCLING)—and also considering the interest shown in things Oriental in the early 1970s (see ACUPUNCTURE, CHINESE LOOK).

Even today in the Orient—in cities like Singapore, Hong Kong or Penang—in the quiet of the night, you can still hear a strange clicking of tiles. This is no unearthly spirit returning from beyond the grave (except perhaps the spirit of that captain of the Chinese fishing boat). The clicking is the sound of the playing of mah-jongg, which still thrives in the Far East.

Legend has it that a captain of a Chinese fishing boat invented mah-jongg to keep his sailors from being bored while they were at sea. This was back in ancient times, but people in every nation and at every time have always wanted interesting distractions. And in the 1920s Americans, having learned that those Chinese fishermen might have been on to something, began to while away some of their hours playing mah-jongg in great numbers, too. It may well happen again. You never know when it comes to fads, and mah-jonggers of today maintain that more and more people are becoming interested in the game.

Dance Marathons (1923–41; High Point, the 1930s)

They draw you near the dance floor, dancing couples there where laughs fill the air . . . if it's midnight or morning—some are laughing, some are yawning.
—Song, Take Me to the Dance Marathon (1932)

Some people called them treadmill grinds, speedathons or walkathons, but nearly everyone knew them as dance marathons and always wanted to know the same thing—what numbered couple would last the longest and win the prize money (usually from $1,000 to $5,000, depending on how much money the promoters had put up). They were announced on the radio with come-ons like "Hear Uncle Jim Harkins describe the dreaded cruel treadmill grinds, contestants chained together until the end of the contest" (this is a bit of an exaggeration; no one was chained to anybody in a dance marathon—but grueling it was). Newspaper coverage, too, was exhaustive. At the end of the thirties, Greta Garbo, the movie queen, danced for a little while in the Hollywood National Marathon. But the Swedish beauty was not a serious marathoner.

Serious marathoners danced for months at a time in a crowded hall or in a crowded section of a fairgrounds. They were allowed only a 15-minute rest period after every hour (in the last stages of the marathon, this was sometimes shortened to 3 minutes); were poked at by the judges, who watched everything going on on the floor closely to make sure the contestants didn't fall asleep; and were taunted by the master of ceremonies to go faster. Yet the marathoners kept it up—for a number of reasons. There were those who saw the contest as a way to earn money; this was true of many marathoners during the midst of the Depression, which started in 1929. There were also marathoners who were trying to make it as entertainers and saw the grind as an opening to establish some contacts by showing how good they were. There were people running away from dullish former lives and people who thought they would be able to find a marriage partner in the dance marathons, (this did happen, always accompanied by great publicity from the marathon promoters and the newspapers). And there were people who did it for the fun of it—to prove to themselves how long they could take it. For instance, there was the marathoner from Miami who kept on dancing even after he found out that he had just received a $50,000 inheritance.

Between 1923 and 1941, despite constant efforts by police and civic officials to close these contests down, dance marathons flourished in America and could be seen in auditoriums, campgrounds, boardwalks and dance halls. As many as 40 might be going on throughout the United States at any one time. To watch a marathon, you could usually get in for a couple of dimes or a quarter, and you could stay as long as you wanted. Some marathons on occasion let you in for nothing if you got there between midnight and 6 a.m. You could buy daily passes, two-week passes and season passes. But even if you didn't get there, you could always hear it on the radio.

It's true enough that dance marathons excited a cruel curiosity. As they looked up at the scoreboard to see how many hours of continuous dancing had elapsed and how many couples remained, watchers could also throw coins at their favorite contestants. One very popular attraction was "cot night," when spectators were allowed to see contestants lying down in exhaustion on their cots.

But it must have happened frequently that spectators at the marathons would get the urge to be marathoners themselves. What were the requirements set forth in the application forms? First, you had to be at least 18 years old to enter. Second, you had to promise to look neat and clean at all times. Some applications also asked prospective contestants "What entertaining have you done?"

Contestants who were accepted signed a contract that they would abide by the rules of the marathon—for instance, that they would stay away from the Master of Ceremonies' platform, that they would get out on the floor at the sound of the bell and get out of their cots at the sound of the siren. Some contests also charged $5 a week for room and board.

Most marathoners danced in couples, but they could also dance solo, if they wished. The names and numbers of the couples and the solo dancers were published in the newspapers.

But whether they danced as part of a couple or alone, marathoners were still checked out by a physician daily. One such doctor said: "They'll be all right if they escape insanity. This music may get them, but otherwise they should last."

Sometimes they didn't. Three deaths were attributed to overexhaustion during marathons. Two happened on the dance floor, and the third was a drowning, which resulted because a weary marathoner in Atlantic City during the allowed morning dip had lost his capacity to swim. It was definitely a strain to dance 40 miles a day, as the average marathoner did.

As a result, the health authorities and the police, considering the marathons dangerous, tried to stop them; the struggle to do just that was often front-page news. Yet the promoters and the dancers carried on,

sometimes changing the locale of a marathon when it was threatened with being closed down. At Madison Square Garden's Dance Derby of the Century, in the high-spirited 1920s, the couples were stopped after 481 hours, but many continued to hoof it up in nightclubs.

It wasn't until the late 1930s that dance marathons began to fade out of the American scene, but this was due more to a decline of interest than to opposition by government authorities.

Before this happened, though, the dance marathon craze spread from America to Europe, with marathons in Paris, Edinburgh, Marseilles and Budapest. And in America itself a number of dance marathon variations became prominent. Among them were a kissing marathon, a combination skating and dance marathon, and a marathon in which troupes of people danced on the highway from Bridgeport to New York or from Providence to Boston.

The dance marathon fad ended slowly. But by the late 1930s people were losing interest. And after Pearl Harbor in 1941, when many an eligible young man went off to fight, the craze for dance marathons ended completely.

During its long heyday, the all-time endurance record for dance marathons was 3,780 hours, or approximately 158 days.

KING TUT (1923–1929; 1976–78)

When the tomb of Pharaoh Tutankhamen—known affectionately as King Tut—was unearthed near Luxor, Egypt in November 1922, a treasury of gold, jewelry and furniture was found. And of course, people raced to adopt the fashion of 1358–1340 B.C. (circa). The profile of the Boy King (who would die at 18) would become as well known as that of Yankee home run slugger Babe Ruth or heavyweight champion Jack Dempsey. You could smoke a King Tut nickel cigar while wearing a King Tut hat.

The 1920s in America were characterized by a whole different conception of beauty than that of the decades immediately preceding it. Cosmetics were introduced on a large scale. Women wore short skirts instead of long gowns and bobbed their hair instead of wearing it long. The unearthing of the tomb of King Tut and its ancient Egyptian wonders added yet another really new and exciting element to the scene. No wonder intense interest was generated by the newspaper accounts of this excavation, done by the English

Tutankhamen's gold coffin

archaeologist Howard Carter. Newspapers published the latest finds, sometimes on a daily basis.

So King Tut fashion became quite the thing. Society ladies wore gowns of turquoise, gold and silver adapted from the jeweled garments in the pharaoh's tomb. At the same time, they may have thought they looked like that recent movie beauty Theda Bara (see VAMPIRE THEDA), who wore this kind of ornate dress in the silent movie blockbuster *Cleopatra*. Chairs that looked like Egyptian thrones became the right thing for the head of the family or his consort to sit on. Not only that, but parents were known to name their children after King Tut. And should the entire family ever

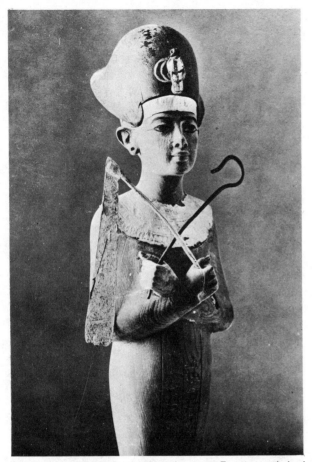

The boy king, Tutankhamen, holding the ancient Egyptian symbols of authority

of a jar depicting a bird in a nest (such as was found in King Tut's tomb) for a mere $190.00.

It was definitely most desirable—indeed something that gave instant status—to get to see the King Tut stuff at first hand. You needed a special ticket for this, and in order to get one, you had to wait in long lines. It was typical for people to give up after an hour and leave before getting the ticket. But it was just as typical for people to wait many, many hours; some waited all night.

After the treasures went back to Egypt, the steam went out of the fad.

It is still possible, however, to see movies about Tut's immediate milieu: mummies. These movies, originally produced in the 1930s, have often featured the curse of King Tut's tomb. A King Tut character also appeared in the television series "Batman" in the 1960s (see BATMAN).

Probably an interest in things ancient and Egyptian will always be with us. But like it was in the 1920s and the 1970s, that may not happen again for a long time.

CROSSWORD PUZZLES (1925)

Since crossword puzzles have become an essential diversion of modern daily life, it is hard to believe there was a time when they were a most extraordinary fad. Yet so they were in 1925. One newspaper, commenting on the crossword's contagiousness, called it "a fierce little black and white checkered microbe." It was also often a cause of domestic discord. In one marital action a judge ordered a Chicago husband to limit his crossword puzzles to three a day, so that communication and peace in the home could be restored.

Crossword puzzles first ran in the Sunday section of the *New York World* in 1912. Though many readers liked them, they caused no great stir. This was not the case when the first book of crossword puzzles appeared in late 1924, however. It led to a chain reaction in which not only was the crossword puzzle the thing everyone was doing, but marriage ceremonies used crossword puzzles; religious sermons used crossword puzzles; and colleges offered crossword puzzle courses.

This mid-1920s marvel was said to have had its origin in the spring of 1924. In a New York City apartment house, editors Richard Simon and M. Lincoln Schuster (who was known familiarly as Max) were supping with Dick's aunt, who innocently asked if they

decide to move, they could find an apartment house named after the boy pharaoh.

The Egyptian craze continued—though slightly abated—through the 1920s and didn't really end until the Great Depression started in October 1929.

But King Tut would rise again in the 1970s, when the treasures of the tomb were shown once more at a number of major American museums, in Washington, D.C.; New Orleans; Seattle; Chicago; Los Angeles; and New York. He would not only rise again but would spawn a whole spate of items in his image. There were King Tut sheets, King Tut puzzles, King Tut rugs, King Tut T-shirts and King Tut tote bags. There were also King Tut posters, King Tut ice buckets, King Tut playing cards and King Tut stationery.

You could get a King Tut item pretty cheaply (a T-shirt, for instance, was $3.50), but one could also call for a bit of cash. A gold King Tut mask would run you $2,700.00; a special King Tut hieroglyphic plate could run you $2,800.00; while you could get a copy knew of a crossword puzzle book she could give to her niece. No such thing, replied Simon and Schuster. And a good reason to create one, they decided. Little did they realize they would bring forth a national institution.

Simon and Schuster's crossword puzzle book, known simply as *The Crossword Puzzle Book*, was the two gentlemen's first publishing venture to come before the American public. Moreover, they didn't really want to become too closely identified with the little game book, so they said the book was published by the Plaza Publishing Company rather than by Simon & Schuster. There was no evidence that they were embarrassed by the book's huge success, though. And why should they have been? The book's writers—all from the staff of the *New York World* (Margaret Petherbridge, Prosper Buranelli and F. Gregory Hartswick)—certainly had not toiled in vain.

Not by a long shot. *The Crossword Puzzle Book* was everywhere. It penetrated the world of commuting and long-distance travel. One railroad, the Baltimore & Ohio, bought a stock of dictionaries for all its passengers who were looking for an *X*-letter word for anything you can think of. It penetrated the world of the courts; trials were said to have been slowed because all the court attendants were doing crossword puzzles. It penetrated the world of office procedure; secretaries wore pocket dictionaries like bracelets around their wrists, the better to do crossword puzzles. There was also an attempt to penetrate the world of high fashion. In the winter months of 1925, women began to wear dresses with crossword puzzle designs. However, this was really only a rage in Paris.

One typical incident neatly illustrates the lengths to which people were willing to go to get the time to fill those empty squares with letters. One patron stayed at a restaurant until the wee hours of the morning because he was engrossed in a crossword puzzle. When the proprietor asked him to leave so he could finally close the place, the patron refused. He was apprehended by the police and the next day was sentenced to 10 days in a four-letter word for a place of involuntary servitude—*jail*. The man said, "That's great. Now I'll have a chance to work puzzles in peace and quiet."

Crossword puzzles attracted people because they were something everybody could do; yet at the same time they showed a special intellectual mastery. Also, they were said to be great time-killers during an era when people were getting more and more leisure time. This probably hasn't changed over the years and may have been the reason why the ancient Greeks and Romans enjoyed their crossword puzzles, too (for they were said to have had them, or something very similar).

The crossword puzzle rage directly followed the rage for the Chinese game mah-jongg (see MAH-JONGG).

To do a crossword puzzle, though, you didn't need to worry about the things you had to be concerned with when you played mah-jongg—like how to interpret the beautiful but confusing-looking tiles or which rules you should play by (mah-jongg rules were constantly changing). All you needed was your native intelligence and, if you liked, a dictionary. No wonder crossword puzzles caught on the way they did.

However, within a few months in 1925, crossword puzzles ceased being a big topic of conversation. What people had become interested in was something exciting, something that would really grab them—like dance marathons (see DANCE MARATHONS) or flagpole sitting (see FLAGPOLE SITTING) or the Charleston (see CHARLESTON AND CHARLESTON VARIATIONS).

CHARLESTON (1925–26) AND CHARLESTON VARIATIONS (1926–37)

The Charleston was the dance rage of the 1920s. Moving on the balls of your feet, standing pigeon-toed, swinging the body from side to side, and knocking the knees with your hands was a continual activity of girls and guys alike. Young people were known as "flaming youth," after a silent movie of that name, and the Charleston was one of the things they did. But the Charleston was hardly limited to young people; nearly everyone was doing it. It was as frequently observed as bobbed hair, short skirts and bell-shaped hats known as cloches—other really popular items from the 1920s.

Popular, however, does not mean the same thing as accepted; like the turkey trot and the other animal dances immediately after 1910 (see TURKEY TROT AND OTHER ANIMAL DANCES) and the tango, from 1914 to 1916 (see TANGO), the Charleston was looked down upon to the point of intense hostility. Frank Borden Jr., mayor of Bradley Beach, New Jersey, said, "I have no objection to a person dancing their feet off, but I think it best that they keep away from the Charleston." It was banned at the College of William and Mary because it didn't emphasize "grace and beauty." At Goucher College it was banned, along with radios, bare knees and cigarettes. When the dance hit Nebraska, a number of social organizations pronounced it vulgar and tried to stop it.

Then, in the midst of the craze, 44 Charlestoners were killed at a dance hall known as the Pickwick Club, in Boston, Massachusetts, when the building suddenly collapsed. The tragedy was blamed on the stress that

49

Two Charleston dancers from Charleston, South Carolina. They are with the city's appreciative mayor, Thomas P. Stoney

This spirited girl has just won a Charleston contest

the Charleston put on the building. The Charleston was then banned at a number of dance halls because of their structural flimsiness.

Yet nothing dampened the Charleston's popularity. People who wanted to learn it filled the dance emporiums. Also, Charleston marathons became a fixed part of the grueling dance marathon scene (see DANCE MARATHONS). The dance gained a popularity that spread worldwide. In England the Prince of Wales (who later became King Edward VIII) did the Charleston with great abandon. European students who came over to America to study or to work brought back Charleston records. One young German, who later settled in America in the late 1930s, remembered how his older brother had done just that, and how his house in Germany was filled with the sounds of the Charleston.

The origin of the Charleston is not completely clear. It is usually maintained that the Charleston was first danced at informal gatherings of blacks who lived near Beaufort, South Carolina; some, however, claim that the Charleston came from the levees near New Orleans. In any event, the dance master of the Ziegfeld Follies, Ned Wayburn, saw it done in the South and introduced it in New York City. There it was first performed in a revue, *Runnin' Wild*, in October 1923. Choreographed by two black artists, Cecil Mack and James Johnson, the Charleston would then become popular at the El Fey Club and the Club Richman in New York. Then it took the country by storm. Everybody was singing the song Charleston, Charleston, Give Us Charleston.

There were said to be 400 different types of steps in the Charleston. The dance surely did lend itself to variations.

The American Society of Dance Teachers tried to modify it, too, in the interests of giving the Charleston "dignity," or so they said. They agreed that the Charleston would be fine without "the kicks" and as long as the toes were not raised from the floor. All this did was eliminate most of the fun.

However, it was another variation of the Charleston, the black bottom, that replaced the dance when it went out of fashion in 1926. This was also a knee-swaying, thigh-slapping, heel-scooting, hip-moving dance. As with the Charleston, it isn't certain where the black bottom got its name; though it may have been named after a section in Nashville, Tennessee known as the black bottom, where the dance was first done. It may also have been named after the black soil in the Mississippi Delta. Its faddishness followed the dance's appearance in the revue *George White Scandals of 1926*.

In the 1930s there arose another very popular dance derived from the Charleston—the shag. The shag consisted of a continual series of stepping and hopping: One minute, you would step and hop with your left foot; the next minute, you would step and hop with your right foot.

The Charleston and Charleston variants continued until 1937, when a squarelike dance with a caller caught the national fancy: the Big Apple (see BIG APPLE).

While the Charleston can still be danced today, it would most likely be done as nothing more than a curiosity. There have been revivals of 1920s clothing items, like raccoon coats in the 1950s and white suits in the 1970s, but never any extensive revival of the Charleston. But in case there ever is, here are the instructions that used to be given for the Charleston in the revue that made the dance popular, *Runnin' Wild*: "You have to learn to toe in. . . . Then stand on the balls of your feet, pigeon-toed . . . your body swings from side to side . . . the knees knock when they come together . . . make it very snappy."

OXFORD BAGS (Fall 1926)

The gals wore short skirts, cloches and bobbed hair to show that they were really "with it" in the Roaring Twenties. By all means, the guys had to do something, too. So in the medieval courtyards of Oxford University in England, fashionable swains began to appear in long, floppy pants, which got the name of "Oxford bags." They seemed so inappropriate there that the authorities tried to ban them.

What was good for merry old England was good enough for America. Oxford bags became the campus rage in the States. You could doff your raccoon coat and show yourself in all your glory—in Oxford bags. Or you could go Charlestoning (see CHARLESTON AND CHARLESTON VARIATIONS) in your Oxford bags, though they might prove a bit burdensome when you had to sway your knees.

The fad for Oxford bags lasted only a very short time, though. Maybe they were just too ungainly.

In the late 1970s long, floppy pants came back. This time, it was young girls who took them up. They were called baggies. These, too, were soon returned to the closet.

INTRODUCTION

There isn't much good to be said for the 1930–50 period. It began with the cataclysm of the Depression and ended with the terrifying prospect of the nuclear age, ushered in by the explosion of the first atomic bombs, followed by the post-World War II American-Soviet rivalry. In between, the term *Hoovervilles* (the improvised shanty towns of the Depression) had entered the American vocabulary, while the world's vocabulary had grown to include such now chillingly familiar place names as Treblinka, Bergen-Belsen, Auschwitz, and Dachau. There have been better times in which to try to survive.

Yet if we step back from the big picture, we again see Americans trying to make their way as best they could—still seeking passing pleasures, even during the hard times of the 1930s. Perhaps the most famous American fad of them all, goldfish swallowing, made its grand—if gluttonous—entrance in 1939. This was surely a fitting climax to a fanciful decade that began with such diversions as endurance golfball bouncing, endurance water bobbing and miniature golf. The latter, of course, is still with us, but today's miniature golf is not what it was in the early thirties—a doughty attempt by average Americans to enjoy life and not let economic misery overwhelm them.

Were Americans exuberant in the grim Depression decade? Hardly. They just found ways not to be dour. In 1931 many a woman flipped over the prospect of owning a fancy feathered chapeau known as the Eugenie hat. What's more, the thirties proved to be a golden age of appealingly creative imaginary characters in animated cartoons and on radio. It was the time of Mickey Mouse (followed shortly thereafter by Donald Duck), Betty Boop and Charlie McCarthy. Here were spunky characters who let nothing get them down. Could Americans be blamed for wanting to emulate them?

From 1935 on, the tone of American pastimes shifted to something resembling a search for a refuge. For the second time in just a little over two decades, Europe was drifting toward war. At the same time there were storm clouds in the Far East, coupled with the Spanish Civil War, the Japanese invasion of China, the Sudetenland crisis and the overrunning of Poland by the Nazis. Although Americans had already proved themselves isolationist enough in the 1920s, even when there were no warlike crises brewing, the events of the 1930s gave good reason for a renewed isolationism—a desire to withdraw within the protective confines of a big, secluded continent-island. One notable expression of this newfound native identity was Americans'

rediscovery of their traditional country dances, with all-American square dancing capturing the popular fancy.

Yet fancies had to be put on hold following Pearl Harbor and the entry of the United States into World War II. The war years were marked by only one domestic craze: the zoot suit. It was a very strange garment indeed, and news of it even reached American troops, for there are pictures of G.I.'s decked out in zoot suits.

After the war passing pleasures took on a completely different quality. Stunting—which went back to flagpole sitting of the 1920s but had perhaps become increasingly important during the 1930s as an exciting form of escapism against a backdrop of distress—was passé. Also, for the first time since 1910—after the obsession with animal dances, the craze for the tango and its variants, the Charleston fad and its variants, and the revival of American square dancing—dance no longer commanded everyone's attention. (Nor would it again in any truly overwhelming way until the advent of the twist in the 1960s.)

The big new attraction in America debuted late in the 1940s—television. This would, of course, change everything. TV brought new figures to be adulated, laughed at or imitated. It was the time of Milton Berle, Howdy Doody and, soon enough, Hopalong Cassidy. Before the era of television, it took a while for personalities to become established in the public consciousness. But the new medium brought people the opportunity to see such personalities easily and often. Thus, when Milton Berle casually referred to himself as "Uncle Miltie" in one of his Tuesday night broadcasts, the nickname caught fire, with Boston fans (who happened to be construction workers) calling out to "Uncle Miltie" upon seeing the entertainer walk by the following day. "Uncle Miltie" it had become by the power of "the tube"; and "Uncle Miltie" it would remain.

But just as television could beam the disguises of Milton Berle into the living rooms of the nation's families, so it could beam in the latest Cold War developments. Americans would soon be able to glance up from their bowl of breakfast cereal to view the blossoming mushroom clouds rising from atomic bomb tests in the Nevada desert.

Way back in the 1890s, you could use the antique stereopticon to view humorous pictures or battle scenes, motionless and silent. Now, all you had to do was flick on a dial to see and hear the pratfalls, the guffaws, the whine of shrapnel, the flash of artillery. Life itself may not have changed, but midcentury technology had—for good or ill—given that life a hitherto unattainable immediacy and vitality.

AMERICAN ORIGINALS— NAMELY, PEANUT PUSHERS, GOLFBALL BOUNCERS, PEPPER EATERS, PICKLE EATERS, SEESAW SITTERS, WATER BOBBERS AND TREE SITTERS (Circa 1930)

I sit to show that women can sit in trees as well as men.
—A 9-year-old who had been sitting up the
same tree for a long, long time

Dazzle, dazzle, dazzle. Despair, despair, despair. In 1930 Americans couldn't really decide whether they just had been through a cataclysm (the Depression of 1929) that positively had to make their lives dreary or whether it was a time for them to do daring, crazy, really unheard-of deeds for a little money—like to win a $50 bet or to collect a prize from a local newspaper that was looking for something extraordinary to write about. It was the time of the stunt lads and lasses: a raw-egg eater, a golfball bouncer, a nonstop pickle eater who would only consume pickles of a certain size, a peanut pusher who inched his way up a mountain and more. This was hot stuff—a real three-ring circus that spanned an entire nation.

First, however, a word of explanation about these American originals, whom the prolific and very good contemporary writer Nunnally Johnson called "nuts" and whom other historians have also tried to figure out. This is just an attempt, but one that has to be made, because figuring out why these originals acted this way—with their bizarre egg eating, pickle chomping, peanut pushing and golfball bouncing—is very important.

Crazy stunting to win a little money was not new to American life in 1930; there had been the dance marathon for many years (see DANCE MARATHONS), and there was flagpole sitting (see FLAGPOLE SITTING), with its hero "Shipwreck" Kelly, and there was a transcontinental race with 199 contestants in 1928, which became known as the Bunion Derby. Yet a dance marathon and a transcontinental race—albeit certainly grueling for those who took part in them—were not really peculiar things. As for "Shipwreck" Kelly's flagpole sitting, huzzah for "Shipwreck," but he was a Hollywood actor and stuntman from way back, and this was what you might expect from him.

In other words, before 1929 American life was settled. Oh, it had its weird edges, which gave it its color, but for the most part it was settled. Not so in 1930, as shown by the American original folks with their surreal stunts, which really were so very personal. They reflected the catastrophe—a catastrophe made of nothing more than paper (things like stocks and bonds), in a faraway city, at a place called Wall Street. Who could understand it, and who could understand why these American originals did what they did for more than just money?

Take, for instance, the pickle eater from Illinois. Now, it is no great thing to eat pickles; lots of people just love them. But this particular pickle eater insisted that each of his pickles be at least 5 inches long; and he proceeded to consume 25 at one continuous sitting. In the middle of the disastrous Depression, the fellow is thinking about eating pickles, and they must be 5 inches long!

Or consider the St. Paul, Minnesota man who regarded himself as something of an aquatic soul. He got near some water and proceeded to dunk his head up and down 1,843 times. During at least half that time (when he was under water), he couldn't even see the audience that was looking at him, unlike those dance marathoners or flagpole sitters, who could watch their audiences anytime they wanted to. And surely it is no pleasure filling with your gills with water. But he did it all right. Somehow, a thing like that just looks like desperation, like beating your fist against a wall. It couldn't have been fun, and he couldn't have gotten much money out of it. But it was better to do something crazily inventive like that than to just sit around hoping.

Then there was the fellow who, to win a $50 bet, pushed a peanut up Pike's Peak with his nose. This took 30 days. Yet this was America, supposedly the land where people were practical, so he made sure that his peanut-pushing feat was made easier by a "specially designed steel nose extension," as Nunnally Johnson reported. Nothing crazy about this man's deed—he had harnessed technology.

Now, how about the competition in New Jersey between two men to see who could eat more green peppers at a single sitting? The winner—who collected a $50 prize—ate 80, and the loser ate 74. Nunnally Johnson said the moral of that story was that "a good big man will always beat a good little man," because the winner weighed more. That might have been one moral. Another could have been that in the chaos of America in 1930, it paid to excel in such exotic pursuits as pepper eating.

And what could have gotten into the girl who took it upon herself to bounce a golfball 2,710 times?

And then there were the meditative pastimes: seesaw sitting and tree sitting. Both allowed world enough and time to ponder the American economic debacle with the patience of a sage. Of these, tree sitting was the closest to the spirit of the Roaring Twenties, because it really was just a variation on flagpole sitting, the sitter being appreciably higher than the ground. And throughout the nation, tree sitters sat. Paul Sann, in his *Fads, Follies and Delusions of the American People*, has recorded how the tree-sitting record grew as people took to the branches in Wisconsin, New Jersey, Pennsylvania and Indiana. The line of reasoning must have gone something like: America has turned topsy-turvy, so let's go roost in a tree.

Or consider the two young Illinois girls who sat on a swing for 18½ hours and only quit because they thought that their parents would be worried. These misses must have known there was craziness in the air then.

Craziness there was, but not only on the part of the American originals, who did everything from eating 5-inch pickles to spending three-quarters of a day on a swing. Think of the reporters who were sent out to cover these events to make sure there was no cheating. Was there a reporter around to see all 1,843 times that the St. Paul man dunked himself in the water? Was there an official on hand to measure and vouch for the size of each 5-inch pickle? This, too, was pretty crazy.

American originals continued to appear throughout the 1930s, but 1930 was their big year. By 1931 the craziness had perhaps moved up a degree—from the world of the stunt to the world of fashion. In the summer of 1931, when Americans were not just one year into the Depression but two, the big news no less was the profusion of women who had begun to appear in the Empress Eugenie hat—a special feather chapeau resembling that worn by the 19th-century royal Frenchwoman, the Empress Eugenie (see EUGENIE HAT). Now this was a sure sign that Americans were finally settling down again and getting practical!

Miniature Golf (1930)

What a racket they make! Why boys and girls in evening dress come on the course late at night and play until 3 or 4 in the morning.

— Chicago police commissioner on disturbances created by miniature golf

Miniature golf—also known as Tom Thumb golf, Lilliputian golf or pygmy golf—really got started on a mountaintop in Tennessee, just like backwoodsman

Davy Crockett, whose coonskin hat inspired a fad of its own many years later, in 1955 (see DAVY CROCKETT AND HIS FUR HAT). There, on the grounds of Garnet Carter's Lookout Mountain hotel in Chattanooga, guests could choose a trusty putter and confront the roller coasters, subterranean passages, miniscule pyramids, doghouses and seesaws of the miniature golf course. This was in 1927. Within three years miniature golf was everywhere. A diversion of the flapper age had become the first recreational fad of the Depression. Mini-golf courses were fun, entertaining, cheap and a great place to bring a date.

Miniature golf first became popular in the South, then in the West and then in the East. You could find courses adjoining hotels and gasoline stations, or in barns or skyscrapers. Zoning commissioners of both cities and towns became very upset at the way vacant lots were becoming miniature golf courses. Many cities tried to ban Sunday miniature golf playing and to enforce a midnight curfew. In Chicago there was some suspicion that the notorious Al Capone gang was charging miniature golf proprietors protection money. It was only supposed to be $5 a month, though. That wouldn't pay the water bills for cleaning the golf balls these days.

Miniature golf could be as chic as you wanted to make it. In Salt Lake City society men and women wore tuxedos and gowns at private miniature golf parties at a spread known as Covey's Cocoanut Grove. Also, if you wanted, when you played miniature golf, you could even have a caddy, who, it was generally accepted, should be paid 75 cents a round. If you could bear to carry your own clubs, though, a round would cost you 30 cents in the afternoon or 50 cents at night.

In 1930 miniature golf was the cure for the Depression blues, both for players on the links and for owners of the courses. The metropolitan New York City and Los Angeles areas alone had 1,000 courses. Altogether, over 40,000 courses had sprung up across the nation, employing over 200,000 people. Creating a miniature golf course was a whole different enterprise than laying out and tending a genuine course. All you needed for the pint-sized version were bricks, boards and drainpipes. The artificial surface was made up of crushed cottonseed hulls, a process that had been discovered in the 1920s.

Yet by 1931, perhaps due to overexposure, miniature golf had become passe. *Miniature Golf Management*, a periodical for owners of miniature golf courses that lasted one year (from 1930 to 1931), cited that in California not one miniature golf course showed a profit in the winter months of 1931. To give the public a new novelty, driving ranges were introduced.

Miniature golf, of course, is still something that you can do in America. It has never again become the

rage that it was in 1930, though, when what was happening on miniature golf courses was featured in magazines and newspapers.

In any event, the fad for miniature golf showed that Americans could still have a great old time laughing at themselves, even in the midst of an economic depression. Miniature golf was sort of a spoof on country club golf, just as the 1930s cartoon character Betty Boop was a spoof on flappers. If you couldn't afford playing that emerald green fairway, well there was a great miniature golf carpet just around the corner. If you missed that picturesque water hazard, there was a great windmill in town that you could shoot through.

And you needn't ever feel that a taste for this pastime excluded you from the upper crust. After all, miniature golf courses graced many an ocean liner, and the next British monarch, Edward VIII, then the Prince of Wales, played it at every opportunity.

BETTY BOOP (1930–34; High Point, 1934)

Anyone care to boop-oop-a-doop with Betty Boop? How can you boop-oop-a-doop? It's easy. All you have to do is move around any which way and sing "boop-oop-a-doop" whenever you please—just like Betty Boop did in such animated cartoons as "Betty Boop's Penthouse," "Betty Boop's Big Boss," "Betty in Blunderland" or "Betty Boop for President." Betty was quite a sensual chick. As the pen-and-ink creature said in an interview with *Screenland Magazine*, "Would you mind if I skipped all that hooey [about being an actress] and talked about my love life?"

What was this creature, Betty Boop? Well, she wore scanty little black dresses and had a slightly disheveled, curly pixie haircut, a suggestive single garter strap and a soft voice. In a time of Depression, Betty Boop was like one of those high-spirited seductive females of the 1920s, a "flapper" (see BOBBED HAIR); and—judging from the teasing way she treated her male friends—she was also something of a "vamp" (see VAMPIRE THEDA).

What's more, Betty didn't become a human dame immediately, having started out in her first cartoon, Max Fleischer's 1930 "Dizzy Dishes," as something that looked like a female dog, with big ears, huge jaws and a black button nose, and with "cute feminine legs on her," as Fleischer recalled. By 1932 Betty had become all woman and even looked like one of the 1920s "flapper" girls. And why did Betty Boop go boop-oop-a-doop? She did so because she was based on showgirl Helen Kane, who called herself the boop-oop-a-doop girl ever since she boop-oop-a-dooped for the first time when rehearsing a song, That's My Weakness Now, for Paramount Studios. Later, though, when Helen Kane sued Max Fleischer Productions for appropriating her boop-oop-a-doop act, she lost the case. It was shown that there were even earlier boop-oop-a-doopers in the 1920s.

No boop-oop-a-dooper ever reached the celebrity fad status of Betty, though. One magazine observed that "She Boops to Conquer."

Betty Boop was everywhere. There were Betty Boop dolls, Betty Boop handkerchiefs, Betty Boop chocolate and nut candy bars, Betty Boop sweaters, Betty Boop tea sets, Betty Boop bathing suits and Betty Boop marbles. You could play that new craze, contract bridge, with Betty Boop playing cards, listen to sweet-singing crooner Rudy Vallee on a Betty Boop radio and light up a smoke from a Betty Boop cigarette case.

She was an idol in the midst of the Depression. In the middle of her cartoons, she would suddenly break into joyful, and slightly provocative, song, which could really make a person happy. A lot of folks even preferred the somewhat risque Betty Boop to Mickey Mouse (see MICKEY MOUSE).

In the mid-1930s interest in Betty Boop began to flag. And in 1937, when Max Fleischer moved his operation to Florida, Betty Boop was discontinued altogether. Betty's sweet voice-over, Mae Questel, wanted to stay in New York.

It is still possible to get Betty Boop stuff, such as charm bracelets, necklaces, buttons and shirts. For a time in the late 1970s, Betty Boop was even something of a fun idol to young girls once again. But the animated cartoon character (which had once been only a dog), with its unique booping joy of life, has never been revived.

A miniature golf course underneath the mountains

A miniature golf course in the city

MICKEY MOUSE (Early 1930s; Middle 1950s; 1970s)

Mickey Mouse is a national treasure and has been so for 53 years now. He cannot properly be called a fad, yet there were certain times in which Mickey was so glorious and so influential that he cannot be passed unnoticed, either. Here, a few of these overwhelming moments will be recounted. Or as the illustrator Maurice Sendak recently said of Mickey: "He was our common street friend. My brother and sister and I chewed his gum, brushed our teeth with his toothbrush, played with him . . . best of all, our street pal was also a movie star."

Sendak was recalling a time when he was young, and when Mickey was very young, too, in the 1930s. Mickey first appeared on November 18, 1928 in Walt Disney's cartoon "Steamboat Willie." He was popular immediately, so much so that when there was no Mickey Mouse cartoon preceeding a movie feature, there arose a common American lament, "What, no Mickey Mouse?" which soon became an American catchphrase. Well, if for some reason you didn't find him in a particular movie theater on a particular day, you could still find him nearly everywhere else. You could see little girls in Mickey Mouse dresses or perhaps playing with Mickey Mouse dolls. You could lather yourself with Mickey Mouse soap, blow up Mickey Mouse balloons, eat Mickey Mouse candy and step out with Mickey Mouse moccasins. And of course, the most famous item was the Mickey Mouse watch; 2.5 million of them were sold in the 1930s, at only $2.95 each. You could also get Mickey Mouse belt buckles, ice cream, bathrobes, alarm clocks, banks and much more. A Mickey Mouse wind-up handcar saved the Lionel Company from going bankrupt.

If you wanted to spend only 10 cents, you could get a Mickey Mouse item of costume jewelry. But if you were a true plutocrat and really loved the mouse, you could also spend $1,200 on a Mickey Mouse bracelet.

Walt Disney did not always tell the same story about Mickey's origin. He said the idea of a cartoon mouse came to him on a train trip he took with his wife in 1927. He thought of the name Mortimer for the mouse, but she said that this was just too fancy and he should stick to Mickey. But he has also explained Mickey's origin in more professional terms, saying: "I can't say just how the idea came. We wanted another animal. We had a cat; a mouse naturally came to mind." On January 13, 1930 Mickey Mouse appeared for the first time as a comic strip in the newspapers.

The Mickey Mouse wristwatch

Also, with the great popularity of Mickey Mouse, a number of Mickey Mouse clubs were born—a phenomenon that would be seen once again in the 1950s.

Mickey Mouse's pluckiness became a symbol for Americans during the Depression, in the 1930s. In a time of considerable distress, he did make people laugh. President Roosevelt was said to have been a great admirer of Mickey's. Those Americans who could afford to travel to Europe could find a wax Mickey Mouse at Madame Tussaud's in London. However, he could not replace the real Mickey, the hero of cartoons like "The Barnyard Broadcast," "The Klondike Kid," "Touchdown Mickey," "Mickey Mouse's Service Station" and "Two-Gun Mickey."

Mickey was so popular in the 1930s that he spawned other Walt Disney favorites—like, in 1935, the cocksure Donald Duck.

Still in 1944 it was M-i-c-k-e-y M-o-u-s-e that was used as the password when the Allies landed on D-Day. On one of America's greatest days, this fantastic rodent was again remembered.

In the middle 1950s Mickey Mouse became really important once more with the television program "The Mickey Mouse Club," whose name was taken from those clubs of the 1930s. It was the thing for kids to wear mouse ears, just like the kids on the show—like Annette, Karen, Jimmy, Darlene, Cubby, Lonnie and Doreen, who were known as the Mouseketeers. In fact, it was Mickey Mouse who threatened another great kids' idol, the cowboy puppet, Howdy Doody (see HOWDY DOODY).

Mickey Mouse ears from the 1950s TV show "The Mickey Mouse Club"

In the 1970s Mickey Mouse came back once more. But this time he came back as part of a great nostalgia craze. It became the thing to wear a Mickey Mouse watch for this reason or to have any other Mickey Mouse artifact. This was the Mickey Mouse of the 1930s remembered. But the Mickey Mouse of the 1950s was remembered also, with reruns of "The Mickey Mouse Club" or with the television show being a big item of conversation. As with Howdy Doody, there were Mickey Mouse revivals on any number of college campuses.

Mickey Mouse is going to last a long time. At this very moment people are probably waiting to meet him at Disneyland or Disneyworld. He is so much a part of us that we don't think of him anymore. But there was a time, in the 1930s, when we thought of him a lot, and he helped us, this mouse of whom Walt Disney said, "He's a nice fellow who never does anyone any harm, gets into scrapes through no fault of his own and somehow manages to come up grinning."

EUGENIE HAT (August–October 1931)

The Eugenie hat, the millinery rage of 1931, was so controversial that it even caused pronunciation problems. The *New York Times* declared that if you were going to wear this voguish ostrich-feathered item, named after Empress Eugenie, the wife of Napoleon III, you should say it like the French do: Make it sound like E-ZEAN-EE, not like U-JENNY. This vulgarization was particularly popular in Iowa, sniffed the editorial.

At a time when the Depression was raging madly,

the ownership and wearing of a Eugenie hat could create the illusion of carefree prosperity. After all, once you donned the chapeau, you were commemorating a 19th-century woman of royalty who never wore the same gown twice, making sure of this by building an entirely new wardrobe every six months and getting rid of all those old rags. Which isn't to say that wearers of Eugenie hats were the only ones to see the world through rose-tinted glasses; if you read many of the newspapers and magazines of the time, you would think that life was going on normally—that it was business as usual. But in truth, America had become crazy; even its stunts had gotten strange (see AMERICAN ORIGINALS).

In the 1920s, women had worn bell-shaped hats known as cloches, and indeed, the Eugenie hat—also called the Second Empire hat and the Montijo—was a variation of these, but with one important difference. The hat bore on it a number of ostrich feathers (or eventually plumage of other birds) and was the first hat in a while to have decorations on it. The humorist Dorothy Parker could be seen wearing the Eugenie hat, as could your typical teen-ager in upstate New York, as could all those gals in Iowa who mispronounced it. It could be found in the smartest boutiques as well as in the "little shops" where they sold "cheap copies of the aristocratic headgear" (as a *New York Times* editorial rather snobbishly observed).

It has been maintained that the fascination with the Eugenie hat originated in Paris and resulted from an event that took place at the opera—the presentation of Jacques Offenbach's work *La vie parisienne*. Going to see an Offenbach 19th-century opera has always been a great event in the city of lights, and the 1931 revival of this work, which is one of Offenbach's most lighthearted, inspired ladies to don the Eugenie hat of the period depicted in the opera.

Well, American women were not going to let this one get by without showing that the Yankees could do every bit as well as those *jeunes filles françaises*. In the summer of 1931, everything was really humming at hat factories for a long time (one observer said that it ended the millinery industry depression, as if no one else were in the very same condition). This was true of the Knox Company of Brooklyn and the Stetson Company of Philadelphia, and it was even more particularly true of four hat companies in Waterbury, Connecticut: Mallory Hat Company, George McLachlan Hat Company, H. McLachlan Hat Company and Frank H. Lee Hat Company. These four companies were quite literally running day and night to produce the feathery chapeaux—three shifts a day at eight hours per shift. All craftspeople in the hat industry benefited from this: the dyers, the hat labelers, the feather dealers, the blockers, the hair net people and the fur felt body dealers. There were also said to be more than 300 small shops in New York City that took part in the ostrich-feathered hat boom.

In other words, people who worked at making Eugenie hats were lucky—very lucky at this time. They didn't have to even think of those horrendously sad "Hoovervilles," or their local equivalent. (One has to conclude that the wearers of the Eugenie hats probably didn't dwell much on the prevailing poverty, either.)

However, not everyone was pleased with the Eugenie hats. There were many who were outraged by them. They simply could not stand the idea that birds—not only the ostrich but also the bird of paradise and the pheasant—were being slaughtered so women could deck themselves with feathers. One woman walking in the millinery district in New York City said she was appalled day after day when she considered what happened to the birds and observed that "every human being with any feelings should shudder at the thought of wearing" a Eugenie hat.

Yet by October 1931 the Eugenie hat had proved to be only a passing fancy. No substantial reason has been offered for the sudden lack of interest. Then, on the other hand, perhaps the fad was proving to be just like Eugenie herself. The French princess (born of Spanish blood) never *had* worn the same things for very long.

Also, although the Eugenie hat passed, feathered hats in general did not. The next big hat, Schiaparelli's "doll's hat," used ostrich tips, too, from time to time.

It was, all in all, a decidedly bizarre comment on the temper of the times that Eugenie hats suddenly developed into a full-blown craze in the midst of a cataclysmic economic depression. If nothing else, the fad's equally abrupt demise eased the minds of the hat's detractors, who objected (among other things) to the raffish tilt at which it was worn—one of the very reasons the headgear had been found enticing in the first place.

SHIRLEY TEMPLE (1934–37)

Shirley Temple was more than the most prominent child actress in Hollywood in the 1930s. During the Depression she was a symbol just as much as little Mickey Mouse, who, with his good cheer, could not be resisted. Shirley Temple brought cheer, too. And so, of course, there were Shirley Temple hats, Shirley Temple shoes, Shirley Temple glasses and, most of all, Shirley Temple dolls. People just liked to look at this little girl with her corkscrew curls and engaging dimples. And they also liked to listen to her sing that joyful song The Good Ship Lollipop, from 1934's *Stand Up and Cheer*, a high-spirited movie (just right to get people's minds off the Depression) in which she played the secretary of amusement in the president's cabinet.

President Roosevelt said of her, and of the American public that was so adoring: "It is a splendid thing that for just 15 cents an American can go to a movie and look at the smiling face of a baby and forget his troubles." The people knew more than their chief executive. Shirley Temple was more than a baby. In 1934 she was 5 years old, and in 1935 she was 6. Every year her birthday was marked by many a newspaper. And not only newspaper articles but books were written about her birthday parties.

What caught on most was the Shirley Temple doll. This first appeared in 1934, after Shirley had starred in the movie *Curly Top*. You could get the doll Shirley in a knife-pleated dress or in a dress of red and white plaid (both dolls were 18 inches high). Later there were other Shirley Temple dolls, in a cowgirl uniform or with a bow, old-fashioned hat, old-fashioned dress and plume (this was what the actress had worn in the movie *The Little Colonel*). This was not a time when everybody could afford a real doll for their little girl, so there were cutout Shirley Temple dolls as well, also very popular.

There were Shirley Temple lockets and charm bracelets, too. You could also get yourself a Shirley Temple mug if you bought a box of Bisquick flour. There was also a nonalcoholic drink called a Shirley Temple.

Children were hungry to find out about Shirley Temple, or perhaps it was that adults wanted to tell them about her. So there were books like *Shirley Temple: Her Life in Pictures* and *The Story of Shirley Temple*. To many a child these must have been engaging. They told how she played with her dog Corky or the things she liked to do in the summer, but they also told how she had to have an enclosed patio built because people kept wanting to get close to her.

Beginning in 1937 Shirley Temple was no longer the little child on whom nearly everyone's eyes were riveted. People had become more interested in radio's red-haired dummy Charlie McCarthy and his stinging wit (see CHARLIE MCCARTHY). And at the end of the decade, her mother, Gertrude, announced Shirley's retirement from the movies.

But there was no way that she or anybody else could retire all those Shirley Temple dolls.

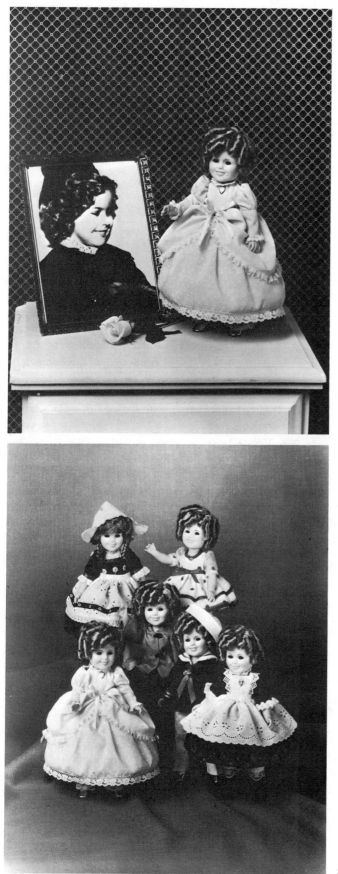

A Shirley Temple doll in a costume based on her film *The Little Colonel*

Six Shirley Temple dolls

BIG APPLE (1937–38)

Looking down from the balcony of the Big Apple nightclub (formerly a church) in Columbia, South Carolina, university students watched black dancers move around in a circle, while a caller instructed them to "cut that apple," "shine," "give your gal a whirl" or "praise that apple." The students were struck by how much fun all these dancers were having, and within a few months after it was first seen, in July 1937, the dance, which was often compared to an old-fashioned hoedown, had become the thing to do. Perhaps it excited in Americans a feeling that "we're all in the same boat together" (the Depression), but whatever it was, nearly everybody was doing it. They were doing the Big Apple in New York City, St. Louis, Memphis, Duluth and Minneapolis; and they were doing the Big Apple, too, in Kansas City, Missouri; Atlanta; Chicago; Omaha; and Dayton. It was an item in the paper in all these places. When President Franklin Roosevelt's son John had an engagement party (he was to marry Anne Lindsay Clark) at the White House, he and his fiancee danced the Big Apple. This, too, was a hot item.

From the beginning of its popularity, the dance was known as the Big Apple, named after the nightclub where the University of South Carolina students had first seen it done. The dance consisted of two parts: first, when all the couples danced together in a circle; and second, when one couple came out to do individual steps, which was known as "shining." As that one couple "shined," the other couples would clap, beat time and shout. The Big Apple also had elements of popular dances of the last decade—the Charleston, the black bottom and the shag (see CHARLESTON AND CHARLESTON VARIATIONS).

One of the most attractive features of the Big Apple was the instructions of the caller, which made it different from the Charleston, a dance that people were beginning to grow tired of after a decade in which it was *the* hoofing thing to do. Sometimes the instructions were really conventional like "give your gal a whirl" or "right foot in, now swing high," but sometimes they were much more fanciful. You might be told to "carry water to the right" (look as if you're hauling a large bucket of water) or "sprinkle roses to right" (looked as if you're scattering roses about). Or there might be a reference to history: "Paul Revere to the right" (look as if you're riding a horse). Instructions of this sort abounded, and they varied from location to location. Sometimes the caller, on the spur of the moment, would make up an instruction. No explanations can be found for such Big Apple steps as "Frankenstein" or "let Roosevelt knock at the White House door," but people knew how to do them.

In 1937 there were 16,000 dancing schools in the United States. One dance that must have brought in a lot of business was the Big Apple.

There was also a variation on the Big Apple known as the little peach. The little peach, however, never caught on.

Interest in the Big Apple waned in 1938, because a British dance, the Lambeth walk (see LAMBETH WALK), had begun to catch on in America.

CHARLIE MCCARTHY (1937–39)

Get that guy out of the way.
—A collective cry that went up from a crowd at Grand Central Station, New York City, waiting to see dummy Charlie McCarthy. The "guy" happened to be his ventriloquist, Edgar Bergen.

At one time, a couple of generations ago, everyone knew Charlie McCarthy, with his pip-squeaking, wisecracking voice, which also sounded sort of like the voice of a little old Boston brahmin lady. They knew him best from his voice because Charlie McCarthy could only be heard over the radio, but they knew him also from thousands upon thousands upon thousands of pictures of the little fellow, with his monocle, his tuxedo and his neatly shined shoes. It was Charlie McCarthy who reigned supreme over radio in the late 1930s, when the Depression was only halfway done, and people still liked any creature with brass and humor, which this red-haired dummy certainly had.

There were Charlie McCarthy radio sets, Charlie McCarthy alarm clocks, Charlie McCarthy dolls, Charlie McCarthy sweatshirts, with wisecracks on the back, Charlie McCarthy playing cards, Charlie McCarthy souvenir spoons, Charlie McCarthy masquerade costumes, and Charlie McCarthy bisque figurines around, in abundance. He was the subject of editorials in the *New York Times* and also the subject of any number of gossip columnists who wanted to know about his private life. Who wouldn't want to have Charlie's good spirits and be able to say to that cranky comedian W.C. Fields, who was on his radio show, "Mr. Fields, are you eating a tomato or is that your nose?" Even Mickey Mouse, who was faddish in the early years of the 1930s, and whose spirit first lifted the pall of the Depression for a lot of people, would not have spoken that way to W.C. Fields. Perhaps people now needed a dummy rather than a cartoon character to warm up to.

Sailors do the Big Apple

This dummy was the creation of ventriloquist Edgar Bergen (real name Edgar Bergrren), who found out, quite by accident, that he had the skill of ventriloquism, and who then wrote away to hone his skills. This was way back in the twenties, when "hooch" alcohol, flappers and flagpole sitting were big. The origin of Bergen's Charlie McCarthy is shrouded in some legend (there are those who say that Bergen bought him from dollmaker Charles Mack—thus inspiring the dummy's name—for $35), but there is no doubt that Bergen traveled the back entertainment circuits like chautauquas, cruise ships and small nightclubs with young Charlie before appearing on singer Rudy Vallee's radio show in 1936. Nor was this the slick Charlie who finally appeared in 1938; the original Charlie kind of looked more cloddish, with his overalls and cap. Yet almost every newspaper in the United States started to talk about that $35 piece of "Michigan pine wood"

that had created such a stir and a merchandising bonanza besides. And there is no doubt that he was a personality; moreover, Bergen did a lot more than routinely trot him out on stage. The ventriloquist really turned him into a charismatic figure at all times and in all places. For instance, when a workman for NBC-radio studios was unpacking Bergen's belongings and moving around the box in which Charlie was kept, Charlie started "screaming for release." All this did was to amuse just one individual—the workman was said to have been taken aback by this strange intrusion—not any general public. It was actions of this sort, however, that might have kept Bergen's imaginative juices flowing—might have prevented the act from growing stale and losing its human touch.

After Edgar Bergen became so successful, Americans experienced a resurgence of interest in becoming ventriloquists.

Edgar Bergen and Charlie McCarthy's own radio show, "The Sanborn Hour" (presented by Sanborn Instant Coffee), began in January 1937. It was the number one entertainment show on the air until 1941. Before 1939 everyone wanted to know about Charlie, and so they learned that his wardrobe cost $300 a year and that he had one silk cummerbund, four dress shirts, two white ties, one camel's hair coat, one beret, two white ties and one black tie; also that the railroad companies insisted that he pay for his own ticket; also that he wore size 3½ hats and size 2AAA shoes. Yet such tidbits came across not only in gossip columns about the show biz world but also on radio itself. Since radio is a medium far different from television (which makes it sort of easy for us—all we have to do is keep our eyes open), Bergen (and others) had to make us visualize through enticing and vivid presentations.

What really stays in your mind about Charlie McCarthy are those jibing conversations with W. C. Fields, with his Irishlike voice, on "The Sanborn Hour." For instance, Fields pretends that he is too, too tired of the hubbub in the entertainment world and decides to spend a very indefinite amount of time camping "far away from the madding crowd" and living in a pup tent. McCarthy asks if he can join him in the pup tent. Fields replies that he "can take a nap in the fireplace and keep us both warm." Or Fields threatening to cut Charlie up into a flophouse for termites: Charlie replies as sardonically as possible, "Oh, Mr. Fields, you make me shudder." This may not be high wit, but one can't help thinking that it has no less substance to it than the dialogues between Archie Bunker and the Meathead in "All in The Family."

In 1939, one year after Charlie McCarthy got his animated features, consisting of moving elbows, moving shoulders, moving wrists, moving hips and moving knees, as well as his new cosmopolitan look, with its tuxedo, flower in the buttonhole and shiny shoes, he started to lose some of his riveting popularity. Edgar Bergen introduced another dummy—a real hayseed type named Mortimer Snerd; the papers talked about their conflict, and Charlie was said to be very jealous. The conflict did not go down in the annals of history, however; nor was it even roughly comparable to that between the Hatfields and the McCoys. In 1941 "The Sanborn Hour" fell to number three in the ratings for radio shows. But by December of that year, war had broken out, so no one cared very much about ratings. Like Mickey Mouse, Charlie McCarthy conscripted himself and was seen wearing military clothing.

After the end of World War II, the television age came soon enough, and Edgar Bergen and Charlie McCarthy did not become part of it, unlike so many other entertainers who went from radio to television without a hitch, like Milton Berle, Jack Benny, Hopa-

long Cassidy, Amos 'n' Andy and the Lone Ranger. Charlie became passe, and when he made an infrequent guest appearance on television in the 1950s, he really seemed dated.

Yet even though no definite link has been established, it is hard to think that Charlie McCarthy and the whole "Sanborn Hour" did not have a distinct influence on that most popular children's puppet show of the late 1940s and the 1950s, Howdy Doody (see HOWDY DOODY). With his red hair and freckled features, Howdy was very much like Charlie, even though he was much more the goody-goody and really did not have much of a sense of humor. Dilly Dally, a sidekick of Howdy's, was also a ringer for Mortimer Snerd, with his hayseed ways. And old Phineas T. Bluster, who was always trying to puncture Howdy's hopes, was always being mean to him and was always scheming to make him look like an idiot, acted the way none other than Mr. W. C. Fields had acted with Charlie McCarthy.

Now, well into the 1980s, Howdy has already been rediscovered by the nostalgia buffs. Charlie McCarthy, however, has not yet been rediscovered. Yet it is possible that if they play back those old radio programs featuring this red-haired shrewdie, a star may be reborn—even if W. C. Fields did call him a flophouse for termites when he was in a mean mood and "my little twig" when he was trying to be affable.

LAMBETH WALK (1938)

The Lambeth Walk was a dance in which many couples strutted forward, linked arms, reversed position, faced each other, clapped and then, as a final step, jerked their thumbs over their shoulders, saying "oi" for no apparent reason—it just made the dance more fun. It came on the scene when the Big Apple, with its couples in a circle, its caller and its unusual and sometimes improvised instructions (see BIG APPLE) was really popular. To some extent, the Lambeth Walk replaced the Big Apple and became more faddish.

As the Lambeth Walk was a dance originally done in Great Britain, its popularity might have resulted from the fact that some Americans wanted to favor a European dance rather than a homegrown step at this time. In England the dance was known as the "cockney strut" and was said to be a variation of another British step, the coster walk of 1918.

It was a number of New York socialites who introduced the Lambeth Walk at a dance at the fashionable St. Regis Hotel in July 1938.

The Lambeth Walk only caught on for a very short time and never achieved the popularity that the Big Apple did. By 1939 homegrown dances had once more become voguish. These were square dances with do-si-dos, promenades, sashays, bowing to your partners and bowing to your corners. The Lambeth Walk was really just an unusual interlude in the history of popular American dance.

For a short time after its brief popularity, the Lambeth Walk was replaced by a dance done very much the same way, known as the pickle (see PICKLE). But instead of saying "oi," the dancers exclaimed "It's a pickle."

PICKLE (1938)

The pickle was a short-lived dance fad that came after the Lambeth Walk, that dance which was originally born in London (see LAMBETH WALK). Like the Lambeth Walk, there was much strutting forward, linking arms, reversing position, facing your partner and clapping in the pickle. Also, like the Lambeth Walk, in the final step you threw your thumbs over your shoulder and made a declaration.

And therein lay the difference. In the Lambeth Walk the couple said, "oi." But in the pickle the couple said, "It's a pickle."

The pickle was too much like the Lambeth Walk to last when the Lambeth Walk itself was no longer appealing. People wanted to do something more American—perhaps to get their minds off what was happening in Europe, where war was obviously coming—and they turned to square dancing for their hoofing pleasure (see DEPRESSION SQUARE DANCES).

But be that as it may, you had to say one thing for the pickle: It had a catchy name.

A couple does the Lambeth Walk in the late 1930s

GOLDFISH SWALLOWING (1939)

The fad for swallowing goldfish began at Harvard College about a month after Groundhog Day on March 3, 1939. One of the most madcap of all American fads and one particularly typical of college high jinks, goldfish swallowing resulted from one young lad's remembrance of things past. He was Lothrop Withington Jr.,

who had seen goldfish swallowing done on a Honolulu beach 10 years earlier, when he went to visit his grandma. He was then only a boy of 10; little did he realize that as a Harvard College senior, he would swallow a goldfish in the college union to win a $10 bet. A couple of college buddies had challenged him to gobble up the little fishy.

Goldfish swallowing might have remained forever obscure—a stunt among friends—had Withington's pals not gone public with their dare. They told the student newspaper, *The Harvard Crimson,* about it. The regular Boston newspapers were also soon alerted, and sure enough someone from each of the various city rooms came to witness Withington's devouring deed.

67

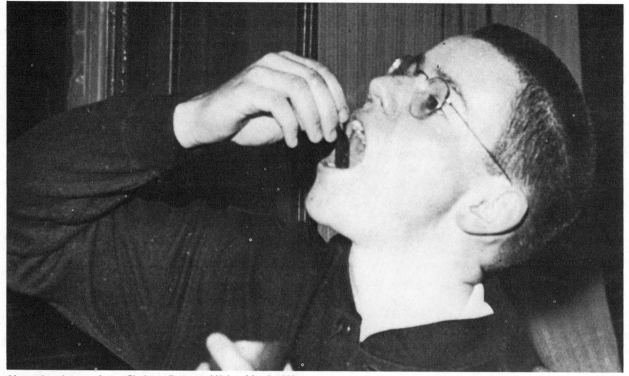

Harvard sophomore Irving Clark swallows a goldfish in March 1939

Once they reported it, goldfish swallowing suddenly came to seem the fashionable thing to do and to be seen doing.

Throughout the nation, in that spring of 1939, there must have been a true ransacking of aquariums. Goldfish swallowers from Franklin and Marshall College, the University of Pennsylvania, Kutztown State Teachers College, the University of Michigan, the University of Missouri and Texas Western in El Paso all dived in. Often the goldfish swallowers did it to win bets. Other times they did it just for the sake of the sport. (Sport?)

Like many another pioneer before him, Lothrop Withington Jr. blazed a trail that later travelers took even farther. Withington had swallowed only one goldfish. If one, why not more? Indeed, why not?

So the record for goldfish swallowing went up and up. First to 3, then to 24, then 25, then 29, then 42, then 43 at one sitting. It was a way of earning accolades from one's fellow students and maybe making girl friends (the goldfish swallowers were usually boys, not girls). The swallower of 43 goldfish, though, was suspended from his school, Kutztown State Teachers College in Reading, Pennsylvania, for "conduct unbecoming a student."

This was not the first time that an administration

had looked on goldfish swallowers with a jaundiced eye. At Boston College, where goldfish swallowers sought to outstrip the achievements at nearby Harvard, they were advised by the dean of discipline that consuming such a repast would lead to "drastic punishment."

At the same time, medical authorities speculated on what goldfish swallowing might do to one's digestive tract. A professor at the University of California in Los Angeles reached the conclusion that one might swallow 125 to 150 goldfish at one time, but no more.

The state of Massachusetts also tried to introduce a humanitarian note. Its Department of Conservation made an effort to ban goldfish swallowing because, after all, it really was pretty unfair to the goldfish.

The goldfish swallowing craze of 1939 lasted little more than a month before college students looked for a variation on the crazy theme—like eating '78-speed records, as was done at the University of Chicago, or munching magazines, as was done at Lafayette College in Pennsylvania.

Goldfish swallowing, however, did make a lasting impression on the national imagination. There was a revival of it in the late 1960s, and it would be no surprise if you were to read about yet another revival today, tomorrow or next week.

DEPRESSION SQUARE DANCES (1939–41)

Let's bring grandfather's old dances back, but let's bring them back alive.

> —Lloyd Shaw, author of *Cowboy Dances* and square dance popularizer

The great popularity of the Big Apple dance (see BIG APPLE) in 1937 and 1938 proved that Americans were excited by group dances that used a caller and featured a lot of stomping and swinging your partner. But at the same time, the Big Apple was accompanied by jazz music, just like the Charleston and its variations, the black bottom, the shag and the lindy. And what Americans wanted now was something really old-fashioned—not only old-fashioned steps but also country songs of bygone years.

No wonder square dances became big. They allowed people to do-si-do, promenade, sashay, bow to their partners, bow to their corner and allemande to their hearts' content. At the same time, they could hear old-fashioned songs like Turkey in the Straw, The Wag'ner, The Old Oaken Bucket and In The Shade of the Old Apple Tree, played by an elderly fiddler.

Square dances were something brand new for most Americans and a lot of fun. In the cities people had mock barn dances and often came wearing straw hats, bandanas and sunbonnets and frequently smoking corncob pipes. There were square dance organizations all over the country: for instance, in New York City in the East; Chicago in the Midwest; El Paso in the Southwest; and Denver in the Rockies. Women's colleges like Bryn Mawr, Vassar and Smith featured square dances. Rounding out the square dancing many a time were old-fashioned country activities like potato peeling and corn shucking. At city barn dances, people made chicken coops out of cartons, as they had learned to do from magazine articles—thus adding to the country atmosphere.

This was a time when Americans wanted to remember exciting and unusual things from their distant past (the Depression, from their recent past, was a rather sad experience to have lived through). They may well have been reacting to the events in Europe, too, where World War II had just started in 1939. In their square dances, perhaps Americans were saying that they didn't want any part of the violence—that here was camaraderie, good feeling.

The prominence of the old-fashioned square dances was not without its humorous aspects. Sometimes city kids went out into the country to take part in square dances there. One old hand said: "The city kids pick it up fast, but they don't do it really right.

Square dancers in Rhode Island in the late 1930s

They cat-howl and roughhouse through the changes, and they're in a hurry. Us old-timers mind the caller." Obviously, the old hands were amused at the city kids picking up on their doings but were not always pleased.

The first popular book on square dancing, and the one that played such an important part in its national revival, was a collection of dances called *Good Mornin'*, selected by none other than the inventor of the Model T, Henry Ford, with the active collaboration of a square dancing expert, one Benjamin Lovett. Lovett said of Ford, "I knew he was interested in old American dancing, but he had hardly taken a step [of old American dances] since courting days." Ford and Lovett's book was to be very popular, and you could get it for 50 cents.

There, you could learn how to promenade in a single file, how to dive for the oyster, and how to flap those girls and flap like thunder. Henry Ford proved to be almost as single-minded in his dedication to

69

country square dancing as he was to the creation of his old Model T, the first popular automobile to roll off an American assembly line. At the New York World's Fair in 1939, the auto pioneer insisted that his staff members be proficient square dancers.

The country square dance, which was so big in the late 1930s and early 1940s, and which has always been an important rural diversion, is something we think of as peculiarly American; yet it was derived from French dance forms. Do-si-do comes from *dos-a-dos* (back-to-back), allemande from *à la main* (by the hand) and sashay from *chasse* (strut). These forms, while practiced in the old French court, also became perennially popular in America.

Interest in the square dance waned after the bombing of Pearl Harbor in December 1941 and the entrance of the United States into World War II, although soldiers and sailors continued to square dance during the war in USO and military camp social gettogethers. After World War II the square dance came back, but it was not to flourish as it had in the prewar years.

HORN AND HARDART BRACELETS, DIRNDLS, PEARL NECKLACES, RED TOOTH CHAINS AND OTHER BRIEF HIGH SCHOOL FASHION CURIOSITIES FOR GALS (1940s)

The 1940s were a period that started with economic depression, followed by four years of war, followed by a postwar revival of spirits and even postwar prosperity. In fashion the 1940s encompassed the crazy zoot suit and Christian Dior's elegant New Look of 1947. Yet there were also a number of much more short-lived fads that thrilled high school girls for a while. Here is the cavalcade.

In New York City one cheap place to eat was Horn and Hardart's automat, where you would put a coin into a slot after choosing what you wanted, then remove the dish once you opened a little door. A lot of girls also liked Horn and Hardart for another reason: They would take a spoon when they ate there and later twist that spoon into a bracelet. No one really knows the reason why not just any spoon from any place would do—perhaps it was that they wanted their friends to see the inscription *Horn and Hardart* around their wrists.

Also in the 1940s, pearls were big, just as they had been in the 1920s, when they were worn by stylish young girls known as "flappers." However, the gals of the 1940s had their own variation. They wore a short string of pearls in the day and a long string of pearls at night.

Sometimes, also, the gals in that decade wanted to affect the Bavarian look. So they wore cotton dirndls. But at the same time they wanted to look rumpled. Something had to be done with the dirndls to make that happen, so they were soaked and wrapped around a broomstick.

When girls wanted to impress their boyfriends, they could do so very easily if they could get ahold of one of the young lad's teeth, which might have fallen out—say in a football or hockey game—or been extracted by the dentist. Now that old tooth might become part of the stock of romance. The girls used blood red nail polish on the tooth, hung it on a chain and presented it to their boyfriends. Although this wasn't quite the same thing as wearing razor blades on chains—as was done in the 1970s to show that you took drugs (or wanted people to believe that you did)—the fad captured something of the same defiant flavor.

Sometimes the young girls wanted to look "tough." For a while in the 1940s, a way to do this was to wear cardigan sweaters backward.

Girls also sometimes wore white muslin beer jackets. They did this because their friends (or even their enemies) could write their names on them, and the girls could then treasure the jackets as a memento of this time in their lives.

BRAZILIAN BOMBSHELL AND TUTTI-FRUTTI (1940–45)

Her real name was Maria do Carro Miranda de Cunha; her stage and movie name was Carmen Miranda; and people also knew her as the chick-a-boom-boom girl, after the chorus of a song she performed. But whatever name she was known by, her appearance was always unforgettable: She wore enormous bunches of fruit on her head, on her shoulders, on her wrists—everywhere. There were bananas in stalks (she is best-

Carmen Miranda, the tutti-frutti songstress, in typical attire

known for bananas), raspberries, strawberries and cherries. In the musical movies in which she performed, like *That Night in Rio* (1941), *Down Argentine Way* (1940) and *Weekend in Havana* (1941), Miranda would appear all fruited-up many times. People today who have memories of those movies or who have seen her on reruns on cable television loved her both for this look and for her enthusiasm.

Because of all that fruit, because of her sensual way of performing with all that fruit on her, and because she was from Brazil, Miranda was known as the Brazilian Bombshell.

But it wasn't just that she thrilled moviegoers, who left her movies feeling excited. It was all that bizarre fruit on her head and everywhere else. Buying crazy Miranda-style artificial fruit novelties (or tutti-frutti) became a fad. Fake bananas, fake grapes, fake cherries, fake raspberries, fake strawberries were fashionable in kitchen, living room, den, bedroom. Some people might call it tacky, but it really was just fun-filled. Tutti-frutti had entered American life. Among other things, there were banana cookie jars, banana earrings and celluloid cherries dangling from celluloid chains. There were also Carmen Miranda cut-out dolls, which gave any young person an opportunity to build a sensual woman complete with bananas on her head.

Carmen Miranda, who was born in 1909 (her father, ironically, was a very successful entrepreneur in the fruit business), did any number of Brazilian films between 1933 and 1939. Then, in 1939 she got her big American break when she did an engagement at New York City's Waldorf-Astoria. American movies then made her a celebrity, creating an exotic, Latin image for her. In the Brazilian Bombshell it all fit in: the singing and dancing, and the fruit (particularly bananas), which people associate with tropical regions. Carmen Miranda had some verve, and in fact, she was performing her routine on the "Jimmy Durante Show" on television in 1955 when she collapsed and died.

As for the tutti-fruitti fad itself, this began at a time when people were anticipating the coming of war. You couldn't blame them for wanting to put it out of their minds and do something a little bit foolish, like buying banana gewgaws for every room of the house. Even after World War II began, tutti-frutti remained popular, but people's minds were really on other things.

During Carmen Miranda's prime, Walt Disney came up with a parrot with a top hat named Jose Carioca, who was a good-natured parody of the Brazilian Bombshell. Jose was popular, too, though he never wore bananas on his head.

ZOOT SUIT (1942–43)

The legs of the pants bagged below the knees; the cuffs were pulled around the ankles. In short, the zoot suit—which was originally called the root suit—looked more than a little bit strange. All the more reason for it to be the male fashion rage of the early war years in America. It might also have taken people's minds off all the bloodshed going on overseas.

To be really fashionable in your zoot suit, you would likely wear it with a chain and a wide-brimmed hat; or with a long jacket, sometimes known as a "juke coat"; or with fancy suspenders.

Unlike other fashion items that have lasted only

briefly over the years, the zoot suit was so bizarre that wearing it was perhaps more a stunt than anything else.

In any case, it was worn primarily by teen-agers, because most of the older men had been called into service. Many people wondered how the guys could fit their feet into this awkward getup.

Zoot suit people had their own lingo. They called themselves "hepcats" (a term that continued to be heard well into the 1950s and even the early 1960s). The suits were called "threads." Their girl friends were "jills."

However, being a zoot suiter didn't mean belonging to a secret society. If you were a teen-ager at that time, all you had to do to turn a regular suit into a zoot suit was to take in the pants at the cuff. Many houses must have been doubling as tailor shops at the time.

If you were a zoot suiter, you might well have found yourself sparking a lot of protest. There were riots against the zoot suits in both New York and California. Finally, their use was curtailed when the WPB (War Production Board) ordered that men could only use a certain amount of inches of fabric in their suits. (The WPB was also applying the same restrictions to women's clothes.) This was known as the L-85 edict, and one of the most exciting things about that revolution in women's dress known as the New Look of 1947 (see NEW LOOK) was that it threw L-85 into the dustbin.

No derivation of the term *zoot suit* has ever been established. The suit itself was first worn in Harlem in New York City, and then its popularity spread nationwide.

There was something of a revival of the zoot suit in the 1950s in England worn by a group of British teen-agers known as the "Teddy boys."

However, in America the zoot suit disappeared once and for all in the 1940s. The "hepcats" took to wearing different "threads."

NEW LOOK (1947–49)

Christian Dior was a little-known French clothing designer who worked for the house of Lucien Lelong. And in February 1947, when sensibilities of elegant dress were reawakening from the Second World War, Dior set forth an idea in Paris. It was called many names—the most popular being the *New Look of 1947*—but it was revolutionary under any moniker. It was perhaps the most exciting thing to happen in the

Five zoot suiters of 1943

Teenage zoot suiter and long-chain wearer of 1943

world of fashion since the 1920s, when the "flappers" (as young girls were known then) wore short skirts, bobs (see BOBBED HAIR) and bell-shaped hats known as cloches. One American buyer said of the Dior line after getting a preview of it: "God help the buyer[s] who bought before they saw this. It changes everything."

Which, indeed, was true. Since the 1930s, skirts and dresses had been somewhat humdrum, with no great or surprising impact on people. Suddenly, with the New Look, skirts and dresses had become longer and more flared, accentuating the leg. Also, Dior skirts and dresses were fasioned to highlight tiny waists, as opposed to earlier styles, which were more loose-fitting. Finally, items in the Dior wardrobe used a lot of fabric, which, to be sure, showed that the war was over: During World War II a government regulation, L-85, forbade the use of excess yardage in garments.

The New Look had yet another characteristic: It had a significantly lower hemline than the skirts and dresses that came before it.

All these aspects of the New Look had one effect: They caused quite a tempest. Some 300,000 American women formed, in outrage, something called the "Little Below the Knee Club," named after the length Dior had abandoned. Many men formed something known as the "League of Broke Husbands," because at first a Dior dress easily ran more than a pretty penny. Within three months in 1947 the New Look was a topic in nearly every conversation and also something that nearly every woman who saw herself as fashionable wanted to have in her wardrobe. Perhaps for this reason, a woman could soon get a copy of a $400.00 Dior dress for $8.95. In fact, it may well have been the New Look that brought about the great interest in mass-market designer items. And it is unquestionably true that Ralph Lauren, Oleg Cassini or Halston would not be the big names they are today if it had not been for Christian Dior. (Not that Dior the man looked glamorous to anyone. A designer said upon meeting him: "I'd been waiting for this chic, dashing character, and what do I find? A French undertaker!")

The preeminence of the New Look continued through the late 1940s and into the 1950s, though it wavered a bit then. But women really did not pull away from the New Look until 1958, when there arrived from Paris another great dress fashion, which looked nothing at all like any creation of Dior. This was known as the sack look (see SACK LOOK).

SLINKY (Late 1940s)

Slinky® is a small, coiled-wire toy, which, through the force of gravity, slinks around: Its most famous attribute, for example, is that if you set it on a flight of stairs, it will slink down by itself, end over end. This is certainly a curious enough maneuver. Or so many people must have thought, because Slinky was so popular in 1948 that a floor at Macy's department store in New York City was so filled with Slinky-wanters that it became a fire hazard. And not all the warnings could diminish the crowd; its members wanted Slinkies that badly.

Slinky is still popular today, but it no longer cre-

A Slinky® display

ates a rage. There are now Slinky caterpillars, Skinky dogs, Slinky elephants, Slinky frogs, Slinky hippos, Slinky kittens, and Slinky trains. All of this "Slinkyalia" was originally wrought by Richard James's simple wire acrobat.

An engineer in the Philadelphia shipyards, Richard James was an inventor in his spare time. In 1943 he came up with the Slinky, and the first thing he told his wife, Betty, about it was how it went down stairs. Then he worked on Slinky some more for a couple of years, while his wife tried to interest people in it. But it was World War II, and a pretty somber time for the introduction of novelty items.

After the war, however, Betty James persuaded Gimbel's department store in Philadelphia to display Slinky for just a little while, while she would try to sell it. It certainly worked. Within 90 minutes, all 400 Slinkies that she had brought with her were gone. And this was just the beginning. The Slinky was a toy to be reckoned with. On March 4, 1947 an official patent was registered for the little device.

Richard James no longer had to work in the shipyards, for James Industries, featuring the Slinky, had become a thriving enterprise.

Slinky is now almost a staple item among toys because it is so enticing. It has never needed much ballyhoo. And the idea can be attributed to someone who didn't have market experience, who was just your typical individual with something cooking in his basement (or with something slinking stealthily down his basement stairs, actually).

HOWDY DOODY (High Point 1948–53; Revival 1971)

Howdy Doody. Was he a bear?
—Comment heard in 1982

Howdy Doody was a red-haired television puppet who had 72 freckles, wore cowboy togs, displayed an engaging smile and blinked his eyes constantly. He was the first great puppet hero of the television age, and in the late 1940s and early 1950s, you could find Howdy everywhere. In the summer you could see Howdy Doody swimsuits, while in the winter you could see Howdy Doody snowsuits. Not only were Howdy Doody clothes a wildly popular item, but Howdy's gestures were also copied. One angry mom wrote NBC television (Howdy Doody's network) to complain about Howdy's constant blinking: "Now my son goes around all the time blinking."

Howdy Doody came on at 5:30 p.m. One mother remembered that it was the only time there was peace and quiet among the kids in the household. "It's Howdy Doody time," the first words in the theme song at the start of the show, became almost a national slogan. Even civil court judges recognized how significant Howdy was. In Paterson, New Jersey, for instance, one such judge ordered a father to let his children watch Howdy Doody. It seemed that daddy was hogging the set to follow the fortunes of baseball's New York Giants.

Howdy Doody emerged on the American scene because of the spontaneous enthusiasm of very young kids. In the early days of television—1947 to be exact—there was a show called "Puppet Playhouse Presents," with a character named Elmer, whose voice was supplied by Bob Smith, the veteran entertainer. The first thing that Elmer said was "Howdy Doody, kids." The kids really liked this, and they also thought that Howdy Doody was the name of a person, not a form of greeting. They demanded to see more of Howdy; letters kept coming in to NBC. And so Howdy Doody was invented. Elmer was no more. As for "Puppet Playhouse Presents," it became "Howdy Doody." Bob Smith, whose real name was Robert Schmidt, became Buffalo Bob. ("Buffalo" because he came from the city of Buffalo, New York.)

So this was the origin of a national romance with a friendly looking cowpoke puppet—a romance that would find kids winding Howdy Doody wristwatches, putting their belongings in Howdy Doody handbags, living in rooms with Howdy Doody wallpaper, perhaps sleeping with Howdy Doody night-lights on. One Brooklyn girl remembered watching Howdy with her younger sister while both of them ate dinner sitting in Howdy Doody chairs and eating from Howdy Doody trays.

Not that Howdy's supporting cast, consisting of both puppets and humans, was ignored. There were rabid fans of Dilly Dally, a slightly absentminded, gangling lad; of Flub-a-Dub, who was supposed to look partly like a dog and partly like a duck; and of Phineas T. Bluster, an old man who was more like Howdy's enemy because he resented all the attention Howdy got. And that was only the puppets. With respect to the humans, there were fans of Buffalo Bob; the clown Clarabell, who was constantly honking a horn; and the Indian Princess Summerfallwinterspring, with her two long, dark braids. Clarabell bicycle horns were a big item. And one lady remembers going to a childhood Halloween party dressed as Princess Summerfallwinterspring.

At first Howdy Doody looked only like a distant cousin of the Howdy Doody of the red hair, freckles, constant blinking and cowboy togs who became so popular in the late 1940s. The original Howdy had blonde features and a Pinocchiolike nose, not that small, snub-shaped sniffer of the later Howdy that America got to know so well.

The grown-up reason for Howdy's new freckled face, introduced in 1948, was that NBC faced a lawsuit in which the network was threatened with losing the rights to Howdy altogether. Evidently, Howdy needed plastic surgery. The kids were told that he was getting a face-lift so he could defeat Mr. X, the handsomest man in the world, who was running against him for "President of All the Boys." (This was also the year that President Harry Truman was reelected in that upset victory over Governor Thomas Dewey.) While Howdy himself did not appear, there were bulletins in the show about the progress of his campaign.

The transformed Howdy won big! With his new face, he collected well over a million votes (and there were only 100,000 television sets in America at the time). As for NBC, it never feared losing Howdy again.

And what a popular face it turned out to be! A Howdy Doody look-alike contest, won finally by a Patchogue, Long Island lad, was featured in *Life* magazine. The contest had been so popular that girls also sent pictures in. When Howdy appeared at Jordan & Marsh, a Boston department store, 20,000 kids waited in line. When Howdy's horn-tooting sidekick, Clarabell, appeared in the clown's native West Virginia, it was a great day for the mountain state and was featured in national magazines. Even that old villain Phineas T. Bluster, who constantly made life difficult for Howdy, would have excited a crowd.

In the early 1950s, the nation's small fry seemed like one peanut gallery (the peanut gallery was that select group of kids lucky enough to see the show in person) for Howdy Doody. Everyone knew about Howdy, Buffalo Bob, Mister Bluster, Clarabell, Dilly Dally and Flub-a-Dub. One of Howdy's favorite expressions, "thingamajigs" (items promised by Howdy in his presidential campaign—like free lollipops or three Saturdays a week), became part of the American vocabulary.

Yet by the middle of the 1950s, Howdy's time seemed to have passed. Mickey Mouse came back on the scene with the Mickey Mouse club, and many a youngster preferred mouse ears to that whole gang on puppet strings. And on September 24, 1960, after 2,543 shows, Howdy Doody went off the air with that daily farewell song, "So long, small fry, it's time to say goodbye."

Howdy and all the gang were taken to an attic in Connecticut. One day in 1961 it was reported that they had burned up in a sudden fire. The next day, however, the puppets were found inside a barrel that was untouched by the fire.

In the spring of 1971 the Doodyville gang returned. And once more, the kids spontaneously brought it about, though this time they were college kids remembering their early years, not real youngsters. It was part of an obsession with nostalgia that also included watching "Hopalong Cassidy," "Lone Ranger" and "Sergeant Preston of the Yukon" reruns. But old Howdy turned out to be bigger than any of these reminders of bygone days. There were Howdy dolls, jewelry, lunch boxes, crayons, watches and sweaters, as before. But this was a new, sexy generation. There were Howdy hot pants, as well.

It all got started because an undergraduate at the University of Pennsylvania wrote in and convinced Buffalo Bob to revive the show. Buffalo Bob did, and the Quaker youth loved it. Then the college kids in San Francisco, New York City, Boston, New Orleans, West Point and all through the nation tuned in. Howdy even played the White House.

But it was a new generation, of course. One young man asked Buffalo Bob if Howdy would have smoked "grass." "He tried it," Buffalo Bob answered, "but it stunted his growth." Deep down, these kids knew that this nostalgic kick for Howdy was only a temporary amusement. They really weren't as wide-eyed as when they were tots. Or, as one young lady put it, "I felt sad that here we are acting like three-year-olds . . . but I like it."

The Doodyville gang wasn't the same, either. Buffalo Bob showed film clips, but he didn't bring back the original Howdy Doody. The craze ran its course, the young kids turning to other forms of nostalgia—like remembering how it was to be a greaser, or wearing sweaters like they did in the Roaring Twenties.

There were revivals of the Howdy Doody TV show with new puppets in 1972 and then again in 1976. Kids watched it, but it never reached the craze proportions of the late 1940s and early 1950s.

Howdy Doody has earned a niche in American life. But somehow he has been divorced from all of Doodyville (the place where the gang had its intrigues and where Buffalo Bob, Clarabell and Princess Summerfallwinterspring also cavorted). One 18-year-old girl knew all about Howdy Doody but had never heard of the peanut gallery. Other young kids in the early 1980s had never heard of Buffalo Bob. Most had never even seen the red-haired, freckled cowboy puppet at all.

In the 1976 television revival, "Howdy and His Friends," a new Howdy Doody puppet was introduced. (None of the original puppets was used again after having been retired to Connecticut in 1960.) He had a lot fewer freckles than the old Howdy and seemed a little taller. Nor did he sport cowboy wear. He really looked more like Huckleberry Finn than like Howdy. He even sort of looked like he should have been called Elmer.

In the show's heyday one of Howdy Doody's puppeteers, Rhonda Mann, said of Howdy, "We wanted Howdy to be symbolic of all little boys." Years later, Howdy Doody remains symbolic still, perhaps of an innocent, uncomplicated way of life that has long since passed.

MILTON BERLE MAKEUP KITS (1949)

It was a time when every day could be Halloween. You could put on a red wig. Or you could sprout whiskers. Or you could surprise with a false mustache or a false nose. Or, like a pirate, you could don an eye patch. You could find all these little items in a makeup kit—priced at $3.98 that let you look like a clowning Uncle Miltie. This was how Milton Berle, the star of Tuesday night's "Texaco Star Theater" and television's first tremendously big comedy figure, was popularly known. (Berle adopted the engaging name *Uncle Miltie* when one Tuesday evening he used it at the end of his show. He didn't think about it much at the time, but the next day in Boston, he was walking down the street and a construction worker called out, "Hey, Uncle Miltie." And so, Uncle Miltie it became.)

Berle's show was such a hit that if you wanted to shop between 8:00 and 9:00 on Tuesday evening or stop off at a bar for a nightcap, you might likely find the place closed because the owner was watching Uncle Miltie on TV.

The attraction of the Milton Berle makeup kit was that you could have fun and mug right along with Miltie. Like him, you could put on a red wig, whiskers, different kinds of mustaches, various noses, false teeth or an eye patch. It was all for a laugh and all for showing off. In this sense the fad was a lot like the one in the 1970s when gals wore flowered decals on their legs (see LEG DECORATION) or the 1982 fad known as deely bobbers, or Martian ears, antennae that people put on their heads and that bobbed happily around (see DEELY BOBBERS).

As for Uncle Miltie, the nation's obsession with him slowly passed, ending around 1953. Yet part of him remained—particularly for those who owned Berleish wigs, whiskers, noses and eye patches.

Shmoos (1949–50)

Shmoos looked like a cross between Casper the Ghost and a misshapen dinosaur. They were discovered in the Valley of the Shmoo, and did they ever cause havoc. Soon after they appeared in Al Capp's cartoon strip *L'il Abner* in 1949, L'il Abner said of them, "Wif these around, nobody won't nevah hafta work no more." And it wasn't terribly hard to find them, either. Or as L'il Abner declared, "Why, thar's more shmoos in th'world than anything."

It was what the shmoos could do that was really amazing. On demand—and they loved to do it—they could lay eggs, produce butter or give grade A milk in a bottle. When Dogpatchers (inhabitants of Capp's mythical cartoon realm) broiled them (shmoos loved to be broiled), they came out steak; and when Dogpatchers boiled them (shmoos loved to be boiled, too), they came out chicken.

It was hardly surprising, then, that the shmoo was not only popular in cartoon Dogpatch but also in real-world America. For your home you could get shmoo ashtrays, shmoo clocks and shmoo pencil sharpeners. You could wear shmoo socks and carry a shmoo umbrella on a rainy day. You could don a shmoo tie, eat shmoo candy and go to special shmoo meat sales at the market. Shmoos were worth a lot in Dogpatch. But they also proved to be of great value in America. By the fall of 1950, shmoo items had brought in $25 million. Which was enough to fill a great number of shmoo piggy banks, yet another item commemorating this most generous beast.

Of course, the shmoo couldn't last forever. Dogpatchers might have liked the life of ease that the shmoos promised, but Al Capp's greedy, exploitative tycoon, J. Roaringham Fatback, felt threatened by the shmoos and ordered them exterminated. Thus, one fine day in Dogpatch, a shmooicide squad arrived and shot the shmoos down.

The whole story of the shmoo was, of course, written and drawn in Al Capp's inimitable satirical style, which had been displayed in *L'il Abner* since 1934, when the strip first appeared in the *New York Daily Mirror*. *L'il Abner* was one of a number of comic strips or animated cartoons that were born in the Depression, perhaps to get people's minds off their troubles. Among the others were Betty Boop (see BETTY BOOP), Little Orphan Annie and Popeye. Mickey Mouse won his greatest acclaim during the Depression. Some people liked *L'il Abner* the best, though, and now—added to Capp's L'il Abner, Daisy Mae, Pappy Yokum and General Jubilation T. Cornpone—there was the shmoo: enough shmoos, in fact, "to supply everybody on earth with all they can eat forever."

After the shmooicide squad shot the shmoos down, they disappeared from the comic strip. In the 1960s, though, the shmoos made a comeback. This time, however, they stayed in Dogpatch. There was no chance of getting yourself a shmoo umbrella or freshening your room with a shmoo deodorizer.

The most popular cartoon figure of the middle 1960s was the luckless Charlie Brown (see CHARLIE BROWN, SNOOPY AND THE PEANUTS GANG), who had a hard enough time taking care of himself. In fact, one thing that Charlie Brown could have used was a shmoo.

INTRODUCTION

The fifties certainly proved to be a vintage decade for fads, including some of the most legendary: hula hooping, Davy Crockett fur hats, 3-D, frisbee throwing, telephone booth stuffing and panty raids. In contrast to the previous two decades, the 1950s represented more of a high-spirited, devil-may-care era—despite the Korean War, which continued through 1953.

Modern television comedies like *Happy Days* and *Laverne and Shirley* may be romanticized versions of the fifties, but they are still true to the spirit of the times. Most people just didn't want to be bothered by controversy then. Anyone who recalls the cockeyed plots of a 1950s TV show like *My Little Margie*—featuring scatterbrained Margie; her equally scatterbrained boyfriend, Freddy; and her hard-working, harassed father, Vern Albright—will understand this perfectly.

The 1950s, for the most part, was no time for eccentricity. The bohemian life was really looked down upon, earning the name *beatnikism*. People joked about the beat-niks' sandals, beards, poetry readings or interest in Eastern religious philosophies like Zen Buddhism.

Another great bugaboo during this period was the fear of widespread juvenile delinquency, usually known simply as J.D. In the middle 1950s (roughly between 1954 and 1958), articles on J.D. abounded, with their tales of gang wars and school disruptions. People—older people, at least—felt threatened by the J.D. manifestations, for they craved stability above all.

But for many of the young, stability was on the way out. Just as youth of the early 20th century repudiated the sedate waltz in favor of the uninhibited animal dances, so the youth of the 1950s turned away from the crooners' sound to the raucous rhythms of rock 'n' roll. Elvis Presley was a national sensation, and millions of adults regarded him as a menace. Nor was he the only figure emulated from the Atlantic to the Pacific. Equally threatening to the older generation was the kids' imitation of the dreaded J.D.'s. Even if using a switchblade was the last thing that would ever cross their minds, such kids would sprout sideburns and swagger around wearing leather jackets and garrison belts, in the manner of antiestablishment movie types like James Dean or Marlon Brando.

Not everything about the fifties can be seen as some kind of sociological comment, though. Certain activities simply took on a zany life all their own. In areas of Arkansas, Missouri and Oklahoma, for instance, college students in 1959 indulged in hunkerin'—the practice of squatting meditatively on their haunches. That same year, by way of South Africa and England, telephone booth stuffing became the rage. While it couldn't have been terribly pleasant to be squished among the many bodies crowding into a telephone booth, did it ever make an interesting story afterward! And what about the striking articles of dress that at one time or another were prominent during the decade? One year, crazy beach hats featured everything from burros to tennis players. Another year, bowler hats made a resurgence. Then guys and gals took to wearing raccoon coats, in a burst of nostalgia for the 1920s—a rage followed by the rise to fashionable prominence of British bobbies' cast-off capes.

Games became important once more, capturing the attention of the entire nation in a way that had not been seen since mah-jongg in the 1920s. First canasta came along, with its multitude of wild cards; then came Scrabble, with people struggling to land a big word on a triple-word score. Canasta had captured the public's attention immediately after arriving from South America, but a prototype of Scrabble had been around since the 1930s without anyone's paying it much heed. You never can tell when a fad will finally catch on!

There are a couple of other fads that illustrate the special quality of the 1950s. Panty raids took the nation's campuses by storm, beginning in 1952 on an early warm spring night at the University of Michigan. Then, at the end of the decade, fast gunfights were held at bars where people (men, mostly) fired blanks and wax bullets at each other as if they were in Wild West showdowns.

Now, those masculine forays into feminine quarters to snatch a few ladies' undergarments showed how far the country was from the time of the institutionalized coeducational dormitories and the pill. The mock gunfights, too, so casually accepted in their time, showed how far the late fifties were from the very different world of the sixties. The assassination of President Kennedy in 1963, followed by other assassinations and widespread domestic violence, made such diversions as fast gunfights suddenly lose their macho charm. Momentous events and dramatic social developments do have a way of obliterating many a fad.

CANASTA (1949–52)

Four years after World War II, the wounds of that great conflict had really begun to heal, and people were looking for a new kind of card game to intrigue them. It was then that a game in the rummy family, canasta, became an obsession.

Oswald Jacoby, that gentleman from Texas who became known as an expert on all card games, said of canasta, "After you have played your first game, your chief problem will be how to stop." His 1950 book, *How to Win at Canasta*, was a number one best-seller that year, even though he warned that readers read his little manual "at your own risk." Millions of daring canasta mavens were taking every possible opportunity to cut and shuffle the 108 cards (for canasta used two decks of cards and four jokers), hope for the wild deuces or the red or black 3s, and make a score in the thousands of points. (Canasta was a game in which people were always laying a multitude of cards down, and for that reason it was very pleasant for a child to play with an older person, as one of the authors did with his grandmother.) Both privately and in official card clubs, canasta was played day and night, and as often as not with no break for dinner, which was brought in on a tray.

It was Uruguayan card players who originated this round-the-clock wonder in the early 1940s, based on rummy, with its melding of cards, throwing out of discards and trying to figure out when to pick up the stock of discards. In fact, the name *canasta*, or basket, came from the tray of discards used in every game.

From Uruguay canasta spread to Argentina and then, in 1949, to the United States. Quickly passing contract bridge as the most popular card game, it also spurred a merchandising bonanza. The tools of the trade alone demanded those special canasta trays and score sheets, and even fancy canasta decks, with their two jokers apiece. Canasta cards went from $1.19 a deck to $2.25 a deck; and Atlantic Playing Cards sold 1 million canasta decks in 1950 alone. Among the top seven nonfiction books during one period in 1950, four dealt with canasta. Even the United States government benefited from all this traffic in canasta. In one year—July 1949 to July 1950—the federal tax on playing cards increased from $319,000 to $859,000.

There were also canasta hats, canasta dresses, canasta jewelry, canasta table covers and canasta overcoats. The last were designed by Christian Dior, the creator of the fashionable "New Look" (see NEW LOOK), with its long, sensual garments, and were advertised as having "pockets big enough to take your winnings home." Most people, while hooked, didn't gamble at canasta, however.

One such soul was Ralph C. Combs, who wrote a book entitled *Who Called Me a Canastard?* This was no ordinary instructional aid, but a humorous account that tied canasta in with the reigning preconceptions of the day. Women always beat men at canasta, for instance, because they were more emotional beings, and if emotion failed, they would wear low-cut dresses to upset concentration. Between jibes, Combs explained the nuances of the game.

None of the other rule books, however, was woman-teasing. They sure were numerous, though. Everyone wanted to know how to meld cards, how to throw away the right discards and when to pick up the entire discard tray. Oswald Jacoby and Ely Culbertson, another great card expert, argued about the merits of canasta and contract bridge, and millions were interested. In England, Americans and Britishers played a canasta tournament in a glass cage, so the horde of canasta fans who were looking on could be kept at a distance from the competitors.

Though *Life* magazine featured canasta lounging pajamas on one of its covers in 1952, the obsession with canasta had already begun to pass that year. Some former canasta enthusiasts began to think that canasta was too much of a game of luck and started to turn back to contract bridge. And then, in the fall of the year, scrabble (see SCRABBLE) arrived, and everyone became concerned with words, not wild cards. It was a much greater coup to be able to put *canasta* down on a scrabble board—it was worth 50 points, a total you could get if you used all seven of the letters in your rack—than slamming down your hand and declaring "Canasta" when you had seven of the same card.

Even Oswald Jacoby, who popularized canasta, confessed it wasn't his favorite card game. When asked what game he liked best, he replied that he would take draw or stud poker.

DOE EYES (1950s)

After they came over from Paris, doe eyes were a pretty big thing in cosmetics. Also called 1950 eyes, doe eyes were eyes made up to look like those of a female deer. The idea was that with doe eyes, you would exude a doelike aura of intrigue. Not everyone liked it, of course. But, then again, in the 1920s, when lipstick was introduced on a large scale, many people were horrified by that, too.

A doe-eyed look was achieved by using a lot of eyebrow pencil, shadow and mascara. The shadow could be applied in a heavy or light tone, but it was used from the center of the eyelid out. The pencil would be used to subtly draw the continuation of eyebrows, while mascara would be used to lengthen the eyelashes. Finally, a line would be drawn along the bottom of the eyelid, while eye shadow would serve to soften the entire effect.

The effect itself was probably less complex than the process of creating it. One woman, for instance, remembers liking it so much that she bought over $30 worth of makeup at a clip—all for the purpose of getting beautiful doe eyes.

Some women thought that sultry Sophia Loren sported doe eyes in the 1958 movie *Houseboat*, in which, as Cinzia Zaccardi, she played opposite Cary Grant, cast as Tom Winston. Tom Winston lived on a houseboat on the Potomac River because he couldn't get a house in the country; Cinzia was an acquaintance of Tom's son, then Tom's housekeeper who loved his children, then—to the surprise of both—Tom's sweetheart. This was a very romantic movie, and Sophia's doe-eyed look made doe eyes popular once more. Fortunately, the women who wanted it didn't have to take second best (a houseboat instead of a country estate); they had no problems getting the real thing in their local department stores. One woman jokingly said about adopting the doe-eyed look: "Sophia Loren is the only woman my husband would leave me for, so I want to eliminate the competition."

Doe eyes, while never becoming a famous cosmetic effect, were a greatly desired look for a while. A lot of women insisted on it. Many may have since gone back to more standard cosmetic styles, but they still fondly recall their days of being doeish.

HOPALONG CASSIDY (1950)

Kids have always wanted to have their heroes, and when they came along, kids insisted on owning things that brought their heroes to mind. After television began to be a fixture in the American home in the late 1940s, the first great cowboy hero was Hopalong Cassidy, or as he was quite frequently known, just plain Hoppy. In 1950 nearly every young boy or girl wanted to have Hopalong Cassidy shirts ($2.95), frontier suits ($8.95), spurs ($1.95), holsters ($1.95) or hats ($1.95). Or sleep in Hopalong Cassidy pajamas. Or play with Hopalong Cassidy play money. Or belong to a chapter of Hoppy's Troopers, which had become more popular than either the Boy Scouts or the Girl Scouts.

Popular Hopalong Cassidy was usually black-hatted, black-shirted and black-booted, though he rode a pure white horse named Topper. He was also sort of an old cowpoke, played by Bill Boyd, who had had silver hair for years. Boyd had been playing Hopalong since the 1930s, when he made the first of his 52 Cassidy movies, among them *Law of the Pampas*, *Range War*, *Silver on the Sage* and *Partners of the Plains*. A luminary from the beginning as Hoppy, it still took television to turn Boyd's cowpoke into a full-fledged fad. For TV could do what movies could not: In a single instant it could create nationwide attention.

Hoppy became as familiar as your kindly favorite uncle (in fact, that is how Bill Boyd saw him) and shot a nasty outlaw only as a matter of last resort. Bill Boyd said of him: "I have tried to make Hoppy a plain and simple man, in manner and in dress. . . . He is not illiterate, nor is he smart-alecky." Was it any wonder that this nice guy attracted crowds of up to 350,000 in cities where he made appearances? At the same time, Hopalong was proud that his crowds were so well-mannered, just the right response for a nice old gunman: "They all want to touch Hoppy . . . crowds never pull at Hoppy. . . ."

Move his hips like Elvis Presley? Hoppy? Never!

The Hoppy TV episodes lasted from 1948 to 1953, but 1950 was definitely the big year. It was the year of the Hoppy peanut butter. The Hoppy cookies. The Hoppy wallpaper. And the Hoppy bicycle.

Hopalong Cassidy got his name because in the original stories about the cowpoke, written by Clarence E. Mulford at the turn of the century in Brooklyn, Hoppy had a limp. He used to say to the rest of the cowhands, "Oh, I can hop along with the rest of you." When Bill Boyd assumed the role, he took the name but not the limp.

Hoppy became part of American folklore. In the middle 1950s, there was a hard-charging back on the Ohio State football team named Howard Cassidy. He was promptly dubbed "Hopalong." Bill Boyd may well have been very pleased.

By 1953 Boyd had become tired of his 20-year run, which had started in movies and then gone to radio before making the big splash on TV. Mounting his white horse, Topper, Hoppy rode off into the sunset. At the same time, a new idol had really come to replace Hopalong Cassidy among American kids—the cowboy puppet with all the freckles, Howdy Doody.

It wasn't just that Howdy was much younger than Hopalong, and thus represented the future, not the past. It was also true that Howdy was a television hero who had been born on television. Hopalong Cassidy had been in many movies before and had already been a great celebrity there.

This just went to show that television was ready

to attract people and also to break new ground. An era in American culture was really beginning.

BIZARRE BEACH HATS (1951)

In 1951 what magazine articles dubbed "crazy beach hats" were quite the thing. These were straw hats with an unquestionably special effect. For on top of the hat itself were little chairs, ladders, pails, tables, brooms, rugs or burros bearing riders. For the sports-minded, there were also bizarre beach hats with golfers, tennis players and autos.

Consider the straw hat topped with a burro and rider for just a moment. This showed that one of the places crazy beach hats originally appeared was Mexico. At the same time, they were turning up in the Caribbean. Then they began to be seen in California, and finally, they spread throughout the United States. In this country they would cost you between $6 and $20.

If you were lucky enough to get them in Mexico, however, you could snap them up for the equivalent of just $2.40.

The fad for crazy beach hats only lasted that one year. Perhaps they were just too gimmicky to have true staying power.

TWO-TONE HAIR (1951)

In 1951 many women wore two-tone hair. This meant that blondes put platinum streaks in their hair or brunettes put in streaks of pale blonde. Dye was used, and hair was often dyed to match the color of an evening dress, too.

It was a time when women were considering new glamour effects, also shown by a new cosmetic look known as doe eyes (see DOE EYES). Though six years had already passed since the end of World War II, in some ways people were still living under its sad shadow, trying to escape it by sporting exciting items like two-tone hair.

The fad, as was still true of most items of high fashion in those days, started in Paris. Then it came to America.

Two-tone hair did not last very long—nothing like

the great craze for wigs in the late 1960s (see WIGS FOR WOMEN), for instance. The kind of woman who might two-tone her hair in 1951 was perhaps the same kind who adopted the new long gown look of 1947 (see NEW LOOK) before it was completely accepted. Still, there were enough women who two-toned their hair and wanted to be in the forefront of things to raise the practice to respectably faddish proportions.

PANTY RAIDS (1952)

Some called them lace riots; others called them silk sorties. But mostly they were known as panty raids, and they were the hit of the 1952 spring season at America's colleges and universities. By June 2 students attending at least 52 institutions of higher learning had participated in lightning raids of ladies' lingerie—taken from clotheslines around girls' dorms and from drawers in the girls' rooms themselves. No wonder the police were often called out to quash them. A mob of boys with one object in mind—female underwear—could be downright imperiling.

Certainly, a panty raid or two or three must have taken place before 1952; it was just not that original an idea. However, it was in 1952 that panty raids really broke out. According to one account, in *Life* magazine, it all started at the University of Michigan on the evening of March 21. On this pleasant first evening of spring, a trumpeter, a trombonist and a "foghorner" began to play outside casually on their instruments. Other students tried to quiet them. This not only got nowhere but also sparked about 600 other men students to come outside and mill around. All of a sudden the cry went up, "To the women's dorms," and before you could say "Spring is here," the mob had broken into a gals' dormitory, the guys making their way into the rooms to get lingerie.

This must have struck a sensitive copycat chord among American male students: There quickly followed panty raids at the University of Missouri, the University of Tennessee, the University of Vermont, the University of Nebraska, Northwestern University, Indiana University, the University of Miami, Stanford University and Columbia University, to name but nine of the most prominent. A typical picture from the period shows a couple of guys triumphantly holding stolen girdles while they prepare to leave a cloisterlike residence hall. Sometimes the boys were a force that could not be resisted. At the University of Miami they broke down a heavy wire fence to get at the girls' dorms. But sometimes the seizure was all too easy. At Indiana

Some proud panty raiders at the University of Nebraska in 1952

University the director of women's residence halls left out a barrel of girls' lingerie in full view, which could be taken by the handful for the plucking.

And not infrequently, the tables were turned. At the University of Michigan, where it all began, 500 girls broke into the men's dormitories; what was good for panties was also good for boxer shorts. One night at Georgetown University, an exclusively male school in Washington, D.C., the boys suddenly found themselves facing a convoy of girls who had slipped in to get at the male undergarments. Now it was the male clotheslines and chests of drawers that were the targets of rifling.

In its time panty raids were not quite seen as a harmless diversion. The police were often called out to stop the men students, and people who were seriously concentrating on their books or others who may have felt their privacy to have been seriously invaded may well have been upset. There were panty raids that got out of hand, with great numbers of windows and doors being broken and other items stolen, like silverware and cigarette lighters. This was, of course, nothing like the campus riots in the 1960s, but who could have predicted that then? To many, panty raids seemed obnoxious enough.

For instance, consider this response to panty raids. In 1952 American troops were still involved in the Korean conflict. Along came the panty raid on the home front. One magazine, *U.S. News & World Report*, put forth the query: "Why aren't they [the pantyraiders] in the army if they have so much energy and so little to do?" The article further listed the number of American war dead in the season of panty raids. It was not an altogether unconvincing argument. And it was repeated two years later at Northwestern, when at a raid late in the undergarment-snatching fad, a dean asked the names and draft numbers of the raiders. This caused them to disperse.

In any event, though panty raids continued through the 1950s, they ceased being the stirring attraction they were in 1952. Why had they first come about? Probably simply because of high spirits, and because spring does this kind of thing to people. Why did they end? Probably because the end of the academic year follows closely upon the beginning of spring. Why hasn't there been a really big revival? Probably because the age of sexual permissiveness has rendered such symbolic action as this meaningless.

No matter. Panty raids—like the fads of telephone booth stuffing (see TELEPHONE BOOTH STUFFING), flagpole sitting (see FLAGPOLE SITTING) and goldfish swallowing (see GOLDFISH SWALLOWING)—have now become part of American legend.

SCRABBLE (1952–53)

I wanted to invent an alphabet game with a balance between all skill like chess and no skill like dice.

—Alfred M. Butts,
Scrabble inventor

Scrabble® is a very frustrating game. To take one uncommon but perfectly possible example, if you have a Q and a Z on your Scrabble tiles—both letters are worth 10 points, the most valuable in the game—and you have an I also (worth 1 point), you get 44 points by making the word *quiz* on a double-word score. But you don't have that U (worth 1 point). Should you wait, or should you throw in your Q or Z, very hard letters to place on the board? In 1953 everyone wanted to address questions like this, and there was even a waiting list at your local department store to purchase Scrabble games. When your turn came, you could get a plain wooden set for $3 or a fancy wooden set for $10. In the meantime you had to comfort yourself by playing with the neighbors or amuse yourself with the stories told about Scrabble—like the one that reported how in Hollywood they played Scrabble with just dirty words.

This mad rush for Scrabble took place some 20 years after the game was invented in 1933 by one Alfred M. Butts, a New York City architect who lost his job as a result of the Depression. Butts thought that he could make ends meet by coming up with this word game (after all, weren't crossword puzzles—which are a little bit like Scrabble—the rage only eight years earlier?). No such luck. No manufacturer was interested in a word game with 100 tiles, placed on a board where different squares represented different point values. The only scrabbling done in those old days was between Butts and a number of his friends, who received the games as gifts from the inventor himself, who handcrafted them on an old jigsaw. Butts said that he gave away some 500 of these sets in the early prebonanza years. Originally, Butts called the game Lexico; then, in 1938, he began calling it Criss-Cross.

One such friend was James Brunot, a social worker who wanted to have his own business. In 1947 Brunot entered into an agreement with Butts whereby he would have the game manufactured. It was Brunot also who chose the name Scrabble for the game. The word meant to scrape, paw or scratch with one's hands or feet.

And sometimes it must have seemed to Brunot that this is precisely what he had to do to make a profit on Scrabble. Mr. Brunot's Scrabble game, which he took from Mr. Butts, was always in the red, never in the black. In 1948 only 180 sets were sold. In 1949 sales went up to 2,251 sets, but Brunot still lost $450.

Things were very quiet in James and Helen Brunot's small Scrabble factory-warehouse in Newtown, Connecticut.

And then in 1952 things began to go crazy for Scrabble. People had suddenly developed a craving for accumulating points for building words on a board, hoping that the luck of the draw would give them good letters. The Connecticut shop couldn't keep up with all the orders coming in, or as Brunot recalled, "There was no room for anything but boxes, racks, and tiles." There was no way that Brunot could satisfy the 2,500 requests a day he was getting. And the number was climbing.

Brunot just could not deal with this, and he saw that he really had no choice but to sell out, which he did to Selchow & Righter, a manufacturing giant that could easily mass-produce the item. And that is exactly what it had to do, for in the first three months of 1953 alone, 51,480 Scrabble games were sold. Scrabble was something that was on nearly everyone's mind. Parents cajoled young children into going to bed by getting them to promise that they would permit themselves to be tucked in peaceably if they could play just one final Scrabble game. A television situation comedy, "The Goldbergs," showed our nationwide obsession with Scrabble. In one of its installments, about a romance that was in the air, what better way was there to present this to the public than by featuring a Scrabble game in which all the words played were about romance?

Scrabble-mania abated in 1953, but the game has become a fixed part of the American cultural landscape. There are Scrabble columns in newspapers and little portable Scrabble-like games you can carry around with you. On the other hand, students at the University of Massachusetts played on a 2,000-foot Scrabble board. There are also Scrabble swimming pools.

In 1953 a German company subcontracted by Selchow & Righter turned out 120 million Scrabble letters; the count must be well into the billions now.

There is a little-known sidelight to the Scrabble story. Forty years before Alfred Butts went to work with his jigsaw, and 60 years before Scrabble became a supreme American fad, families in the Gay Nineties could play a game called klova, which also featured picking letters at random and combining them into words. In this game there were no double or triple word scores, and all letters counted one point. There is no evidence, however, that klova ever caught on.

CREW CUTS AND OTHER SHORT HAIRCUTS (Early–Mid 1950s)

It is commonly held that the short haircuts for men that were fashionable in the early to middle 1950s were styled that way because people were more conforming, more regimented then. Not so, as the variety of teen-age fashions makes clear (see JUNGLE JACKETS).

Men wore their hair short because they thought it was natty, elegant; it was the faddish thing to do. There were many kinds of short haircuts around, all vying to be named as the most stylish. These included cuts like the crew cut, the butch, the Caesar, the boogie, the flattop and the Detroit. If men did not have the hair to sport one of these cuts, they affected them with toupees. In 1955 bandleader Xavier Cugat and movie actors Humphrey Bogart and Van Heflin all had crew cut toupees.

These were the cuts: the crew, which left anywhere from one-half to one inch on a man's head; the flattop, which left the hair long enough on top to brush only the sides straight back; the butch, in which the top, sides and back of the hair were cut particularly short, and which was said to make the wearer look like a "tough guy." Or consider the Caesar, which had a fancy swirl or part, and which some people had in order to cover up bald spots.

At the same time, there was also in popular vogue a certain type of mustache wax that was used to make sure that the hairs stood up to a precise height (see HAIR WAXING).

In other words, the variations on short hair were as stylish and as faddish as the variations on long hair were only a little bit more than a decade later.

It took Elvis Presley, the rock and roll singer, to change all this in 1956, when he began to wear sideburns. Sideburns then became the voguish thing for young men to wear (see SIDEBURNS), though many people were horribly offended. And then, in the 1960s, long hair came along, which for many years put the barbering business into great decline. Short hair also got the reputation of being really unfashionable. Besides being a decade of protest and significant social change, in the 1960s the young tried to rewrite the history of hair. This was revisionism straight from the top.

3-D (1953)

The pictures really stepped out—away from the background; they actually moved. I have made 3-D my new hobby.
—A.D., Soldiers' Home, Vineland, New Jersey,
after looking through 3-D Movie Magazine

Put on those cardboard eyeglasses and get a lion in your lap, a locomotive bearing down on you, a rattlesnake biting you, a maiden stroking you and more. This was 3-D (or three-dimensional) cinema, which made it possible for millions of moviegoers to experience countless optical kicks while perhaps coming down with about as many headaches.

In 1953, in movie theaters throughout America, 100 million people donned polarizing lenses, for which they paid about 10 cents, over and above the usual admission price. This was the kind of effect that the movie business was looking for, because when 3-D was introduced, cinema going had reached a post-World War II low (people preferred staying home and watching that relatively new video invention, television), and studios like Warner Brothers, Paramount and United Artists were looking for something big to give them a boost. They thought they had found it in 3-D.

For a while 3-D was really something. One 8-year-old from the state of Washington was so frightened by the horror movie *House of Wax*, (being boiled in oil with the young girls on the screen was a highlight) that he didn't go to another movie for four years. About the same time in Illinois, a scientist put Polaroid glasses on a bunch of chickens to see how they would react to 3-D: They pecked at the screen.

How did 3-D, or "depthies," work? In contrast to "flat" movies, where there were only two dimensions, length and width, 3-D provided in addition a sense of depth with these special glasses, consisting of one lens with a red coloration and one with a blue coloration. Two projectors beamed the film from the screening room, and the viewer, with the filtering and polarizing effect of the glasses, was able to pull the two images together. Though theoretically hard to understand, the actual effect was pretty clear. You would feel as if you were right there and could touch the lions in the first 3-D movie, *Bwana Devil*, as they were ready to jump on the engineer and his girl.

In the early 1950s no major film studio took the idea of 3-D very seriously, and none played a part in the production of *Bwana Devil*, which was made for $300,000 at the World Jungle Preserve near Malibu, California. The movie was the work of exscreenwriter and inventor Milton Gunzburg; his brother, eye surgeon Julian Gunzburg; and prolific radio dramatist Arch

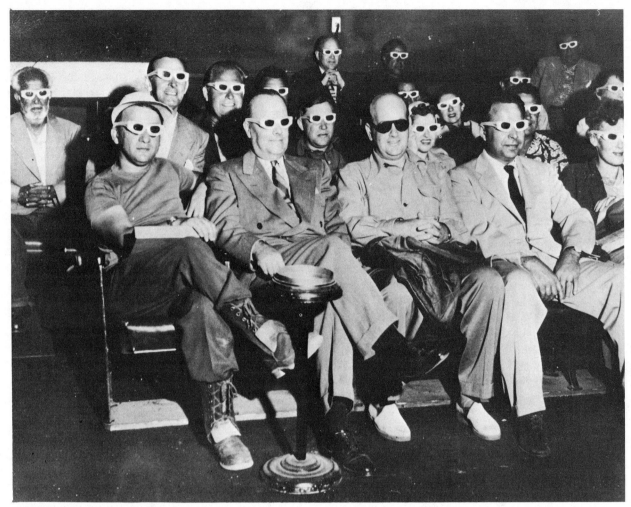

Enjoying a 3-D movie, March 1953

Oboler. They called their 3-D process "natural vision."

Bwana Devil, which premiered the first week of December 1952, was a smashing success as it played to capacity crowds and extraordinary waiting lines at two Paramount theaters in Los Angeles. As one of the movie house managers related to Milton Gunzburg, "It's the most fabulous thing we've ever seen: They're standing four abreast all the way down to the Roosevelt Hotel in Hollywood." The rights to the picture were bought up by United Artists, and the movie hit the rest of the nation in March 1953, as a $300,000 investment became a $15 million bonanza. A movie gossip columnist said of 3-D, "Nothing since the atomic bomb has struck the motion picture industry with such force." The Polaroid Company, which made the 3-D glasses, saw its stock jump from 24 cents to 32 cents a share. These were some of the responses that made 3-D people think their investment in 3-D was just the right medicine to guarantee them a rosy financial future.

Moreover, the New York Herald-Tribune said of 3-D that it "made every man a voyager to a brave new world," while accepting the fact that "flat" movies were out and that 3-D movies were in. In the spring months of 1953, nearly everyone wanted to see those 3-D movies, House of Wax and Man in the Dark. In House of Wax they could feel like the young girls stalked by a mad museum owner, and in Man in the Dark they could feel like the man lying injured on an operating table, waiting for brain surgery (and then the scalpel would plunge . . .).

And that wasn't all there was to 3-D. For kids comic book companies ran 3-D issues of Captain 3-D, Superman and the Three Stooges, among others. Fans of movie magazines could now see in full 3-D a muscular Kirk Douglas astride a rock or a sensual Debra Paget lying on a couch doing a modified push-up. for the handy artists' set, do-it-yourself 3-D cameras became the newest thing in photography.

And there was more. Sports fans could see a 3-D rerun of the heavyweight title fight between Rocky Marciano (his name is perhaps the inspiration for Rocky Balboa of *Rocky*, *Rocky II* and *Rocky III* of the 1980s) and Jersey Joe Walcott. The problem was that the film was 18 minutes long, while the fight itself had lasted only 2 minutes and some seconds. Or if you had business with beans in Chicago, you could find yourself at an in-house commercial promotion for a beanery done in 3-D. Indeed, 3-D had reached faddom.

Still, full-length movies were mostly what 3-D was all about. Movie moguls—all sporting the Polaroid cardboard glasses, were shown sitting together in a nondescript production room watching the rushes of *House of Wax*. A policeman was hired to make sure that the two 3-D movie projectors were always protected. The first three 3-D movies—*Bwana Devil, Man in the Dark* and *House of Wax*—all grossed over $15 million. *Time* magazine gave 3-D its front-cover treatment on June 8, 1953, while *Life* magazine showed a movie house filled to capacity, the audience staring intently with their cardboard glasses.

Yet if you couldn't shell out a buck for a 3-D movie, *Life* magazine ran pictures of *House of Wax, Sangaree* and *Fort Ticonderoga*, complete with instructions for how you could get the full effect of 3-D just by using a hand mirror.

Also, due to the overwhelming interest in 3-D, another moviemaking process was invented that made the audience feel like it was being drawn into the screen: cinerama. Cinerama, however, never was used as a process in commercial suspense or horror movies as 3-D was, but rather was used ordinarily in educational-type films such as travelogues.

While 3-D made it big in 1953, it was hardly a new idea. It had first been experimented with by American movie studios in the 1930s, and German and Italian 3-D movies were also made in that same decade. In the 19th century and the early 20th century, there was the stereopticon viewer (see STEREOPTICON VIEWS AND VIEWHOLDERS, HAND-HELD), which was a precursor to 3-D movies. And a long, long time before this, in ancient Greece, there was the mathematician Euclid, who supposedly was the first to discuss 3-D principles.

In the spring of 1953, however, only Darryl F. Zanuck, the boss of 20th Century-Fox, didn't have the urge to compete with the other studios in the production of 3-D films. Zanuck said: "I have been supplying my own third dimension all my life. What we need is to open up, open up wide." He planned that Fox would go completely to the wide screen, Cinemascope, beginning with a blockbuster film about early Christians, *The Robe*. And that was one of the things that brought about 3-D's decline and confirmed the prediction of

movie actress Gloria Swanson (who had been around since the silent movies) that "3-D is a flash in the pan."

By February 1954 people were growing very tired of the contrived special effects of 3-D. In February 1954, in San Francisco, for instance, one angry moviegoer who had gone to see *The Nebraskan* slugged the theater manager because he didn't like being boiled in oil or having arrows shot at him. True, one wonders why he went to *The Nebraskan* in the first place, but it is also a fact that the 3-D special effects were often almost shameless. In *The Charge at Feather River*, you could get bitten by a rattlesnake and live to tell about it. So it was hardly surprising that when *Kiss Me Kate*, a musical based on Cole Porter's Broadway show, was released in October 1953 in both a 3-D and a "flat" version, the "flattie" did 40 percent better at the box office.

Nor did audiences continue to really like those cardboard glasses. Some people complained that the glasses gave them headaches, while others said that the colors blurred with them and a disjointed image was sometimes seen on the screen. In Chicago the Board of Health closed 3-D theaters because the glasses were full of germs, while New Yorkers complained that they smelled. The idea that 3-D was going to save the movies—which in the early 1950s were really threatened by television—turned out to be a mirage. Judging from the cold, dry numbers showing attendance, 1953 finally turned out to be a worse year than 1952, which had been bad enough. This was not exactly what the movie studios were hoping for.

Still, 3-D did not fade out completely. In late 1953 doctors wearing polarized glasses based on 3-D principles studied the anatomical movement of joints. And the tradition of 3-D special effects was well represented by three 1959 movies that battered the senses. In *The Tingler* seats were wired electrically to give shocks during the film; in *The Scent of Mystery* and *Behind the Green Wall*, viewers were smothered by a host of unexpected smells. This was know as Smell-O-Vision.

In the 1970s and again in the 1980s, there was a 3-D revival, but it created nothing like the big news of 1953. In the 1970s Andy Warhol did *Frankenstein's Bloody Terror*, and there was also an X-rated movie, *The Stewardesses*. In the early 1980s there were adventure or horror movies like *Coming at Ya* or *Friday the 13th III*. Most recently, in March 1983, a number of 3-D movies were being planned: *Spacehunter, Amityville 3-D, Phantom Empire*, and *Rock Hotel*, the first rock 3-D production. And in July 1983 *Jaws 3-D* opened. How this killer shark movie does as a "depthie," will determine if the cinematic waters around Hollywood, California become infested with many a 3-D thriller or teaser.

BERMUDA SHORTS FOR MEN (1953–54)

Let no one mistake the fact that Bermuda shorts had to fall two inches above the center of the kneecap. This was as much a part of their very English pedigree as their having first been worn by British military officers in Bermuda in the 1920s, when they were known as Bermuda walking shorts. In the middle 1950s, however, you could see Bermuda shorts being worn by American men on the street, in railway stations and in offices. In fact, they were quite the thing to wear during those years. Now, no one gives Bermuda shorts a passing thought, for they have become institutionalized. Then, they were the rage.

Sometimes, these shorts, originally brought back by American tourists to Bermuda, caused an extraordinary furor. Police were called out in New York City to prevent a Bermuda-shorted fellow from getting into the Palladium dance hall. The illustrious Plaza Hotel in New York City didn't allow men in Bermuda shorts, either. Nor did the Copacabana.

If you were a man in 1953, wearing Bermuda shorts cast you in the limelight. A reporter from Boston's *Christian Science Monitor* wore Bermuda shorts to a press conference given by President Eisenhower. A few journals reported what his question was, but most were much more interested in writing about *those shorts*. Without a doubt, Bermuda shorts were considered daring.

Being seen in the presidential Rose Garden showed that Bermuda shorts had come a long way. Those British army and navy officers wore only rather plain flannel Bermuda shorts; American men could now get them not only in flannel but in denim, linen, corduroy or Italian silk. If an American had happened to own a pair before the middle 1950s, you might have seen him sporting them while playing tennis or golf. Now, you might find him wearing Bermuda shorts in a bank's boardroom.

Yet after a couple of years, no one gave Bermuda shorts a second glance. They had come to be considered part of the American landscape. In 1960 *Women's Wear Daily, the* paper of the fashion industry, included them among the clothes worn by the pillars of the community. Anyone who wanted to be considered avant-garde couldn't possibly take them seriously.

Yet before Bermuda shorts became old hat, they did accomplish one thing that in 1953 was still considered the exception, not the rule. They were an item of clothing that allowed men to dress as provocatively as women. They gave rise to jokes in the newspapers, such as one woman saying to another, "Wonder how I'd look in that. My legs are better than his," or "Get a load of those knees! They'd laugh at us." The old sexual stereotypes had begun to drift away.

JUNGLE JACKETS, COLONEL TIES, MAMMOTH CUFF LINKS AND OTHER BRIEF HIGH SCHOOL FASHION CURIOSITIES FOR GUYS (Early 1954)

In 1954 some of the clothing items that are traditionally associated with the 1950s and would become really big—like motorcycle jackets, blue suede shoes and white bucks—had not yet appeared. This was because that greater stirrer of kids, rock and roll, had not yet appeared, either, and also it was not yet considered fashionable to look like a juvenile delinquent (or a soul alienated from his or her parents, uncomfortable with the world). At the same time, the image of the 1950s as a period of conservative, conforming dress was not true, either; the kids of the early 50s make one think of the mod era, and sometimes they even looked like dandies. Consider the examples listed below of this explosion in teenage fashion. Needless to say, the parents didn't like it much; or as one father asked the manager of Sam's Clothes Shop in Lynn, Massachusetts, which specialized in this apparel, "What do you mean selling my son a get-up like this?" The simple answer was that his son wanted to look like the other kids, who had taken up certain elegant sartorial fads.

Sometimes, a guy wanted to look like he was the slickest creature in the jungle, and so he donned his jungle sports jacket. This had leopardlike spots from neckline to waistline. It would be a nice outfit to pick up your date in; she, in turn, might be wearing the ankle bracelet you gave her, a crinoline skirt with rhinestones on it or an angora sweater with seed pearls.

Then there was the colonel tie, which was fancy and looked like a combination of a bow tie and two small string ties, leaving a space in the middle of the shirt for the buttons. The kids often wore the colonel tie with a design of small dots on it.

Or consider the humble cuff link, which one normally does not regard as an item of high fashion. In 1954 the chic high school guys wore mammoth cuff links, which looked like they were the size of golf balls.

And these were only a few of the things that you would have seen, first in shop windows and then in the corridors of the high school and at parties. There were many other things, too, that we usually do not associate with the conforming 1950s—pink top hats, yellow and pink shirts at a time when hardly anyone had ever heard of such things (this, too, would have to wait for mod) and neon-blue suits. All these items caused "the bitterest family rows," as the manager of Sam's Clothes Shop said. This, however, hardly prevented the clothing entrepreneur from carrying them. In the case of the colonel tie, for instance, the store had to buy them the moment they hit the market, or it would find itself without colonel ties—which meant losing money.

Life magazine showed how the "with-it" high school man of 1954 looked very much like the well-dressed and fancy gentleman of 1851. This does not fit the conception of motorcycle-jacketed guys, which often seems to be the most common image of the 1950s. Within a year (1955) the motorcycle look and the juvenile delinquent style had begun, and they swept away everything that came before it—jungle jackets, neon-blue suits, mammoth cuff links and all.

DAVY CROCKETT AND HIS FUR HAT (December 1954– December 1955)

On December 15, 1954 TV's "Disneyland" showed an hour-long episode in which General Andrew Jackson commissioned Major Tobias Norton to find backwoodsman hero Davy Crockett and enlist his aid against the raiding Creek Indians. This episode, entitled "Davy Crockett, Indian Fighter," was the first of a three-part series, which would include "Davy Crockett Goes to Congress" (January 26, 1955) and "Davy Crockett at the Alamo" (February 23, 1955). Walt Disney didn't expect to clear a profit from the series in America (any money he might make, Disney thought, would be from release of the films in other countries).

Things didn't turn out quite that way, though. By May 1955 most kids were singing and humming the show's theme song, Davy Crockett, King of the Wild Frontier, and wearing Davy's favorite headgear, a coonskin cap. And that only scratched the surface of the great Davy Crockett obsession. You could find the image of the King of the Wild Frontier on baby shoes, wallets, bathing suits, jigsaw puzzles, pajamas, lunch boxes, ukuleles and ladies' panties. Typically, a department store would merchandise Davy Crockett towels as follows: "Mom, your bathroom struggles are over. Your kids will run to Davy Crockett towels." Quite simply, Davy Crockett items made up a $100 million market.

The Davy Crockett fur hat was, for the most part, a fad for the very young. Teen-aged guys who sported DA haircuts (see DUCK TAIL, OR DA) or tough-looking garrison belts (see GARRISON BELTS) or gals who just loved to tootle around in poodle skirts (see POODLE SKIRTS) did not find wearing Davy Crockett fur hats quite the voguish thing.

Yet the kids really believed in Davy Crockett. Wearing a coonskin cap was a must, and when a Seattle television reporter offered to trade anything he had for one, no school kid was interested in the deal. They fought for Crockett, too. When Murray Kempton, columnist for the *New York Post*, attempted to discredit Davy's legend, youngsters from Coney Island picketed the newspaper. One of their protest signs read, "Davy killed a b'ar [bear] at three; what did Murray Kempton ever shoot—except the bull?"

The Davy Crockett craze responded to a national desire for a folk hero—a desire that adults also shared. They admired the courage and earthy humor of the Indian fighter, the backwoodsman who became a congressman from Tennessee (1827–31, 1833–35) and the leader at the battle for the Alamo, where he died in 1836. Not that Crockett worship was new to America. In the 1820s Congressman Crockett was celebrated in books and songs (and also given an honorary degree by Harvard College); between 1834 and 1836 books attributed to him excited widespread interest; and from the late 19th century through the Depression, a number of plays were written about his exploits. The last of these was *Davy Crockett: Half-Horse, Half-Alligator* (1932).

So in 1955 Davy Crockett became a hero once more, though the Davy Crockett people admired was the one played by ruggedly handsome Fess Parker (according to Hollywood legend, Walt Disney said immediately after seeing Parker, "That's the man I want for Davy Crockett"). The nation began to hum with interest in Davy. The Washington press corps gave President Eisenhower a Davy Crockett tie. Members of New York's Police Athletic League reenacted the legend of Davy Crockett's childhood bear-killing feats. Historians wrote two new books on Davy Crockett, *The Story of Davy Crockett* by Enid La Monte Meadowcroft and *Davy Crockett* by Walter Blair, both for adults.

In all this ballyhoo, it was sometimes hard to remember that the 1950s Davy Crockett was created for kids. The kids, however, did not forget. From coast to

A four-year-old boy adjusts his Davy Crockett coonskin cap

coast they donned Davy Crockett fur caps, while also wearing Davy Crockett buckskins and toting Davy Crockett rifles, which they filled from Davy Crockett powder horns. Sometimes, wanting to be more like Davy Crockett than any other kid on your block created problems. The best kind of fur hat to wear was of raccoon, but in the spring of 1955, the supply of raccoon tails ran out. Some kids just had to make do with fur hats of muskrat, rabbit, wolf or fox. The kids' song was King of the Wild Frontier, and it sold over 4 million copies. For a number of weeks it topped the hit parade.

And it was the kids who really introduced the mania for Davy Crockett about the end of April 1955. Between the second and third episodes of the Davy Crockett series, they deluged the Walt Disney studios with letters pleading "not to let Davy die," knowing exactly what was going to happen at the Alamo. This was in the second showing of the Crockett series— installments on April 13, 1955; April 27, 1955; and May 11, 1955—but it was the one that made Davy extraordinarily popular. This may have been because most children find it difficult to be frontiersmen in the dead of winter.

Through the summer of 1955 the fad continued, the kids having fun in their backwoods buckskins and their coonskin hats, the adults enjoying a new folk hero. Sometimes, interest in the folk hero took a decidedly satiric turn—for instance, spoofing the opening lines of King of the Wild Frontier. The catchy first lines all about Davy Crockett's Tennessee mountaintop birthplace became, in a New York City version, "Born in the wilds of Delancey Street / Home of gefilte fish and kosher meat." And in a California version, "Born in Chihuahua in 1903 / On a serape out under a tree." Later there came along the Davy Crockett mambo, after the Latin dance that caught on in the early winter (see MAMBO).

The decline and final demise of the fad is somewhat harder to figure. According to *Variety* magazine, "Davy was the biggest thing since Marilyn Monroe and Liberace, but he panicked. He laid a bomb." And overexposure was certainly a reason. It was, however, not the only one. Most significantly, Davy's heroic image began to be tarnished.

There had always been rumors that Davy did not actually die at the hands of Santa Ana's bloodythirsty Mexicans at the Alamo but rather surrendered and was later executed. As time passed, this story—as well as others to the effect that Davy bought his way out of fighting, abandoned his wife and was a habitual drunk— gained more and more currency. (These stories were not new but went back almost to the time of Davy Crockett himself.)

In any event, disillusion with Davy became wide-

Senator Estes Kefauver, a Tennessean like Davy Crockett, in a coonskin cap

spread. One young boy, perhaps anticipating the no-holds-barred antiestablishment posturing of the sixties, wrote of Crockett: "We looked him up in books and found that he really fought, but he was no hero. . . . It was a lot of cheap publicity. I'll bet Disney made a fortune."

Moreover, a new Davy Crockett episode (the fourth), "Davy Crockett and the Keelboat Race," which aired November 16, 1955, only served to further discredit his image. Instead of presenting Davy as the Indian fighter or the Nathan Hale-like patriot, the Disney writers pictured him merely as a guy out to win a big boat race from one Jim Fink, a loudmouth who claimed to be "King of the River." Antiheroism was not yet in (it wouldn't be until the late 1960s), and it was painful in every way that this Davy Crockett was a lot more trivial than the earlier one. By the time of the last episode, "Davy Crockett and the River Pirates" (December 14, 1955), the fad was over. It didn't much matter that Davy was once again performing some heroic exploits that benefited America, or that he had a more serious Jim Fink at his side.

Or maybe it was just that kids had become tired of playing frontiersmen.

Whatever the reasons, the long-expected Christmas 1955 Davy Crockett bonanza never materialized in the marketplace. Davy Crockett T-shirts, which had gone for $1.29 when everyone was clamoring for the King of the Wild Frontier, could be had for 39 cents. Merchandisers had no idea what to do with all that Davy Crockett counter space. And the coonskin caps could be picked up for a song. By that time there were probably few who bothered to ask whether they were the real raccoon article or were made of wolf, fox, muskrat or rabbit instead.

CONTESTS—25 WORDS OR LESS (1954–59)

When you're washing clothes, think: What's different about this soap? Does it make things whiter? Does it make socks smell cleaner?
—Mrs. Nita Parks, winner of many
.25-words-or-less contests

It is difficult to look down on competitions that made people think, and the 1950s were a time in which people could win lavish prizes for writing in 25 words or less why a product was tasty, was beautiful, was really comfortable, was great for children or was any number of other things. How many people were turning out these two dozen and one words?—Twenty million. It was said to be second to stamp collecting as a hobby. Were they doing this for the sport of it? Well, not quite. Winners could find themselves with a 1960 Rambler station wagon or a Sunbeam automatic electric can opener or an electric frypan. And these were the premiums for only one contest: "In 25 words or less tell us why Heinz Ketchup is red magic on foods and in cooking." All you needed, with your phrase, was a box top or label to return to the company to prove purchase.

The middle and late 1950s saw lots of contests like this. There were jingles to be written and sentences to be finished, but for the most part, it was "In 25 words or less . . ."

In a typical contest, the first prize was $10,000; the second prize was $5,000; and the third prize was a new car (which had a market value of about $3,000 then). Other prizes included kitchen appliances, pots, pans and clocks.

Take Mrs. Parks, one of the biggest winners of these contests. Mrs. Parks, who discussed in great detail for national magazines how she would sit down and really concentrate when she started to think about the short statements she was preparing, won a Sealy Posturpedic mattress when she came up with a mattress slogan, fancy pots and pans when she came up with a Birds Eye slogan, a washer and dryer when she came up with a Rinso slogan and a Ford automobile when she came up with an Oxydol slogan. Even if you weren't in Mrs. Parks' league but were pretty good at turning a phrase, you could win $859 in these 25-word contests—which isn't at all bad.

The prizes could be your commonplace trip to the Riviera, appliances or college scholarships, but they could certainly be a lot more exotic. You could win a square inch of land in the far reaches of Alaska. Sealy Posturpedic feted its winners with a "slumber party" at the gold suite of New York City's Savoy Plaza.

Sometimes the contestants had modest aims. One Chicago housewife bragged that she had won numerous contests and was the proud owner of six steam irons. A man in Omaha won a house, a car, a swimming pool and a trip to Hawaii. Now he may well have been one of the biggest winners of them all.

These 25-words-or-less contests also had their altruistic aspects. There was a national organization, called Winsiders, of shut-ins who played the contest games and who were helped by people like Mrs. Parks.

Since everyone thought that he or she had an equal chance to walk off with the winning, companies sponsoring the contests tried to make very sure that there was nothing wrong with them. One major independent organization, the Reuben Donnelly Company, was hired to judge the entries. It made sure, for instance, that one person in a blue uniform would open the envelope with the entry, while a second person in a blue uniform would pull the entry out.

Yet by the end of the 1950s, interest in these contests had waned. There were stories about how people hired organizations to come up with the phrases, paying them up to $100. The investment wasn't worth it: These organizations would likely send the same phrases to great numbers of people (which, one might say, served people right for hiring phrasemakers in the first place rather than toiling over original material).

And the companies must have grown tired of promoting their products in this way. So the task of creating jingles and catchy slogans was once again given back to the advertising agencies.

Somehow, the termination of these contests seems like something of a loss to American culture. It was certainly more interesting than collecting strips of green and blue stamps at your local grocery store and sticking them in books. That only demanded a knowledge of how to lick stamps.

CRINOLINES (Mid-1950s)

In the mid-fifties crinolines and hooped skirts kept girls standing at attention for fear of sitting and having their skirts pushed from behind over their heads. The fuller the skirt, the more stylish. The girls starched them and wore as many of the crinolines under their skirts as needed to hold the skirts high and wide. Some were made from horsehair, and most were truly uncomfortable, but still the girls starched them and added layers just to be in fashion.

One reason given for their popularity was the residual effect—even a decade later—of the movie about the genteel 19th-century South, *Gone With the Wind*. Any young girl could look like Scarlett O'Hara.

Crinolines were popular but bothersome. Articles were written in ladies' magazines giving helpful hints on care and storage of the precious accessory. They were made in many different fabrics, including a few brand new synthetics. Some crinolines had to be dry-cleaned; others were hand-washable only. Customers were advised to "ask the saleslady for advice when choosing a crinoline." Just to keep them fluffy and stiff, crinolines were to be stored on skirt hangers and be allowed plenty of room to save a lot of pressing. So important was the fullness of the crinoline that tags were inserted warning the wearer not to fold it into a drawer. Moreover, crinolines of nylon net and organdy had to be hand-rubbed when washed due to their delicate makeup. They required more care than almost any other accessory but played an important role in dressing up a young woman.

The style didn't outlive the fifties, but while they lasted, crinolines commanded universal attention.

GARRISON BELTS (Mid-1950s)

In 1954 young high school guys still wanted to look a bit like fashion plates. So they wore clothing items that we do not remember at all these days—items like jungle jackets, tiny colonel ties, neon-blue suits and mammoth cuff links (see JUNGLE JACKETS). It was only about 1955 when that image of the "tough guy" or the "pseudo–tough guy"—which so many people knew so well as the image that typified the decade—began to appear. Goodbye mammoth cuff links, jungle jackets and tiny colonel ties; goodbye swanky high school look. Hello tough look. Just consider, for example, the garrison belt, one of the newest fad items, and one of the toughest.

A 2½-inch wide black leather belt with an oversized metal buckle, the garrison belt was an accessory that a tough guy just *had* to have. Although it could be used as a weapon, it was also part of the tough-guy apparel, which included as well a duck tail haircut (see DUCK TAIL, OR DA) and a leather jacket (see MOTORCYCLE JACKETS)—all of which items reflected the look sported by heroes like Marlon Brando in *The Wild One* or James Dean in *Rebel Without a Cause*. All the national magazines were full of talk of juvenile delinquency (or "JD," as nearly everyone called it). A lot of kids wanted to be JDs (juvenile delinquents) or to at least look like JDs.

Having a garrison belt was one way of doing so. One New Jersey fellow remembers the oversized belt and the effect it had: "I was sent home [from school] to change my clothes to something more proper. I was an instant celebrity with the other guys and even the girls." This fellow, no JD, had just wanted to look like one.

The copycat JD with his garrison belt sure looked tough. But you would want to steer clear of the real JD with his garrison belt. He actually was tough and could use this hard, wide buckle to hurt you. You could get badly gouged.

The garrison belt itself was gouged out of the fashion picture by the late 1950s. By the 1960s alienated youth no longer felt garrison belts, leather jackets or being tough JDs were what set them apart from their elders. Rather, they felt alienated because they had a political cause and no one was really listening to them. They weren't interested in mean gestures, just in changing society—and you needed a lot more than a garrison belt to do that.

Although the garrison belt had originally been worn by men in the military, it never became known for that. Instead, it was to gain lasting notoriety as an endorsement sported by some JDs and by a lot more JD look-alikes.

HAIR WAXING (Mid-1950s)

Most young people these days can only remember a time when men wore their hair long or, if not long, of moderate length; yet in the 1950s it was the thing to wear one's hair short. But there was short hair and there was short hair. In the middle 1950s, if you were really with it, your hair at the top of the head would be able to stand on end for hours at a time at an ideal height of 1¼ inches. And there was one way to accomplish this: Keep it waxed, with an effective mustache wax. This was true if you were wearing a crew cut, fuzztop, butch, flattop or heinie—all fashionable hairstyles of the period (see CREW CUTS AND OTHER SHORT HAIRCUTS). Just keep that hair waxed—that was the thing to do.

People had, of course, been using something on their hair to keep it up for a long time. Yet it wasn't as perfect as this 1¼ inches, nor did it stay up for as long a time. In terms of styling short hair, previous oils were to hair waxing what a sand castle is to a chateau.

This era of very sophisticated hair waxing was the first time that mustache wax had been popular since the early 20th century, when your gentleman about town sported a mustache.

Using the hair wax was easy enough. All you needed to do was catch some hair in a comb and brush on the wax. This would up the hair for hours and hours. And the wax only cost $1.50.

This was big in colleges but caught on with older men, too. Some of them said it made them look younger and minimized their balding.

One had to be wary of the occasional prankster, however. Sometimes the wax was mixed with a bit of paste, and unsuspecting victims would brush their hair with the mixture, only to find their scalps soon bristling with solidified spikes.

Of course, mustache hair wax was used for mustaches, too. One of the most famous of the waxed-mustachioed was comedian Jerry Colonna. He was known for going into a piercing yell from the depths of the throat at the beginning of his act—a yell that went "a-a-a-a." (This may also have been the response of those poor fellows who had been fooled into doing some pasty hair waxing and had found they were going to be stuck with a spiked top for a long time.)

Hair waxing belonged to a period in the fifties when the short hairstyles were big. But that time was passing. More college kids wanted to look like Elvis Presley, who was not into crew cuts or hair waxing, or they wanted to sport sideburns (see SIDEBURNS). Some weren't interested in hairstyles at all, turning their attention instead to such concerns as acquiring a really tough-looking leather jacket.

WEARING DAD'S SHIRTS OVER JEANS (Mid-1950s)

A typical afternoon in 1955, and a teen-age girl could be seen walking down the street in jeans, rolled up above the ankle, with a large shirt flowing over her small frame. Why was the shirt so big? Had the girl or her parents forgotten how to shop? No such thing. It was considered faddish for a young lady to wear her father's shirt over her jeans. It was just the height of casual attire.

You could always see it done on television's "Father Knows Best" and "The Donna Reed Show," in which there were scenes of a teen-ager bounding down the stairs wearing her dad's shirt. Donna Reed would exclaim, "Can't you put a dress on if you're going out

on a date?" And the girl would respond, "But I *am* dressed up." And so the fashion hit the street, the malt shop and the sock hop.

By the early 1960s wearing dad's shirt over jeans was no longer done. In a way the 1950s were kind of an innocent era. By the time the 1960s came along, all the talk was of the "generation gap" between parent and child. In no way would a young girl be caught putting dad's shirt on. Dad would be lucky if she said hello.

MOTORCYCLE JACKETS (Mid–Late 1950s)

Movie actors Marlon Brando, of *The Wild One*, and James Dean, of *Rebel Without a Cause*, folk heroes of the young in the 1950s, helped turn the black motorcycle jacket into a symbol of rebellion and toughness. *Wanting* to be a "hoodlum type" caused such an upsurge in the wearing of the black leather jacket that by 1958 even children in grade school were sporting this tough-guy look.

One over-30 executive remembers having a motorcycle jacket in high school and recalls that the day he bought it his father told him he was to get rid of it immediately. After much discussion he was finally allowed to wear it—but only on weekends, never to school and certainly never to church on Sunday.

An expensive clothing item for the 1950s, the jacket could cost about $50 to $75.

School authorities—especially those in private and parochial schools—banned the wearing of the jackets to school or school-related activities. It was not the jacket itself but the connotation: The jacket stood for all that was antiestablishment and all that was rebellious.

The jacket was made of heavy black leather with a thick zipper front and large snaps. A thick black belt known as a garrison belt was attached to the jacket; it bore a large buckle. The leather epaulets on each shoulder gave the wearer an even tougher look. Sometimes black leather gloves were slipped under one of the epaulets and carried there. Of course, not everyone could carry off the tough-guy look. Often, skinny adolescents were seen sporting the jacket and looking incongruous in such garb.

There was also many a variation on the black leather motorcycle jacket look. In 1961 one of the prized possessions of one young girl who entered a college in upstate New York was a red jacket like the one that James Dean wore in *Rebel Without a Cause*.

Interest in the motorcycle jacket has continued to the present day, but in recent years it has been regarded as a high-fashion item, not as a great symbol. In the middle to late 1950s, though, motorcycle jackets, along with a DA haircut (see DUCK TAIL, OR DA) or a garrison belt (see GARRISON BELTS), showed, if you were young, that you were "with-it"—definitely at the place you wanted to be.

POODLE SKIRTS (1955)

A poodle skirt may sound like a garment designed for a dog, but by 1955 many a fashionable teen-age girl was wearing these full skirts made from felt. Attached to the front of the skirt was, for example, a large patch in the shape of a poodle with a furry tail hanging off the surface of the skirt and rhinestones for the poodle's eyes and around its collar. Some of these felt skirts had likenesses of 45 rpm records attached to them, and one girl in Brooklyn, named Marie, had a skirt with images of two squirrels and real walnut shells glued on.

The proper accessories to be worn with these skirts included bobby sox, saddle shoes, a white shirt and a small scarf tied at the side of the neck. The wearer might also have an ankle bracelet (see ANKLE BRACELETS).

The female dancers on television's "American Bandstand" were not only celebrated for being a part of the popular teen-age dance show but were real trend setters besides. What's more, they often wore poodle skirts.

As a variation on this theme, pop singer Connie Francis, appearing on the "Ed Sullivan Show" one Sunday night in 1956, wore a very full felt skirt with flowers embossed throughout.

When the skirts were at their faddish peak, they were covered with everything from kittens to hot rods and even radios. They were most popular among young teen-age girls, but within a few years these same girls grew up and out of the poodle skirt. The next generation of teen-agers was beginning to wear more casual clothes. There were new fads to be started.

ANKLE BRACELETS (Middle–Late 1950s)

Ankle bracelets: thin gold chains, about six inches in length; some plain, most with gold hearts, two often overlapping. The links were sometimes attached by pearls but mostly by hearts, which were usually engraved. Whatever their form, ankle bracelets signified teen-age love in the 1950s. The ankle was, of course, the place to display it. So you would see many a girl striding down the street proudly—knowing she had her ankle bracelet: on the left ankle if she was "going steady" (an exclusive relationship), on the right ankle if she was "going steadily" (that is, with a boy who could still be replaced).

People have memories like this of this mid-1950s item: It's 1957, and a boy of about 16 gives a girl friend the small bracelet. She rushes to put it on her ankle, wanting to let other boys and girls know right away that she is going steady. Many of the luckier girls had inscriptions across the bar of the bracelets—phrases like "Forever" or "For Eternity." Of course, girls who were more cynical about life, and who wanted no part of an exclusive relationship (as "going steady" was also known), dubbed the sweet little ankle bracelet a "slave bracelet," because it marked the girl as the property of the boy. You'd almost have to regard such cynics as cold-hearted, considering the money a guy might have to shell out for an ankle bracelet: $50 for a solid gold bracelet, $3 for a costume jewelry version.

But it wasn't only cynical young folks who weren't crazy about the faddish ankle bracelets. Some parents didn't think it was the greatest thing for their daughters, either. One Brooklyn housewife, given an ankle bracelet in the 1950s, described her experience like this:

I was thrilled! Not only did it mean a boy liked me a lot, but my girl friends would be so jealous. . . . I really had to be careful that my father didn't see it; he'd kill me. So every day after school, I would take it off and hide it in a shoe box. One day I forgot to take it off, and I realized that I had it on when my father walked in. Well, I sat on my legs, Indian style, for an hour before he left the room. I could barely walk when I finally . . . [limped] to my room to take it off.

Yet by 1959 ankle bracelets were definitely on the decline. Jewelry shops were so anxious to sell them (or so concerned because suddenly they weren't) that they would give you a free engraving on the bracelet if you bought one. This kind of thing later happened when pierced earrings got to be the rage, with a slight difference—buy the earrings at the jeweler's, and he or she would pierce your ears free of charge (see PIERCED EARRINGS).

Nothing seemed to work to revive ankle bracelets, though. Since going steady was not in vogue, this token of love was relegated to the jewelry box.

The fad was kind of touching. In the 1980s, when everything seems so temporary, the sensitivity of this fad, its almost "ball and chain" mentality and its innocent promise are particularly striking.

Yet who is to say that ankle bracelets are gone forever? In late 1982 the New York newspaper *The Village Voice* ran a picture of ankle bracelets and said that at some shops they were a fashionable item once more. And who is to say what the next step will be? Perhaps the ankle bracelet fad will reassert itself. And if it does, will tradition be followed—with a bracelet worn on the left ankle signifying "going steady" and on the right ankle signifying "going steadily"—or will the new ankle bracelet wearers make a daring break with the past?

SIDEBURNS (Mid-1950s; Early 1970s)

Elvis Presley had them; James Dean certainly wore them; even pop singer Tom Jones framed his face with them. What were they? Sideburns—facial hair which men grew past the ear in the mid-1950s and the early 1970s, giving the face a dramatic look. Juvenile delinquents and the more numerous group of 1950s JDs manque, with their tough look—which consisted of a leather jacket, a DA haircut and/or a garrison belt (see MOTORCYCLE JACKETS; DUCK TAIL, OR DA; and GARRISON BELTS)—thought very highly of sideburns.

The conservative and acceptable length for sideburns had, up until the mid-1950s, been short, even as trimmed as a quarter of an inch below the hairline. This is not to suggest that other male hairstyles of the 1950s were so "establishment-conscious" as to be uninteresting. There were many variations of men's haircuts to consider (see CREW CUTS AND OTHER SHORT HAIRCUTS), and those who think that in the present century unusual trends in man's hairstyling only began with long hair in the 1960s should think again.

During the 1950s, when Elvis Presley sideburns were in vogue (see DODGSON ELVIS HAIRDO), they were grown longer than an inch and a half and were quite thick; ideally, they were perfect rectangles in front of each ear. The 1970s version of the sideburn was grown

as long as the earlier fashion, but the sideburn itself was sculpted to the cheek, almost to a point at its base.

The conservative business world in the 1970s took the trend as a sign of sheer decadence. A conservative Wall Street firm forbade its employees—lawyers as well as clerical staff—to wear the hairy look. On the other hand, many teachers, advertising executives and retail store owners were seen with conspicuously long sideburns, a little more tapered than the younger set but still an acceptable length to be considered a sideburn.

Also, one accountant from Chicago stated that since accountants had a rather stuffy reputation, he wore sideburns to let everyone know how in touch with the times he was. He was more daring than many people in the business world who—just a few years earlier—had donned fake facial hair to keep up with the long-haired or mustachioed look by night, but who by day had remained straight as a ruler (see FAKE FACIAL HAIR FOR MEN).

One teacher in a New Jersey high school, however, commented with a sly smile, "They're good for grabbing onto when disciplining a troublesome student."

Easily grown and even more easily shaved off, sideburns were a style many men tried, then shaved off and sometimes grew back again. But as time passed, they began to disappear. Difficult to keep trimmed, sideburns lasted only a few years, and by the mid-1970s, just as had happened at the end of the 1950s, short sideburns were once again the rule.

DODGSON ELVIS HAIRDO FOR GIRLS (1956) AND OTHER ELVIS PRESLEY FAD MANIFESTATIONS (1955–57)

Flashback 1956: In Grand Rapids, Michigan about 25 high school girls are lined up on the main street, all with identical Elvis haircuts—their hair plastered back on the sides, a little tuft beside the right ear that resembles a sideburn, and another lock of hair over the forehead. What's more, the hair is dyed black to look like Elvis's (the irony is that Elvis's own hair was naturally light, and he dyed it black, too). No one can say that any of these girls really looked like the rock and roll idol, but they were all doing him homage, just as millions of other kids did in the middle 1950s. Or as

Eddie Condon, the band leader, said of Elvis, "I've been in this line of work 30 years, and I've never seen anything to equal the grip he now has on kids."

Surely there were a lot more than 25 high school girls to adopt the Elvis cut that spring in Michigan; that small group was just part of one typical day's work at one of Glenwood Dodgson's salons in Grand Rapids. There were enough girls to keep 77 barbers busy with cutting, clipping and creating sideburns. Why Grand Rapids was not so far away from other Michigan towns, like Lansing, Muskegon and Battle Creek, and even the metropolis of Detroit was not exactly on another continent. Immediately after Mr. Dodgson made it known that his salons were giving Elvis haircuts at $1.50 apiece, the girls didn't have to content themselves anymore merely with watching Elvis in the movies or hearing Don't Be Cruel, Heartbreak House and Hound Dog, his smash songs, over and over again—they could actually be like Elvis. They could think about that as they were waiting eagerly in one of Dodgson's waiting rooms.

At Grand Rapids some parents must been upset when their young daughters came home with their new hairdos, and some boyfriends may have been upset also, but it did not cause violent controversy. After all, 3-year-old girls went to the beauty salon for an Elvis treatment, and so did 60-year-old women.

Elvis was in fact a real outlaw from 1955 to 1958, when he found himself inducted into the Army. He created mob youth hysteria wherever he went and appeared and sang; it was all because he moved his hips suggestively, which really titillated the audience—titillated it into screams. Nor was this an act (at least at first) on Elvis's part; in the beginning, when he had just begun to record in the South, he moved naturally, caught up in the spirit of his own music. Then, in 1954, he did it once before an audience in Memphis, causing the crowd to go wild. He mentioned this afterward to his entourage in puzzlement and learned that he had been moving his left leg during the performance (he wasn't aware of it).

And soon enough after that, among parents, among authority figures like police officers, and among many an editorial writer, Elvis was considered a beast—quite an accomplishment for someone who only wanted to be a gospel singer. Parents were just overjoyed if their sons or daughters by any chance preferred the more soothing sound of fellow southerner Pat Boone (see PAT BOONE'S PARTICULARLY WHITE BUCKS).

But wherever the monster went, there was a monstrous reaction. On one occasion a bunch of young girls absolutely defaced Elvis's three-month-old Cadillac by writing their names on it in lipstick from hood to fender, and maybe some mushy messages as well (the whitewalls must have been really something!). A

disc jockey offered to give up seven strands of Elvis's hair and got 18,400 soliciting replies. Girls owned "Hound Dog Orange" lipstick or wore blue jeans with Elvis's signature on the back or showed a wrist with an Elvis charm bracelet. While to them, Elvis might have been a heartthrob, to the elder American citizenry, he was one big heartburn.

It is easy to understand why. Elvis had suggestive movements as well as an air of defiance of authority at a time when adults worried a great deal about juvenile delinquents. Consequently, parents began to be concerned even about the harmless JD look-alikes (perhaps their own sons and daughters) who were trying to keep up with other harmless JD look-alikes (perhaps their neighbors' sons and daughters). (See GARRISON BELTS, MOTORCYCLE JACKETS.) If you were an old-fashioned sort of person and preoccupied with your imperiled children, you just had to take action—like making sure that Elvis would be shown on television only from the waist up! No swaying hips allowed!

What was needed was youth with a different point of view, less susceptible to the influence of all this guitar work, hollering and sweet singing, brisk shaking of legs. And so in April 1957 this breed suddenly emerged, wearing "Combat the Menace" (Elvis) buttons and "I Like Ludwig" (Beethoven) buttons. Supposedly there were 20,000 members of this "I Hate Elvis" kind of organization on about 100 campuses. This was a vivid counterreaction to a fad, and it was a precursor of the mad counterreactions of the late 1970s and early 1980s. It was to Elvis what 101 Uses for a Dead Preppie was to preppies (see PREPPY, PREPPIER, PREPPIEST) and 101 Uses for a Dead Cat was to felines (see CATS).

But in terms of the Elvis obsession, the "I Hate Elvis" clubs had precious little influence.

Then, by a combination of circumstances still not entirely understood, Elvis Presley found himself drafted by the United States Army in 1957 and was inducted in early 1958. The defiant wild boy with the moving leg, the provocative voice and the sideburns was in Uncle Sam's armed forces. All the magazines and newspapers made a big thing of his healthy new image—and so did Elvis. At Fort Chaffee, Arkansas in March 1958, Elvis said as he was about to make a bed in an army bunk in front of the cameras that "It's my first experience in bedmaking." (No doubt true, as Elvis Presley was a very sheltered individual.) And then the coup de grace—the stunning blow witnessed by camera upon camera upon camera—Elvis getting his hair cut at the military barber salon by one James M. Peterson, a native of Oklahoma. (Life magazine took over 1,000 pictures of this event alone.) As the shears went clip, clip, clip, a whole generation sighed, and Elvis made something of an attempt at punning humor: "Hair today, gone tomorrow." There was also many a picture of the hair that had fallen on the floor of the military salon.

When Elvis came back from the Army, in 1960, he continued in this new mainstream image and, as a result, was not the obsession he had been. In 1963 and 1964 girls in Michigan or anywhere else might have wanted to grow or cut their hair like the Beatles, not like Elvis Presley.

In spite of this, Elvis remained a hero until his death in 1977. And now there is probably many a mother in Grand Rapids or its environs who has told her daughter all about the time when she went to one of Dodgson's salons one fine day to look like Elvis Presley—just when the young girl's thoughts have turned to the idea of getting the latest short punk hairdo.

CALYPSO (1957)

It came to this country in a big way in the early spring of 1957, with songs like The Banana Boat Song (Day-O), which was the first of the style's big tunes in America, Jamaica Farewell and Marianne. When it swept in it sometimes seemed that it would replace rock and roll. This was the music known as calypso, and it came from the West Indies. How extensive was it as a fad? Just consider: The nightclubs of the land featured calypso singers and changed their decor to convey an atmosphere full of bamboo and hammocks. (Never mind that bamboo and hammocks were more characteristic of the South Seas than the West Indies; how many people were expected to know that?) For $25 you could get a set of calypso bongo drums and maracas at your local department store. True, they didn't have the spirit of Trinidadian instruments, but they still made perfectly OK calypso. As for Hollywood, it geared itself up to make the film *Bop Girl Goes Calypso*.

In the West Indies calypso really flourished in Trinidad. However, when it became fashionable in America in the mid-1950s, it was Harry Belafonte, a 30-year-old singer of West Indian extraction who was born in New York City, who made it popular, particularly in a record album simply titled *Calypso*, produced by RCA-Victor. The Trinidadians said of the American form of calypso that it was "slickened up, prettied up and sophisticated." But maybe this was just envy. They might have had a point, however, about the calypso jingle that was used to sell beer.

However, it wasn't the Americans alone whom the original calypso makers from Trinidad made sport of. They also noted how calypso was spreading to all the other Caribbean islands. One Trinidadian wit said of this, "Is getting so dat any small island with a quatro in he name tell people dey making calypso."

Calypso, with its gossipy, satirical lines and its exciting rhythms, first appeared in the West Indies in the 18th century, when African slaves, forbidden to speak what was on their minds, began to sing it instead. In Trinidad, in particular, calypso became a tradition, performed in long festivals when people wore masks and costumes—a tradition that has continued until the present day.

You can't keep a good type of music a secret forever, though. And in 1939 calypso became the rage in New York City. It did again in 1945, with the calypso song Rum and Coca-Cola. Still, the rages of 1939 and 1945 were nothing compared to the rage of 1957, when you couldn't turn on the radio without hearing calypso. One young fellow in Massachusetts first heard it on the way to junior high school and can attest that it had nothing in common with the rock and roll he was used to.

You could also dance to calypso songs. Calypso dance steps, according to West Indian tradition, are very much like Charleston steps, except there are no kicks or hands crossing over knees. Calypso, however, did not catch on as a dance form in the United States the way the songs did.

When calypso emerged as a fad, a lot of people who frankly disliked rock and roll ballyhooed the West Indies music unabashedly. Or as one American-composed calypso song put it, "Elvis might have to go / And Hound-Dog to Calypso Joe."

But calypso was just a bit too exotic to replace home-grown American rock and roll. Yet people have continued to be attracted by that unusual Caribbean music. In the late 1970s *reggae*, from Jamaica, became popular, which could never have happened had it not been for calypso.

The origin of the word *calypso* is unknown. It has nothing to do, though, with the Greek goddess Calypso, who imprisoned Odysseus. She captured and held the famous wanderer for seven long years.

America, on the other hand, was captured by the calypso rage for only a few short months, but you can still hear a song like Jamaica Farewell played often, and you can still enjoy it a lot.

DROODLES (1957)

Droodles were a sophisticated form of doodles—random drawings that were done to pass the time while you were talking on the phone or pausing to think.

Things like curly-Q's and angles, sometimes colored in, were doodles. Droodles, however, were definite whimsical designs that told a story. They could represent nearly anything. You could do a droodle of ants walking through a spilled martini or a fish climbing a ladder on the Empire State Building; all this could be suggested by the shapes you used. In any event, droodles were big in 1957. *Life* magazine featured a story on them and said that there were droodlers from Greenwich, Connecticut, to Jacksonville, Florida, to Hobbs, New Mexico.

The idea of the droodle in the 1950s was said to have originated with comedian Roger Price. And it certainly caught on. Why? Because it was amusing to draw funny shapes that told a story and also, perhaps, because it revealed a little bit about your character, like inkblot tests. Some of Price's first droodles, which became well-known, were things like a spider doing a handstand or germs scattering in a mass away from another germ who has caught penicillin.

Droodles became so popular that Price came up with a variant called "living droodles," which was also featured in *Life* magazine. This was really like pantomime, in that people acted out the droodles rather than drawing them. *Life* showed some Greenwich, Connecticut high school students with their own living droodles. In one, for instance, a student's hands were desperately trying to make his eyes bulge out; this bore the caption, "Darn those contact lenses." Or in another, a man has his glasses on his forehead and a cigarette in his left ear; this bore the caption, "My doctor told me not to inhale."

The late 1950s was a time when people enjoyed doing frivolous things with their bodies like creating living droodles. After droodles, the next physical phenomenon to come along—in 1959—was "hunkerin'," in which people would squat on their haunches in strange ways (see HUNKERIN'). In a certain sense, this was a lot like living droodles, but it was done by a much more southerly part of your body—all below the waist.

A West coast swimmer plays with a Frisbee®

FRISBEES (1957)

It's still common to see frisbees flying around. Nor will anyone think that you're hopelessly out-of-date if you get up and fling one yourself. You can even go to frisbee tournaments. Yet as popular as frisbees remain today, they were a truly faddish obsession in 1957. This polyethylene item, nine inches in diameter, which looked like a plate, could only be deemed the plate of the hour. Not only did they abound outside—a young man who lived in New Hampshire at that time remembers a field full of people throwing Frisbee® flying disks in the air—but they were also flung about indoors at cocktail parties, where, it was said, hostesses retrieved them from under chairs with broomsticks.

The name *frisbee* for the flying plate came from the Frisbee Baking Company of Bridgeport, Connecticut. The connection between the company name and the toy came about in a rather interesting way. After the Second World War, people were beginning to have high spirits once more, and someone must have noticed in the baking company's executive offices or accounting department that a great number of the tin pie plates that came with Frisbee pies were not being returned (the company offered to refund a small deposit when you brought back the container, just as soft drink producers used to do). They wondered what the reason was, and they found out: People were keeping the Frisbee tin pie plates to toss in the air and at each other.

This happened only in Connecticut, though, until the middle 1950s, when Fred Morrison, a World War II pilot, found out about the flying plates and suggested to Wham-O Inc., a maker of toys, that here was something that might catch many people's fancy. And so the Frisbee® flying disk, as we know it now, was born. Wham-O called the item frisbee because, after all, it wasn't so much different from the original pie plate. Frisbees were also known by other names: flying saucers, space saucers, Pluto platters and wrimpleplates. But whatever name you knew them by, they still cost only 79 cents. The disks, it was reported, first flew primarily in the skies over Yale University, then spread to the rest of the country.

The Frisbee flying disk obsession might have continued longer, except for one thing—the hula hoop (also produced by Wham-O), which came along in 1958. People became more fascinated by swaying their bodies than by tossing pie plate-like disks into the air.

Raccoon coats (1957) CALLING ALL RACCOON COATS OF THE 1920s.

In 1957 an invocation of this sort would definitely have been in order. The raccoon coat—that heavy staple of the 1920s worn in football weather—had come back. Or as much as it possibly could, considering the fact that maybe 2 million Roaring Twenties raccoon coats had been completely dismantled to make Davy Crockett coonskin caps, that *big* fad of 1955 (see DAVY CROCKETT AND HIS FUR HAT). A Davy Crockett raccoon fur hat was just as prestigious for a youngster to have in 1955 as a 1920s raccoon coat was two years later for the kid's older brother or sister.

One thing to remember, though, was that this was a rage specifically for raccoon coats first worn in the 1920s, not for some dolled-up imitations made in the

1950s. The coats had to look old, or as department stores would describe it, "shabbily genteel" or "in a state of magnificent disrepair." Though probably no one knew it at the time, the hunt for old raccoon coats would prove to be very much like the hunt for antique clothing that took place in the late 1960s and early 1970s (see ANTIQUE CLOTHING).

It was college kids—first the men, then the women—who initiated the raccoon coat fashion. This took place mostly on the eastern seaboard at first, because 1920s raccoon coats then had only one major distributor, a couple who ran a clothes shop in New York City's Greenwich Village. But were they ever a fad there! In New York City people stood in line from 5 a.m. in order to plunk down $25 for a 1920s raccoon coat. Word got around, though, and soon enough, department stores outside the East—in Tulsa, Los Angeles, Chicago and Indianapolis—couldn't get enough 1920s raccoon coats on their racks.

Which, again, was precisely the problem in the first place. There just weren't enough 1920s raccoon coats to go around because of their dismemberment to make Davy Crockett fur hats. That Greenwich Village couple scoured (or had scoured for them) one warehouse or attic after another in the search for 1920s raccoon coats.

So the fad for 1920s raccoon coats ended—without reaching the height that it might have. The coats were an interesting novelty, though, and people have always liked to bring back fashions of the past when the spirit moves them. In the 1970s the saddle shoes of the 1950s and the white suits of the 1920s (see GATSBY LOOK), among other items, were brought back once again.

Still, college kids continued to look for fascinating apparel. Following the 1920s raccoon coats in their fancy was an obsession with secondhand but genuine capes worn by London policemen, who are known as bobbies (see BOBBIES' CAST-OFF CAPES).

Pat Boone's PARTICULARLY WHITE BUCKS (1957–58)

Once upon a time, near the end of the 1950s, there arose a conflict between warblers: a clash between the sweet and melodious Boone bird and the untamed and raucous Presley bird—or so the newspapers would have had us believe. Pat Boone sang tender songs like I

Almost Lost My Mind, Friendly Persuasion and Love Letters in the Sand, was clean-shaven, wore a varsity sweater and had an audience that adored him but did not act hysterical. Even the police said how well behaved they were when compared to that mad Presley mob (see DODGSON ELVIS HAIRDO FOR GIRLS AND OTHER ELVIS PRESLEY FAD MANIFESTATIONS).

Many people were truly relieved by the fact that Pat Boone was a really popular *non-Elvis* person, so much so that Boone items also became faddish: like Pat Boone watches, Pat Boone bathing trunks, Pat Boone gloves, Pat Boone shirts, Pat Boone record players and particularly white bucks. Any number of white bucks were bought because people were into being like Pat Boone, who wore size 10½. It is also true that Elvis Presley, in some of his first concerts in the South, wore white bucks. But most people just knew white bucks as Pat's thing.

The national magazines built up a big Elvis Presley versus Pat Boone rivalry, and Pat became known not only for his singing voice but for being a dutiful husband and father, a diligent student at Columbia University and someone who was ready to stand on a platform representing all that was clean-cut and dutiful. His best-selling book, *'Twixt Twelve and Twenty*, was all about this.

It is interesting how wrong the stories were about both Presley and Boone. Elvis really was just a homebody with little sexual experience who simply had a lot of charisma, and whose favorite gesture, swinging his pelvis, came about naturally early in his musical life—this was the way he could best feel the pulse of the music. Pat, on the other hand, was much more complicated and uncertain than a plain old "straight arrow."

Sometimes, however, fads really grow on delusion and illusion. And Americans need their diversion. If a little illusion creates happiness in sporting a pair of white bucks or having Elvis sideburns, who would even want to deny it?

BOBBIES' CAST-OFF CAPES (1958)

You could see them in Piccadilly Circus in the heart of London. Or nearby in Trafalgar Square. Or maybe even where the Prime Minister lived on Downing Street. At all these places, you could in 1958 find bobbies—or British policemen—who wore fancy-looking capes as part of their uniform.

These were not the only places you could see the cape worn, but at these other places it was worn without the bobby in it. Where were these other places? In America. For in 1958 genuine bobbies' capes were a hot item in the former Colonies, and you could get them for only $19. It was the female collegiate young who mostly picked up on this rather exotic garb. Perhaps it made them feel nicely silly or even more cosmopolitan—just as the fad of the previous year, 1920s raccoon coats (see RACCOON COATS), might have made them feel daring and part of that "roaring" decade.

Also, getting a bobby's cape sometimes proved to be a bit of a problem (so did getting a 1920s raccoon coat, because most of them had been dismantled to create Davy Crockett fur hats). British newspapers asked how American co-eds were able to get all these capes, but the importer insisted that it was all aboveboard. And it sure grabbed attention. Specials on the bobbies' capes were written up in *Life* magazine, the *New York Herald-Tribune* and *Women's Wear Daily*.

The cape could make a cape wearer feel very British. Each had a police badge with the royal emblem, EIIR (meaning Elizabeth II Regina—Queen Elizabeth), and also an unmistakable British crown.

Still, all this authority was not enough to prevent the bobbies' capes from being only a very short-term fad. It both began and passed in 1958. It was nothing like those big, big British fashion obsessions that were to come to America in the 1960s—like the Twiggy look (see TWIGGY LOOK), named after the gaunt look of the stick-thin model; and the mod look, with its double-breasted suits, wide belts and ties, and lavish print shirts, copied from styles sometimes affected by the Beatles and sometimes designed on London's Carnaby Street.

However, none of those other voguish fashion items featured a helmet. When you got your bobby's cape, however, you could get a helmet, too—a helmet that had also been worn by a real, live bobby.

Wearing bobbies' cast-off capes was, for the most part, a collegiate fad—an item to wear to impress your seminar-mates or dormitory-mates or to wear to a stylish cocktail party. It wasn't high fashion like the sack look (see SACK LOOK), which many women wore to dazzle; it was more like a garment worn as a stunt. After all, not many a lass was in training to become a British constable.

Bobbies' cast-off capes were not the only bizarre costumery fad of that year, however. Fathers were often sporting bowler hats in 1958, as if they were living in Merry Olde England in the early 19th century (see BOWLER HATS). It must have been quite a scene at any collegiate weekend for fathers and daughters—the lass wearing her bobby's cast-off cape greeting her father in his bowler hat.

BOWLER HATS (1958)

Bowler hats were not a national fad in the same sense that hula hoops, Davy Crockett fur hats or frisbees were, but they were prominent enough to be featured in magazines like *Look* and *Newsweek* and for Dick Clark, the master of ceremonies for the rock and roll television dance show "American Bandstand," to say of the old bowler to his teen-age audience: "I just don't dig derbies. The kids might give me a ribbing." Here was yet another illustration of the age-old fight between generations: The teen-agers who watched "American Bandstand" thought that fads like bowler hats that their parents got involved with were silly; just as a lot of parents couldn't stomach motorcycle jackets or songs like Hound Dog or Blue Suede Shoes. If a teen-ager saw daddy coming home from work in his bowler, he or she would just give him the kind of look Daddy gave the kid when he or she spun 45 rpm rock and roll records.

The bowler hat came back in 1958 because men are inclined, from time to time, to wear fancy British apparel. And the bowler hats were really British. They were first fashioned in 1780 by a hatmaker named Bowler. Soon enough, they hit the English aristocracy and were worn by the Earl of Derby and his crowd. It is for this reason that bowlers are sometimes called derbies.

And there was no doubt about the resurgence of the bowler in America; 3,000 bowlers a week were exported to the United States from England in 1958, whereas between 1939 and 1958 only a total of 800 bowlers had been exported. While 3,000 was not a big, big number, it was enough for the bowler to get a lot of magazine coverage and to be found just plain chic. According to one report, the center of bowler activity was Toledo, Ohio, where almost 2,000 men were spotted wearing the hat at one time in 1958.

It all just went to show that both father and daughter could try to be old-fashioned together in the modern 1950s. Dad could sport his bowler hat while his lass could wear a raccoon coat (see RACCOON COATS). In a few years, when the "generation gap" was all the fashion, this could be seen as quaint.

HULA HOOPS (1958)

In the 1950s it wasn't enough for the Australians to beat us yearly for the Davis Cup, the international tennis championship trophy. What more could the Aus-

sies do? They gave us the idea for the hula hoop, that's what they did. And the hula hoop drove Americans into a big faddish frenzy. There were "hoop-ins" in many an American town. People dived into hoops in the water. In Hollywood hoops were kept all over the place so the celebrities could play. Luminary hoopers included Jane Russell, Debbie Reynolds, Red Skelton and Art Linkletter, to name but four. But you didn't need to be a luminary to be a hula hooper in 1958; nearly everyone was trying to put into practice the instructions that came with every hula hoop: "Hug the hoop to the backside . . . push hard with the right hand . . . now rock . . . swing it . . . sway it. . . . You got it." By September 1958, 30 million kids were said to be turning, swishing and swaying. One hula hoop maker said of it, "It's bigger than Zorro, bigger than Davy Crockett, bigger than anything in the toy business."

The polyethylene hula hoop, which was the cause of all this swishing and swaying, was very much different from the hoop Australians used in their gym classes. Those were three-foot bamboo rings, which were soon to be sold in Australian stores as well.

But somehow, news of this kind of hoop spread to California, where two entrepreneurs, Richard P. Knerr and Arthur K. Melin, picked up on it. (One year earlier, Knerr and Melin's company, Wham-O, had come up with the frisbee; see FRISBEES.) They refined the Australian bamboo hoop, first trying something made of scrap wood, before turning to polyethylene. For the hula hoop, after it was determined it should be polyethylene, all systems were go. Millions upon millions were sold at $1.98 to $2.79 apiece. Soon enough there were not only Wham-O hoops, but also Hoop-Zings and Hooper-Doopers. Only the name was different; your body swished and swayed in them in exactly the same way.

Hula hoops made people feel good, or as Jules Feiffer, the cartoonist, showed it when he drew a young girl with her hoop: "I was feeling lonely and unnoticed. But then I got a hoop." Spinning around in a hula hoop was rather like intoxicating continual motion. While you could hoop it up alone, there were also giant-sized hoops in which a couple could gyrate together. It was news when someone swayed his body in 14 different hoops at the same time. It was news when a young Michigan boy made 18,200 turns in a hoop at one session. The hula hoop was many things to many people: It was a mode of self-expression. It was an excuse for getting together with your friends. Also, a psychologist suggested that the hoop was attractive because its shape reminded kids of the warmth of the "family circle." It could be just an engaging stunt, too.

At the height of the hula hoops' popularity in 1958, 2,000 a day were being sold at a Boston department

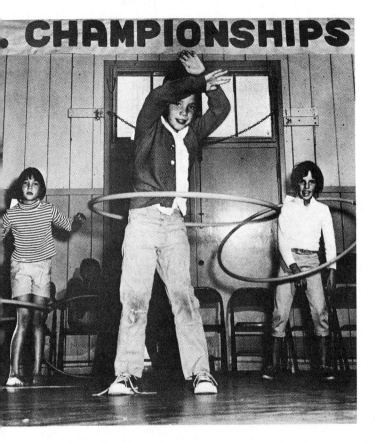

Three kids hula hoop it up

store, where a majorette demonstrated how it was used; at the other end of the continent, where it all began, 1,800 a day were being sold at a Los Angeles department store.

Yet the hula hoop, "one of the sweetest merchandise phenoms I ever saw," as a West Coast retailer put it, was mostly a summertime fad, and by the middle of the fall, the craze had begun to die out. Or as the *Wall Street Journal* put it, "Hoops Have Had It."

You could also tell what was happening from the prices. In the period of the hoops' boom, they had started at $1.98 apiece and gone up to $2.79, and still demand outstripped supply. But when the hoop fad collapsed, prices fell—first to $1.49, then to 77 cents, then to 56 cents, finally to 50 cents.

The kids had become bored, or as one said, "How many ways can you twist around?" As the market dwindled, hoop makers tried to come up with twists on the hoop that would revive its popularity. One manufacturer came up with a hoop that made a musical sound; another came up with a hoop with bells; still another came up with a hoop that doubled as an umbrella or a sail. But nothing seemed to work.

Yet while the hoop was declining in America, it was becoming a worldwide fad—the biggest fad to come from the United States since the time of the yo-yo. In Jordan the Queen Mother spun it around, and in Japan, the prime minister. A great fan of the hula hoop in France was the novelist Francoise Sagan. In Finland there were hoop marathons.

And in a time of "Cold War," the Soviet bloc of nations also became fascinated. First in Yugoslavia there were four hoop-making factories. Then in Poland the official magazines called admiring attention to it and urged the Ministry of Light Industry to embark on production of hoops immediately. The leaders of East Germany said the hoop was good for physical fitness. Only the Soviet Union stood aloof, its citizens not encouraged to swish and sway.

When there was a Belgian expedition to Antarctica, 20 hula hoops were taken along.

Though the fad for the hula hoop lasted only a part of one year in the United States, it is still not difficult to find a hula hoop, and no one would think you were too terribly silly if you swayed around in one. People continue to remember the hula hoop as one of the biggest fads there ever was.

It is uncertain, though, whatever happened to those three-foot bamboo rings, once used in Australia, that were the start of it all.

105

SACK LOOK (1958)

Designers jeered at it; men said they never saw such a thing; and many older women said it was only fit for teen-age girls. All it did was sell. No matter what unflattering name its detractors gave it—like *bag, balloon, pear* and *pickle.* And of course, *sack*—sometimes even *sad sack.*

Still, le sac was the latest spin of the fashion wheel, and it had the added advantage of being quite comfortable for women to wear. A loosely fitting, unbelted dress (often described as chemiselike), the sack was easy to slip on. Women were ready for something different from the superelegant New Look, with its garments hugging the waist or bosom, or with its great amount of fabric, which had been popular since 1947 (see NEW LOOK). Perhaps women wanted to be considered as something more than fashion plates. Which is not to say that a lady couldn't get a sack that was most fashionable. For instance, there were taffeta chemises; short, satin evening chemises; and chemises in black Persian lamb.

Whether women wanted an easy garment to put on, or just the latest fashion, the sack really was the rage. Women in the East, Midwest and Far West were all avid buyers, as sales in New York, Milwaukee and San Francisco showed. In the 1958 catalog the sack was Sears Roebuck's biggest-selling dress.

The sack look was first designed by the Spaniard Balenciaga and the Frenchman Hubert de Givenchy, and was first introduced in Paris in September 1957. From France, just like the New Look and many another fashion during this century, it spread to the United States.

Yet the sack look lasted only a year. Perhaps it declined because there was something about the look that was just too austere. It has also been maintained by a number of fashion writers that the sack declined because it was a type of garment that was not only easy to make but also easy to make poorly. Those writers noted that too many shabby sacks came on the market, and women were turned off.

In any event, the sack look suddenly ceased being the vogue. One woman who was in her twenties during the 1950s ruefully remembers this. She said of the baggy garments that she had "loved them." She felt that when sacks were popular, she really didn't have to dress up. Now she had to dress up again.

FAST GUNFIGHTS (1958–61)

The legend of the Wild West has always figured prominently in American life. In the 1950s, television shows like "Gunsmoke" (with Sheriff Matt Dillon), "Wyatt Earp" and "Have Gun Will Travel" rode high, all featuring the shootout, or the good guy against the bad guy, when life was at stake. And long before television, historical characters like Billy the Kid and Bat Masterson had entered into the mainstream of American folklore. Children played "shoot 'em dead" after school. It was no wonder that fast gunfights were a rage from the late 1950s to the early 1960s. You could find them being played at many a nightclub or bar—by men and women alike—by westerner and easterner alike.

A fast gunfight was not conducted with real bullets but with blanks and wax bullets. The idea was to pull the gun out of your holster and shoot in the quickest time possible. For instance, $13/100$ of a second was an acceptable speed, but $9/100$ of a second was really good. Though his speed at the draw is not known, Sammy Davis Jr. pulled a fast gun on the "Jack Paar Show," the forerunner of Johnny Carson's "Tonight" show. One million people belonged to various fast-gun clubs, and journals like *Gunsmoke Gazette* and *Gunslinger's News* could be found anywhere that fastgunners happened to meet. A serious fast-gunner might spend as much as $158 for a nickel-plated gun. Fastgun devotees not only attracted people who wanted to prove that they were the fastest on the draw but also people who were interested in history. A truck driver from Mississippi, for instance, said he liked to play fast gun for exactly that reason—that "he read a lot."

Playing fast gun was such an obvious activity that it was of course not really invented in the 1950s. Yet it was popularized then. According to many accounts, this popularity is attributable to the efforts of Dee Woolem, an Oklahoman, who became a crack fastgunner while working as a train robber at a Los Angeles amusement park with a Wild West theme. His skill drew such wide attention that he and his gunplay appeared on Los Angeles television in 1954. And slowly but surely, fast gunfighting caught on nationwide. An article in *Sports Illustrated* showed that by 1961 it was being done by missile technicians, salespeople, plastics workers, millwrights and dentists. Many of these sported Western clothes, since they declared that "it was part of our sport." A most unusual costume worn by an Oklahoma missile technician consisted of a beaded suit of red velvet.

Soon enough there were fast-gun competitions as well. In Las Vegas, where the 1961 fast-gun competitions were held, there were 185 gunslingers. This was a far cry from the early 1950s, when only 12 gunslingers had entered.

There was also many a fast-gun club in the late 1950s and early 1960s, which resulted in large part because of the active promotion of such clubs by Colt Industries, the gun makers.

Fast gunfighting continued through the early 1960s, though less was written about it; it probably continues even to this day. Yet as a diversion, the interest in fast gunfighting and drawing probably really began to slow down in November 1963, when President Kennedy was assassinated. This rocked American life to its foundations, particularly since it was followed by a string of other assassinations, and a lot more resistance was shown by much of the general public to gunplay as a type of sport. Somehow, it no longer seemed like a game, once so many somber events had transpired.

HUNKERIN' (1959)

To hunker meant to sociably squat on your haunches, and it was a big fad in the Ozarks—southwestern Missouri, northwestern Arkansas and northeastern Oklahoma—among college students in 1959. In fact, in that time of Cold War between the United States and the Soviet Union, it was suggested that the president of the United States, Dwight Eisenhower, and the premier of the Soviet Union, Nikita Khrushchev, should do a friendship hunker together. This meant that they would squat on their haunches while putting their arms around each other's shoulders.

Hunkerin' was big in the fall of 1959, about six months after the telephone booth stuffing craze (see TELEPHONE BOOTH STUFFING). Hunkerin' was much less bone-crushing than telephone booth stuffing and also more amiable—even almost meditative. You could daydream while you were hunkerin'; you could quietly concentrate. In fact, there were many forms of hunkerin', of which concentration hunkerin' was one. In that one you sort of sat on your haunches and looked out like Rodin's sculpture of *The Thinker*. There must have been many scholarly types at the University of Arkansas in Fayetteville, at other colleges in the Ozarks and at Memphis State College, not so far away in the Mississippi Delta region, who did a lot of concentration hunkerin'.

But hunkerin' was not only for intellectuals—far from it. There was telephone stand hunkerin', in which you squatted on a telephone stand, and piano top hunkerin', in which you roosted atop a piano. There were also jockey and modified jockey hunkers, in which you looked more or less like a jockey on a horse (more for jockey hunker; less for modified jockey hunker). There was a hunker known as the Hornibrook Special Hunker, named after an undergraduate; it was a position that only really accomplished hunkerers could carry off. There were also many other kinds of hunkerin', and new styles could always be improvised. Not that hunkerin' was something to be taken lightly. There were many different views on "how high off the ground a hunkerer's posterior should be," as one national magazine, reporting on the squatting, put it.

Hunkerin', a word of old Norse origin, probably lasted only a short time; there is no account of how or why it disappeared. Perhaps it was just more difficult to hunker than to sit normally.

But somehow, it is probably also true that it caught on in the first place because hunkerin' sounded like a really esoteric experience. If it had been called just plain squattin', no one would probably have given it a second thought. And certainly no one would have recommended it for Eisenhower and Khrushchev.

Hunkerin' was a quiet fad, and very personal. It was much different from other fads of the 1950s, like telephone booth stuffing, panty raids and hula hooping, which almost demanded group participation. Hunkerin' sort of foreshadowed the introspective seventies.

KOOKIE (1959)

Kookie was kind of a wild young television hero in the late 1950s, who was known for three things—that he had blond hair, that he was always grooming it with his pocket comb and that he had his own personal lingo, which sounded very bohemian, although Kookie himself (Played by 25-year-old Edd Byrnes, an actor from Manhattan) looked like a surfboarder. He was particularly fond of the suffix *-ville*: When he talked about being sick, he was in "illsville"; when he talked about having to be around too many people, this was "antsville"; and when he talked about being in a dull situation, why this was none other than "squaresville." And the bonanza this young parking lot attendant on a detective show, "77 Sunset Strip" (an address in Los Angeles), brought to merchandisers was moneysville. Six-foot, 165-pound Kookie was just the charmer of the year, and for the boys it became a fad to want to be like Kookie, while for the girls it became stylish to perhaps give their boy friends combs.

This is the only time in recent memory that a pocket comb—just a simple pocket comb—caused long lines at department stores. After the faddish items—like the Davy Crockett fur hat, the hula hoop, the raccoon coat and the frisbee—that had been big in the last half decade, whoever could have dreamed that a humble pocket comb would follow? Yet there it was, selling in the many thousands. When a guy combed his hair like Kookie, it wasn't just that he wanted to get rid of any unkemptness—he was trying to be really slick, as he ran the comb through his hair with almost artistic motions. Yes, indeed, at high school, he would be sure to show all the girls that he was continually combing his hair.

Not that the pocket comb was the only Kookie item that became popular as the fifties were winding down; there was also a song that quickly streaked onto the hit parade, Kookie, Kookie, Lend Me Your Comb. This line was sung by a bunch of ecstatic young girls any number of times during the course of the short 45 rpm, as if to show that Kookie's pocket comb was the only thing they had to think about. The record sold over 2 million copies.

Kookie was a sex symbol, but nothing like Elvis Presley, who caused girls to scream as he sang and swayed his pelvis, or Marlon Brando and James Dean, who were "hoods" with their leather jackets and their tough ways of strutting around and taking no baloney from anyone. Yet though much tamer, Kookie was not so tame that any teen-ager would ever think that he inhabited squaresville. What's more, he showed that you didn't need to be a JD (juvenile delinquent) to attract girls; Kookie, after all, worked with a couple of detectives, played by Efram Zimbalist Jr. and Roger Smith, to clear out the Los Angeles underworld. Neither of the detectives quite had Kookie's style, however; you would never catch either of them telling a pretty young lady that she was the "ginchiest" (very lovely) or, when he was ready to knock off at the end of a hard day, that he wanted to "pile up some Zs" (get some sleep). This was strictly Kookie's lingo.

The interest in Kookie passed in the early 1960s, with a waning of interest in "77 Sunset Strip." Although Arthur Fonzarelli (alias "the Fonz" or "Fonzie") of television's hit comedy show "Happy Days" (see THE FONZ), with his perfectly groomed D.A. haircut and his distinctively wisecracking style, did follow in Kookie's footsteps in the late 1970s, no one since has quite succeeded in living up to Kookie's image. And certainly no one since has managed to inspire a hit song featuring a pocket comb.

TELEPHONE BOOTH STUFFING (1959)

Well, everyone began laughing so hysterically that no one could answer the phone, even if they could reach it."

—Penn State student, about the moment during a telephone booth stuffing when the phone rang

Telephone booth stuffing is one of the most illustrious American fads. Never mind that in its origin it was not American at all—it was thought up in South Africa—or that it only caught on intensely in the western United States; when one thinks of the all-time great fads, telephone booth stuffing ranks high on the list. This may be because it is so unmistakably unique: all those outstretched bodies, arms and legs trying to wedge into the confines of one telephone booth.

Telephone booth stuffing was principally a fad for men students. It was guys who squeezed into the telephone booth, and it was also guys who watched the telephone booth squeezing done; pictures show that few girls even watched the event. From time to time, there was an exception when it came to female participation in telephone booth stuffing. In Fresno, California a number of coeds in one-piece bathing suits created a lovely sight by squeezing into a telephone booth submerged underwater in a pool.

The first telephone booth stuffers did it in Durban, South Africa; the stuffers were 25 men strong (some news reports said that all the students were at least 6 feet tall). This inspired the young men of England, but they came up with only 15 to 19 telephone booth stuffers at one time. Then at Oxford University the Britishers went on a diet, which resulted in a respectable 22 stuffers making it in.

However, the English stuffers also had a beef with the South African stuffers. They maintained that the object of telephone booth stuffing was not only to squeeze as many bodies in as possible but also to be able to make an outgoing call (some Britishers further held that this call had to be made by someone in the middle of the collection of stuffers). The South Africans—they said—were just interested in the stuffing; it was much too easy the way they did it!

In any event, telephone booth stuffing became the rage, which spread to North America—probably to Canada first, then to the United States. At the University of Calgary in Saskatchewan, 40 young Canadian men squeezed themselves into a telephone booth. However, this achievement, too, had its detractors: The booth was non-regulation size, being 10 feet high. A conventional booth is 7 feet high. Hence, a lot more

Telephone booth stuffing at Memphis State University. Usually done by fellows, girls showed that they could do it every bit as well.

bodies could be squeeze in; hence, this particular telephone booth stuffing should be disregarded.

In the United States in the early spring of 1959, American students began stuffing telephone booths. Most of the action took place in California, although some took place in the Middle West, and the only student theorizing about telephone booth stuffing took place at the Massachusetts Institute of Technology. In sheer numbers, for instance, phone booths were stuffed by 17 people at UCLA and by 18 students at the College of St. Mary's in Moraga, California, while there were 19 phone-booth stuffers at MIT, where the mathematics of the thing had been worked out far in advance.

Then Modesto Junior College in Modesto, California came up with 34 telephone booth stuffers. Was this to be considered a record? No. Why not? The telephone booth in question was not standing up but had been laid on the ground. Again, this made it possible for extra people to fit in.

Nor was this the end of controversies about how to stuff a telephone booth or what counted as a stuffed body. Sometimes it was maintained that a stuffer could have his legs dangling outside the booth, but other times it was maintained that a stuffer had to keep his legs inside the booth. This last arrangement was known as the sardine position and was highly respected wherever you went.

Somehow, these burning issues were never settled before the fad came to an end in the year in which it began, 1959.

A few years later, a fad quite similar to telephone booth stuffing came along: VW, or Volkswagen, stuffing. This never really caught on like telephone booth stuffing had. Perhaps it was because it lacked controversy. There was no doubt that a VW stuffer had to fit his body inside the car. There was no funny business about wedging into the trunk or sitting snugly atop the motor.

109

WHITE LIPSTICK (1959)

White lipstick was popular in the United States in 1959, but the fad didn't last very long. A number of women have been asked about white lipstick recently, and none remembered it. Yet back in the 1950s Revlon Industries and 29 other companies were heavily into the cosmetics producing shades like white pearl, white lustre, white frosting and winter white.

Why would many women who had used red and pastel-colored cosmetics all their lives suddenly switch over to white lipstick? Because it was a new thing, and one that could make a woman look unusual or exotic in the sea of ladies around her with red lipstick—perhaps. Charles Revson himself said, "It's just that with white and light shades a woman has more chance to look individual and different for different places and times of day."

There was perhaps another reason why white lipstick caught on in 1959: The Food and Drug Administration, in April of that year, had warned people against using a number of lipsticks that contained coal tar colors because their heavy use of dye was considered something of a health hazard. So if a woman felt misgivings now about wearing a vibrant red shade, there were striking white shades around that could be every bit as enticing. What's more, there was a lot less coal tar in it.

Michel Cosmetics of New York City is said to have been the first company to distribute white lipstick on a large scale. The magazine *Printer's Ink* said that "Michel's shady doings are on the lips of sophisticates everywhere."

Americans came late to white lipstick. It had first become chic in Europe in the early 1950s. Yet in America its effect was short-lived. Most women thought that it was just too macabre to have ghostly lips. There was nothing beautiful about this; it was merely outlandish.

BARBIE DOLLS (1959–Early 1960s)

Dolls have usually been thought of as rather innocent, just like miniature people. In the late 1970s and early 1980s, this kind of image has been true of Strawberry Shortcake (see STRAWBERRY SHORTCAKE), with her red freckles and pleasant fruity smell, and the Muppets (see MUPPETS), whether it be the sleek Miss Piggy or the urbane Kermit the Frog. Just before World War I, the very popular kewpie doll, which first appeared in light children's poetry for magazines (see KEWPIES), was really innocent.

But in the late 1950s, there was one outstanding exception to the innocent-little-person doll—an exception that became faddish: the Barbie® doll. She was tall, full-figured, long-legged and complete with glamorous wardrobe. She became popular not because girls wanted a doll that was cuddly but because they wanted one that was more realistic and more sexy. They wanted an 11½-inch doll that looked as if it was about to become a woman.

Many a New York City woman has recently been asked about what it was like to own a Barbie doll. A secretary remembered the doll's perfect girlish size; a writer remembered that Barbie was the type of creature who knew her way around boys; a graphic artist remembered that her Barbie had an independent life, wasn't someone to cuddle up to as you might do when you comb an infant's hair; and yet another artist was so taken with Barbie that she made all her other dolls Barb's maids. Barbie was someone really unusual, quite unlike other dolls. No wonder she became so very popular.

How popular is popular? Consider Barbie in the early 1960s. By 1964, 5 million Barbies had been sold in California alone. There were Barbies (there still are) to fit every temperament and every conception of beauty—like Barbies with blond hair, platinum hair or brunette hair.

Although the Barbie doll herself cost $3.00 in 1961, what was a Barbie without a dazzling wardrobe, for she was meant to be a young lady ready to step out. There was Barbie in a strapless black gown, Barbie in a natural mink jacket, Barbie in a sequined bolero jacket, Barbie in a magenta satin dress, Barbie with rhinestone earrings, Barbie in a skiing outfit, Barbie in a skating outfit, Barbie ready to make her professional mark as an airline stewardess, and an altruistic Barbie in her hospital volunteer uniform, no less. There was even a stay-at-home Barbie who changed diapers. Particularly popular was Barbie's wedding trousseau, which cost $35.00 for everything but only $1.25 to $5.50 for the wedding dress itself. There were also Barbie bras and Barbie girdles.

Just looking at the figures on Barbie doll costumes, 100,000 a week were sold, and the factory was barely keeping up with the demand.

Barbie was a Pisces and was first introduced by Mattel Inc. on March 1, 1959. She was named after Barbara Handler, the just pre-teen-age daughter of Ruth and Elliot Handler (the brains and money behind Mattel Inc.), who had always liked to dress up paper dolls. Mrs. Handler began to think, as she told it many times,

"Wouldn't it be nice if there was a three-dimensional doll which could be dressed in miniature fashions?" And so, after much experimentation and considerable scoffing by people in the doll business that a doll with almost full-sized breasts would never catch on, Barbie appeared. Soon enough, there.was a Barbie magazine with 100,000 subscribers and Barbie fan clubs from the United States to Afghanistan.

The Handlers thought that this adult Barbie® doll, with her flirtatious ways, would be seen as something of an outrage. This really didn't happen, though some parents were upset that this new stranger in their young girls' dollhouse was a bit more racy than the other dolls, and some parents tried to avoid Barbie's being put by their little girls into sexually suggestive situations. There were even a few columnists who took the Handlers to task for Barbie's explicit physique. For the most part, though, Barbie was welcomed without a tiff and, since she was unique, became faddish.

And where did all this interest in the Barbie® doll lead? It led to the creation of Ken, a boy doll, also almost like a man—in other words, not just a cherubic innocent. This took place in 1961. Ken and Barbie together—now that was a whole lot different than a female baby doll and a sweet kewpie doll together (kewpies were, according to their creator, Rose O'Neill, always boys). Parents tried to establish limits about what Ken and Barbie could do together, but you can't always go into a little girl's room, and you can't hire a full-time spy.

Still, parents kept a sense of proportion about the matter. The popularity of Barbie was not like the second coming of the Charleston or the turkey trot, which were seen as very sinful when they were danced earlier in the 20th century. No religious figure complained that little girls were playing too much with their Barbies on a Sunday rather than coming to church, as ministers had done when the bicycle became voguish in the 1890s. All this may have showed how far Americans had come.

And now consider how much money there is in owning an original: One original brunette Barbie doll created in 1959 goes for $750 today.

As for Barbie, her popularity has remained so high that she has inspired a whole collection of Barbielike imitations. She has become a tradition, which is something different from what was she was in the early 1960s, when having a Barbie doll was an obsession with almost every little girl. While little girls with their Barbies might be having some fun now, their mothers had Barbies at a time when the doll's every new hairdo and wardrobe item made her a figure of romance. This was an American doll such as there never was. Not just any female doll can inspire a Ken. Can't be done.

THUMPER
(Late 1950s; Early 1960s)

During the late 1950s and early 1960s preprotest era, a very innocent college drinking game was played on many a campus, though it wound up with one and all getting "plastered." It was a beer-consuming diversion known as thumper, for no obvious reason, and it was played, for instance, at Hofstra University on Long Island in New York, at Clemson University in South Carolina and at Loyola University in Chicago. At all campuses the only equipment needed was lots of beer and enthusiastic players. If it were played in the 1980s, it might be said that both the players and the beer itself had the gusto.

Thumper was a game that required a good memory and coherent thinking, which just goes to show that people did more than arm wrestle when they were getting drunk, which is what the beer commercials would sometimes have us believe. While the drinking of beer is done as a group, every now and then one of the beer-guzzlers is pushed into the spotlight and asked by everyone else, "What's the name of the game?" He or she must reply "Thumper is the name of the game," and if that isn't hard enough, he or she must spell out T-H-U-M-P-E-R. If the drinker goofs up and spells out T-H-I-M-P-E-R, for instance, he or she must down a mug of beer.

Eventually, everyone is going to make a lot of mistakes and become really "swished."

And if that isn't hard enough, thumper players also had to remember codes as they were answering questions. For example, one's signal might be a pull of the earlobe. A mistake here could also lead to downing a lot of beer.

As for records, in one fraternity in upstate New York, there were said to have been 34 drunken players at the end of one particular competition. Also it was said that a marathon thumper game could last as long as 24 hours. There were breaks, of course, so the drunkenness would not happen too quickly. Maybe there were also breaks to write papers and prepare for tests.

Thumper was not a collegiate drinking game that caught on for too long a time. It was more like other short-term collegiate fads of about the same period— bed racing (see BED RACING) and the Ozark squatting game of hunkerin' (see HUNKERIN'). Still, it required a lot more gusto than the famous telephone booth stuffing, which came along soon enough. You couldn't have fit a can of beer into those crowded telephone booths, much less any number of six-packs.

INTRODUCTION

Anyone who lived through the sixties will not easily forget them, for those years surely constituted a period of profound unrest. It was a time of political assassinations: John Kennedy, Martin Luther King, Robert Kennedy, Medgar Evers—all were slain, and all, to many, were symbols of the prospect of a more humane American future. It was a time of great social upheaval in American cities and a time of the Viet Nam War, the first conflict in modern American history to meet with widespread domestic hostility. All these developments had an effect on the fads of the decade.

This was true, for instance, of the business coloring books of the early 1960s, which spoofed the serious ways of ambitious corporate professionals. Although this predated the assassinations, civil chaos, war and other disturbances, it showed that a kind of antiestablishment sentiment was already in the air. A similar effect could be seen in the growing popularity of the twist (and its later variants like the frug, the monkey and the watusi), which initially resulted from teen-agers' determination to go their own rebellious way in cultural matters. Another popular gesture of defiance was the wearing of iron crosses. At first, the wearing of miniskirts could also be counted among the defiant gestures, but within a few years miniskirts were the standard garb—and, indeed, it became a defiant gesture for women *not* to wear them.

At the same time, hero worship played an important part in the creation of the decade's fads, jusst as it always has. In the early 1960s Jacqueline Kennedy was a revered figure, with many women sporting bouffant hairdos and pillbox hats in imitation of the first lady's characteristic fashion style. Yet awe of Jackie was not the only big force on the faddish horizon. There were also the Beatles, who made their flamboyant entrance in 1963, together with the whole mod scene from England, which would bring us bellbottoms, Nehru jackets, turtlenecks and even the Twiggy Look. And then there was the "hip" counterculture (the nature and extent of whose effect it would take volumes to explain), which manifested itself in love beads, dayglo, long hair for men and the taking of drugs.

Yet these powerful social forces and instances of personal magnetism, as loaded with cultural dynamite as they were, do not account for many of the fads of the decade. They do not explain the importance of surfing or any of its offshoots (which included skateboarding, a prominent variant, and pier-roulette surfing and pypo-boarding, minor variants). The surfing group of fads seems attributable to the long-standing human tendency to try new athletic feats. Nor do they explain superball, a simple but incredibly bouncy little sphere, or G-R-O-N-K-I-N-G, a popular cry serving as a release from the tension of intensive studying that hit the nation's campuses in 1965. Nor do they explain op talking, a kind of private form of communication among teen-agers in 1963 that boasted its own special grammatical rules centering around the use of the omnipotent *op* sound.

Just as there is such a thing as art for art's sake, could it be that there is such a thing as fads for fads' sake?

BOUFFANT (1957–64; High Point, 1961–63)

The puffed-out bouffant was what Jacqueline Kennedy adopted as her hairstyle when John F. Kennedy was president from 1961 to 1963, and consequently it was the bouffant that became the chic cut from coast to coast. On the head of the most admired woman in America then, the bouffant had a festive history. It was pictured in all the papers when Kennedy was inaugurated and when the Kennedys were shown greeting President DeGaulle of France. Then it had a sad history, for Jacqueline Kennedy was wearing the bouffant when her husband was assassinated in Dallas in 1963. In fact, after the assassination, the bouffant lost a lot of its momentum as a fashionable style to adopt. It had been linked to a time when people had thought of themselves as young and gay, and now many thought of themselves as sad.

In contrast to hairstyles in the 1950s, which often favored the "poor boy" or urchin look, in which the hair was cut severely, the bouffant had a stagy or regal look. In fact, it looked just right on a woman like Mrs. Kennedy, who was rather a democrat-aristocrat. There was no end to the articles attesting to the first lady's style and radiance. And for instance, when she took to wearing a pillbox hat with her bouffant—the hat sort of nestled atop the hair—the pillbox hat became really popular, too (see PILLBOX HATS).

The revival of the bouffant went back to 1957 in America—earlier in Europe—when *Life* magazine showed pictures of women in bouffants who were also wearing elegant jewels or feathers. The article pointed out a number of things that any woman who was experimenting with the bouffant must have known already —namely that to shape the bouffant just right, curlers had to be used, some of them 1¾ inches wide. In addition to the curlers, hairspray was often used to keep the bouffant in place. These surely were artificial procedures and took a lot of time. Yet women were beginning to do them often, and when Mrs. Kennedy came to the White House she put the bouffant (which was also known as the bubble) over the top.

Yet by 1964 the bouffant had passed as a significant part of the American beauty scene. Mostly, it probably had to do with the unhappy events in 1963, but it was also true that it had become the fashion to act spontaneous, and certainly not to give the impression that you had labored long to arrange your hair in artificial fashion. And the bouffant was, if nothing else, artificial.

Some women thought the bouffant made them appear too tall, while others simply did not want to take the time to use curlers (also known as rollers).

One college girl told *Seventeen* magazine, "I just don't like rollers."

As an important style, the bouffant has not reappeared since 1964. Perhaps people just don't feel regal enough about themselves yet.

PILLBOX HATS (Late 1950s– 1963)

The pillbox hat looked like a box that held pills. Yet in the early 1960s this sort of medicinal look was favored by the most fashionable lady in the land, Jacqueline Kennedy, and was thus favored by great numbers of women who wanted to do what Jackie did. Not only had a New Frontier—as Jack Kennedy's presidential administration was known—appeared in national politics, but Jacqueline Kennedy heralded a New Frontier in fashion. The pillbox was one of those new items, though in fact it had also been worn in a somewhat different form in the 1930s. When Mrs. Kennedy appeared in a pillbox hat at her husband's inauguration, while Mrs. Dwight Eisenhower and Mrs. Richard Nixon wore more conservative kinds of hats, the interest in pillboxes was on.

Pillboxes were worn by older ladies, young matrons and teen-age girls. Sometimes these women wore a bouffant (see BOUFFANT), too, a hairstyle that Jacqueline Kennedy also made popular. A famous song tells of how a sonnet could be written about "your Easter bonnet," but when Jack Kennedy was president, gals were likely to wear pillbox hats at Easter time, not bonnets. If you wanted your pillbox in satin, it would run you $35.

Though Jacqueline Kennedy made the pillbox hat popular, she was not the first person to wear it, even around 1960. The wife of the president of Mexico was seen wearing one a year before Mrs. Kennedy did.

The fad for pillbox hats lasted through the early 1960s, with women wearing them to work and when they went out on the town. There was even a game played at parties in 1962 called pin-the-pillbox-hat, which made fun of Mrs. Kennedy's penchant for wearing that chapeau (see PIN-THE-PILLBOX-HAT). And guitarist and lyricist Bob Dylan wrote a song making fun of the style: Leopard Skin Pillbox Hat.

In 1963 interest in the pillbox hat died out. When President Kennedy was assassinated in November 1963, Mrs. Kennedy was shown wearing her pillbox hat while in a state of great shock. This image was very bleak and must have caused the pillbox hat to have

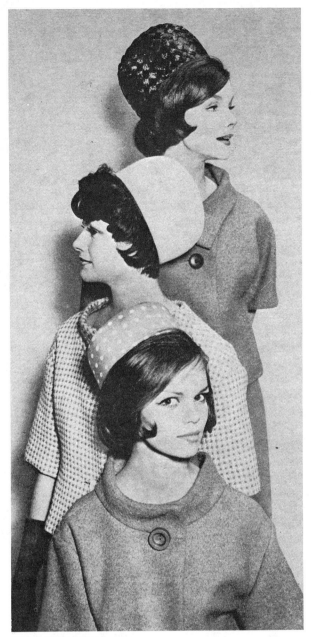

Pillbox hats of 1961

an unpleasant association for many women (and men, too).

Also, a major occurrence in fashion would soon take place: Women started to go hatless, reversing a trend of many decades.

Still, women remember the pillbox hat with pleasure. When one New York lady was asked about her pillbox hats, she answered, with a gleam in her eye, "What, are they coming back?"

WOODIES (Early 1960s)

The woodie was a most important possession of the surfer in the early 1960s. Both practical and popular, the woodie was a carrier of surfboards and a carrier of dreams—finding the perfect wave to surf on and taking in the rays of the sun both being experiences to luxuriate in. For the woodie was the modish vehicle that kids transported themselves in if they wanted to go surfing—that Hawaii and California sport which had such an impact nationwide.

Not that it was written in any constitution that you had to take your woodie to a nice surfing place. In certain parts of California, you and your friends could take your woodie to a place where you could do pier roulette surfing (see PIER ROULETTE SURFING)—a dangerous sport indeed. Or in Washington state and perhaps other parts of the Pacific Northwest, you could use a woodie to carry your stuff to go pypo-boarding (see PYPO-BOARDING), a tame sport done in very shallow waters. And no one ever said you couldn't throw a bunch of skateboards into a woodie, either.

All that aside, it was still considered best to use the woodie for ocean surfing.

Called a "woodie" due to its wood-paneled sides, the vehicle was usually a late 1940s version of a station wagon. Chevrolet was said to be the most popular make for the woodie, but whatever the make, there was usually seating for about eight people. But the woodie of the surfers was not the same station wagon that was used for a Sunday picnic with the kids. More space was needed for the surfboards.

So most of the seats were removed from the woodie, as was the back sometimes, and also even the windows and doors. Then surfboards and other surfing paraphernalia were easily tossed in the back, and the driver and his or her cohorts could be off to the beach or even use the woodie to follow the waves. On a long trip the driver could use the woodie to sleep in, too.

Though they were most popular on the West Coast, there were a lot of woodies in the Northeast and Southeast, all the way down to Florida. In fact, the woodie became so popular that there weren't enough wooded station wagons to handle the traffic. Customized pickup trucks were also used as woodies, as were some vans. These were called "woodies" after the doors were removed and wood panels were attached to the sides. It was obvious that woodies were not only a useful thing but a thing of beauty and status. In the early 1960s young surfers were very important romantic figures on the American landscape, and this was their conveyance.

A 1949 Chevrolet, turned woodie, would cost

about $800. Stick shift, radio, but with no other ex-
tras, they did not hit very high speeds. That wasn't
their purpose. They were dependable, sturdy vehicles,
even if they were sometimes clumsy-looking. After all,
what mattered was that they could hold a number of
surfboards. Or as one California surfer said: "I would
drive my woodie up and down the coast for months
at a time. I'd sleep in it, eat in it. It carried my surfboard, and I partied in it. It was my best friend."

Yet this mode of conveyance for man and surfboard, which was also part status symbol, began to
fade away by the late 1960s, after some woodies had
traveled as much as 150,000 miles. Why did the
woodies began to fade out? Perhaps because the
wholesome pleasures of surfboarding (which still remained popular—just not so obsessive) and tootling
around in the old woodie had begun to pale. It was
getting to be a time of long hair on youths which
troubled adults, and dances with suggestive motions
like the twist. The songs sung were much rougher than
Surfer Girl. And youngsters wouldn't want to climb
into a woodie to get away from the harshness. In the
lingo of the time, that would be too much like "cop-
ping out."

TRAMPOLINES (1960)

They had names like Jumpsville U.S.A., Jump for Joy,
Jumporama, Jump Fun and the Big Jump, and what
they had in common was that they were the center of
trampoline action. And were trampolines ever big in
1960, particularly in the spring! What a great thing it
was to flip, flop and twist in the air! An activity that in
the 1950s was used principally in junior high school
gymnasium classes was now the thing to do. *Life* magazine ran a feature showing people from 18-month-
old toddlers to the 69-year-old comedian Joe E. Brown
jumping on trampolines. It also gave instructions on
how to do a stomach drop or a front flip.

Trampolines, trampolines, trampolines—you could
find them everywhere. In Los Angeles, San Diego, Miami, Phoenix, Houston, Oklahoma City, St. Louis,
Reno, Boston, Washington, Atlanta and Richmond, to
name just a few places. As *Popular Science Monthly*
also showed, you could create your own trampoline
in your backyard. A 5-foot by 7½-foot trampoline could
cost as little as $50, though it was also a good idea to
get protective pads for the frame, which cost between
$60 and $100. However, a really decent-sized trampoline—such as the 7-foot by 14-foot ones used in
trampoline parks—went for between $500 and $1,000.
Wherever trampolining was done, however, it was

thought to be the most engaging kind of exercise, and
it was certainly a lot more active than fads like droo-
dling and hunkerin' (see DROODLES, HUNKERIN'), which
had been big in recent years and demanded nothing
more than the ability to use a pencil or sit on your
haunches. When one considers that there was many
a magazine article in the 1950s that talked about how
unpleasant it was (in the eyes of a great number of
people) to take the time to do some physical exercise,
the interest in trampolining was indeed a refreshing
change.

And so as trampolining became important, it is no
surprise that television segments were devoted to
trampolining and to interviewing trampoliners. For instance, a couple of young boys who were jumping in
the air on two trampolines were asked what they liked
best about it. Their answer: "The feeling of being air-
borne—that was the best."

Another attractive thing about trampolines—particularly to trampoline park owners themselves—was
that creating a trampoline park was inexpensive,
needing an investment of as little as $10,000. In this
respect commercial trampolining was somewhat similar to the miniature golf craze (see MINIATURE GOLF), in
which owners of these courses needed only to get some
pipe, some carpet and throw together a few interest-
ing-looking hazards. For trampoline park owners this
was good for another reason. They could use the
money to promote trampoline park competitions in such
skills as jumping the highest, doing the greatest number of turns, turning somersaults in the air and jumping rope while trampolining. You could win plastic
trophies or transistor radios, which weren't exactly a
king's ransom—but consider the exhilaration of jumping . . .

Some of the first commercial trampolines for use
in parks were designed in the 1950s. And it has been
maintained that the very first trampolines were created
by one Bill Sorenson in the basement of his father's
home. This sort of brings to mind the Philadelphian
Richard James, inventor of slinky (see SLINKY). Mr.
James had also worked in his cellar. In fact, slinky
walked (or should we say "slinked"?) down the stairs.
Now if someone could get slinky to trampoline, that
would really be something!

Yet by the middle of 1960, the interest in trampolining had begun to wane. In the Los Angeles area
alone, 40 trampoline centers closed down during that
summer. A trampoline park owner said of this, "Who
wants to bounce in the heat when there is a swimming
pool nearby?" Moreover, it was hard to make money
when as little as 40 cents per person was being charged
to jump on a trampoline for half an hour.

Yet there was one other big reason for the decline
in trampolining—people began to conclude that the

sport was unsafe. There were neck injuries, back injuries and ensuing lawsuits as a result of trampolining. Doctors said that many of these injuries were caused by backward flips improperly done.

Trampoline centers were made aware of guidelines that would make jumping less dangerous. No one should be allowed to jump for more than half an hour at a time; no horseplay or wild jumps should be allowed; jumpers should stay at the center of the trampoline at all times. All this surveillance took a lot of the spontaneity out of trampolining.

The rage for trampolining started in southern California, where there came to be 175 trampoline centers in Los Angeles alone. It ended all over America at about the same time.

You can still bounce on trampolines—huge cots with metal frames and cloth webbing. But you can no longer find a place to do it on nearly every block.

Yet there's no reason why you shouldn't soon be able to again, considering how activities have a way of losing favor and then coming back strong in a really faddish way. At any time, some movie star or athlete might say that he or she keeps a sleek build by trampolining. And then the rush to jump, twist, flip and flop will be on once more!

BED RACING (1961)

There doesn't seem to be much of a reason for pushing a bed for as many as 317 miles at one time, but on the other hand, why should anyone want to swallow goldfish, sit on flagpoles or stuff telephone booths—other stuntlike fads that took place in the 1930s, the 1920s and the 1960s, respectively (see GOLDFISH SWALLOWING, TELEPHONE BOOTH STUFFING, FLAGPOLE SITTING). Yet bed racing enjoyed a slight vogue, first in Canada and then in California, in 1961. It just went to show that you could do more with a bed than catch 40 winks.

Some students from the University of British Columbia were the first to try bed pushing. They got ahold of a plain old hospital bed and proceeded to push it 42 miles. Other Canadian bed-racing groups followed and also began to record their elapsed time. There were the students who went 70 miles in 8½ hours with their bed, and then another group who traveled 105 miles in fewer than 12 hours with theirs. All this took place in the dead of winter. It might have been a very good idea to have brought along a jug of hot toddies to warm those hard-working bodies.

Then came the bed-pushing event in Canada to beat all bed-pushing events. At Ontario's McMaster's University, 100 students got together to push a bed 317 miles in 13 hours. Of course, they kind of bent the unwritten rules, just as teams of telephone booth stuffers did earlier when they used oversize booths (see TELEPHONE BOOTH STUFFING); when it came to bed pushing, the new wrinkle was that the bed had bicycle wheels. Still, all was not clear bed pushing. For six hours this McMaster's crew lost its way on a frozen lake.

Meanwhile, this type of journeying was considered so intriguing in California that University of Southern California college students decided to get into pushing beds with bicycle wheels themselves in April 1961. The two fraternities involved, Delta Chi and Tau Epsilon Phi, decided that the appointed course would run from the California border to Las Vegas. And furthermore, Delta Chi and Tau Epsilon Phi each pushed a bed with a young female movie hopeful on it.

The outcome? Delta Chi's bed-pushing team covered the 42 miles before Tau Epsilon Phi's team did.

The bed-pushing craze was not picked up. Perhaps college students thought that even for a fad, it was really terribly foolish. In 1962, though, some high school kids in southwest Michigan picked up on the fad and tried pushing a bed from Augusta to Benton Harbor—not so very great a distance. But they performed their push along a superhighway—not exactly the type of roadway for such a conveyance—and were stopped by the police.

To all this we may add a historical note. Bed racing showed that at least one thing remained of the influence on American ways of Great Britain and the British Commonwealth: They inspired fads. After all, telephone booth stuffing came ultimately from South Africa, and piano smashing originated in England.

BUSINESS COLORING BOOKS (1961–63)

Dennis Altman, Marcie Hans and Martin Cohen—Chicago advertising copywriters all—had an idea. They would market a spoof of children's coloring books, for adult executives. They each chipped in $300 for production and publicity for the *Executive Coloring Book*. What they did was make a killing. By November 1961 its first printing of 1,600 copies was sold out. By October 1963 1 million copies of the *Executive Coloring Book* had been snapped up. People were intrigued by it and gladly dug out their crayons to fill in pictures with captions like, "I am an executive. Color my underwear important."

The *Executive Coloring Book*© was 20 pages long and pervasively satirical in nature. It jibed at the clothes executives wore, the commuter trains they took and the customers with whom they had to deal. But it was also attuned to a philosophy that was gaining currency at the time—a somewhat antibusiness philosophy that mocked at things like people striving to climb the corporate ladder. This could be seen in works as diverse as Billy Wilder's popular film *The Apartment* (1961) and the well-known academic studies written by sociologist C. Wright Mills, *The Power Elite* and *White Collar*.

The *Executive Coloring Book* poked fun really harmlessly, though. Maybe this was the reason it spawned a lot of imitations. Architects could whip out their crayons for an *Architect's Coloring Book*. Psychiatrists could fill in drawings in a *Psychiatrist's Coloring Book*. There was a coloring book for bartenders, brought out as a premium by the Schweppes Company, and Texas even tried to promote the entrepreneurial glories of the Lone Star State by sending out coloring books. A helicopter company kidded its sales representatives in a coloring book, one of whose captions read, "We've sold a helluva lot of image. Maybe, this year, we'll sell a helicopter."

At the same time, in 1961 and 1962, current events hucksters picked up on the trend, and soon there was a *JFK Coloring Book* and a *Nikita Khrushchev Coloring Book*.

Making fun of the Russian premier was like making fun of the bogeyman (no one likes the bogeyman much anyway), but making fun of the president—his youth, his New Frontier policies and his wife, Jacqueline—was all in really pleasant spirits. For instance, his wife, Jackie, was very fond of sporting a pillbox hat (see PILLBOX HATS). In 1962 party givers came up with a nice little game burlesquing this. It was called pin-the-pillbox-hat (see PIN-THE-PILLBOX-HAT), and anyone who knew how to play pin-the-tail-on-the-donkey could pick it up easily. (The pin-the-pillbox-hat game was nowhere near as popular as the *JFK Coloring Book*, though).

Yet by 1963 the adult coloring book was on its way out. Perhaps adults had thought for a while that coloring like a little kid was fun, but the pleasure soon paled. Also, with the assassination of President Kennedy in November 1963, the national mood became a whole lot more gloomy.

In any event, you could now get the *Executive Coloring Book* for as little as $1.00. Back when everyone was pulling out their crayons, you had to plunk down $9.98.

TWIST (1961–65)

You can talk about inhibitions, release of cold war tensions and all that jazz but I think it's mostly that adults are beginning to find out how much fun the kids are having.

—American disc jockey Dick Clark,
on the popularity of the twist

The twist, whose origins went back to rock and roll in the 1950s and jitterbugging in the late 1930s, was definitely the dance to do in the early 1960s. As its name implied, the dance was done with a lot of twisting around. Chubby Checker, the Philadelphia singer who made the twist the rage, said that twisters moved their hips as if they were wiping themselves with a towel as the first step. The second step was to move their bodies in one direction and their hands in another direction. And the last step was "to ad-lib energetically." This was the twist done in its most pure and perfect manner. When it was done in practice on the dance floor, though, people pretty much twisted around as they pleased. It was often compared to hula-hooping without a hoop. (Hula-hooping was the fad of a few years earlier; see HULA HOOPS).

However, longtime crooner Nat King Cole didn't think that it was unusual at all. When he was young, Cole said, he and his friends were always doing it, except they called it the "mess around."

So who twisted? First, it was the teen-agers who twisted. They had seen it done on "American Bandstand," a midafternoon rock-dance show emceed by Dick Clark, and introduced by Chubby Checker in July 1960. Chubby had sung a song called Let's Do the Twist. Chubby Checker's real name was Ernest Evans Jr. He took the name Chubby Checker because one of his heroes was the singer Fats Domino.

In any event, the twist caught the mood of the moment. Within months, you could get twist chairs, twist cufflinks, twist hats and twist pajamas. Twist dolls were big in the Christmas season, and you could watch them gyrate to that fast-moving 45 RPM disc Jingle Bell Twist.

The free-wheeling movement of the twist made it easy to do and a lot of fun. It was also a dance in which you did not touch your partner. All these attributes made the twist somewhat exhibitionistic and kind of a prelude to the "let it all hang out attitude" of the sixties. A number of social psychologists approved of the twist, saying it was a good release from the tensions of everyday life and served to allay the anxiety regarding the Cold War between the United States and the Soviet Union. However, try telling that to the mother in Queens whose 3-year-old daughter was already doing the twist—and what did she know about Cold War tensions?

The focal point of twisting action, where both teenybopper and tycoon alike came to twist, was the Peppermint Lounge in New York City (just as in the late 1970s disco dancing at Studio 54 in New York City made disco particularly stylish; see DISCO). But the dance spread far beyond the confines of New York City—and even far beyond the confines of America. They twisted in France and England, and they also tried to twist in both the Middle East and the Far East. This didn't work out so well. In Syria the Union of Bellydancers prevailed on the government to ban the new dance because its members feared that it would throw them out of work. In Indonesia the twist was prohibited, along with fashion shows, beauty contests and songbird contests.

This didn't make this Asian country so terribly different from the venerable dance hall Roseland in New York City, which wouldn't allow the twist on the grounds that it was inferior dancing. (Roseland also tried to ban disco but relented on that one.)

Meanwhile, in the United States, in places other than the Roseland ballroom, socialites and other adults were picking up the twist from the teen-agers. One barmaid, watching the celebrities twist at the Peppermint Lounge, decided that "Society men don't get the twist as good right away like the society women." In any case, the Duke and Duchess of Windsor, Leonard Bernstein, Truman Capote, the writer, and Lee Radziwill, the sister of Jacqueline Kennedy Onassis, all twisted. They even had their own special teacher, Killer Joe Piro. When twister luminaries arrived at a party thrown at the Metropolitan Museum of Art in New York City, the director of the museum quickly disowned the gyrating hoofers, though, declaring, "I did not invite them." Former President Eisenhower didn't think much of the twist, either; he was certain that no American pioneer would ever have done such a thing.

After the adults started co-opting the twist, the dance began to die out as the *rage* because it was no longer any great novelty. The teen-agers turned to dances with really exciting names and movements to match, like the mashed potato, the fly, the monkey, the jerk, the swim and the mule (see TWIST VARIATIONS). There was also a brief interest in the bossa nova (see BOSSA NOVA), a Latin American dance completely different from the twist and its variants.

The rage for the twist, which was a very erotic dance, showed how open-minded authority figures had become as far as new kinds of dancing were concerned. If you had done the turkey trot in the second decade of the century (see TURKEY TROT AND OTHER ANIMAL DANCES), you could have wound up in jail. You could expect no such harassment when you did the

1960s dance fad. You might have been deemed silly, but you could at least go home without a summons after gyrating your hips.

After the twist—and its variations—the dance world became more or less dormant and created nothing obsessive until disco came along in the late 1970s.

BOSSA NOVA (1962)

The bossa nova, which means the latest thing in Portuguese, was a Brazilian dance that excited America for a short time in 1962. The dance was in almost flagrant contrast to the frenzied, pelvis-thrusting twist (see TWIST), which attracted teen-agers of both the teenybopper and nonteenybopper variety, followed by their moms and pops. Like the samba and some early 20th-century Latin dances, the bossa nova depended on an elegant backward-and-forward stepping. After the excitement of the twist, the bossa nova really was kind of quiet. But it had something else going for it that made its faddom inevitable—the first lady, Jacqueline Kennedy. When she showed she liked the bossa nova, it became the rage, just as when she had showed she liked bouffants and pillbox hats (see BOUFFANT, PILLBOX HATS), they became the rage.

The jazzy bossa nova tempo was introduced at the White House on November 19, 1962. Stan Getz, the saxophonist, had brought it back from Brazil, where it had been popular since 1958. The great interest in the bossa nova really dazzled Getz, who was quite overwhelmed when, soon enough, every nightclub worthy of its name was playing bossa nova songs or using a bossa nova orchestra, which might consist of drums, guitar, flute or trombone. Killer Joe Piro, the fashionable teacher of the twist, became the fashionable teacher of the bossa nova, as well. But even if you couldn't afford Killer Joe or go to high-priced nightclubs or have an entree to one of Jackie's parties, you could still do the bossa nova to most any old jukebox. What's more, you could do it while wearing bossa nova-style lipstick and bossa nova-style shoes.

In November 1962 bossa nova was all the rage. Everyone was bossa nova-ing to none other than the song Do the Bossa Nova.

But the dance was really only a very brief passing fancy. Even at the outset of the fad, a record company executive said of bossa nova, "I'd give it another month—it won't be anything like the twist."

The problem with the bossa nova was that, after the free-spirited twist, bossa nova was just too hard. A

Minnesota teen-ager said of it, "It's too fast for slow dancing and too slow for fast dancing." Another teen-ager remarked, "You can't fake it as well." And yet another teen-ager, an Illinois lass, put bossa nova in its place (it was not a favorite in the teen-ager's eyes), saying, "The only reason people know about it is because it was played at the White House." Yet another Illinois teen-ager said of it, "It doesn't swing enough."

And the good old days when people at least 20 years old were creating dance fashions were gone: The teen-agers were the trend setters now. As for the adults, they soon realized that they didn't like the bossa nova much better than some of the traditional Latin dances: mambo, samba, tango. The trendy step became the passe step in almost no time at all.

People became much more interested in doing the twist once more or in trying some of its variations—the swim, the monkey, the slauson, the shaggy dog (see TWIST VARIATIONS).

The prediction of that recording company executive had been right on the money.

NIM—THE MATCHSTICK GAME (1962)

Nim, a game played by two people, was the big amusement of the spring of 1962. In offices it was played with paper clips. At bars it was played with swizzle sticks. At cocktail parties it was played with toothpicks. If you were enjoying the spring, you could even play it with blades of grass. All you needed were 16 small throwaway-type objects, which were set up in one basic configuration: 7-5-3-1. You won this game by making sure that it was your opponent who had to remove the final object from the playing surface; this final object was not necessarily the item in the 1 row, but just the last remaining entity on the board. You were allowed to remove as many objects as you wanted in any one turn, but only from one row. You and your opponent played in turn.

Though nim was an ancient Chinese game going back to 3000 B.C., it only became the rage in A.D. 1962, after it was played by a couple of anonymous players in the French movie *Last Year at Marienbad.* (Originally named nim in the early 20th century by Charles Leonard Bouton, a Harvard mathematics professor, the diversion was tagged "the matchstick game" because matchsticks were used in *Last Year at Marienbad.*) The movie, shot at ornate Central European spas, used unusual cinematic techniques and was

puzzling. There was no uncertainty, however, about the extraordinary faddishness of the game.

In the movie one of the nameless strangers always won, and the other always lost.

The fate of real-life players of the game was somewhat similar. In the final analysis, it was anything but fair. If he or she knew the combinations, the person who went last always won, because 7-5-3-1 itself was a losing combination if you had to play it. However, a nim shark, even if he or she went first, could turn the tables by capitalizing on the very first mistake of the nim novice—this would be fatal.

In other words, once you knew the winning combinations, the game lost its attraction. Or when an experienced "nimmer" was playing someone inexperienced, the game was grossly unfair, and when two experienced "nimmers" were playing each other, the game was really a bore. By the summer of 1962, nim was no longer the rage.

The next big puzzle hit was Rubik's Cube (see RUBIK'S CUBE), of the early 1980s, which was a lot more complicated than nim and was in no way unfair.

MARIENBAD CUT (1962)

It looked something like a 1920s bob. But a section of hair was allowed to fall over the forehead. This was supposed to convey a look that was both sophisticated and little girl-ish. And it was the haircut rage of 1962. In New York City it was worn by the socialite Gloria Vanderbilt, and in Washington, D.C. it was worn by none other than Jacqueline Kennedy, at times when she forsook her beloved bouffant (see BOUFFANT). Was it any wonder that thousands of women wanted to wear the Marienbad cut also?

The cut was first seen in the French movie *Last Year at Marienbad* and was worn by its female lead, played by Delphine Seyrig. This puzzling movie, with its unusual cinematic techniques, was also responsible for another fad that year—the matchstick game, based on an old Chinese puzzle and played by two people (see NIM—THE MATCHSTICK GAME).

Though a popular fad, the Marienbad cut never excited the extraordinary attention that the bouffant got. After the Marienbad cut was no longer fashionable, the bouffant was still around.

PIN-THE-PILLBOX-HAT (1962)

Pin-the-tail-on-the-donkey is a very old game; there exists, for instance, an extensive account of a variation on it that Brooklyn, New York young folk played in 1891. Another form of it arose just over 70 years later: pin-the-pillbox-hat. This was a spoofy sort of game, because it made harmless fun of first lady and trend setter Jacqueline Kennedy and the hat she loved to sport, the pillbox (see PILLBOX HATS). According to *Seventeen* magazine, playing pin-the-pillbox-hat was the rage at many a party in 1962.

There really was very little difference between pin-the-tail-on-the-donkey and pin-the-pillbox-hat. In donkey a blindfolded person tries to feel his or her way around and then affix the tail to the four-legged beast whose picture is tacked to a wall; the blindfolded person might wind up placing the tail on the eyes, on the hoofs—anywhere. In pillbox a blindfolded person is sent on his or her way with a pin, moving in the direction of an enlarged picture of Jacqueline Kennedy in her pillbox hat. Now the dicey part is that the person might stick her eye or her nose or even one of her up-to-the-minute dresses.

This must have been an amusing thing to do—for an about an hour. And if you were a dyed-in-the-wool Republican, maybe you might even want to pin Mrs. Kennedy in just the wrong places.

If the pin-the-pillbox-hat game had lasted until November 1963, it could not have lasted much longer. For in the third week of that month, President Kennedy was assassinated, his wife at his side in a pillbox hat. To have played it after that would have been just plain ghoulish.

TWIST VARIATIONS: WATUSI (1962), MONKEY (1963), SLAUSON (1963), SWIM (1964), JERK (1964) AND SHAGGY DOG (Circa 1965)

The twist and Chubby Checker got everyone going (see TWIST). But soon enough, people wanted to dance the twist without doing it exactly the way it was introduced or the way it was done by those who fre-

quented New York City's Peppermint Lounge, so they came up with variations that seemed really exciting.

There was the Watusi, in which you really moved your shoulders around; the monkey, to a song like Major Lance doing Monkey Time while the dancers made like monkeys—there were movements aping monkeys climbing trees, shaking trees and even peeling bananas; or there was the swim, to Bobby Freeman's C'mon and Swim, in which the dancers would move as if they were swimmers—a crawl, a backstroke or a dog paddle, among others.

Or there was the slauson, to the well-known song Louie, Louie by The Kingsmen. In a time when motorcycling was still important, this reminded many people of what it was like to start a motorcycle. In the opening steps the dancers' fists were clenched just as a motorcyclist clenches his or her fists on a handlebar. There was also the jerk, which included many jerking motions. And there was the shaggy dog, in which the dancers' heads kept shaking.

These twist variations of the 1960s made one think of the animal dances of the early 1900s, which were also full of activity and which were intriguing because they involved pantomiming the movements of the creatures after which they were named—dances like the turkey trot, the buzzard lope, the kangaroo dip and the chicken scratch. And like the animal dances, you didn't have to do the twist variations quite right (one couple's swim might be another couple's jerk); all you had to do was think that you were doing them and have fun.

By 1966 the interest in the twist and its variations had not disappeared, but it had passed for the most part. Dance was no longer an obsessive thing. It was now the fashion to be donning some love beads or letting your hair grow really long or trooping off to San Francisco's Haight-Ashbury district or making Haight-Ashbury come alive in your own college, your own town or even your own home. It was the time of the "heads," sometimes known as the "hippies" (see PSYCHEDELIC TRIPS).

LOVE CHAINS (1963)

Love chains were also known as idiot chains, although their motivation was really rather touching. What they should have been known as was chewing-gum wrapper chains. But whatever name you wanted to give it, *Seventeen* magazine reported in January 1963 that the chains had become somewhat widespread, even faddish.

The chain worked like this. It was made of a whole bunch of folded chewing-gum wrappers linked together by a girl for her beau. She would make the chain as long as her boyfriend was tall: If he was 5 feet 4 inches, she would make him a chain 5 feet 4 inches long, and if was 6 feet 9 inches, she would make him a chain that long.

At this point accounts differ as to what was done with the love chain. It seems that sometimes the chain was burned, and the young girl kept the ashes around her "to insure a long, happy romance," as *Seventeen* put it. Or (and this makes more sense) she would give it to the young man and then get it back when and if they broke up.

In any event, making a love chain of chewing gum wrappers was quite an undertaking.

Also, the gal had to be something of an artist if, for instance, she got a new steady boyfriend. No boy would like to see his chain look jagged, as if parts of it had been snipped off; every boy wanted to receive an original, not a 5-foot 9-inch version cut down from a chain first made for someone 6 feet 3 inches tall.

Maybe burning the chain was the best idea after all!

PIANO HACKING (1963)

Piano hacking was a slight fad indulged in by college students in 1963, but slight as it was, no one can deny that it was rather violent. The object was—with the use of axes and sledgehammers, and preferably with a crowd watching—to demolish a full-sized piano so that all its parts could be stuffed down an opening no bigger than eight inches in the shortest possible time. Now that was precision work! The students at Caltech could do it in 10 minutes and 44 seconds. Impressive? The students at Wayne State University in Michigan halved their time by smashing a piano and fitting its fragments down that little hole in 4 minutes and 51 seconds. That record stood.

It was a time of student protest, and one of the Caltech smashers called the hacking a comment on "the obsolescence of society." Now it was a very energetic student who would choose to take part in piano hacking in order to show his or her disillusionment with society. A more passive sort might have contented himself or herself with a spoofy fad like the *Executive Coloring Book* or the *JFK Coloring Book* (see BUSINESS COLORING BOOKS).

As a fad, however, piano hacking was not an American first. Students at the University of Derby in England had dismembered a piano and tried to squeeze all its pieces down a small opening before anybody else.

In America piano smashing has been used, from time to time, as a nightclub act. Rock singer and pianist Jerry Lee Lewis did it as he played his best-known song, Great Balls of Fire, to a driving rhythm. Some years before that, the celebrated comedian Jimmy Durante—or the Ole Schnozzola, as he was known—did it as well.

Durante and Lewis, however, did their piano smashing alone. At the universities piano hacking was done in teams. You had to get some people to wield the axes and others to wield the sledgehammers. Also, someone had to be delegated to go out and get the pianos. At Caltech, for the day of the piano hacking, four pianos were bought for $60.

One piano-hacking group, in keeping with its academic aims, called itself the Piano Reduction Study Group.

A *Life* magazine feature writer called piano hacking "Andante on a Choppin' Theme." He also pointed out that the finale was chopsticks.

Piano hacking was faddish for only that one year. Nor were there any unusual variations during the run of the fad or following it. No reduction study group came up with the idea of demolishing a single harpsichord, organ or cello.

PIER ROULETTE SURFING (1963)

Pier roulette surfing was a variation on surfing that was practiced in California, and it was a really daredevil form at that. To be a pier roulette surfer, it would really help if you were a "hot dog" (that is, very outstanding on the polyurethane board).

Pier roulette surfers would surfboard beneath a pier jutting out to sea. These piers were made of concrete pilings, with nasty barnacles on them. As a wave was breaking near these pilings, the pier roulette surfer would attempt to ride his board while avoiding all this concrete. If you "wiped out"—meaning "fell," both in surfing and then in skateboard parlance—you would be "dashed against concrete," as a February 1963 issue of *Popular Mechanics* put it.

It has not been established why this fad ever came about. But it is not difficult to hazard a guess. People have always been daredevils and doers of stunts, and surfing was a very popular thing at that time. And if the surfer couldn't do his or her thing and be courageous riding in a 20-foot wave, there just had to be other things to do—like pier roulette surfing.

Yet one important aspect of riding those big waves was the sense of beauty it gave the surfer; many surfers talked about the overwhelming sense of nature they had as they took these sea monsters.

Pier roulette surfing, on the other hand, just presented a man-made perspective of drab concrete. Well, you couldn't have everything. If you wanted to be a "hot dog," you had to put up with a little ugliness.

Pier roulette surfing did not travel as an obsession to the Atlantic Coast the way regular old surfboarding did in the summer of 1964. It stayed among the piers of California, where it lasted only a short time.

REQUIRED INSIGNIA FOR MONDOES AND COLLEEGES (1963)

In 1963 in much of Rhode Island, the high school mondoes were mondoes and the high school colleeges were colleeges, make no mistake about that! If you were a mondo, when you went to the barber, your hair would be trimmed short; when you went to the shoe store, you would buy boots; and when you went to school or returned from school, you would hold your books at arms' length. All this went with the tough, practical image of being a vocational high school student.

But now a colleege—that was something else again. A colleege would go to a barber and get his hair styled long; or he would go to the shoe store (some mondoes probably thought that some colleeges had their own private cobblers) and buy moccasins; and when the colleege would be going to school or coming back, he would hold his books close to his chest. He supposedly did this because he was in a college preparatory program. Needless to say, there was no law requiring mondoes and colleeges to behave the way they did. It was just the thing to do in the Ocean State in 1963, from industrial Narrangansett to opulent Newport.

This may have been some kind of fad, but a lot of kids complained about it. One young woman said that it reminded her of the rigid caste system in India, while a young man complained that he wanted to wear his hair styled any way he pleased and wished that people would just get rid of that mondo and colleege distinction.

No doubt there could be no future for mondo and colleege uniforms. It was abominable, and it just had to go. But history has a way of justifying foolishness. In the 1970s, when short hair had become big once more, Rhode Island folk getting to be in their late twenties would probably all say that they were "mondoes." However, when moccasins became big with the upsurge of the preppy look in the early 1980s, the folks getting to be in their thirties would probably all say that they were "colleeges." One hopes that their children were not confused.

INDIAN-STYLE RAIN DANCE PARTIES (Late 1963)

There was little rain that year in the part of Texas slightly southeast of Dallas. Moisture-invoking measures had to be taken. So reasoned the Eustace, Texas high school kids.

What was needed was a rain dance party. The kids decided to gather outdoors, dance to drumbeats and dress in Indian-style robes. And to top it off, they would play a game called corny finish (a race determining who could eat a bowl of dry corn flakes the fastest).

Rain dance parties spread far and near, even to big cities in the Southwest where there was lots of rain. It seemed that every high school kid wanted to dance to drums, look like a big chief or squaw, and consume corn flakes speedily.

It rained again in Eustace, Texas.

By early 1964 southwestern high school kids were having different kinds of parties. But who wouldn't want to dance and invoke rain at least once in their young life?

OP TALKING (Early 1963)

Op talking was not shorthand for the operator saying that he or she was on the line. It was a teen-age code so that people like adults or younger brothers or sisters wouldn't understand what the adolescents were saying to each other on the telephone. Op talking resulted when the sound *op* was put before each vowel, except if the vowel came at the end of the word, in which case the *op* was dropped, and it was English as usual.

For instance, if Jill wanted to secretly tell Jack, "Dog Fido has fleas," it would come out in op talk something like "Dopog Fopido hopas flopeas." (And with something like that, you'd want to get him to the veterinarian really quick!)

It is not clear from the discussion of this phenomenon in *Seventeen* magazine whether op talking had a basis in how things were spelled or how they were sounded. Take, again, the word *dog*, as in "dog Fido"; the *o* is pronounced in English like *aw*. Does this mean that in op English, "dog" should become "dopawg"? In this case, some people might think that a pig needed to be taken to the veterinarian.

In any event, the teen-agers didn't talk about dogs; they talked about dates and schools—mostly about dates. Maybe they talked a little about pimples, too (popimples in correct op spelling; pihimples in correct op sounding).

Op talking was said to have been inspired by pig Latin, in which the first letter of a word is dropped, and the new word is formed by the remainder of the word plus this first letter plus *ay*. In other words, "Dog Fido has fleas" becomes "Ogday idoFay ashay easflay" (this last word might be noted as an exception, but *fl* are two letters that are thought of together, and thus together they go to the end of the word preceding the *ay*).

By 1963, however, most young people had given up any idea of demonstrating a classical education with pig Latin, and so op speaking it was.

Now that that's out of the way, here's a little quiz on your knowledge of op. (After all, what would you do if you were stranded on a desert island, and your companion spoke only op?) What is the English equivalent of the following op expression? (To avoid confusion, correct-spelling op is used, not correct-sounding op. Answer is written backwards in English at the end of the entry.)

Sopave the lopast dopance fopor me.

Op was only spoken early in the year 1963.

Give up on that quiz question? Answer: Evas eht tsal ecnad rof em.

STYLED WHITE BOOTS (1963–65)

They looked like the kind of boots that high school majorettes would wear during the half-time of football games when they twirled their batons; but these they were not. They were the first 1960's high-fashion boots for ladies; before the white boots, boots simply served to keep a girl's feet dry during heavy rain and snow. And then these white boots designed by the Frenchman Andre Courreges became the rage. Some ever-vital Parisian girls, known as go-go girls, began to wear them, and before you knew it, they were big in America, too, because we still followed the Parisian lead in these matters.

Styled white boots became part of the frenzied twist scene (see TWIST) in one of its bizarre variations; people in these white boots would dance aloft on platforms or cages while they looked down on the other dancers below. This was known as platform go-go dancing, and it was first practiced in France (see PLATFORM GO-GO DANCING). They were also fine apparel to wear at a party; however, American business offices had not yet reached the stage where they would accept them.

Not only were there white boots, but there were also pink boots. There were stylish British vinyl boots as well, and the American designer Rudi Gernreich came up with boots with a giraffe print.

In time the white boots themselves passed from the scene, but the idea of fashion boots had come to stay.

There is no way to consider latter-day boots without thinking of those first white boots. The brilliant red boots, pink boots and lime green boots of the 1970s, the boots with gold buckles on the instep (they went for a cool $375), the trendy Frye Western boot and the slick and more pointed high-fashion cowboy boot all owed their existence to a piece of footwear that looked as if it had walked away on its own when it should have been on the gridiron marching to a spirited fight song.

PYPO-BOARDING (SUMMER 1964)

Pypo-boarding was a variation on surfing that was practiced in Aberdeen, Washington and quite likely in other parts of the Pacific Northwest, where there really is next to no surf. It was mostly high school kids who went pypo-boarding, and it consisted of riding a wooden disk in the spume at the water's edge. The pypoboards were compared in shape by *Life* magazine to pizza boards, were made of wood and were 28 inches wide. The thing to do was to put the pypoboard in the spume and ride it.

Pypo is supposed to mean "kick" in a Hawaiian

dialect, and perhaps pypo-boarding got its name because it was a good idea to scoot along the spume with a kicking start. Also at Aberdeen it was done using a bicycle with a towline pulling the pypoboarders. This type of pypo-boarding was a lot like waterskiing.

Pypo-boarding probably became popular in Washington soon after surfing with the big balsa or polyurethane boards in the high waves became popular in California in the early 1960s, but it was first noted after surfing became really big in 1964. Pypo-boarding was only written about once. But it is such a good diversion, and not potentially dangerous, that it is probably still being done somewhere, if not in Aberdeen, Washington.

FOLK JUG BANDS (1964)

The 1960s was a time when kids were really interested in singing folk songs; Joan Baez was very big, particularly her first two record albums, and so was Bob Dylan, who was not yet into rock and was far from being into religious singing, which he is in the 1980s. Guitars were numerous on every campus, including many old-fashioned acoustic guitars, without electric amplification.

A variation on this was what was happening at many a high school in Massachusetts in 1964. There, kids would form folk jug bands and play away on kazoos, washboards and jugs (which you blew into to make melody). This was not as slick as some hootenannies—gatherings where people sang folk songs at colleges—but somehow it reminded you more of all those country people in the 19th century who would get together and sing.

When these Massachusetts kids went to college, though, it was electric guitars all the way. If you mentioned that they had ever played kazoos, many of them would probably have been acutely embarrassed.

TELL-ALL FEATHERS (1964)

Tell-all feathers, which flourished among teen-agers in Memphis in 1964, had absolutely nothing to do with whether you were ready to pass the peace pipe or whether you were short of wampum or whether your mother's young papoose had wrecked your room;

however, if you were a squaw, tell-all feathers told a lot about what you thought of the braves. For as a young squaw, you would wear two feathers side by side on your head if you were "going steady" with a brave, one feather in front and one feather in back to indicate that a date was acceptable, feathers above both ears to indicate that a date was being solicited (or as *Seventeen* magazine put it, you were "on the prowl") and feathers crossed to show—again in *Seventeen*'s words—"dated tonight, try tomorrow."

Tell-all feathers were a lot like ankle bracelets (see ANKLE BRACELETS) of a decade earlier; both gave a sign of what social state a girl was in—wearing an ankle bracelet on one ankle meant she was going steady; on the other, it meant she was going steadily.

Yet you could do more with feathers than with ankle bracelets, perhaps. Ankle bracelets were definitely a feminine thing. But there is no reason why boys couldn't wear two tell-all feathers to show what they were up to—down Memphis way.

LBJ 10-GALLON HATS (1964–65)

When Texan Lyndon Johnson first became president, the Texas 10-gallon cowboy hat became popular. A traditional item of dress in the West, Easterners, like people in Washington, D.C. and New York City, took to wearing it, too. When they donned the hat, it represented high fashion, as opposed to when kids did it (in Connecticut or Colorado) because they wanted to play cowboys.

The prices reflected just how high fashion the 10-gallon hat had become: They ranged from $17.50 to $250.00. The $250.00 model was mink-trimmed.

Of course, the LBJ 10-gallon hat was never popular in the extraordinary sense that the Davy Crockett fur cap was in 1955 (see DAVY CROCKETT AND HIS FUR HAT), nor did it catch on quite as much as the pillbox hat did in the early 1960s because Jacqueline Kennedy wore it (see PILLBOX HATS). But it was nonetheless a status symbol in 1964–65, as could be seen by the fact that sales of these Western-style hats were greater than they had been in two decades.

Sometimes, the 10-gallon hats were known simply as LBJ hats (for Lyndon Baines Johnson).

You could even get a 10-gallon hat made by President Johnson's own hatter, Byer-Rolnick of Dallas. The hats were custom-made and inside them you could find a map of Texas, on which the LBJ Ranch in Johnson City was highlighted. The president was very pleased that the hats were popular, and it was rumored that people wore them in Johnson's presence to curry favor with him.

The flourishing of the LBJ hat showed that Western items could be just as voguish as the latest Paris fashions. Though not part of the fad for Western-style things that began in the late 1960s, the LBJ hat did presage it. A few years after the cowboy hat interest, country and western music swept the nation.

Then, in 1980, all sorts of guys were seen wearing another kind of cowboy hat—a black cowboy hat like that worn by J.R. Ewing, the evil lead character in television's prime-time soap opera "Dallas" (see "DALLAS" FAD MANIFESTATIONS).

PLIN DRAWING (1964–65)

Plin drawing was a type of systemized doodling that took high schools by storm in the middle 1960s. It probably encouraged many an art teacher to think that he or she had better plin drawers than an art teacher in another high school or an art teacher in a neighboring town, or even that he or she taught the best collection of plin drawers in the whole state. Here is how many a day was whiled away while plins were made.

To come up with a plin drawing, you started with a basic shape that is roughly similar to that of the bobby pin (as we have seen, the bobby pin was invented in the 1920s to take care of that new rage, bobbed hair). At that point, the challenge began, because shapes were added to this bobby pin-looking sort of object so that it would become an amusing representation of a well-known person or thing. For instance, if you added a bunch of stubble below the plin and put something like a beret above the plin, you could call the drawing beatnik plin. Or if you turned the plin into a stick figure with arms and legs but also made sure that the legs were gyrating, you could call it twisting plin. You could do anything you wanted with a plin, and for about one year, that's what people did. In its Teen Scene section *Seventeen* magazine included a plin column, which more or less asked the teen-agers, "Can you top this plin?" In response, plins were sent in from all over the country—month after month.

The origin of plin drawing is not known, but it really was not that unusual an activity. Only seven years earlier, in 1957, high school students had got themselves quite involved in another kind of doodling that told a story; these drawings were known as droodles (see DROODLES). Droodles were much more free-form than plins were, because they did not demand one basic shape to start with. Oh, you might see something like a plin in a droodle every once in a while, but most people droodled without ever thinking of plinning.

By the end of 1965, however, plin drawing was seen by kids as being on the stodgy side and was on its way out. The big thing then was using day-glo or fluorescent paint (see PSYCHEDELIC TRIPS) or, failing that, using vibrant colors on items both usual and unusual. Though some may differ with this view, kids had apparently become less interested in a witty drawing exercise than they were in self-expression. And so frivolous plins were no longer interesting. Much more interesting was coloring glass pop bottles so that they looked like a swirling configuration of flowers or fish, or even an American flag, as was done by some Salt Lake City teen-agers; or spraying paint on oval stones found on the beach to make them resemble an 1890s girl with a lot of ribbons, or to make them spell out a name, as was done in Portland, Oregon. In New York City, when this was done to a multitude of subway cars, it was known as graffiti.

SKATEBOARDING (1964–66)

Hanging five. The toes of one of your feet are over the edge.
Hanging ten. The toes of both your feet are over the edge.
Coffin. You make a free jump.
Wipe out. You fall down.

These were only a few of the terms you would have known if you had gone skateboarding in the 1960s. A Queens, New York girl said of skateboarding, "There's no place you can surf, so this is the next best thing." Living in the city as she did, she may have been skateboarding in parking lots or streets.

The skateboard craze came from California in the 1960s, and the nature of its extraordinary popularity was indeed surprising. Skateboards were originally designed for surfers to practice on when they had to be on dry land, and the first skateboards were made for Val Surf, a North Hollywood, California specialty shop (hence, the name that skateboarding was originally known by, *sidewalk surfing*). There had even been a few skateboards produced commercially in the 1930s.

Why could the skateboard rage be called a sur-

Two young boys go skateboarding.

prise? Consider. An Illinois manufacturer was asked if he wanted to turn them out. He said no. Another manufacturer (who would eventually produce skateboards) was every bit as skeptical at first, saying, "Somebody showed me a skateboard last year and I thought they were nutty."

These men, who must have been savvy to the ways of the American consumer, should have known better. After all, if you couldn't surfboard, why not get out your skateboard? This urge would affect the multitude of lads and lasses not near any ocean—in places like Iowa, Minnesota or Arkansas, say. If you couldn't brave a 20-foot breaker, why not dare a most precipitous hill? You could still use the same attractive lingo, with only a slight difference in meaning. If you "wiped out" in surfboarding, for instance, you would find yourself under an onrushing wave; if you "wiped out" in skateboarding, you would find yourself down on the rough pavement.

And so skateboarding did indeed become the rage in 1964. A Philadelphia manufacturer said of them, "They're selling like popsicles." At Princeton Univer-

sity a really good skateboarder could win himself a bottle of champagne. There was a skateboarding meet between the New England colleges of Amherst, Wesleyan and Williams. But skateboarding had not just hit the East alone: It was all over the nation.

You didn't even need to plunk down any money for a skateboard. You could make one yourself. All you needed was a tapered piece of wood flexibly mounted on roller-skate wheels. Most people, however, bought their boards. You could get them for as little as $2, but most boards cost significantly more than that. A motorized skateboard cost $50.

Skateboarding had a number of attractions. It was based on surfing, and young kids often loved to surf. It looked really daring, because a skateboarder had to be able to use his or her hands and body very carefully to avoid "wiping out." For proper coordination on the board, you would have to combine the action of your hands and your body weight. The hands were used essentially to balance, while the body was used to change direction. People who skateboarded had more than a bit of daredevil in them. Or as a demonstration-

129

skateboard girl (she worked at Macy's department store in New York City) said of the life's work she had chosen (and for which skateboarding prepared her): "I want to be a movie stunt girl—anything from falling off horses to stock-car driving."

Yet another great attraction of skateboarding was not only that it looked dangerous but that people also tried to prevent skateboarding from being done. The National Product Safety Council emphatically discouraged the use of skateboards, while skateboard injury statistics compiled by hospitals began to create a big furor. Both police officers and government officials began to ban skateboards.

This is not to say that surfboarding itself had never been charged with being dangerous. In certain parts of California some surfboarders had indulged in a variant called pier roulette surfing (see PIER ROULETTE SURFING), in which they rode right near concrete pilings that jutted out into the sea—a practice that could lead to a nasty, nasty crack on the head.

Yet the skateboarders held on. One Brentwood, California boy said, for instance, about the risk of injury: "I've had a couple of concussions—nothing serious, though; had to stay out of school a couple of days, that's all." Skateboarding was just too much of a pleasure to give up, whether you were going down a hill, just skateboarding along a flat pavement or making like a skiier on the slope, slaloming between empty beer cans instead of poles.

Some 10,000 people turned out to watch the skateboarding championship events held in May 1965 in Anaheim, California. There they could see the "boarders" doing coffining, head stands, kick turns, slalom and jumping over a bar. A song about skateboarding recorded by Jan and Dean, Grab Your Board and Go Sidewalk Surfing with Me, sold 700,000 copies.

However, the tide that had turned against the sidewalk surfers just rose and rose. The chief of police in Mahwah, New Jersey said of the skateboarders, "They scare the wits out of drivers and pedestrians." In Shrewsbury, New Jersey the first time you were caught skateboarding, you were given a warning; the second time the police gave you the slat of your board back but kept the wheels. But skateboarding was in trouble beyond New Jersey; it was also banned in 20 cities throughout the nation, including Fort Lauderdale and Chattanooga, as well as on many college campuses.

The nation's press voiced its disapproval, too. *Consumer's Bulletin* and *Good Housekeeping* ran articles on the injuries that skateboards could cause. So did *Life* magazine. Just 11 months earlier, *Life* had been describing skateboarding as an innocent pleasure.

All this proved to be too much, and interest in skateboarding began to wane. Sales of skateboards fell dramatically, with warehouses said to be full of skateboards and skateboard parts. A skateboarding magazine, *Skateboarder*, folded.

But skateboards did come back in the middle 1970s. Often these had polyurethane wheels, which made the skateboards safer. Prices were also somewhat more expensive. A really fancy model could run you between $100 and $3,000.

But in the 1970s skateboarding was only one possible diversion among many. In the middle 1960s it had almost seemed like an obsession.

TOE RINGS (Mid-1960s)

The middle and late 1960s were a time in which a group called flower children flourished. These were usually young girls who wore flowered leg makeup or flowered tattoos, all meant to show that one should be peaceful—make love, not war. For this was in the midst of the ambiguous, bloody Vietnam conflict, where—no doubt about it—there was war.

Toe rings also came along then. One girl remembers her ring as having had elastics on the bottom to hold it on her sandals. She also remembers how flowered it was. She wore it off and on for two months, then gave it away.

Toe rings were like the ankle bracelets of the 1950s (see ANKLE BRACELETS)—something unusually decorative with which to adorn oneself. Moreover, the flowered pattern added a political statement, which was very important in the 1960s.

Toe rings died out quickly, though—more quickly than leg makeup or flowered tattoos or decals.

COMMUNES (1964–70; High Point, 1967–69)

Together we watch the flowers come with the early days of spring. . . . In fall we gather [together] to make wine in crushing the grapes and storing them in barrels. . . . We help each other with what needs to be built—a house, a stove, a porch, a septic tank.

—20-year-old girl, quoted by Ramparts *magazine on life in a California commune*

Communes have a long history; the early Christians formed communes of sorts, and so did people in Indiana in the 19th century, when they founded Robert Owen's New Harmony, a place where people gathered to share a simpler and less hostile life. When communes were revived in the late 1960s, mostly by young people disenchanted with American society, it was hardly surprising; nor was it surprising that commune dwellers were all popularly classed as a bunch of "hippies." A cover story in *Life* magazine was typical: Commune dwellers are shown in a full-color spread gathered together in the midst of a forest, where everyone wears love beads; the men have long, long beards; the women have granny dresses; the babies are always naked; and there is an aura of togetherness that could never be found in suburbia.

This was sometimes true, but mostly this had as much in common with commune life as a papier-mache fish has in common with a real live trout. For instance, take what happened at Oz Commune in Meadsville, Pennsylvania in the late 1960s. There, many of the local people distrusted all these commune dwellers, who went around barefoot and slept all together on the floor, and for some reason or another, intrigued people like doctors, teachers, lawyers, salespeople and car dealers, who came to Oz on the weekends—sometimes out of idle curiosity, sometimes because aspects of their lives were beginning to prove empty. Some local Meadsville people tried to block the roads leading to Oz; others were very nice to the commune dwellers, bringing them fresh fruit and vegetables. But the Oz commune members finally decided they had to move on if they were to survive. Not that the "uptightness" in this little Pennsylvania town meant that you would only find inhibitions and hostility near the eastern seaboard; in carefree California (near San Francisco), where a group of craftsmen and craftswomen lived together in rather well-appointed houses, any number of old civic regulations were dusted off and used to root them out.

One commune member said of the way his style of life was spreading, "In a few years, there'll be a whole network of communes from coast to coast." He knew all about the grit and hard reality of living on a commune; yet for him and for others, it was the only place to be. There were communes in California, Arizona, Maine, Oregon, New Mexico, Pennsylvania and Vermont, to name only a few states.

Ever since the first communes of the turbulent 1960s began to appear in California in 1964, commune dwellers shared a certain attitude that the commune was at once a very private place and also a place where they could become closer to others. One commune dweller said of Hog Farm in California that "It was the holiest place I've ever been. Another said of

the nice sense of isolation, "I often get up at 6 a.m. just to wander around by myself when everyone else is sleeping." And a third commune member said it encouraged intimacy: "When you can get past the cat and mouse stage [the way life is lived outside the commune], you can learn to be friends."

Yet there were problems with communes—problems that always exploded into the spotlight because of the unusual nature of the life-style there, when contrasted to the rest of mostly urban America. Many a commune tried to keep out runaways from the family, but sometimes they failed; at other communes runaways were enthusiastically welcomed. This caused problems with civic authorities. Many a commune outlawed the use of drugs, but many others let drugs flourish, and the reputation of communes as drug havens was in some ways not unwarranted. Many a commune outlawed free love, but many others thought that this was what intimacy was all about, and you can be sure that this latter type of commune found itself on the front pages and in the editorial pages. Almost all communes strove to find a leader with profound knowledge of human relations—a guru—to guide them; on one momentous occasion this led to disastrous results and really marked the end of the image of "flower children," who made up many of the commune dwellers.

On a more trivial level, many people were suspicious of young kids and others who lived by barter, making hammocks and raising grain to sell in food stores, when they could be earning many dollars an hour toiling on an assembly line, handling litigation or just running a business. There were many people who still believed in this, outmoded as it was, as the rightful order of human affairs.

Yet communes continued to influence the shape of the times. What was the Woodstock festival of 1969 but one very, very big communal activity, where intimacy was paramount? And what was the intention of all those "free stores" (particularly on the West Coast but also in New York City), where food was given away, except as an example of the communal spirit? And then in August 1969, Charles Manson and other members of his "family" murdered Sharon Tate and a number of other Hollywood celebrities in the bloodiest way possible. The "family" was not exactly a commune in the strict sense of the word, but yet—with its obsessive intimacy and its aura of being excluded from society—all the elements were there. This act made a lot of people think more sourly about communes, and things did change. Because of a random act of slaughter that had nothing to do with growing your own food with the help of others or the sharing of clothes, money and other worldly goods that are the aims of the commune, innocence was lost. Beginning in 1970 a lot less

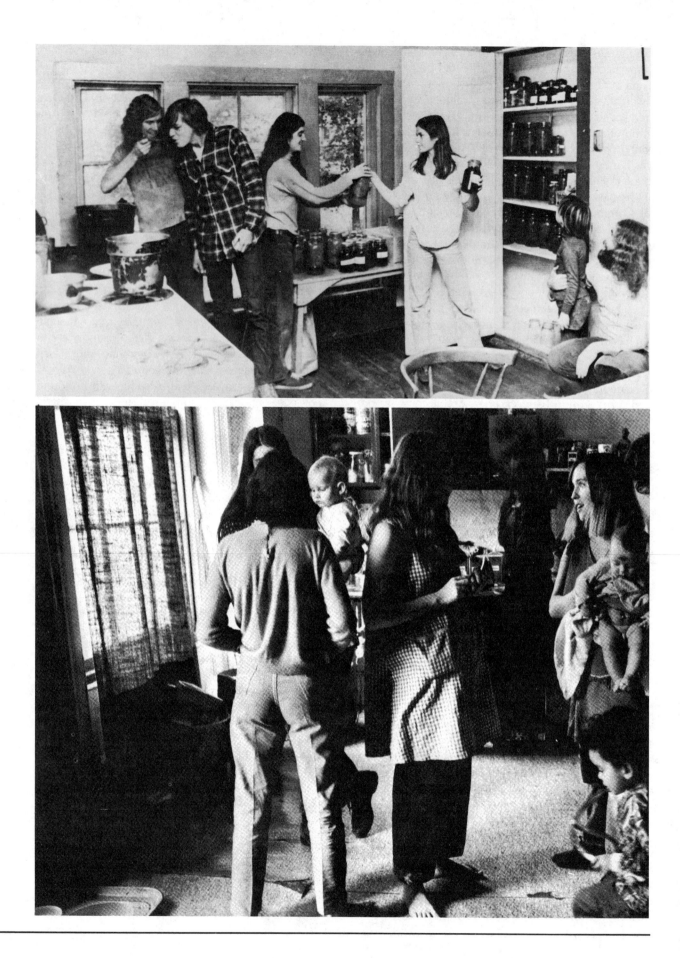

Tasting and putting away the food at the Brotherhood of the Spirit Commune in Northfield, Massachusetts

Commune dwellers at Hog Farm, California.

interest was shown in communes, and by the middle of the decade, most had collapsed.

Surely, this had something to do with the fact that the temper of the times had changed and that people were much less interested in what was proestablishment and antiestablishment; it is also true that many people had become more interested in building careers than in joining communes. Yet there was no denying that the romance had been lost. Or as a member of a northern California commune said, "Right now we do not know where we stand." This collection of sharing people had gone adrift.

PSYCHEDELIC TRIPS (1964–70; BANANA SKINS (1967); DAY-GLO (1964–70); TRIBAL APPAREL (1965–73); AND LONG, LONG HAIR (1965–70)

I'm just taking it easy, floating along.
— The driver of the "heads'" Haight-Ashbury bus in San Francisco, 1967

During the middle 1960s and even into the 1970s, when "flower children," long, long hair, mantras, trips on substances like LSD, peyote or mescaline, granny glasses, flowered vans, day-glo and be-ins all flourished, one sometimes got the impression that this era—or the Aquarian Age, as it was sometimes called—would never end. But end it did. Today, in 1983, you ask someone what day-glo is in New York City, the hub of a lot of the "head" action (or "hippie" action or "counterculture"—it's all the same thing), and many a person does not even know. Or take the "diggers," a group of people who adopted that many-named lifestyle but who also got and distributed free food to a lot of others living it, particularly in cities like New York

and San Francisco. The "diggers" are only a name out of the past now, mostly unremembered. They have really gone the way of the love beads, the derisive flag blankets and flag posters, and sunflower seeds.

This is a narrative about fads, not about life-styles; about the items people are fond of for a while, not the deep-seated attitudes they have toward existence. This is Marum's recollection of these deeply felt passing fancies.

Way back in the spring of 1962, the author, while in college, first learned about marijuana (or "pot" or "grass"). No big conversational deal was made of the fact that this little weed was illicit to smoke; rather, you were just asked things like, "Have you tried marijuana?" or "You want to smoke pot?" You just had to do it at least once, because that's what nearly everybody else was doing. And it was always the same kind of scene when it happened. People would gather together in a room in a state of high anxiety and be quiet, not because they were afraid of getting busted but because that secretive thing was approaching them—the marijuana "joint." It was rolled between paper in the shape of a cigarette, passed around like a peace pipe and taken in the mouth (the author frankly never learned to inhale it). It was really kind of amusing, and everyone looked like a bunch of decadent penguins contentedly blowing out their cold breaths on some remote icy region. And marijuana became big on campuses nationwide.

Politics was also a ruling passion. The author remembers wanting to take part in bringing about some improvement at a black ghetto in a nearby New York county seat, but so did a lot of other people, and to do it he had to be selected by a committee of both black and white student leaders. He was not selected and went behind the old ivy-covered building where he was interviewed and sat down and cried.

Yet in the early 1960s, another passion—and a very overwhelming one—began to stir, almost by accident. At Harvard University psychology Professor Timothy Leary and his associate Richard Alpert were seeing what would happen when students tried a drug known as LSD (lysergic acid diethylamide). Well, what it did was induce hallucinations or, at the very least, make perceptions and sensations more intense, as both friend and foe of the drug will readily agree. Leary and Alpert were asked to leave Harvard because of these experiments (they first went to suburban Newton, Massachusetts to continue the tests), and the legend of Dr. Leary was born; born, too, perhaps was a desire among young kids to try the drug (and without controls) because it created such a furor. Who knows what the landscape of American life would have looked like in the 1960s had Dr. Timothy Leary been allowed to stay at Harvard?

133

The drug that Leary (and others) tested became known as psychedelic, which freely translated from the original Greek, meant mind-showing (later, it was commonly called mind-altering); this was true of LSD and of other drugs like peyote and mescaline. In any case, it made colors look different, solids look different, odors smell different and foods taste different. And it was a "trip" to experience these sensory thrills after taking LSD or the other drugs. And whether LSD was poison or panacea, it was featured in many a national magazine—like *Time*, *Newsweek*, *The Nation* and *Glamour*—by 1966, or about two years after it became a not uncommon item on campuses. LSD and its cousins peyote and mescaline separated the men, who would take them, from the boys, who stuck to marijuana or took nothing at all. What's more, though it may not have been as widespread in terms of people doing it, LSD perhaps was the 1960s what the Charleston was to the 1920s—overpowering, impossible to ignore. It was both a vogue and an emblem of the times.

While the author's memory of the exact lineaments of the time is vague, one event is still almost as clear as light. In 1964 he knew somebody well who was on a whole gamut of psychedelic drugs (somebody who was a "head"). The "head" was a man who had lost interest in school and politics, formerly things that obsessed him. Everything he did was, in a word, strange. One day, he was carrying around a huge cactus plant. Was it peyote? The author still doesn't know. Another day, he would, in a rage, write strange words on the author's dorm door. For him, the psychedelics were bad—very bad.

This is memory, not commentary; in America you just could not escape from the world of the psychedelics in the middle to the late 1960s. People talked about being "busted," which both made the drugs more of a menace and served as a greater enticement. The *New York Times* reported that stockbrokers, playwrights and business executives took LSD, perhaps buying a $5 sugar cube that was spiked with a droplet of the stuff; and of course, poets and musicians took it. A songwriter said that it made an orange he was eating seem "to burst through my mouth," while a "young poet" reported that "It's all over town. You can get it anywhere, if you know the right people." And so it continued until 1968, as one reporter wrote of a gathering of "heads" in Central Park in July; there was, for instance, one who took LSD and was "goofing [playing around in a bizarre way] with a frisbee."

Such incidents were among the many things that were happening in the middle to the late 1960s because of the explosion of LSD, a chemical whose effects were discovered quite inadvertently by a Swiss chemist who was experimenting with a derivative of the fungus ergot in 1943. Now this derivative of ergot contained a form of LSD, but the chemist did not know of LSD's dynamite effect. He was to find out, however. First, he had most unusual perceptions in the laboratory, and then he found it was impossible to bicycle home. And there the tale of LSD sat until Dr. Leary got ahold of it, and the rest, as they say, is history.

By 1970, though, LSD had either lost much of its vogue, or great numbers of people did not want to stimulate themselves by using it. One former "head" who used it told the *New York Times*: "I got bored with acid. I had other things to do"; another said: "All we talked about were prices, shipments, who got busted. It is a very finite topic [of discussion]."

During its great heyday, the obsession with psychedelic drugs among that great number of "heads" spawned an interest in a type of fluorescent paint known as day-glo. Eventually, day-glo was used by far more people who wanted to affect the guise of being "heads" than by the "heads" themselves, but in the early days— particularly in San Francisco—day-glo was a simple little way of showing how unusual your senses could be when you used psychedelic drugs. Day-glo was sprayed on your face or your body in all kinds of swirling or strange patterns or combinations of colors that would come extraordinarily alive after the drug had begun to work itself out. Dolls were day-glo colored, as well as vans, trunks of trees, military helmets, kitchen tables and anything else that you could think of.

In 1967, though, day-glo and the rest of the "head" life-style and paraphernalia were taken almost bodily into the national and commercial bloodstream of America (or to use a word of the late 1970s and the 1980s, they were "co-opted"). You could get day-glo colors for yourself at nearly any shop dealing in novelties, paints or "head" items, and you just might go home, put the paint on, sit in the bathtub, watch it come off and see how that old tub became a swirl of colors. There was many a day-glo poster of the cultural heroes of the time, like Bob Dylan or any of the Beatles. Day-glo became a part of those light shows in cities, which grabbed the young and made them think that they belonged for that one night to that hip, absorbing, bizarre "head" culture. The author's brother-in-law, in 1970, who was then only in his midteens and had no more intention of taking a trip with LSD than of taking a trip to Lahore, Pakistan, had day-glo colors in his own basement room, which was a light show, too, a lot of the time. Day-glo had come to everybody; everybody soon became familiar with it, decided it was much better when it was part of the secretive "head" guild and discarded it because it was passe. People now ask, "What was that day-glo stuff?"

By 1967 being like the great gathering of "heads"

134

was really in fashion. In San Francisco the "hippies" (this was now the common term for "heads") went around the well-known Haight-Ashbury district, which stretched 40 blocks from the black Fillmore section in the Bay City to the Golden Gate Park, via free rides on a 1930 bus with a bathtub as one of its rear seats. And so in June 1967 a similar conveyance, though a little bit more modern and without a bathtub, was purchased by New York City inhabitants for $5,200 to begin traveling around the streets of Gotham in the middle of July. There was one slight difference: The New York City bus, which was to be painted in day-glo colors, was a commercial vehicle with the most up-to-date goods, all of which could make you feel like a full-fledged hippie. It sold incense, Indian bells, water pipes, bead necklaces, forehead jewels and stick-on tattoos (as well as yo-yos, for some odd reason). One of the four entrepreneurs who bought the bus said that he got the idea from the *Wall Street Journal*, which said that "psychedelic stuff" was big. To find that out, though, he needn't have gone so far as to flip through this photoless though most authoritative newspaper; all he had to do was turn on the tube or leaf through a color spread in any magazine while browsing at the newsstand. His partners, the other three entrepreneurs, were duly impressed and called him "an idea a minute man." However, his was not the type of thinking that LSD especially encourages. This was a more old-fashioned high—one called making a cash killing.

At the same time, in every other part of the country, "head shops," or hippie emporiums, were springing up. This was a phenomenon that was certainly not overlooked anywhere, either by the young consumer, who wanted his or her love beads and day-glo paints, or by the reporters, who considered it one whale of a story. Well, most of the journalists got the same line from these heterodox businesspeople. We think of our hippie life-style first, but really, we don't mind piling up a bunch of money on the side.

This was also the time that the light show was invented, for people who wanted to experience artificially the effects of an LSD high. The colors and the light and the motion in these halls would do the trick. In every way, these light shows were the forerunner of disco clubs (see DISCO) in the vibrancy of their setting. Yet the *New York Times* wryly observed that a real "head," who often depended on the efforts of "diggers" to survive, could not afford the $3.50 entrance fee to the Fillmore West, a very popular light show in San Francisco.

Meanwhile, in San Francisco itself, the public mode of transportation known as the Gray Line bus had a very popular itinerary: a trip into "Hippieland," or Haight-Ashbury. This wasn't quite on the same level as those European tour buses, with the guide sol-

emnly announcing, "We are now approaching Chartres Cathedral, perhaps the greatest monument to Gothic art in France," but perhaps it wasn't all that far off.

No wonder that the gathering of real "heads" was almost mortified by all of this and held a communal funeral for "Hippie," complete with flowers, flower children and all, in 1967. Yet Haight-Ashbury, with its milling thousands of "heads," remained a magnet. A popular song of that year was If You Go to San Francisco, Wear Flowers in Your Hair.

It was in October 1967 that the author himself set off for San Francisco, because he always wanted to see it, not to gaze at or be part of the throng, as he said. And see it he did. He saw the hippies passing by in the Haight district, all with long, long hair or beads or Indian ponchos, which really was not all that different from coming back from a Big 10 football game and seeing every single couple holding hands in exactly the same way. But to get back to San Francisco, he saw all that was typical of the "head" life, the giving of flowers, the lying down of the whole family, including a baby, in the Golden Gate Park grass. But also he saw many a glazed eye, including meeting a former girl friend of sorts who had been innocent in college but now appeared just utterly zonked out.

This was, of course, why the hippie life-style was so frightening to parents. The roads were filled with vagabonds from the family who were just fed up at this particularly alienated time in American history. One New Jersey 15-year-old was given permission because he was an "A" student to travel out to the Haight to see what it was like, but this was clearly the exception. Most kids who went there were not about to bring home their new awareness to Mom, Dad or Sis. In one runaway's words, "I got so tired of people mooning over me because I was Mrs. So-So's son," as a reporter for the *New York Times* was told.

And contrary to popular belief, which sometimes held that the "heads" were like pied pipers trying to attract the gullible young, this influx was not encouraged by Haight-Ashbury denizens. Rather, it was asked through underground channels that the young swelling crowd of "head" aspirants stay away. What's more, a letter from the "head" newspaper, *The Oracle*, to the influential *Village Voice* asked just that. The letter went on to say that if a young vagabond's mind was made up, he or she should bring money for rent and food, a sleeping bag or rucksack, and warm clothing, because San Francisco can be very cold. However, it also sort of undercut the message, because it told the vagabond to bring bananas, too. Bananas were a drug—of sorts.

Now starting in New York City, and due to a radio broadcast by a disc jockey on a WBAI show, in the spring of 1967 getting a "high" from the white fiber of banana peels was the latest thing. What you did was put the skins under heat or in any oven and then when they were oven-dryed enough, smoke them, after rolling them into a "joint" or putting them in a pipe. The *Village Voice* wrote about this "electrical banana," and people from all over the East Village gathered in Central Park and smoked them. It also got to the point where the police would patrol these outdoor gatherings, insist that the kids (and sometimes just the old-fashioned "beatniks" from the fifties and perhaps an 80-year-old poet or two) throw away the skins of the bananas and then allow them to eat the rest of the banana to their hearts' content. Not that the police could really control the consuming of bananas or that anyone was busted for eating this fruit. This was against an international agreement.

The fad for bananas lasted about six weeks.

Banana smoking really was one harmless aspect of the "hippie" scene, but it wasn't the only one, because the feeling between the hippies and the common run of the citizenry was not always one of bitter strife. In both San Francisco and New York, there were days in which hippies were allowed to do exactly what they pleased at certain places. When they had a "be-in" (a celebration of hippies together "doing their own thing") in New York City's Central Park at the end of March 1967, no one touched them. In San Francisco, then-Mayor Joseph Alioto issued a proclamation that a certain day in that spring of 1967 would be a hippie day.

Yet there was enough animosity, too—perhaps more than enough. In a gathering in San Francisco at Golden Gate Park, where at least 25,000 "heads," "hippies" and "flower children" (what have you) came together, there were arrests. Later, in New York City, there were arrests because "heads" were just milling around the East Village in Manhattan, and also, when "heads" decided to have a "be-in" in Grand Central Station, arrests were made there. This continued from the beginning of the days of "head"-dom to its end.

The gathering of "heads," or "hippies," was known as the "gathering of the tribes." There was perhaps a Haight-Ashbury "tribe" (or perhaps many of them) and a tribe (or many of them) from Manhattan's Lower East Side; tribes could come from anywhere: Boston; Austin, Texas; Seattle; Duluth, Minnesota; Wilkes-Barre, Pennsylvania; Birmingham, Alabama. They called themselves "tribes" because they identified with the American Indians. Sometimes, however, the American Indians didn't identify with them. In the summer of 1967, the Hopi Indians refused to let the "head" tribe of San Francisco come down and camp out in part of the Grand Canyon.

In any event, the look of many—if not all—of these tribes was much the same, and even as the tribes

began to die out in the early 1970s, individuals would still continue to sport the same old apparel. There were headbands aplenty, love beads and Indian print dresses, and the only places that the hippies really seemed to sleep were mattresses on the floor, and there were granny glasses, and there was always long, long hair. Now this hair was different from just plain long hair, which extended down to the shoulders and caused great horror among parents, school authorities and at offices. This was long, long hair worn by men, which often went all the way down to the buttocks.

Now all this appears like one almost unforgivable stereotype, but in picture after picture, not only in color spreads in national magazines but in dull and drab dailies, the look is repeated again and again and again. "Hippies" were interested in bonding together, not in standing out from other similar people, which is the aim of much of fashion.

Obviously, people who were once horrified by the counterculture were beginning to tune it out after a while—to accept it and just go on. This may have happened as early as 1968, with the success of the Broadway production *Hair*. Nothing can kill exotic uniqueness like a Broadway musical sometimes.

So the "head" scene began to die out in the early 1970s, but not right away, of course, because in 1970 you could still see at any newsstand in the East Village any number of colorful underground newspapers, as they were called, from all the cities in the nation where "tribes" gathered. But die out it did.

Why did it die out? Hard to say. Perhaps people were just tired of being exotic in a way that took so much energy. Maybe the lotus-eater attitude of many of the "heads" was becoming less popular. Maybe the winding down of the Vietnam War did something, and maybe the horrible events at Kent State University, when four students were killed by the National Guard, did something also. In any case, people became interested in more individual pursuits like 10-speed bicycling or jogging or hang-gliding or whatever; and if they wanted to show how bizarre they could be, they could do so by giving someone a pet rock (see PET ROCKS).

At the same time, the "head" attitude, which was so much about living in the here and now, was replaced by an obsessive interest in wearing clothes of the past and in bringing back the television heroes of the past. People looked in particular toward the decade before the 1960s, the 1950s—the time of Howdy Doody, Hopalong Cassidy, motorcycle jackets and steady dating. This was called nostalgia, and it didn't involve such fond recollections as, "Hey, you remember that 'high' we had on LSD two years ago in July?"

The surprising thing is that when the "head" scene finally passed, it was as if someone had drawn a curtain over it or, better still, as if it was hidden in a closet, a skeleton not to be thought about. It is strange, because no one can deny it was a time of real self-expression and a time when the byword was *love*. Now, in 1983, much of the shame about the "head" scene inexplicably remains.

Pass/Fail Grading (1964–74)

The grade has generally been a most important consideration. A common question asked from grammar school to graduate school is "Whatdja get?" accompanied by a battery of other queries like "What's a soft course?" and "Who's an easy marker?" For 10 years, in the 1960s and 1970s, however, pass/fail grading often took the place of A, B, C, D, F. College students said things like, "I'm sure I can at least pass it. I'm enjoying the course more than almost any other course I've taken"; while college faculty members said things like, "[I] don't need to play a game of grades with my students, have a guerrila war." Competitive grading was still used but was looked upon as kind of hidebound. By 1971 about ¾ of the nation's colleges and universities were using pass/fail as an alternate form of grading.

Comparative grades were first eliminated in a few public schools in 1964. This may have come about because of a lot of criticism hostile to traditional education, expressed in such books as A.S. Neill's *Summerhill: A Radical Approach to Child Rearing*, about an experimental British school.

However, it was when pass/fail was introduced in colleges and universities that this new mode really caught on. At the California Institute of Technology, one of the first institutions to use it, a pass/fail system was mandatory in introductory courses in math, physics, chemistry, English and history. Stanford, the University of California at Berkeley, the University of Michigan, Oberlin College and Princeton soon followed suit in offering a pass/fail option. By the next year it was so widespread that the practice was featured in national magazines like *Look, Seventeen* and *Newsweek*.

Pass/fail grading seemed so desirable because in the 1960s college students were changing their attitudes about life. More and more students looked down upon going to law school or business school, or competing with fellow students for a grade. Expressions like "climbing the corporate ladder" elicited sneers. And many students thought that was all getting good grades meant.

At the same time, the Vietnam War put grades in very poor repute, because draft boards would often take students with bad grades and pass over students with good grades. Pass/fail grading seemed to be a way of making sure this wouldn't happen, or as one professor put it, "I know of no way to measure the value of a given human life." She quit teaching at her college because it would not adopt the pass/fail system.

Editorials in college newspapers praised pass/fail and condemned traditional grading.

By 1971 pass/fail grading had seeped down to high schools and grammar schools as a general method of evaluation. Also, other types of grading began to abound in colleges, like secret grading, blanket grading and contract grading.

Yet by 1974 students began to lose interest in pass/fail, with a resurgence of students choosing traditional grading in order to get into professional schools, which had become popular once more; the corporate ladder got to be in vogue again, too. One faculty member, in noting the declining interest in pass/fail, called it "a noble experiment that didn't work," while another teacher called it "an academic bubonic plague." In fact, to many of the students, traditional As, Bs, Cs, Ds and Fs were a new and exciting thing, since from grammar school to junior high to high school, they had experienced only pass/fail grading. Also, the Vietnam War was all but over.

Frug (1965)

You do the frug by yourself, perhaps as a defiant gesture of independence in an increasingly homogenized world.

—Ivy League professor

Frug away and reestablish your identity. You can even go beyond the bounds of having a dance partner. Now *that's* rebellion. Just throw your pelvic weight around, first to the right and then to the left or, if you prefer, first to the left then to the right. In the middle of doing your frug, you could thrust your index finger in the air. Another new variation on the dance scene? Nope, though many of the fruggers might have thought so. The same finger thrusting was done in the fashionable Lambeth Walk—which we copied from England—in the late 1930s (see LAMBETH WALK). When it was done in the Frug, the finger movement was known as the "I told you so" gesticulation; in the Lambeth Walk all the dancers said was "oi."

137

The frug was the big dance of the collegiate young in 1965. You could see them doing it to any music they wanted to, though you would hardly expect to see such movements done to anything resembling a waltz tempo. Chubby Checker's I Need Your Loving or Having a Party or the Beatles' Can't Buy Me Love or the Rolling Stones' Can't Get No Satisfaction were more like it.

In its time the frug must have been thought both exciting and enticing. In the Broadway musical Cactus Flower, a plain Jane dentist's aide, played by Lauren Bacall, turns into a provocative siren. Among the ways she shows her real glamour is by doing the frug.

The frug first appeared in upstate New York, at Syracuse University. In that big eastern state, down-staters (like people who live in Manhattan) sometimes regard people who live upstate as out-of-touch—what used to be known as "square." Well, those Manhattanites learned a thing or two; the Syracusans were so out-of-touch that they came up with a dance that spread nationwide.

The frug was a good dance to do when people were "into" anything nonestablishment, for the frug was definitely nonestablishment. When it had first appeared, some people made a big thing of the fact that you don't need a partner to do the frug. Well, the fact is that you don't need a partner to do disco, either. Thus, while the frug itself quickly passed from the scene, the concept of partnerless dancing it introduced lived on.

GLASSLESS GLASSES (1965)

Glassless glasses were a big fad among the kids in southern California in the summer of 1965. They were obviously a spoofy sort of thing, making fun of the intellectual look, such as that sported by those television commentators or politicians who wore glasses on the tips of their noses. It is no wonder that the kids who did this—as Seventeen magazine reports—called themselves a collection of BEEK (or Big-Eyed Egg-heads of California).

One wearer of glassless glasses had a really inflated idea of how important this strange bespectacled look was. For this youth it was "the biggest fad since surfing" (though these two activities might seem to have little in common).

One might think that glassless glasses would have touched off a storm of teen-age burlesques, like having tieless ties and pocketless pockets, but that it did

not. However, what soon followed glassless glasses among the young was another bizarre optical look. These glasses had lenses all right, but the lenses seemed to come straight out of the Gay Nineties. The look was called granny glasses (see GRANNY GLASSES).

Because of the relative brevity of the fad, one important question prompted by glassless glasses was really left unanswered: If it is true that "men don't make passes at girls who wear glasses," as a humorist once observed, what if the girls were wearing glassless glasses?

Glassless glasses were the kind of fad that seemed out of place in the very serious and not terribly ironic 1960s. The humor that prompted them was more like that which prompted the briefly popular merchandising items that were found in the middle 1970s, like pet rocks or bottled money (see PET ROCKS, BOTTLED MONEY).

GRONKING (Spring 1965)

That cry you just heard, G-R-O-N-K, was a way of relieving academic distress. You could hear it at the eastern colleges in the spring of 1965. Who knows? Maybe the students were expressing their unease about a Western Civilization examination. Or one in Biology. Or a French test. Or perhaps they were afraid they wouldn't recognize half the constellations on the Astronomy quiz.

There was only one thing to do: yell G-R-O-N-K.

Here's the procedure: The students would get together in a group to pore over the books. Soon enough they would get tired of studying, reach an impasse or just plain get scared of a coming examination. A parley among the students. A decision: It was gronking time.

Then all of the students would count 1-2-3-4 in unison. At the count of 4, a yell would be heard: G-R-O-N-K.

Then maybe they would settle down again. And then maybe again, sometime later, they would burst forth with another G-R-O-N-K.

One collegian said of gronking, "It's a great way to let off steam quickly—and sociably."

Gronking was an end-of-the-academic-year fancy. Some gronkers may even have quit earlier. Perhaps they thought that if you shrieked one G-R-O-N-K, you shrieked them all.

Gronking was an old-fashioned kind of fad, and it was not the type of innocuous thing that was done by just everybody. It was not the sort of thing done by kids who were weary of the mainstream of American life and were turning to taking psychedelic "trips" (*see* PSYCHEDELIC TRIPS), for example, nor would you associate gronking with long hair, though there is no reason why a gronker couldn't have long hair. A gronk was never a political statement, either, as were psychedelic trips and long hair.

This just goes to show that there never has been just one type of fad; there have always been fads to fit every type of temperament—and there always will be.

the smell of a "dead rabbit." (He was, however, a boy and perhaps not a connoisseur of the fine art of ironing hair.)

The New York girl quit ironing her hair after two months because she found that she was ruining her hair, which was becoming too dry and getting split ends. This may well have been a typical reaction.

Girls got tired of ironed hair as other hairstyles took its place. It turned out the curly look could be just as popular as the straight look.

IRONING HAIR (1965)

For young girls in 1965 having straight hair that hung over your face was very popular. But a lot of girls had curly hair. What to do? Easy. Just whip out an ironing board and apply a hot iron to the hair. That would quickly change the curly look into the straight look. A Connecticut girl told how widespread the process had become: "Everybody in school is ironing their hair. Even the people with straight hair are ironing it to make it straighter." A New York girl remembered that she started pressing her tresses because all her sisters and friends were doing it.

A gal could iron her hair by herself, but this was by no means as simple as pie. First, she would haul out the ironing board. Then she would take a section of her hair, bend down and put this section on the ironing board. To prevent being burned, she would then cover the section with a towel and apply the iron, holding it there for a few seconds and moving it up and down the section. She would repeat the same process for three or four other sections of hair. Sometimes, two girls would do the hair ironing together. One girl would lay her hair on the ironing board while the other ironed it, an inch at a time. This whole process could take as much as an hour but might take only about 15 minutes for a girl who had done it many times.

The New York girl repeated it every day or every other day. Her straight hair didn't last very long, though. When it was washed, its curliness immediately came back.

To maintain the effect of ironed hair, jumbo rollers, larger than tuna fish cans, as one girl remembered, were used, or the hair was wrapped up.

In some ways, the whole operation was amusing. The New York girl remembered that "trying to keep the towel on right was a real riot." Also, ironing hair created a burning odor, compared by one observer to

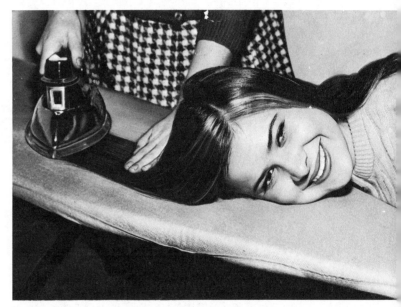

A young Colorado girl has her hair ironed

GRANNY DRESSES (Fall 1965)

Way back in the Gay Nineties, women wore long dresses. And then the gals threw off all that excess baggage, declaiming against the dresses and, in general, feeling a lot more comfortable. So what were all those California and other western lasses doing wearing those floor-length dresses in 1965? Why weren't they in miniskirts?

To what extent had granny dresses (as the long dresses were called, because they had been worn by the girls' grandmothers—really it was probably their great-grandmothers) replaced minis? Consider this. When the Beatles played the Hollywood Bowl in the fall of 1965, they looked out at an audience of young girls wearing granny dresses, not minis.

It might have started a few weeks earlier because of an incident on a teen-age dance show in Los Angeles. The MC had kidded the teens on the show because of their short skirts. En masse, the teen-age girls decided they would show their elders, who thought they knew everything about the young, a thing or two. They would wear long dresses just like their grandmas.

And so they did. However, it wasn't as if they could just buy a long dress of the old style off the rack. They couldn't find them anywhere. So they sewed the granny dresses themselves. They were that intent on wearing them.

The granny dress fad swept the land. Designers began to create and sell them themselves. Teen magazines gave instructions on how to make them, while telling how all the girls were wearing them.

Just about the same time that the teen-agers were wearing their granny dresses in Los Angeles, they were also strolling around Disneyland. You could see them in Frontierland, Adventureland, Tomorrowland and Fantasyland. (Other tourists must have thought that they were living in 1890s-land.) Their appearance in the number one amusement park helped spread the fad.

The granny dress, however, was only a temporary diversion. Looking like the Gibson Girl, that fashion plate of the late 19th century (see GIBSON GIRL), was fine for a month or two, but a steady diet? No way. The mini would return. The legs would be back.

PLATFORM GO-GO DANCING (1965–66)

Platform go-go dancing was part of the twist scene (see TWIST) of the 1960s, which included, besides this no-touching and gyrating dance step, miniskirts, jump suits and high boots—but it was a very special part. You could twist without doing platform go-go. Yet in 1965–66 platform go-go was still very popular. It was really an exciting thing to dance on platforms or in cages—sometimes resembling bird cages—that were aloft, suspended above the dance floor. Or even to change garments in cylindrical "his" and "her" booths that hung from the ceiling. Now, all this was being a bird, and a high-stepper besides; in fact, gal dancers often wore the trendy new white boots, which had begun to entice lots of people (see STYLED WHITE BOOTS). It was particularly statusy to platform go-go dance in places like Cheetahs or the Peppermint Lounge in New York.

Platform go-go dancing, or dancing on platforms above the dance floor, wasn't always something that your average chic nightclub dancer out for an evening on the town took part in. In the early 1960s the practice began in France, which gave us the term *au go go* to describe it. Then, a little bit later, in America women began to dance on the platforms and in the cages, wearing boots and jump suits; but these gals were go-go dancers—professionally trained, paid performers. It was only in 1965 that the dancers on the floor wanted to start doing these things, too. And so they did. First, they imitated the movements from above the dance floor. Then, they wanted to climb into their own cages and platforms.

This became very popular. One man remembers that on December 31, 1965—in other words, New Year's Eve—he was all set to do some platform dancing himself. But he came down sick, and his friends had to go to the nightclubs without him.

However, by mid-1966 people had begun to lose interest in platform dancing as something to do themselves. They began to be more interested, for instance, in nightclubs with an intriguing light show (see PSYCHEDELIC TRIPS). The twist continued, but platform dancing lost its vogue.

While the term *go-go dancers* was still used through the 1970s and into the 1980s, it referred not to ordinary dancers doing a special go-go step, but to professional dancers—go-go girls—doing it just as a job.

CHARLIE BROWN, SNOOPY AND THE PEANUTS GANG (1965–67)

Way up on the 57th floor of a Manhattan skyscraper near Wall Street, hidden away in a little office, hangs a poster of the beagle Snoopy, lying on top of a his doghouse. The caption: "I think that I'm allergic to the morning."

Snoopy has always belonged to the battered and bruised *Peanuts*© gang, headed by his master Charlie Brown and also consisting of the tease Lucy, the musician Schroeder and Linus, famous for his blanket. Popular from the mid-1950s to the present day, the *Peanuts* gang, particularly Charlie Brown, reached overwhelming faddish proportions in the mid-1960s. Benjamin Spock, the most revered pediatrician of them all, said, "I care about Charlie Brown very much." There was a Broadway musical called *You're a Good Man, Charlie Brown*. There were well-known little books like *Home Is the Top of a Doghouse*, *Linus, on Life*, *I Need All the Friends I Can Get* and, most famous, *Happiness Is a Warm Puppy*, which sold in the millions. A theologian even wrote *The Gospel According to Peanuts*.

Not to mention all the little *Peanuts* gewgaws you could get—like Charlie Brown dolls, records, calendars, pajamas, pillows, T-shirts, hats and paper cups. You can still get them today, of course; but back then they were a very special and overwhelming rage.

Peanuts, as everyone knows, was not merely for children. It dispensed humorous words of advice, which, in many ways, were not dissimilar to the advice dispensed by the great numbers of self-help books in the 1970s. Lucy may have been a real terror to Charlie Brown, but her 5-cent psychoanalytic booth was not a budget killer like lying on an analyst's couch, and a lot of adults must have thought Lucy's insights would do just as well.

Ironically, at its outset, the cartoon was not all that comforting, but really was a bit savage. In the first strip ever featuring the gang, Lucy slugs Charlie Brown. After he falls down, she observes that girls were made of sugar and spice. Later, in another strip, when Charlie Brown writes the initials of his girl friend on a tree, the tree topples over. This may have been a trifle too mean-spirited. Charles Schulz's characters did mellow.

Schulz, *Peanuts*' cartoonist, was little-known until the 1950s. In a few newspapers he drew the kids who would make up *Peanuts*, but he called the strip *L'il Folks*. For a time the strip was also known as *Rats and Good Grief*. As any reader of *Peanuts* can attest, both these phrases remained prominent—"rats" for any-

thing that really overwhelms the characters and "good grief" as in "Good grief, Charlie Brown" (when any of his friends want to tell him that he has messed up again).

When Schulz's work was picked up by King Features Syndicate, the strip was renamed *Peanuts* (Schulz has always said he dislikes the name) and caught on immediately.

There never has been a character named Peanuts in the strip. As for Charlie Brown, Schulz has often said there is a lot of Charlie Brown in him, remarking on at least one occasion, "I guess I am 100 percent Charlie Brown."

Many, many others must have thought of Charlie Brown much the same way, for people can always be heard talking about how Charlie Brown's qualities relate to their own. No wonder Charlie Brown and the *Peanuts* gang were a $15 million industry in 1967. Shoe stores also used Snoopy as an emblem to boost their sales.

In fact, in the late 1960s, Snoopy really asserted himself. Often, this was shown in daring aerial battles with the German flying ace known as the Red Baron—which, too, led to dolls, records, calendars and posters.

SUPER BALL (1965–67)

Oh, if Galileo had only dropped a super ball from the Leaning Tower of Pisa instead of the leaded weights with which he proved the law of gravity! It might have bounced back up to the old scientist, who could then have proved the theory of the miraculous bouncing ball. History could have been altered, and it could have been 17th-century Italian youth, not 20th-century American youth, who would take part in the super ball fad. Or grave Italian political counselors in their *palazzos* rather than McGeorge Bundy, special adviser to President Johnson, in the basement of his Washington home.

Super ball, that small, black synthetic rubber sphere about the size and weight of a squash ball, would bounce back high in the air or for a duration of over a minute, if dropped the right way. Kids from coast to coast dropped it to see how high it would go. The thing only cost 98 cents. Invented by one Norman Stingley, it was produced by Wham-O, those people who a decade earlier had given us the hula hoop (see HULA HOOPS) and the frisbee (see FRISBEE). Made first on the sunny shores of California, super balls were bounced by stockbrokers of the Pacific Stock Exchange, who were among the first to play with them.

The fad died out because, as one Wisconsin lad put it, "How many times can you bounce a super ball?" The effect was admittedly somewhat repetitious. Also, since the ball was so hard, it was found that a bad bounce might cause injuries. Within a few years the same thing was said about clacker balls, two hard plastic balls connected by a cord (see CLACKER BALLS). These, too, became a fad among the kids. In fact, the Wisconsin lad who had bounced the super ball would soon be striking clacker balls. He got tired of them both.

In any event, super ball did make one lasting contribution to contemporary American culture. In 1967 Lamar Hunt, the oil tycoon and owner of a professional football team, was home thinking about a name for the championship game to be played between the winners of two major football leagues, the American Football League and the National Football League. To say that he was stumped is putting it mildly. Then, all of a sudden, this ball owned by his young son went shooting high in the air. "What in the world was that thing?" asked Lamar Hunt "Super ball," answered his son. And from that moment on, the football game that has become one of the most important American sports events was dubbed Super Bowl.

No super ball was taken onto the field, however; the players kept their pigskins. In fact, after 1967 there were few super balls to be seen anywhere.

COMPUTER DATING (Heyday, 1965–Early 1970s)

Searching for romance? Mind-Mates offered "the enlightened versatility to match flower children and Wall Street tycoons." Just take advantage of its trusty computer, or that of Selectra-date, Compatibility, Affinities, Team, Icebreaker, Match Mate, Update, Operation Match or Contact. Employing the latest hardware, like IBM's 360/40, computer dating blossomed from being a college fad in 1965–66 to being a national cure for loneliness by 1967. One fellow called computer dating "the greatest excuse for calling up a single girl that I've ever heard." Sometimes the comments were more restrained: "Everybody was trying it." "It sounded interesting." "There was nothing to lose and maybe something to gain."

The idea of computer dating had probably been germinating in many people's minds for some time, but it was two Harvard College undergraduates, Jeff Tarr and Vaughn Merrill, who would make it a reality in February 1965. The original aim was modest: to make intercollegiate dating more possible, since it was "so difficult to meet new friends." In other words, as a *Look* magazine article described it, "punch bowls were out and punch cards were in."

Tarr and Merrill's system first attracted 8,000 young men and women, each of whom paid $3 for the names of five dates. They called their service Operation Match, and it was probably directed at those colleges known as the Ivy League schools (Harvard, Yale, Columbia, University of Pennsylvania, Cornell, Dartmouth, Princeton and Brown) or "the seven sisters" (Smith, Radcliffe, Wellesley, Mount Holyoke, Barnard, Vassar and Bryn Mawr). Soon afterward, a student at the Massachusetts Institute of Technology, David De Wan, developed Contact.

The way any of these systems worked was simple enough: You were asked personal information, which was fed into a computer along with the answers that others had given. After comparing information, the computer chose the names of dates likely to be compatible. On occasion, this boomeranged, even on the true believers. David De Wan, who made Contact a brisk business, lost his girl friend after listing her attributes in the computer. And for some, there couldn't be too much certainty. One young woman threatened to break her engagement unless her fiance, whom she had met through computer dating, could prove to her that their cards were "flawlessly identical in every detail."

Perhaps the reason computer dating caught on big was because it applied sophisticated technology to solve a problem that interested almost everybody: how to get a date. What's more, it was somewhat easier for a guy to pick up a phone and talk to a potential date about Mind-Mates, Contact or Compatibility than to approach the matter cold turkey. And perhaps it was somewhat easier for a girl, too.

In any event, the romance computer organizations varied in the emphasis of their questionnaires. Some were directed at college youth, while others sought all the "single, divorced and widowed," like Compatibility. That firm's "personal inventory"—the series of questions whose responses were fed into the computer—had a distinctly conservative hue, inquiring about such matters as "Is organized religion a great force for good?" or "Are shows with semi-nude performers a corrupting influence?" But if Compatibility was old-fashioned, Affinities was "with-it." Affinities asked if you identified with Mao Tse-tung, the leader of Communist China; Eugene McCarthy, the Democratic senator from Minnesota who challenged President Johnson in 1968; Che Guevara, the Cuban revolutionary; or Spiro Agnew, the 1968 Republican vice presidential candidate (and later vice president). It really wasn't expected, though, that many Affinities clients would claim to identify with Spiro Agnew, who was hostile to the counterculture. The computer dating organization known as The Love Generation was much the same way: Its advertising copy said if "Cambodia withdrawal," "legalizing pot," "Earth Day" and "Woodstock" were "your bag," The Love Generation was your place to seek interesting dates. Like any other successful idea, computer dating caught the pulse of its times.

Not everyone in the love generation itself used computer dating, though, popular as it was. Many young people who were very much into the counterculture of "heads" (see PSYCHEDELIC TRIPS) would often gather together in parks and in their own areas of cities to perhaps smoke some "dope," spray some day-glo, listen to some rock music or maybe just show their friends how long their long, long hair had grown. These meetings, which were known as the "gathering of the tribe," were also situations where people would just pair off. No computer dating, no punch cards, no phone calls that began awkwardly "'Compatibility' told me that you . . . "—none of the advanced technological formality was necessary.

A variant on computer dating in 1966 was a harmless game called the "hunt" or "hunters and victims," which was played on college campuses (see HUNTERS AND VICTIMS). This included ingenious ways to carry out mock assassinations. The game itself was based on the movie *The Tenth Victim*, but the bringing together of hunters and victims by computers mimicked the premise of computer dating.

Yet computer dating—this "most adventurous experiment of our time," as one dating outfit billed itself—became subject to widespread abuse. Often the lonely got trapped, as in the case of a mother who shelled out $400 for five years' worth of dates for her incapacitated daughter. The young girl was to receive only one phone call. There were government investigations into such cases, but generally, no conclusions were ever reached.

Nonetheless, it was changing times and not questionable practices that led to the decline of computer dating (which was, at its height in 1970, a $20 million business). Single people began to look for other, more interesting ways to meet. Compared to "communes," "be-ins" and "encounter groups," computer dating was tame. It was keyed to a time when people were still shy about sex, and that time was passing.

When Jeff Tarr, one of the founders of computer dating, had said, "We're not trying to take the love out of love; we're trying to make it more efficient," people took him seriously. Even after the vogue for computer dating passed, men and women still sought to make romance less a matter of chance. Arranging dates based on videotaped interviews began in the 1980s—a trend that would probably never have occurred had it not been for computer dating.

MINISKIRTS (1965–72)

The miniskirt was a real eyepopper. What did it do? It showed a lot of leg, that's what it did. To define it in an unexciting but perfectly accurate way, the hemline of your commonplace miniskirt was at midthigh, while the hemline of the mini's first cousin, the micromini, was much higher than that. Girls wore the miniskirt to school, which in the early days many administrators tried to prohibit. Girls wore the miniskirt to work, which led one reliable polling organization to conclude that they lowered office efficiency. One gal from Iowa who was working in personnel in New York City said that her bosses approved of miniskirts, as long as they weren't too far above the knee. And another office worker put it this way, "Even at your desk, if you swing around sometimes to your typewriter, you reach a state of high indecency."

While the miniskirt was provocative and sexy, it also served another function, much like long hair did on young men. In the beginning the miniskirt was worn principally by young women, who were also making their own kind of statement, to the effect that they would do as they pleased. It was a way, too, of sneering at the proper people who made all the rules at a time when the stings of war (the Vietnam conflict) and injustice (the object of civil rights demonstrations) were constantly being felt. Let the establishment not like the miniskirt; look at what they've done with the world!

So the miniskirt was enticing, controversial. But was it ever a hot item! By 1967 it was about the only kind of skirt that a female could find without much difficulty on the department store racks. Or as one New Hampshire teen-ager put it, "You just couldn't get a long skirt." In her high school class, any girl who did not wear a miniskirt was kind of sneered at. So she swallowed her dislike and wore them, too—but she wore the longest ones she could find.

Not that most girls had to be dragooned into wearing miniskirts. To judge from a number of memories of them, most of the girls loved them. What was so great about the mini? In speaking of the "let it all hang out" sixties, most journalists and sociologists agree that the miniskirt was kind of a cry, which said something like, "Look at me. I'm free." But it was also thought enticing, particularly in combination with the accessories that accompanied it—like tights; or long stockings with holes in them, known as fishnets; or leg makeup; or boots.

However, when the first miniskirts came over to America in 1964, the style did not catch on immediately. Girls held back from wearing it, and men made fun of it, just as they did with any number of other new fashions at the time of their inception: for instance, the luxurious New Look of 1947 (see NEW LOOK) or the baglike chemise of the late 1950s (see SACK LOOK).

But within a year great numbers of American girls were wearing the miniskirt, just like their counterparts in England, where the miniskirt may well have started, having been designed by Mary Quant in the late 1950s. American youth had adopted the British look, which was known by the term *mod*. Boys had taken their long hair from that pervasive inspiration, the Beatles, and now girls, too, were copying miniskirts from the English.

It is also sometimes claimed that the idea for the miniskirt came from France, having been the brainstorm of the designer Andre Courreges.

But no matter how it started, the miniskirt had caught on big. For instance, between 1966 and 1967 at Joseph Magnin Department store in San Francisco, sales multiplied tenfold. And when fashion designers came up with the long-skirted midi look in 1968 (see MIDI), most women were enraged and held on to their miniskirts. A poll taken as late as 1970 revealed that 8 out of 10 women preferred the mini. It was definitely the style of the day. Oh, from time to time between 1965 and 1970, women flirted with other fashions, like granny dresses, Depression-era dresses, and maxi coats and dresses. But these were only brief flings.

In fact, when a number of young ladies in the middle 1970s were asked what fad they remembered best, most of them picked the miniskirt.

Yet by 1971 women were beginning to grow weary of the miniskirted look as long skirts once again became more elegant and varied. About that time, too, miniskirts were even becoming almost mandatory, and girls were sent home from high school on occasion if they were not wearing them. To say that this detracted from their charm is putting it mildly. It was the longer skirt that now drew the loudest huzzahs in department stores. By the middle 1970s the time of the miniskirt had passed. On a city street, where you might have seen hundreds of minis a few years earlier, now they were scarce.

There was a revival of the miniskirt in 1982, but it didn't reach the point of being the great rage it was in the 1960s. It was more like an amusing novelty this time around.

A young British lass in a mini-skirt.

HUNTERS AND VICTIMS (1966)

With the hunt, campus faddom took a cunning, murderous turn. It was all in good fun, though. No one could get hurt in these secret but well-planned assassinations. At worst, you might be done in by a paper cut at the hands of a sophisticated hunter.

But you could really show how clever you were. In fact, you had to if you were going to entrap that hapless victim. The hunt was based on the 1965 movie *The Tenth Victim*, about society in the 21st century, when war was not allowed. Instead, private assassination was organized, and hunters were provided with a list of victims. The victims knew only that they were on a hit list.

The first collegiate hunters were at Oberlin College in Ohio, where an IBM 1620 matched up hunters and victims—exactly the same procedure as was used in computer dating (see COMPUTER DATING). From there, stalking your prey, academe style, spread to many other campuses. On one campus an undergraduate was choked with a rosary. On another a student was reading a routine business letter sent by the bursar's office and got as far as the last paragraph, which advised him the paper had been doctored with phenylhydrazine, a contact poison. Other students were eliminated by lasers (flashlight beams) or by unexpected screeching noises or by plastic explosives timed to go off when the phone was picked up. Should you answer your date's phone call?

Speaking of dates, one hunt organizer said of the game, "There isn't much social activity on the campus, and this is a good way to meet girls." The rationale for the hunt in the movie was that since there was no war, people could use the assassinations to release their aggressive instincts; college organizers of the hunt also said that the game released academic tension. But maybe the game released both academic and interpersonal tensions. Couldn't a guy get the girl and at the same time diminish his worries about grades?

The hunt was a game played by both faculty and students. At times, though, faculty members kept track of the ground rules and awarded points to the craftiest hunters. In one typical hunt game, the prey was stalked for four days. At the end of that time, when all the cunning carnage was completed, the hunt directors evaluated the slayings. One point was awarded for an adequate killing and two points for a most resourceful one. You lost one point if you were killed by your victim and two points if you happened to kill somebody who was not on your list. The hunter who first got 10 points was declared the winner, or a "decathlon," like in the movie. And then everybody went to a party given for that best killer.

The hunt was a springtime sport, and it ended with the spring semester. When the students came back in the fall, it was not resumed. You might say that stalking your prey had become passe.

IRON CROSS (1966)

You can't do much on Lake Michigan. If you can't have a surf, and you can't have a board, at least you can have something.

—A 17-year old Chicago lad
on why he liked to wear his iron cross

Wearing the iron cross caught on big, first with the motorcycling set, then with the surfboarding set and then among kids who might have lacked a cycle or a surfboard but could still look as if they were ready to VAROOM out onto the highway or ride in with the last wave at sunset.

The iron cross, of course, had a somewhat suspect history. During and before World War II, the iron cross was the highest Nazi military decoration that could be earned. There was no denying that this turned on some youngsters, who wore it to get their parents' goat, this being the time to get involved in anything nonestablishment. Other kids, for instance, were doing the frug, that dance you did all by yourself, which went against all dance traditions (see FRUG).

However, a lot of young people didn't know about the history of the iron cross. When one distributor was asked about the year 1939 (which happened to be the year that Nazi Germany invaded Poland) on an iron cross, he said, "I just tell them it was a big year for surfing." So the iron cross became a fad of 1966. Let's let the social historians figure out if and how it was some form of protest.

And since there weren't enough iron crosses to go around, they were soon made of copper, wood, enamel and silver, too. Only a sandbug (the term antisurfers were known by) would dislike the iron cross. Yet, as with other items of jewelry, kids grew tired of the iron cross (or its copper, wood, enamel or silver equivalent).

But in its time, maybe the iron cross made motorcyclists feel more dynamic, surfboarders more free and everybody else who wore it more important. It really was harmless enough.

PIERCED EARRINGS (1966)

One jeweler reported proudly that he had pierced the ears of all the nurses who worked on a certain floor at a New York City hospital. This was in 1966, when ear piercing was new and had not yet become part of the American popular beauty scene. Of the fad for pierced ears, it was said that it "was going like an avalanche." Gals in all age groups—high school, college and older women—wanted to wear pierced earrings. But it was truly a laborious and even sometimes a painful process.

Piercing could be done either in a jeweler's shop or at home. At a shop the jeweler would spray on some kind of solution to freeze the earlobes temporarily and then insert the new earrings. One New York gal remembered closing her eyes at that point in the operation. Another gal, who had the piercing done in Nantucket, remembered that it really hurt. She was among those who would never want to have their ears pierced again. But there were also many who never regretted pierced ears—who liked the fact that they could sport new jewelry styles without fear that their earrings would fall off.

Piercing done at a doctor's office would be handled like this: The doctor "shot" in the studs (small earrings that had to be worn for about eight weeks so that the ear tissues would not grow together again) with a little "gun" after first marking their desired location on the earlobe. One quick "zap" and the earrings were inserted. However, this usually cost a little more than if it were done at the jeweler's, where piercing would sometimes be performed free with the purchase of a pair of earrings.

The home piercing method was perhaps even more difficult and painful than piercing done in the jewelry shop or by a doctor. A girl would have someone else freeze her earlobes with ice cubes, and then a heated needle would be stuck through. Nor would she be able to put on her new pierced earrings immediately. For a couple of weeks, the holes would be kept open, first by the needle and then perhaps by straws from an old whisk broom, as one girl remembered. This young lady said of the operation that "it was disgusting," but she liked the end result and has been wearing pierced earrings now for 16 years.

Way back in 1966 the majority of pierced earrings were rather small studs. As time went by, more and more styles of pierced earrings appeared: antique earrings, large and crescent-shaped earrings. A gal could get a pair of pierced earrings from under $10 to $350.

Why did girls pierce their ears? For two reasons: style and convenience. The pierced earrings were new and stunning. As often happened, an older gal in a family might start it, and then her younger sisters would want pierced earrings, too. Or among a group of friends, it might have been the thing to do. As for convenience, pierced earrings couldn't fall off.

In fact, pierced earrings have become so popular that traditional earrings had to assume a new name—clip-on earrings. Interest in pierced earrings shows no signs of waning, and today many a young lady already has her ears pierced as an infant.

Yet pierced earrings are not something every gal prefers. One woman, who has liked traditional (clip-on) earrings all along, jokingly said that she would only get her ears pierced if someone gave her diamond studs.

In the middle 1960s pierced ears were the voguish thing. In the 1970s they had become more or less accepted. To be seen as sporting something special then meant wearing items like platform shoes, designer jeans or slick leather.

ZHIVAGO LOOK (1966–67)

The Zhivago look of 1966–67 featured Russianlike fur hats, Russianlike long coats, Russianlike muffs and Russianlike tunics. The great urge to look Russian resulted from the popularity of the movie about prerevolutionary and postrevolutionary Russia, *Doctor Zhivago*, a film version of Boris Pasternak's illustrious Nobel Prize-winning novel of the same name.

Getting the Zhivago look could be fit into nearly any pocketbook. A gal could get a Tatar tunic for $25. On the other hand, Russianlike fur hats designed by Halston went for $350.

The Zhivago look—or as it was sometimes known, the Cossack look—was featured in *Seventeen* magazine. One model was shown strumming a balalaika, the Russian version of the guitar.

The Zhivago look was replaced by something more homegrown, the Bonnie Parker look (see BONNIE PARKER LOOK), with its long skirts, Depression era-like dresses and berets. Bonnie Parker herself was a murderous lady bandit in the 1930s, but when played by the glamorous Faye Dunaway in the movie *Bonnie and Clyde*, she set the latest fashion.

As for the Zhivago look, it really didn't die out completely. Much of it was assimilated into the peasant look of the early 1970s (see PEASANT LOOK), for which items worn by Slavic women served as a significant inspiration.

Batman

BATMAN (1966–68)

From the middle 1960s almost to their end, Batman, the masked marvel, rode again. This was the heyday of the comic book character created by Robert Kane in 1939. And it was made possible by full-size blown-up posters of the bathero, followed by a wildly popular television series. What did it all mean? For readers of

New Yorker magazine, it meant cartoons such as the one in which the wife reproved the husband for taking Batman seriously. For an Omaha, Nebraska department store buyer, seeing how popular Batman was, it meant saying, "Just give me anything that's got Batman on it." For schoolchildren, it meant going to classes wearing Batman outfits. And for one evening in March 1966, it meant the perils of real-life American astronauts were considered trivial compared to what was

147

happening in Batman's struggle against the evil Cat-woman. In short, for better or for worse, Batman had captivated America.

Batman was a superhero with great technological expertise and resources. Unlike Superman—who performed his life-saving exploits with his strength, his flying or his X-ray vision—Batman and his sidekick Robin would use the latest specially made gadgets: Batguns, the Batcopter, the Batboat or Batradio. In the Bat-cave—where Batman and Robin sequestered themselves when they were not saving Gotham City—they had a Batphone and a Batmobile. This up-to-dateness made Batman a particularly attractive hero, and the kids could always get their own toy Batguns, Batboats, Batradios and Batcopters.

Batmania, however, did not stop there. The world of fashion sent forth Batsportsjackets ($27), Batslippers and Battuxedos ($50). The world of musical instruments sent forth a Batelectricguitar ($125). Other worlds of merchandising sent forth Batbubblebath, Batjewelry, Battricycles, Batpens and Batquilts. Not to mention Batcapes, Batguns and Batmasks.

Why did Batmania strike so hard? For 25 years Batman and his younger sidekick Robin had had a respectable enough following. But nothing like this—nothing at all like this. For all those years it was generally acknowledged that Batman was just for kiddies and teen-agers.

Just for kiddies and teen-agers in 1966? No way! When astronauts Neil A. Armstrong (the man who eventually became the first to walk on the moon) and David R. Scott found their lives in peril during a space mission on March 16, ABC broke into its "Batman" television program with news bulletins about what was happening to the two men. In the 10 minutes that the network interrupted "Batman" to bring America the latest on the potential disaster, the ABC switchboard was flooded with calls of protest. These callers were not kiddies and teen-agers, either. They were red-blooded adult Americans interested in Batman and the Catwoman, not Armstrong and Scott. "Batman" was one of the highest-rated TV shows on the air at that time.

Armstrong and Scott escaped without injury; at the same time, Batman dispatched the Catwoman. He probably did so as a succession of ZAPs, OWWWWs, POWs, WHAPs and THUNKs flashed across the screen. Following the style used in the comic books, this replaced the physical violence and was thought extremely witty. Among "with it" adults, humor like this accounted for the show's great attraction.

To them "Batman" was satire. They just loved its combination of action with any number of strange humorous twists. They just loved the character of Gotham City Mayor John Lindseed, such an obvious parody of New York City Mayor John Lindsay. They just loved to see Hollywood luminaries playing rather silly roles. There was Burgess Meredith as the evil Penguin, Otto Preminger as the evil Mr. Freeze, Ethel Merman as Lola Lasagne and Liberace as Evil Fingers. Compared to these heavyweights, Batman, played by Adam West, and Robin, played by Burt Ward, paled. It was no wonder that *Life* magazine featured the "Batman" show on its cover on March 11, 1966.

And given the events that transpired on "Batman," you could easily see how people found the program intriguing. On the very first show—at 7:30 p.m., Thursday, January 13, 1966—the evil Penguin tried to get rid of Batman by force-feeding him into a furnace, while Molly of the Molehill Mob forced the masked marvel to batsui (an obvious parody of the then-fashionable dance, the Watusi) against his will by putting a potion in his orange juice. In another show Professor Egghead (also known as Mr. Egghead) tried to take over Gotham City by means of a legal loophole, but Batman had a way of preventing that catastrophe, too.

So at its height, "Batman" intrigued nearly everybody. Adults were captivated by its zany form of satire and kids by its action and gadgetry.

Yet in 1967 the "Batman" fad began to die out. Its television rating, which had been number 1 or 2 in 1966, fell to number 48 in 1967. Not even creating a Batgirl (Yvonne Craig) with an exploding cosmetic case could stop the decline. You could now get Batman colorforms (a toy with lift-up plastic pieces) for 69 cents, where you used to have to spend a dollar. It was rather like what had happened to Davy Crockett fur hats a little more than a decade earlier (see DAVY CROCKETT AND HIS FUR HAT).

The adults, who at one time almost adored Batman, perhaps became tired of his hokiness. Also, a chorus of older folks joined together to protect their children against the masked marvel. The National Pest Control Association, for instance, warned that little boys and girls should be prevented from touching germ-laden bats, which the kids just might do, thinking that they were fooling around with Batman himself. Psychologists warned that playing Batman made children too intensely aggressive. Schools sought to prohibit children from wearing Batman costumes, so they would settle down more easily in the classroom (what about the Batman posters in the teachers' homes? one might ask). Schoolteachers told any number of horror stories in which kids punched each other just like in "Batman." They didn't think it would cause any harm—just ZAPs, POWs and THUNKs, like on the show. Better, the kids at least used make-believe guns.

"Batman" went off the air on March 14, 1968. In the late 1970s there was a revival of the "Batman" series, and throughout the decade it was possible to see reruns. Yet it never became big time like it was in the 1960s.

When "Batman" came on the air on January 13, 1966, it replaced one of television's old standbys, "Ozzie and Harriet," the nostalgic saga of the Nelson family (Ozzie, Harriet, David and Ricky). But Batman also reached into the past—although its past was comic book heroes and comic book fun. When the fad started in 1965, it was because people went wild over Batman posters. People craved anything larger than life. The protest decade, the 1960s, was also very wearying. Many people wanted to withdraw into themselves and their dreams—a process that continued even after the Batman fad died out. A craze like Batman may have made possible the great popularity inspired by things nostalgic during the 1970s. And the bonanza of its faddom coupled with its light-hearted approach to heroes might have inspired the revival of Superman, who came back in amusing and extraordinarily profitable versions in the late 1970s and early 1980s.

Way back at the end of the 15th century, Batman first saw the light of day in prototypical drawings of a batlike flying machine by Leoardo da Vinci. Leonardo called it an "ornithopter." But there it stayed, on the drawing board until 1939. It lifted off a little bit then. But it really soared in the mid-1960s. Batman truly had made America his home.

LEG DECORATION (1966–68)

Here were some of the strangest lips, butterflies and flowers that you have ever seen, as well as some of the strangest eyes, freckles and even rattlesnakes. Why? Because they were found on bare legs of women. This was a time of miniskirts (see MINISKIRTS) and also a time when it was just the thing to look slightly bizarre as a way of teasing the "straight" world—a time of "heads," with their drug trips, and "flower children"; a time of day-glo (see PSYCHEDELIC TRIPS, BANANA SKINS, DAY-GLO, TRIBAL APPAREL AND LONG, LONG HAIR), granny glasses and love beads.

A girl could get stick-ons for her legs from $3.00 to $6.50. Or she could draw that crazy sketch on very nicely with a ball-point or a felt-tipped pen.

One related voguish item was a silver dress with a rattlesnake drawn on it. This cost $35, and the rattlesnake was crafted by the well-known Joe Eula. When this mini-skirt-length garment was worn, it was almost *de rigeur* to exhibit leg decorations with it.

Leg makeup was featured in *Harper's Bazaar* and in *Life* magazine, which said of it, "The beauty business is going out on a limb these days." Revlon sold a leg makeup kit, which consisted of colors and brushes.

By 1968 the interest in leg makeup had begun to wane. Yet though it waned, the leg makeup boom probably foreshadowed the glorious tattoos that began to appear on women in the early 1970s (see TATTOOS).

PAPER CLOTHING (1966–68)

I liked it until I put it on. I was walking down and it began to disintegrate.

—A comment on paper clothes, as reported by *The Wall Street Journal*

Paper clothes were about the most faddish item in the marketplace between 1966 and 1968, but the first paper clothes, designed in 1962, were about as far away from the earthbound American consumer as possible. Those first paper clothes—or to be more precise, garb of chemically treated paper—were developed for use by female astronauts. After a week of being worn by the ladies, the paper togs could be tossed into the stratosphere. After all, female astronauts did not really have time to worry about high fashion (at least not until the 1980s, when female astronauts manques appeared on the disco floor).

What happened in 1966, though, had absolutely nothing to do with scientific exploration and everything to do with an old-fashioned merchandising bonanza. Paper clothing had proved just fascinating to people who had absolutely no interest in blasting off for outer space. Motel owners gave travelers paper bathing suits to put on when they used the pool (it was sometimes reported that the suits caused an itchy feeling after 15 wearings). A high-fashion designer in California came up with a paper fur coat, which sold for $200 and had only one drawback: You couldn't really clean it; you had to snip off the dirty parts. There were also paper miniskirts, paper raincoats, paper suits for men, sweeping paper gowns, paper wedding dresses, paper cocktail dresses with matching paper coats, and paper bikinis. By 1967 paper clothes were a $100 million industry, in which 60 clothing manufacturers competed. It was definitely voguish to wear these perishable duds, and in January 1967 a shortage of the best paper was most upsetting to producer and consumer alike.

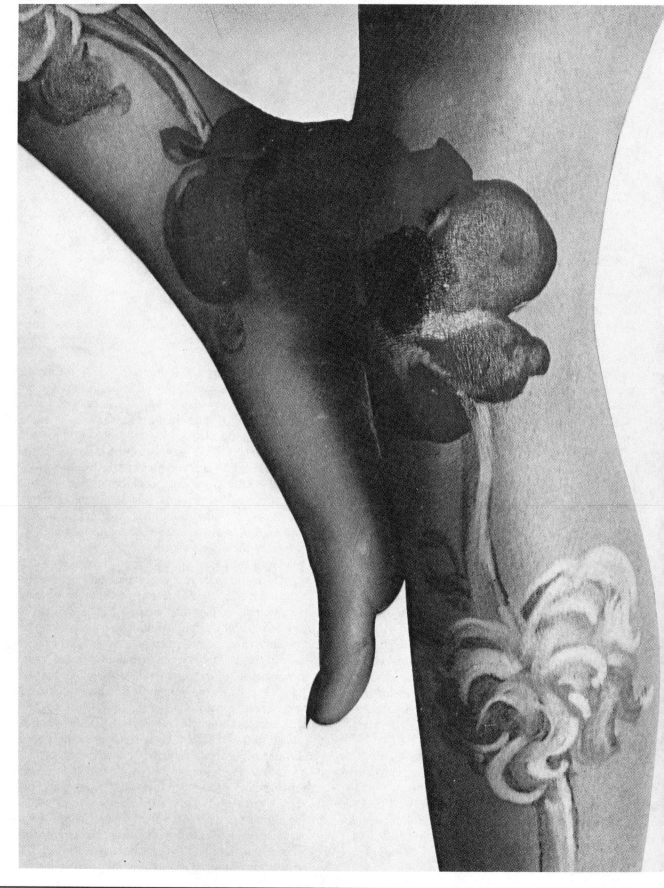

A number of shops reported that they "carried nothing but throwaway [i.e., paper] clothes."

Paper clothing appeared at a time when people were seeking new ways of showing who they were. There was the miniskirt. There was long hair on men, which though already a few years old, was still considered most striking. Paper clothes were also a great departure from the norm and were something of a lark as well. Added to that was their great convenience. You didn't have to worry about sending paper clothes to the laundry or getting a fatal spot on them.

Paper clothing attracted people who were inclined to buy high-fashion items. You could spend $15 and more for imitations of Christian Dior or Halston items. You could get yourself a gem-studded paper robe. Or as one designer put it, "You can do things with paper you wouldn't dare do with regular fabrics."

Yet paper clothing also attracted people who wanted to get their apparel cheap. And could people ever do that! You could get a paper dress for as little as $1.00, a full-length gown for as little as $4.00. In 1966 Scott Paper Company, the first company to go into the paper clothing market, sold 500,000 dresses at $1.25 each. Scott decided not to continue in the business because it didn't want to become a paper dress manufacturer. Other companies, however, picked up the slack and churned out the paper clothing "like sausages," as one manufacturer put it. In fact, another clothing manufacturer predicted that 75 percent of all garments would soon be made of paper.

That just didn't happen. Nowhere near. People got tired of paper clothing. On a number of occasions, the paper clothes proved to be flammable, when it had originally been thought that they were fire resistant. Or it would happen that paper bathing suits would disintegrate in the water, belying the original notion that paper garb was water resistant. Or it was found that they were just plain uncomfortable. Feeling paper next to your skin was not the same thing as feeling cotton, wool or nylon.

So by 1968 paper clothes were no longer a mainstream fad but had passed into the counterculture. For instance, there was a hot-selling item called poster dresses, which included paper clothes with a picture of an eye or of a hand making the peace sign, among other designs.

What paper clothes remained were only those that were 100 percent useful and biodegradable—such as gowns worn by hospital patients or disposable diapers.

BUTTONS (1966–69)

Want to make a comment about sex? Wear a button. Want to make a political statement? Wear a button. Want to state your position on religion? Wear a button. Want to make a comment that makes fun of buttons? Wear a button. Or so people must have thought in 1967, because nearly everyone seemed to be sporting a button—and, of course, not the type of button you use to fasten your clothes on tight. No, this kind of button was a conversational item, or as an owner of a button shop in New York City said, "A button is a social energizer. When you wear one, there's a difference in the way people treat you." He must have had something there. His button enterprise sold 200,000 a month for a while in 1967 and 1968, at 25 cents to $1 apiece.

It is usually maintained that "hippies" were the first group to make buttons popular. But buttons were so attractive that even "conservative" people picked up on them. Schoolteachers might wear buttons; accountants might wear buttons; housewives might wear buttons—there were buttons for everybody. And you could put them on anything: Hippies could put them on fatigue jackets, while young students could put them on schoolbags—or you could pin them on a lapel or a hat. Any visible place was appropriate.

The late 1960s were precisely the time to shout about a cause. The button was just right, with its varying degrees of seriousness. Was politics "your bag" or "your thing" (to use the late sixties idiom)? Well consider "Come Back Truman. All Is Forgiven," "Burn Pot, Not People," "Would You Really Feel Secure with George Hamilton in Uniform?" (George Hamilton was dating President Johnson's daughter.) There was also "Be Kind to Communists. They Mean Well." And there were some so famous that they came to symbolize this generation: "Flower Power," to remind people of the might of the "flower children," who were really into peace. Or "Don't Trust Anyone over 30," the slogan of the alienated young. Of course, you could wear them all. One day you might be in the mood for "Don't Trust Anyone over 30," and on another day you might want to be sexually suggestive—"If It Moves, Fondle It." Many a person could be seen wearing a jacket covered with buttons. Some read: "I Am a Human Being. Do Not Fold, Spindle or Mutilate," or even "God Is a 5,000-Foot Tall Jelly Bean." There was also "Turn On, Tune In, Drop Out," which touted "getting high" on drugs.

From "People Power" to "Poodle Power" and "Draft Beer, Not Boys," the clever slogans, concise but revealing, brought the buttons mass popularity for a few years. Sometimes they really could be downright

151

controversial. At least one lawsuit was prompted by the wearing of pornographic buttons.

No one could say much about "Anti Button," "My Button Loves Your Button" or just plain "Button," though.

In the 1970s shouting about causes became a thing of the past. Of, as the button wearers themselves probably realized, they had made their points, and there was nothing left to shout about.

GRANNY GLASSES (1967)

Granny never looked like that! Small wire-rimmed glasses, the glass often colored with pink, blue or green, the lenses themselves acutely smaller than regular-sized eyeglasses. If you couldn't find a pair in the attic, optometrists were selling them for about $50 a pair—prescription, of course.

Antique shops, thrift stores and flea markets were prime spots to find the old-fashioned glasses. Throughout New England, especially, granny glasses were both extremely popular and accessible.

Two enterprising college students spending the summer of 1968 on Cape Cod sold inexpensively made replicas of the granny glasses in Provincetown, Massachusetts. The tourists must have made their work worthwhile, because the kids reported grossing $3,000 during the course of that summer. That's a lot of glasses.

Worn by both teen-age boys and girls, granny glasses were a necessary part of the antiestablishment dress code. The standard outfit—that is, the more acceptable look with the granny glasses—included a pair of sandals, preferably worn out. Patched jeans were a must, and either a fatigue jacket or blue work shirt rounded out the outfit. This description held for both males and females (see UNISEX).

A New Jersey housewife said: "I still have my granny glasses in my bureau drawer. I can't let them go. They remind me of those important years—the idealism, the rebellion and just plain being different."

Granny glasses, along with the entire antiestablishment regalia, seemed to fade away by 1970–71. The peace movement and the rebellion of the late sixties were dissipating, as was the look that began with the use of recycled clothes and accessories.

Vision centers around the country that had been selling expensive copies of granny glasses reported that sales went from $500 a month in 1966–67 to about $50 a month by 1970.

KNEE WATCHES (1967)

Two years after glassless glasses (see GLASSLESS GLASSES), another fad hit southern California—particularly Los Angeles—which played havoc with reality as most people had come to understand it. This was when high school girls moved from wearing their watches around their wrists to wearing them just above their knees—thus carrying the time around in a much more southerly location on their bodies.

This probably occurred around August 1967. It was exotic and looked good with miniskirts. One girl did admit to *Seventeen* magazine, which recorded the season of the knee watch, that it was done to impress boys, who would be sure to check the time there. Not that the girls would display just any old time on their knees, though, for they made sure the watches were set to the absolutely correct hour.

This may strike us as a rather obvious tease. But maybe it was just luck that girls did not adopt this style nationwide and then throughout the world, for customs do indeed change. Just consider the history of men and their watches. It wasn't until the early years of this century when it became fashionable for men to wear wristwatches rather than carry pocket watches with fobs. Up until the time that dancer Vernon Castle did it (see TANGO AND DANCES OF IRENE AND VERNON CASTLE), wristwatches for men were considered effeminate.

So knee watches passed out of vogue. What replaced them? Something old-fashioned, though not as old fashioned as a pocket watch and fob. No, it was the Mickey Mouse watch once again.

TWIGGY LOOK (1967)

In the early spring of 1967, the rage was for the Twiggy look, for girls who could affect it. Now the model Twiggy herself—really, 17-year-old Londoner Leslie Hornby—was only a little twig of a thing; she wasn't the least bit buxom. About 90 pounds, she had deep-set, sad eyes with distinctive lines under them, which she called "twiggies," too, and pale facial coloring. No matter. Twiggy was the most photographed model in the world, and *Seventeen* magazine said that the fashionable look was "17 and starved."

It was true that a "full-bodied woman" who took on the Twiggy look could perhaps be made to look like a boyish innocent with a pout. Yet Twiggy was what was showing on the covers of *Vogue* and *Newsweek* magazine. It was a time when mod fashion created in Britain was the obsession and when the "flower children" were venerated. In the 1960s many of the old-time values were cast aside, and this included the traditional conception of feminine beauty.

Even Twiggy said of herself, "Hit's not really wot you'd call a figger, but with me funny face, me funny skirts, and me funny accent somehow it all combined to work out just lovely." On one occasion, however, she noted, "I've always been thin, and I've always hated it."

Twiggy first became prominent in 1966 in London, and soon enough in England there were Twiggy clothes, Twiggy perfume and even Twiggy ice cream. That was only the beginning. First, she caught on in continental Europe and then in America. One news account after another concerned itself with the "world's narrowest girl." There she was, all the time, in her beads, double-breasted suits, miniskirts and Nehru jackets. In other words, mod.

Yet the fad for being a Twiggy type lasted only that one year. By 1968 women began to look for more traditional models (or maybe newsmen did)—like Faye Dunaway's Bonnie Parker character in *Bonnie and Clyde* (see BONNIE PARKER LOOK). Now Bonnie might have been a murderess, but she certainly didn't look like a waif.

Also, the Twiggy look didn't catch on with everybody. One young New York City girl was offended when told that she looked like Twiggy, while an Indiana University coed thought the interest in Twiggy was "preposterous."

Even Twiggy ceased to like it after a while. And also, in a few years she outgrew it, which didn't bother her all that much.

NEHRU JACKET (1967–68)

That look has been fantastic; we can't keep them in stock.

—New York City clothing buyer
commenting on Nehru jackets

The many-buttoned, single-breasted and collarless jacket known as the Nehru was a big fashion item for men in the late 1960s. They were featured in all the department stores and were worn by—to name just two celebrities—Johnny Carson on the "Tonight Show" and Sammy Davis, Jr., who claimed to have over 200 Nehru suits in his closet.

The Nehru jacket was part of a "hanging loose" but elegant look, which also included wearing bell-bottom pants. It was, in fact, an outgrowth of the trendy mod look. *Life* magazine ran a spread on the Nehru in which men, women and children were all wearing the jackets.

Men could get a typical Nehru jacket from $20 to $35. It would be very nice to wear the jacket with an ornamental chain (see ORNAMENTAL CHAINS) or with a medallion, as a number of magazines advertised.

The Nehru jacket was named after Prime Minister Jawaharlal Nehru (he governed India from 1947 to 1964), who wore the coat on nearly every occasion. Yet the inspiration for wearing the Nehru jacket bore only a slight relationship to the Indian style of dress per se; the first large number of commercially produced Nehrus were made in England in the middle 1960s. The Nehru was popular because people were "into" other qualities of Indian life as they perceived it—the emphasis on meditation; the greater regard for human life; the unusual, intense music.

The Beatles, perhaps the greatest influence on contemporary life, were often seen wearing a type of Nehru; and when all the Beatles except Ringo Starr went to the Valley of the Saints in order to meditate with Maharishi Mahesh Yogi, people wanted to find out not only about the growth of their spirits there but also about what they were wearing. It was shown in newspaper pictures and reported that George Harrison liked to wear long robes with tasseled hoods, that Paul McCartney liked a long-sleeved Indian garment known as a kurta but that John Lennon still looked more Western, going around "in stupid-color pants and mad shirts." Harrison, McCartney and Lennon were only three of many (though probably the best-known) who went on this pilgrimage to be with Maharishi, and *Women's Wear Daily* even chose who the best-dressed "chela," or disciple, was. It turned out to be Mike Love of the Beach Boys.

At a time when not only fashions but also values were changing quickly, the vogue for the Nehru jacket only lasted a couple of years. To follow was the Mao jacket, which was inspired by the customary apparel of Mao Tse-tung, leader of the People's Republic of China.

A fashionable young man wearing a Nehru jacket

Ornamental Chains (1967–68)

In the late 1960s chains were very popular, first one year among women, and the next year among men. The female fad for chains was called the "New, New Look," while the male fad for chains, although it had no name, showed both the influence of the counter-culture and that men could appear to be daring, didn't have to look staid. The chain was the voguish thing.

In the summer of 1967 it was the girls who took up chains, and in definitely improvisatory ways. They put chains on their sandals or on their bikini tops or on the backs of their sunglasses. Or they hung them from their bags or their shoes. A chain could cost a girl anywhere from 79 cents to $30.

In 1968 girls were no longer sporting these chains in any great numbers—which didn't mean that chains were no longer a most fashionable item. On the contrary: The men had taken them over. These chains were not so experimental as to be worn on shoes, sandals or sunglasses—they just went around the neck, their traditional place. But if a guy wore a chain, he really cut a romantic figure.

The counterculture, or hippies, had first taken up chains for men. And by 1968 the hippies were no longer thought to be so bizarre. Much of what they did and what they wore was found to be attractive. Like ornamental chains for men.

So in 1968 you could see men wearing plain chains or chains with crosses or chains with crescents or chains with medallions. Or a man could put a chain over his turtleneck shirt or turtleneck sweater, a big garment of the period (see NEHRU JACKET and TURTLENECKS). Ornamental chains were also worn over dashikis. Many times a chain had a peace sign on it, for this was a time when antiwar sentiment was widespread because of the Vietnam conflict.

There was never any lack of celebrities who wore chains. Richard Burton was photographed wearing a chain.

Chains for men cost somewhat more than chains for women; you could get them for $7.50 to $10,000.00.

Chains for men continued into the 1970s, but by then not all that many people were paying much attention to them.

Bonnie Parker Look (1967–68)

In the 1930s, when she and her sidekick, Clyde Barrow, were robbing banks in the Southwest and Midwest, people tried to stay out of Bonnie Parker's way. This included people in Abilene, Texas; Oronogo, Missouri; Lucerne, Indiana; Okabena, Minnesota; and Alma, Texas—a few of the towns where the youthful robbers struck. Luminary 1930s hood John Dillinger said that they were punks who gave bank robbing a bad name. How times change! In 1967 and 1968 Bonnie and Clyde had become almost household names. Women tried to look like the youthful gun moll (Bonnie Parker was in her early twenties when she went on her shooting spree), and men, to only a slightly lesser degree, tried to look like the slick Clyde (then also in his early twenties).

It was all due to the popularity of Arthur Penn's film *Bonnie and Clyde*, in which Florida-born movie actress Faye Dunaway, in her first major role, played the murdering ma'am. Warren Beatty played Clyde Barrow.

The Bonnie Parker look, which was the rage not only of America but also of Western Europe, was displayed by wearing long skirts, Depression-era-style dresses and a beret. The Bonnie beret was particularly big. One hat manufacturer told Theodora Van Runkle, the high-fashion couturier who designed the beret, as well as other items that made up the Bonnie look, that "If it weren't for you, I wouldn't have had any business this year."

In fact, for a few months the Bonnie Parker look almost replaced the ever-present and enticing mini-skirted look (see MINISKIRTS). Its prevalence caused a Parisian policeman to observe of the passing scene, "I hate to see the knees disappear."

The Bonnie Parker look was also known as the "poor look." This was a bit of a misnomer, as garments in the Bonnie Parker wardrobe could cost between $100 and $500.

For people caught up in *Bonnie and Clyde* in the 1960s, Bonnie Parker was no ordinary gun-slinging gal thug. At a time when the establishment way of life was constantly being challenged or baited, her carefree bank robbing sometimes seemed to have struck the right note of defiance. What's more, Bonnie and Clyde did things in the picture—which they also did in real life—that made them appear rather engaging and aware in their outlook. Bonnie wrote poetry, and the two of them took revealing pictures of each other, the most famous of which was of Bonnie toting a gun and wearing a beret, with a cigar in her mouth.

The Bonnie Parker look passed when *Bonnie and*

Clyde was no longer *the* film that people had to see. The next cinema sensation was *Easy Rider*, the 1969 story of drifters up against the establishment, but this had no real effect on the type of fads found in the world of fashion.

Not so *Bonnie and Clyde*, which may have changed the very face of fashion. For the Bonnie Parker look may have ushered in the great fashion war of the late 1960s and early 1970s between supporters of the really high hemline and supporters of the midiskirt (see MIDI), with its midcalf length. Now this struggle would involve angry women and angry men, would confuse department store buyers and would be an object of special attention in nearly every well-known national magazine.

The Bonnie Parker long skirts and Depression-era dresses only barely predated the introduction of the midi length by French and Italian designers. It was indeed possible that its success influenced these European designers. In any case, when the Bonnie Parker look was no longer featured on dress racks, the midi look was.

Another big item made popular by *Bonnie and Clyde* was the fedora for men. Clyde had sported this in the movie.

Way back in the 1930s, in the midst of the Depression, when a lot of people were down and out, Bonnie and Clyde inspired almost as much admiration as they did fear. But they never made any inroads into the world of faddom and fashion then. No high-powered fashion designer was in attendance when they were gunned down on May 23, 1934, in rural Louisiana—far from Hollywood, New York City, Paris or Rome.

TURTLENECKS (1967–68)

A man with a short neck shouldn't wear a turtleneck under any circumstances.

—Amy Vanderbilt

Turtlenecks were the big men's fashion in the late 1960s. Arnold Palmer, the golfer, wore them; and George B. Scott, the movie actor; and Robert Kennedy, the New York senator; and Adam West, who played Batman on the television series; and Johnny Carson, who could be seen nearly every night on the "Tonight" show. But it wasn't just luminaries who wore turtlenecks; the turtleneck was also your typical dating, cocktail-partying and sporting outfit for the average guy. He could spend $100.00 if he wanted a mink turtleneck, but only $3.95 if he was willing to settle for a cotton one.

Turtlenecks were the faddish sweaters and shirts, at a time when the mod look—with its polka-dot ties, wild print shirts, hip-hugging pants and Dutch boy caps—was strong. People in their turtlenecks might don any or all of these other items as they wore this shirt or sweater, with its almost clerical collar.

In fact, they continued to wear turtlenecks when bellbottoms, polka-dot ties and Dutch boy caps went out of fashion. Yet it was 1967 that the men's fashion paper, *Daily News Record*, called "The Year of the Turtle."

CRAZY PETS (1968)

A dog does things to please you, but an ocelot is completely honest.

—a Long Island ocelot owner

The Wall Street Journal featured an article on the numbers of people who chose to own crazy pets in 1968—for example, the ocelot mentioned above. Although some people are always going to own unusual pets, *The Wall Street Journal* felt the trend that year had reached unusual proportions.

So here was the bizarre animal scene in 1968: Some people were buying baby tigers at $3,000 and up. Others purchased baby lions. Also new on the domestic zoo scene were bats, eagles, wolves, coyotes, monkeys, snakes and iguanas. Far from your usual dogs, cats, canaries, parrots and goldfish. A wolf owner from Eagle, Wisconsin said lovingly of his pet, "'Little Red Riding Hood' is the biggest farce ever presented." Statistics showed that in 1968, some 140,000 mammals and 2 million reptiles were sold in the United States. According to *The Wall Street Journal*, this proved it was a boom year for animals. A Miami doctor added that otters are easier to feed, love children more and are more appreciative than either dogs or cats. A Staten Island youth had three boa constrictors.

Not everyone liked the trend of owning unusual animals. Some people complained that pet shops were exploiting these exotic species and that species, some already endangered, were put in even greater jeopardy. As examples, they cited Texas tortoises, golden-headed quetzals and certain types of monkeys.

Buying crazy pets may have tapered off in 1969. In any event, crazy pets were no longer publicized then. The next thing that was heard about any pet rage (aside from 1975's upswing in pet rock ownership) was the obsession with cats that began in the 1970s and has continued more or less unabated (see CATS).

FAKE FACIAL HAIR FOR MEN (1968)

In 1968, due to the influence of the mod British look or the flowering of the counterculture, with its long, long hair for men, or a little of both, it was often the thing for men to have beards or mustaches. At the same time, this was far from being widely accepted, and men often found their jobs imperiled if they had a beard or a mustache, or they found themselves unable to land the job they might want. This kind of situation called for desperate remedies. Solution: fake facial hair. In 1968 a guy could get himself a really well-made beard or mustache (not something you would pick up at a novelty shop for Halloween) at a department store, barber ship or hairpiece shop. One New York City hairpiece shop alone provided any of the following mustache looks: Royal Air Force, French Foreign Legion, Pancho Villa and Errol Flynn—all costing between $10.00 and $15.00. Out West things were more expensive. A Fu Manchu-like mustache cost $17.50 in San Francisco.

So a guy could go to his job looking all clean-shaven by day and then don his facial hair at night or on the weekends. In some ways it was the best of both worlds. At least many men apparently thought so. One million facial hairpieces were sold in 1968, as opposed to 40,000 in 1967.

These happily bearded and mustachioed fellows said things like this, as recorded by *The Wall Street Journal*:

—A Detroit copy machine salesman: "I don't care to be governed in my private life by the conservative style of the businessmen" (who presumably did not have beards or mustaches).

—A New Jersey lawyer: "People tell me I look like an English colonel in mine."

Besides the fake mustache or fake beard, a man could get fake long sideburns. He could even get false eyebrows or simulated body hair. The best-sellers, though, were fake beards and fake mustaches. One Detroit salesman took no chances; at night he glued on a mustache and a Van Dyke beard. Another Detroit fellow, who was a hairdresser himself, admitted that he couldn't grow a "decent-looking mustache" and liked the manufactured kinds. Women often liked them, too: One midwestern radio production assistant said that fake mustaches made men look European, which she found most attractive.

It was not easy to create fake facial hair. It took the same skill used to make wigs—a very, very big item at this time (see WIGS FOR WOMEN). In other words, human or synthetic hair had to be worked into a well-crafted netting. Sometimes the painstaking procedure required almost half a day to create a single hairpiece.

By the 1970s, however, with real beards and mustaches much more widely accepted, there was no longer a need for the fakes, so men grew more hair of their own. But the simulations were so well-done that many guys may just have continued wearing the hair they bought in 1968. Who would ever know?

ROYAL TREATMENT FOR BEAUX, PENNSYLVANIA-STYLE (Spring 1968)

The vintage years for "going steady" among teen-agers supposedly ended in the late 1950s, but every now and again, you found a place that still took this honorable practice seriously and even adopted symbols to show how seriously. For instance, in Memphis in 1964, a girl who was dating steadily might well wear two feathers side-by-side on her head (see TELL-ALL FEATHERS).

And in 1968 in one community above the Mason-Dixon line, Hamburg, Pennsylvania, girls let their steady guys know that they were—quite literally—kings. Well, since monarchy has never really caught on in this country, this, you would think, might present some difficulties. But this is not taking into account the power of playing cards, particularly kings.

What an enamored girl (whose affection, incidentally, was returned) would do would be to get a king from any deck of cards she liked and paste the lucky boy's photo over this monarch of clubs, diamonds, spades or hearts. Then she would give the card to him.

There is no evidence that a guy would do the same with a queen from a deck, although this is something that the girl would certainly have appreciated.

If there was ever a necessity to "break up" and perhaps behead or "dephotograph" the former king, the girl would probably just have to use another king card.

Perhaps if the girl did it too often, boys would think that she was the joker in their deck.

Tots' fur coats (Fall 1968)

Fun fur is the young status symbol now.
—Salesman at Saks Fifth Avenue
department store, New York City

You could see them stepping out in a white rabbit fur. Or in a delightful sealskin. Or even in mink itself. Who were these stylish young women in fur coats? They were just beyond the newly born state—maybe 3 to 5 years old. Tots' fur coats were big in 1968. Or as *The Wall Street Journal* put it, "Young ladies these days are stepping out of diapers into furs."

Nor were these limitations on style, what with fur trench coats for tots, or coats that looked like velvet or Nehru jackets (see NEHRU JACKET). Tots' fur coats became so lucrative that one manufacturer, Daniel Fur Company, made plans to stop making adult furs and concentrate entirely on children's lines. "You're a big girl, now—too bad; our fashion is strictly for little girls," the message seemed to read. There was no arguing with success. Or as one manufacturer of children's furs put it, "I simply can't cope with any more orders."

Of course, there was a spillover effect. A lot of fur coats were sold in sizes 12 and 14 for girls who had reached the advanced age of 11. And that wasn't all. Many small older women found exactly what they wanted in the children's departments. As one such women said indignantly, "It's a free country. I buy all my clothes in children's departments."

Tots' fur coats were the rage for only one season, though. Perhaps they died out because the consumers were not the kids themselves but their parents and grandparents. And since the coats could cost as much as $800, the older folks didn't want to come up with the scratch. Why you could get lots and lots of mini-skirts for that kind of dough.

Needless to say, not everybody could shell out this extravagant kind of money for their trendy tots. Yet at the same time, the fad did catch on enough to merit comment. Those who were involved in it were probably saying, "Enough with this devil-may-care contempt for fashion that's so characteristic of the 1960s. *My* child is going to look chic."

In retrospect, the right kind of mink a tot should have worn and how she should have worn it should also have been documented in a book, like *The Official Preppy Handbook* of 1980 (see PREPPY, PREPPIER, PREPPIEST), so she wouldn't appear too gauche. After all, children are very inquisitive, and you can never start them too young as far as high fashion is concerned.

Unisex (1968)

In the 1960s people really wanted to get rid of old ideas. One such idea was that the man should dress plainly while the woman should dress much more decoratively (after all, wasn't man the dour pursuer and woman the frilly pursued?). The 1960s said no to this. Men began to sport long hair, while women did everything they could not to be seen as hothouse plants. Trendy 1960s people wanted to show that men and women were much more alike than they were different from one another. And so there came Unisex—or couples in identical bellbottoms or in identical Nehru jackets or in identical vests or in matching fatigue jackets or wearing matching jeans, designer scarves, ties or denim. Unisex was widespread and was also known as monosex, uniworld or just plain "look-alike."

There were special unisex boutiques in department stores, where women could buy army jackets and men could buy high-heeled boots. A woman could select the right tie to wear to the office, while a man could scout out the choicest ruffles. For though unisex in its most pure form was only done by couples, you could also make a unisex gesture by wearing men's apparel if you were a woman and women's apparel if you were a man.

Or consider what a high school boy might do to prepare for a date in the late 1960s. He might visit the hairstylist for a lengthy and expensive grooming—get his shoulder-length hair washed, conditioned, delicately shaped and meticulously trimmed. Then, at home before going out on the town, he might apply aromatic colognes, tanning lotion and blemish cream. Then he might step into his tight tweed hip-huggers. All this was the kind of thing women were supposed to do.

Rudi Gernreich, the American fashion designer, thought unisex was very fine, saying of it: "The true statement of our time is the emancipation of women. Unisex is a very important fact; it's the final emancipation." But in a way, he was talking about men, too. Men didn't have to be what they thought they had to be for so many years—to live up to that burdensome macho image.

It was also maintained by psychologists that unisex made young people look at things in more subtle, less black-and-white ways. One physician at the New York Psychiatric Center, Dr. Bruce Buchenholz, added that unisex was consoling: "It alleviated the anxiety of being so different." However, no conclusion was ever reached on whether the psychologists were right about these aspects of unisex. As a fad, it died before the issues were resolved.

Before it faded, however, unisex went worldwide. There were "look-alikes" in London, Paris, Moscow and Prague, as well as in New York, San Francisco, Atlanta and Minneapolis.

Yet unisex as an overpowering fashion gesture was short-lived. In only one brief season—mostly 1968—could you see a lot of men and women in look-alike jackets, vests, jewelry, etc. By 1969 it was for the most part passe.

The fad's downfall may have happened so quickly because unisex vestments remained mostly only a high-fashion item, with correspondingly high prices. It was voguish in one real sense of the word—expensive. Also, though well-known designers took to making garments in the unisex look, no really overwhelmingly original clothes were created.

In the final reckoning of things, perhaps unisex was just too gimmicky. All it really had going for it was the idea that you looked exactly like your partner, and men and women weren't supposed to do that. That kind of thing might get a little boring.

All this together led to the swift decline of the unisex look. By 1969 many a special boutique for unisex fashion had closed. Among them were shops in Los Angeles, San Francisco and New York City. At Gimbel's in New York City, the manager of the former look-alike shop said, "We had our run with unisex, and now we're out of it." The old stalls were turned into new ones that sold high-priced leather.

So "look-alikes" died. Much of unisex has remained, though, and will probably continue in fashion. That men can dress flamboyantly owes a lot to unisex, as does the idea that women can sport ties and three-piece suits. It's not quite the same thing as looking like two peas in a pod, but who is to say it isn't better?

COMBAT BOOTS AND OTHER MILITARY APPAREL (Late 1960s)

Sporting military apparel while having nothing to do with tanks, battleships, barracks or bazookas has often been voguish, as a change from ordinary skirts, overcoats, dresses or trousers. In the late 1960s in the United States, the military look was seen everywhere, but it wasn't just that it was voguish. People were protesting against the war in Vietnam by wearing items like combat boots and military khaki to decry it and ridicule it simultaneously. One New York City librarian remembers, during those times, that she had a neighbor who

always dressed in khaki and combat boots to express his anti–Vietnam War sentiment. During antiwar gatherings many young people who were melodramatically sending messages to Ho Chi Minh wore such khaki and combat boots, too. This was a time of marches on the Pentagon, of burning and defacing draft cards.

Yet there soon came a time when wearing military apparel was more of an homage to fashion than it was a reaction to politics. Just consider the combat boot, not quite a delicate item of footgear, which had to be laced up past the female ankle. Often the combat boots formed part of an ensemble, which might also include long granny skirts, denim skirts, jeans or work shirts. Ponderous to wear, these boots were surely chic, as well. A cynic might well ask why a 90-pound female college student would choose to clump along in these massive boots rather than stride briskly in a pair of noncommital walking shoes. Yet so they did throughout the late 1960s and the early years of the 1970s.

Before the American rage for military apparel ended, the French picked it up. The French sometimes showed it was very high-fashion, indeed, as items normally found in wartime went for as much as $180. The French wearing of military apparel started in St. Tropez, too, about the most "trendy" place in the world. Textile factories ran out of khaki cloth—so great was the interest in looking soldierly.

The French also added another twist that Americans rebuked. They like to wear their uniforms with insignia like stars, stripes, medals and bars on them, while in America it was considered enough just to look like a simple soldier.

Combat boots and military wear may have passed as a fad in the early 1970s, when American involvement in Vietnam was about to end. Yet the fascination has remained. In the late 1970s and early 1980s, camouflage pants traditionally worn by soldiers suddenly appeared at many a place. And it would not be surprising if any night at the disco (where clothes were supposed to be most intriguing) you were to catch sight of people sporting both combat boots and paratroopers' jackets. In such close quarters, you need them for the heavy action.

Maxi (1969–70)

It was obvious in 1969 that the only fashionable direction for hemlines to go was down. The miniskirt, the great fashion obsession that appeared in the middle 1960s, was no longer the fantastically daring garment it used to be. Far from it. It had become so commonplace and acceptable in high schools, for instance, that sometimes girls were sent home if they were not wearing miniskirts.

No wonder, then, that in 1969 girls just took to the maxi, a high-style coat that went all the way to the floor. At one department store a buyer reported that "everybody's asking for them," while a buyer said of them at another department store, "We're having a hard time keeping them in stock. Even short girls are buying them." In San Francisco maxis sold like "hotcakes." Everywhere in the fall of 1969 maxis were big: in New York City, Chicago, Boston, Denver, Dallas, Detroit, Philadelphia, Atlanta and St. Louis.

A really fancy maxi coat could cost a woman $850. But she could get a maxi for $60, too. And all tried to be colorful, coming with capes and dramatic cowllike hoods and being worn with sensual boots. When Ossie Clark, the British fashion expert, predicted in the summer that the maxi was on its way, saying, "This summer will be one last fling to show your legs. Next year the idea will be to wrap 'em up warm," he was

dead right. By winter the maxi—the coat worn from neck to ankle—was the hottest item.

Yet the maxi turned out to be shorter-lived than most people would have thought. The reason was that many women found these big coats rather cumbersome to walk around in, just like what had happened with the hobble skirt in the early 20th century (see HOBBLE SKIRT). The hobble skirt got its name because it seemed to make women hobble. Now, about six decades later, women said they had a lot of trouble getting in and out of cars, climbing on and off trains, and riding on escalators because of the maxis. One fashion designer said that American women didn't know how to walk and therefore couldn't very well maneuver the maxi.

In any case, making sure that your maxi wasn't getting in the way or hiking it to walk up stairs was becoming a bit too much to take for a lot of women.

So the maxi kind of faded out of the picture. And what came next? The direct opposite: hot pants. The only thing the two garments had in common was the high price of fashion. Next to the maxi, which used yards of material, hot pants used next to none. And the hot pants' hemline was about as far away from the foot as you could get.

Hot pants started in the early winter months of 1971. A maxi would have been nice to protect against icy storms, but no one ever thought of that.

160

INTRODUCTION

The present. You're living in it. So what is true today may not be true tomorrow. Early this year (1983), wallwalkers—those eight-legged insectlike devices that crawl creepily down when placed upon a wall—were thought to be the coming fancy, but somehow the centipede craze passed without creating very much of a storm. You could never say that wallwalkers caught on the way slinkies, for instance, did. Video games, too, which with their thousand and one variations have been popular for a while, have at least temporarily reached their saturation point; *The Wall Street Journal* reported in June, 1983 that diminishing expectations of profitability led to the production of 50% fewer games in 1982 and that the "typical" video game lost money. There may also have been a decline in interest because of video games' new image: that they triggered peoples' latent aggressiveness. At the same time, however, Pac-Man has remained as much of a craze as ever, and Donkey Kong has been really popular, too. You'd have to be able to read a crystal ball to know what will happen next.

Back in the 1970s, there was a kind of trend among fads. After the first few years (ending perhaps in 1973), in which the "hippie" counterculture continued to thrive, a reaction set in; the obsession with Love Generation symbols like long, long hair on men passed, as did the general enthusiasm for political controversy. In its stead, people's interests turned to really jokey items. First there was the pet rock, followed by *The Nothing Book*, the mood ring and bottled money—all downright frivolous items. It appeared that the country needed time out after all those years of tension.

In addition to the "new frivolity," three other fad trends were unmistakable in the seventies. The first was (and is) an interest in new kinds of sensual pleasures, such as those that could be experienced in water beds and hot tubs. The second has been a fascination with the past that resulted in a nostalgia vogue. For instance, there was the Gatsby Look and the mania for wearing antique clothing; then, later an interest in the dress and life-style of the fifties took hold, with people doing everything from coveting old "I Like Ike" campaign buttons to clamoring for tickets for Howdy Doody show revivals. This nostalgia kick is still continuing. The third fad trend was the interest in science fiction paraphernalia and movies that followed in the wake of *Star Wars*.

At the end of the seventies decade and continuing into the early eighties, the frivolous trend took on a bookish tone. Overwhelmingly big was Lisa Birnbach's *The Official Preppy Handbook*, which inspired any number of preppie parodies like *The Joy of Stuffed Preppies* and *101 Uses for a Dead Preppie*. The popularity of the 1983 best-seller *Real Men Don't Eat Quiche* would not have been possible but for this revolution in correct personal appearance/conduct instructional books started by Ms. Birnbach.

But now that nearly 3/10 of the 1980s have passed, it appears that (aside from book parodies and put-downs) no really distinct fad theme has emerged—nothing like the way dancing was big in the 1910–20 decade or endurance stunting was big in the 1930s or fads of youthful defiance were big in the 1960s.

What does the future hold? Of course, it's impossible to say for sure, but the popularity of Rubik's Cube and personal home computers may be a hint that the 1980s could become the decade where solving intellectual puzzles all by your lonesome is considered the most voguish thing. The practice of cogitating over mental puzzles could acquire a catchy name (say, *cawjitating*), be hyped on a national television, get a participating movie actor or rock star to lead the way—and it just might be flagpole sitting, goldfish swallowing and streaking all over again!

WIDE-WIDTH TIES (Late 1960s–1970)

Until the late 1960s wearing a necktie was a very commonplace thing to do. Some neckties had more color or more stripes than others, but no necktie was truly eye-catching; it would, in fact, be really inappropriate for a man to wear an eye-catching tie. And then there came to America from England the mod look—with its boots, print shirts, double-breasted suits and Dutch boy caps. And with its ties—flamboyant, with polka dots, flowers and many other kinds of vivid new prints. And their size was flamboyant, too—the width of a man's hand. It was the thing to wear a wide-width tie now. These cravats—also known as elephant ties—had become the fad.

You found men sporting wide-width ties showing poppies, irises, daisies and tulips. Or from a department store you could buy a tie showing nothing less than a rose garden, with other vibrant colors besides. Nor was that the most unusual thing about the rose tie: It was six feet by two feet. This might have been most unusual, but it wasn't a tie that was bought terribly often. Most men were not overly fond of the idea of looking like a billboard—even a mod billboard. This was, of course, just a novelty.

Or you could buy (or be given) other flamboyant wide-width ties, depending on your taste and/or how well the giver knew you. For your delectation there were ties showing Hawaiian scenes and palm trees, or wild paisleys with lush forest vistas. You could also adorn your neck with a tie showing a mountaintop or two. For Christmas of 1970 wide-width flamboyant ties were a really popular and fashionable gift.

What a change! Men who were used to wearing pin-striped suits with regimental-striped ties now decked themselves out in seven-inch ties with a sun-drenched beach motif. Not to mention all the polka dots, big in the late 1960s, which had now become commonplace.

There was even many a tie around that went with love beads or somehow managed to give the right effect to long, long hair.

Yet the elephant ties only caught on in a big way for those few years. Why? One problem was the huge knot that resulted from all that fabric. Another was that the ties made men with short necks look as if they had no neck at all.

So men began to lose interest in the wide-width flamboyant look. Yet like unisex (see UNISEX), the interest in these big, flamboyant cravats proved that men were not going to go back to looking commonplace—just plain dull and traditionally masculine. They would now sport not only wide-width ties but really intriguing bow ties (see BOW TIES) and, at the end of the 1970s, ties so skinny that they just barely covered a couple of shirt buttons. Ties were becoming a remarkably versatile way to make a fashion statement.

ANTIQUE CLOTHING (Late 1960s; Early 1970s)

Fashion-minded young people in the late 1960s began rummaging around in attics, basements and garages and haunting thrift shops to come up with the apparel they really wanted to wear—old clothes. This obsession soon had a name, *antique clothing*, and became one of the fancies that someone might want to participate in. For instance, a couple might go to a rock concert where there was the latest in the many-colored variations of psychedelic lighting (see PSYCHEDELIC TRIPS) in such antique clothing as a fur coat with shoulder pads and a Humphrey Bogart trench coat. Then they might remove their antique outer garments and—lo and behold: bellbottoms or a miniskirt. You could see men in baggy suits from the 1930s and big fedoras from the 1940s, or a gal wearing a blouse with puffy sleeves from the 1930s. To cater to this trade, over 10,000 antique clothing shops had opened across the country by 1969. They carried everything—from hats to scarves, from old-fashioned suits to high-button shoes. Since these cast-off clothes were so popular, their prices skyrocketed. A blouse from the 1940s cost about $35, and a moth-eaten wool coat from the late 1930s could go for as much as $150. While you could sometimes find an antique dress for $5, you might also have had to spend as much as $300.

This was a true rage, far overshadowing the fad of 1920s raccoon coats that suddenly reappeared in 1957 (see RACCOON COATS). That fad stayed more or less in the New York City area or in college towns, but the antique clothing fad spread nationwide. Though not too many people realized it then, it presaged the nostalgia craze of the 1970s, which was to include anything from the past that could be dragged into the present—like Flash Gordon uniforms, Mickey Mouse watches or saddle shoes.

Let's take yet another example of the mania for antique clothing. One of the more striking pictures from the period appeared in *Time* magazine in 1969. It showed a young woman in a very 1940s-looking hat with a black veil covering her face. She also wore a huge fur coat from the same period. Under the coat, however, could be seen a pair of contemporary patched jeans.

There were also hand-crocheted shawls, very grandmotherly and very trendy. Or silk scarves—usually white on white, straight out of a Fred Astaire movie from the 1940s—adorning the necks of many.

Although the antique clothing fashion has continued to the present, the rage has really calmed down. It is no longer like the late 1960s or the early 1970s, when you simply *had* to have something antique to go with your maxi or your hot pants or your Mao jacket or your turtleneck.

Wigs for Women (Late 1960s–1973)

Wouldn't it be smart if you have a blue dress, blue stockings, blue shoes, and a blue wig?

Eva Gabor, President of
Eva Gabor's International Wig Boutique

Wigs went back to ancient Egypt, then first became popular in the modern Western world in the 18th century. In the 20th century, in America, they were biggest in the late 1960s and early 1970s. Women who wanted to be with it wore them, as did women who might otherwise have thought wigs were a silly indulgence. One such austere type from Pennsylvania wore a wig to her daughter's wedding. She left it in the New England town where the wedding took place, and when the wig was sent back to her, she was very embarrassed. And there must have been many a woman like the one who got married in a longish-length wig because her new husband had admired her in long hair and her natural hair was not growing out fast enough.

This was not the typical case, though. Most ladies who donned the purchased hair were quite proud of it and may have owned a number of different wigs. Did the turn of the century Gibson Girl look please her? She could get a Gibson Girl wig. What about a flashy ponytail? That, too, was available. Or long braids. Or an Afro. Or to bring back the 1930s, Shirley Temple ringlets. The hairdresser Kenneth predicted that the wig would be the hat of the 1970s. Theodore Friedman, president of Paragon Hair, said, "Wigs will slowly but surely replace the hair coloring industry."

The wig craze began in Rome in 1968, but by 1969 it had taken the United States by storm. Stores in many of the major cities—New York, Los Angeles, Chicago, Denver, and Houston—all reported that wigs were quite the thing. Their voguish character was so pronounced that both banks and big grocery stores offered wigs as premiums. One typical case was a bank in Muncie, Indiana, where, with a $100 deposit, you would be able to buy a $29.95 wig for $9.95. The officers of the bank said that the response was "overwhelming." Another reaction was that they sold like popcorn.

Wigs were becoming very, very popular at a time when men, too, were beginning to sport fake mustaches and beards (see FAKE FACIAL HAIR FOR MEN). The men probably got their inspiration from the women, but you never know: In one family, it might have been that way; in another family, it might have been the other way around.

When wigs first came out, you could get them for from $15 to $300. Different cities had different best-selling wigs; in Los Angeles, for instance, in 1970 the big wig was called a "lion's mane."

A lot of things made the wig popular. It was new and exciting, and one lady said that a wig was just the thing for her when she was down in the dumps. Another great advantage of the wig was that, supposedly, it didn't cost any money to keep up. But before long, the hairstylists questioned this very notion. They said that women would have to learn that wigs had to be cut and styled, just like natural hair did.

By the early 1970s, wigs had become quite commonplace and were no longer the stylish thing. As a result, the price of wigs dropped. You could get a $50.00 wig for $8.95 if you were really lucky. But even if you couldn't do that, you could easily get a $40.00 wig for $16.90.

Why did the wig lose its compelling attraction? It was partly because the shag hairdo became the style and partly because women no longer found wigs fashionable. In the wig's heyday hairdressers themselves acknowledged that it took several wearings for a lady to get used to a wig. Now a lot fewer ladies saw the need to try them even once.

Flamboyant Bow Ties (Early 1970s)

They were blossoming all over the financial purlieus of Wall Street in the early 1970s, having already conquered the advertising purlieus of Madison Avenue. Perched neatly under the chins of the most respectable businessmen, bow ties had made a comeback.

During the early 1920s, bow ties were so universal that they seemed to be *the* thing that a serious gentleman must wear. They were also considered very dapper. Yet most of them appeared to be black—no lavish pastels or patterns.

Then the bow tie left the scene for a while, only to come back in the early 1940s as an accessory to the zoot suit—that exaggerated-looking, baggy dress suit often worn with chains (see ZOOT SUIT). The bow tie that went with it was also unusual: Generally black, it extended past the wearer's neck almost a quarter of the way to his shoulders.

Not until 1970, however, did the bow tie become really flamboyant, as the successor to the wide-width tie (see WIDE-WIDTH TIES). This was part of the revolution wrought by the mod look from Britain—with all its pheasantlike plumage (which was acceptable for men), such as double-breasted suits, wild print shirts, boots, Dutch boy caps and also giant ties such as the polka dot variety. No really colorful bow tie was introduced with the mod look, but someone must have thought that what was good enough for any other item of apparel was good enough for bow ties, too. And bow ties had historically been considered really natty. Thus, the era of the flamboyant bow tie had arrived.

So in 1969 the new bow tie emerged, and it was both a stunner and a favorite. In truth, it really wasn't exactly a bow tie. It was something almost the size of a bow tie but with a shape that looked like a butterfly; it was thus called a "big butterfly bow." They gave a slightly floppy look, these butterflies that were designed by well-known people like Pierre Cardin and Nino Cerruti.

The butterfly tie was nice but was seen as something of a novelty. Men began to reason that if they wanted a bow tie, why not get a bow tie, and not a close variation on it like the butterfly. So bow ties became unabashedly flamboyant, colorful and even, sometimes, the star of the outer vestments. People would look not at the pants, shirt, or jacket, but at the bow tie. Small wonder. Models were sporting them in *Vogue*, *Gentleman's Quarterly*, and the *New York Times Fashion Supplement*.

A chic bow tie would cost you between $2.50 and $10.00.

Yet the bow tie vogue did not last. Bow ties were replaced in the fashionable male imagination by really pronounced wide-width ties, longer and more flamboyant than the first mod ties that came out of England. Perhaps this was the fashion world's compensation for how little material had been used on the bow tie.

Nothing much would happen with really small ties until the skinny tie at the end of the 1970s (this was the type that made the bow tie look like a monster). But who ever said that times don't change?

COUGHING ASHTRAYS (Fall 1970)

Here was something just a little bit out-of-the-way and slightly morbid—a fad that parodied the smoker's cough. A fun-loving smoker would stub his or her cigarette in this special ashtray. At that moment a battery was activated, causing coughing noises to be emitted from the heart of the ashtray for 18 seconds. The coughing ashtray must have been the life of any number of cocktail parties, or (who knows?) it could have been pulled out at business conferences or at luncheons with easily amused clients.

It cost just $9.

The fad was also entertaining for nonsmokers. With the coughing ashtray they could show their opinion of smokers.

While this was the kind of joke that could last only a season, the fad was at least longer than the duration of a smoke.

Perhaps in the final analysis the fad for coughing ashtrays passed so quickly because it was really kind of nasty, reminding people of the perils of smoking as it did.

APE HAIR STYLE (1970)

One of the first fashionable hairstyles of the 1970s was the ape. It is thought to have been dubbed this because some of the young people who adopted the special cut said it looked like the hair on an ape. The ape cut was versatile, however; it could be shaped in any number of ways. Sometimes the hair fell like a veil, other times like a helmet or even like sideburns. About its extreme popularity, there was little doubt. Between June and October 1970, when ape was in, Ingrid Bergman, Julie Christie, Mary Quant, Jane Fonda and the Duchess of Windsor all sported the look.

Even the most famous hairstylists, like Vidal Sassoon and Alexandre, came up with their own variations of the ape cut. And as far as salons go, they are about as far up on the evolutionary ladder as you can get.

The most common form of the ape consisted of long hair in the back and short hair in the front. The cut itself was compared to a pile of leaves or to a wet mop. Nor were these demeaning terms. Women liked the idea of affecting a little natural unkemptness. As one actress said of the ape's best quality: "It's untidy." The *New York Times*, however, did not look on it so favorably, saying it "looks like the offspring of Mick Jagger and Raggedy Ann."

Posterity never did find out who was right about the ape: The hairstyle was out by 1971.

CHOKERS (1970)

This little item, worn around the neck, looked very much like a dog collar. Chokers were made of suede, beads or even elephant hair, and they cost from $1.50 up.

And maybe as a spoof, they were popular among women in 1970. One Ohio lady said of them, "I love chokers. I wear them all the time, but I refuse to call them dog collars." While another woman added, "Dog collars are a great look. Black velvet ribbon with a cameo is my favorite." Now there was a woman with discerning taste.

This was the kind of look that could last only a very short time.

MUTTONCHOPS (1970)

A man sitting at a desk on Wall Street in the financial district of New York City was dressed in a typical business suit, and no one would have given him a second look until they saw his peculiar kind of sideburns. They were long and full, but they were also shaped to look like a cut of meat, or more precisely, a mutton chop. A standard hairstyle for turn-of-the-century men had returned. It was a time when long hair was going out after a very extended run.

It was the sideburns that were all-important when someone sporting muttonchops went to the barber, and more attention was paid to them than to the hair that sat firmly atop the skull. A man wanted to walk out of the barbershop with his sideburns trimmed neatly and contoured precisely. It got to the point that one Brooklyn, New York barber, who did more of a business in muttonchops than the neighborhood butcher, wanted to put up a joking sign proclaiming "No Mutton Chops Sold Here."

Being styled with muttonchops did not come cheaply. While an ordinary haircut cost $5.00, a muttonchop look cost $7.50.

In a way, it was much harder for men to have muttonchops, for they took extra time to groom. Yet their neatly sculptured look was such a contrast to untrammeled long hair that it is no wonder many men liked them.

Yet, after a while it was also maintained by many men that muttonchops filled out the face too much, making their faces appear overly round and full. This may have been one reason why the look was in vogue for a relatively short time, passing within a year. Another was that men had become much more aware of hairstyling (a trend that has continued until the present day) and wanted to try other cuts that fit their personal temperament better.

MIDI (1970–71)

Midi means a skirt whose hemline is at midcalf length. Sound uncontroversial enough? Well, in the early 1970s the midiskirt was dynamite, for some an item of high fashion, for others something to be abominated—but something in any case on nearly everyone's mind. One Chicago gal said about the midi, "If the midi becomes the style, I'll commit suicide or murder. I'll stay out of the store for four years if I have to." Organizations like GAMS (guys and gals against more skirt), FADD (fight against dictating designers) and SMACK (society of men who appreciate cute knees) bloomed from coast to coast. At a Cincinnati store a mock funeral was held for the miniskirt, a ritual complete with open casket; but the women didn't turn out to mourn. The 1970s may have been a time in which noninvolvement became almost a password, but it was ushered in with one major conflict, at least in the fashion world.

What was the big fuss? The big fuss was that many of the ladies, and many of the gentlemen, too, wanted to continue wearing or admiring the miniskirt, the great fashion obsession of the mid- to late 1960s (see MINISKIRTS). Let there be no mistake, the miniskirt was skimpy, going to three inches above the knee and higher. One Massachusetts girl said of the effect of the miniskirt, "I have pretty legs, and I like to show them." The war was waged not only in the salons and the offices of this country but also on the highways. One bumper sticker read, "MINI, YES! MIDI, NO!"

The midiskirt came on the fashion scene in 1968. Why it did so is not completely clear, because miniskirts were still selling wildly. It may have been that some French and Italian designers decided that women needed a new fashion in dress, but it was also true that a small number of women were beginning to wear a medium length spontaneously. The length of skirt was knows as le long look, or the longuette, because of what was taken as its Parisian inspiration.

As early as 1968 people were warned, "If you like knees, look quick." The luminaries picked up on this, and by 1970 Princess Grace of Monaco, Ethel Kennedy, Jacqueline Onassis and Princess Margaret of England were all wearing midiskirts. A lady could get a high-fashion midi starting at $120.

At this point the big midi furor was kicked off. The influential New York City fashion newspaper, *Women's Wear Daily*, featured the midi look, and other magazines soon followed suit. And sure enough, the midi was big in New York City and San Francisco—but not in too many other places. Negative comments about the midi kept popping up. Things like, "I don't want to look like an old lady," or "The midi is all right in its place, like in a dungeon." The apparent flop of the midi also became a hot item in the press. This news was flashed in *Time, Newsweek, Life, The Wall Street Journal* and *Forbes* magazine.

Well, the journals spoke too quickly. By 1971 the midi had become the rage. An official at Lord & Taylor's department store in New York City said of the midi, "Last year we had [unsold] racks of the things . . . this year, girls come in by the dozens and ask for midis." Perhaps women had become tired of the let-it-all-hang-out miniskirted look after all. There were places, like public schools, in which girls were now required to wear miniskirts, and if they didn't, they were sent home. Intimidation of this sort has never been a contributing factor in what garments become really popular at any given time, though. People just want to wear things they regard as fun and exciting.

Moreover, the midis themselves had become much more varied. Whey they first came out, only their hemline was significantly different from the miniskirts. But now the midi appeared with all kinds of new and intriguing wrinkles—zippers, buttons and slits. Midis with slits were a particularly big item.

As the 1970s continued, midiskirts became slightly passe. However, the hemlines women generally wore were now much closer to the midiskirt than they were to the old mini.

So when the miniskirt came back in the early 1980s, that was hot news. Many girls who wore it then thought they were doing something special. And what about that old 1960s mini? A few puzzled girls asked, "Wasn't that something Mother wore?"

PLATFORM SHOES FOR WOMEN (1970–71) AND PLATFORM SHOES FOR MEN (1971)

We made 'em like doughnuts.
    —Manufacturer of platform shoes for men

Platform shoes for women, called such because the sole of the shoe was raised up like a platform about two inches thick, were a brief fad of the early 1970s. Although they never quite reached the burning intensity of the rage for hot pants (see HOT PANTS), with which they were often worn, they were striking. They were also worn with miniskirts (see MINISKIRTS), maxi coats (see MAXI) and fishnet stockings. *Seventeen* magazine shows illustrations and advertisements—one after the other—of platform shoes.

The heel of the platform shoe was very high—perhaps five inches—dwarfing plain old high heels.

Yet in thinking back on platform shoes for women, a New York officeworker remembers that they really didn't pop his eyes out. This is because platform shoes were not all that different from high heels—a sophistication, perhaps, or a more sensual look, but that's all.

Now platform shoes for men—that was a whole other story. You just don't associate platform shoes with men, and there they were, a very popular item. A *Newsweek* writer said of them, "I was nearly 6 feet tall for the first time in my life," and went on to say that it was the feeling of "instant King-Kong." At a Milwaukee shop 1,500 pairs were sold in three minutes.

There were also platform boots. Shoes usually went for $35, boots for $50.

Three years before 1971 there had been an attempt to manufacture platform shoes for men. This had turned out to be a bust. But during these intervening years, man himself must have gotten more fashion-conscious, wanting to become a "peacock in his apparel," as Meyer Magid, executive vice president of a clothing conglomerate, said. Men just couldn't get enough of platform shoes. To be sure, they were much different from loafers or tie shoes. They were, well, *unusual*.

Often the prototypes for the platform shoe were made in Europe, with cheaper copies being produced in the United States. One manufacturer who used this method admitted that he had "to knock out copies so fast, it's not even funny."

As with the case of hot pants only a little earlier, platform shoes were made for men after they were made for women. Yet the two experiences turned out to be dissimilar. Hot pants for men were immediately taken as a joke and remained a joke. Platform shoes for men, however, caught on. Anyone can devise his or her own explanation for this.

Platform shoes for men were just too unusual a novelty to last for long. Yet a Brooklyn, New York man remembers a time he rode the subway and, in looking all around him, saw what appeared to be a whole carful of men wearing platform shoes.

By 1972 men had reverted to normal-soled shoes. But many of these fellows then adopted shoe styles that made them look not as if they were living in the 1970s but as if they were living in the 1920s and getting ready for a big date with a flapper. As for women, those high platform shoes were also thought to be a trial to wear after 1971; it was just too much trouble to be so provocative. What's more, a normal-sized pair of high heels was found sexy, too. So why be a giant?

TAROT (1970–71)

In the early 1970s one thing that people turned to in order to figure out life's mysteries was the deck of tarot cards. Though its history went back to 14th-century Italy and perhaps even earlier, tarot, with its 78 cards and their mysterious faces, had become contemporary once more. Books like *Ancient Tarot Symbolism Revealed*, *The Sexual Key to the Tarot*, *The Devil's Picture Book*, and *The Windows of Tarot* were published. A rock group called itself The Fool, after a major tarot picture card. In the musical *Hair*, perhaps the best-known celebration of the counterculture, large copies of tarot cards were used as part of the stage set. There was even a game played among teen-agers called strip tarot, although it had nothing to do with physically disrobing. The players would sit around on the floor, deal with the tarot cards and then tell about themselves.

The word *tarot* comes from the medieval Italian *tarocchi*, or playing cards—but these playing cards were also often seen as tablets that predicted fate.

Telling about yourself by tarot came about as a result of interpreting the major picture cards, which have always been known by the name of the *greater arcana*, meaning very secret. So players would analyze cards that depicted death, the wheel of fortune, the magician, the hermit or the moon. There are 78 tarot cards in all, and the greater arcana makes up 22 of them.

There were also experienced tarot readers. A full read by one of them, in which the cards were gone through one-by-one, might have taken an hour and a half. The subject of the tarot would first shuffle the cards himself or herself, thus unfurling his or her own destiny. Magazines like *Time*, *Look*, *Mademoiselle*, *Playboy*, *Rolling Stone* and *Vogue* all discussed the tarot phenomenon.

The interest in tarot was part of a resurgence of an obsession with things astrological in the early 1970s. This was true even though tarot has little in common with astrology, depending upon interpreting a deck of cards rather than the stars in the sky. (One astrologer, when asked about tarot, said that the two had less in common than a surgeon does with a psychiatrist.) Most people, however, saw them as equally intriguing and inscrutable. This was a time of zodiacal highballs and cocktail glasses, of astrological writing paper, of psychic jamborees. About the most popular opener in conversations was "What's your sign?"

Another thing that intrigued people about tarot was the appearance of the cards themselves. Just think of it—a deck of cards that could tell an exciting (or tragic) story, depending on how they were turned: A hanged man could turn up or a burning sun or two lovers (would they be doomed?) or a tower. They were lovely to look at in the 1970s and have been so since they were first printed in the late Middle Ages. You could get a copy of such a deck for as little as $7.95.

The tarot deck was the forerunner of the deck of playing cards we know today. The four tarot suits—cups, wands, swords and coins—have become the hearts, diamonds, spades and clubs. A major picture card, the fool, is now known as the joker. The other arcana cards have been eliminated from the modern deck, though. That is why today's deck of cards consists of only 52 cards and 2 jokers.

Tarot has continued to the present. But the time when college kids in great numbers were interpreting their destiny by tarot in the quiet candlelight seems to have passed. To learn their destiny, all they have to do now is pick up the telephone and dial a recorded horoscope message. And never will they get any of these tarot charmers like the magician, the hanged man, the sun or the tower.

HOT PANTS (January–May 1971)

Hot pants were hot, those women's shorts that went well up the thigh. Hot not only because they were sexy but because they were *the* thing to wear in the early months of 1971. Girls showed up for college classes clad in hot pants, and they showed up that way in offices, too, which sometimes led to a lot of negative feedback from supervisors. Some women embraced this fashion halfheartedly though. One woman remembers going to a movie theater with hot pants on, covered by a coat. She didn't take the coat off all evening—she was that embarrassed.

Yet judging from the fact that hot pants became a fad of multimillion-dollar proportions, sheepishness was not the customary attitude of those wearing them. Rather, the question of the day seemed to be what kind of hot pants should be worn: There were mink hot pants, satin hot pants, cotton hot pants, denim hot pants and leather hot pants, to name just a few of the fabrics that had been "hotted up." A stylish pair of velvet hot pants could cost $60. Sometimes, it seemed that charging the highest price for the least amount of fabric was the name of the game.

One reason for all this was the great vogue for the miniskirt in the late 1960s and early 1970s; this excited the admiration of most men and many women (though not all—that's for certain). However, in the early 1970s, a longer dress known as the midiskirt (see MIDI) had begun to come back. It at first prompted scorn. Well, the designers reasoned, if the miniskirt was out and their midiskirt was not yet accepted, why not hot pants? That may have been their thinking in the late months of 1970, when hot pants first appeared in Europe. In Paris people danced the night away in hot pants, while in Rome hot pants with sequins were a big item.

It wasn't long before hot pants had become big in America, too—about February 1971. Here was a whole new continent, with millions of new customers, whose entire legs suddenly looked almost completely bare, while the pants themselves were skintight. Hot pants action was brisk; consider the reaction of a New York City boutique manager: "The way women are buying [the hot pants] and men are acting, it would seem that legs have been out of sight for ten years, not ten months."

To add to the provocative effect, hot pants were often worn with platform shoes (see PLATFORM SHOES FOR WOMEN and PLATFORM SHOES FOR MEN).

Ironically enough, hot pants became a big item in the midst of a very cold winter. This may have said a lot for women's stoicism in withstanding wickedly chilly winds.

But if the women who wore them were stoical, other people were often less so. You might even say they complained like the dickens. For instance, the Metropolitan Life Insurance Company of New York forbade hot pants for its employees, as did the Irving Trust Company, complaining that the garments lacked

the necessary "decorum." If you worked for the Manned Spacecraft Center in Houston, hot pants were out there, too. Also at any number of banks in Detroit; Boston; Chicago; Dallas; Portland, Oregon; and Atlanta. The same was true of many a school. One school noted that it was bad "for the learning situation," and that "Hot pants would distract boys." In one Atlanta school they were roundly disapproved by administrators who considered themselves quite progressive: After all, bermuda shorts and culottes were allowed. Nor was that the end of problems hot pants wearers faced: Sometimes they couldn't even eat at their favorite fashionable place. One restaurant in Cleveland suggested that a hot pants wearer stay out of the main restaurant and limit herself to the coffee shop.

Yet it was only some of the time or only in certain places that hot pants were outlawed, which added to the prevailing furor. It was a great sport to try to find a place where hot pants were accepted, though there must have been many people who simply got a kick out of causing a scandal. At the Pewter Mug in Atlanta, restaurant policy was to allow "all the hot pants we can get." The manager of Daly's Dandelion, a restaurant and singles bar in New York City, said, "Our customers are definitely wearing them," while a manager of the Broker, a Denver restaurant, observed that "Four ladies came in here yesterday wearing them, and they look pretty exciting to me."

Nor were all places of business so restrictive about hot pants. Stewardesses for Allegheny Airlines were given blue hot pants as part of their new spring-summer uniform ensemble. National Bank of Washington, D.C. welcomed them in its "progressive" tradition, just as it had welcomed boots and pant suits before. Churches were even more open to the wearing of hot pants, for the most part. This was a far cry from the end of the 19th century and the early 20th century, when sermons were sometimes delivered against such fancies as bicycle riding and the tango.

You can't get too much of a good thing, and before you knew it, men's clothing manufacturers also started to turn out hot pants. Two guys, friends who were trying on the very trendy hot pants for men, were overheard in the dressing room of New York City's Bloomingdale's. Their wives were waiting outside the dressing room while the men, sounding like small boys, each encouraged the other to walk out of the dressing room first. Finally they emerged, to guffaws of laughter from their wives. Quickly retreating to the dressing room the fellows changed clothes and rather shamefacedly left the store.

In general, men's hot pants did not fare as well as women's.

Winter ended, and spring came. The weather got to be balmy. You would now expect that if hot pants had been big before, they would now become extra gigantic. This did not happen. Instead hot pants faded—became a thing of the past. Showing legs seemed to be strictly a winter sport. The next time there would be such wild abandon—near nakedness—in clothing would be in summer, though: in 1974, the year of the string bikini.

CLACKER BALLS (1971)

Clacker balls were one of the first crazes children had in the 1970s. They were two hard plastic balls connected by a cord. When the cord was swung rapidly with an up-and-down motion, the two balls would strike together sharply and repeatedly. Kids liked clacker balls because they whizzed rapidly and gave a delightful whirling impression. One young man from Wisconsin remembers that when he was younger he and many of his friends had contests to see who could make the clacker balls go the longest. Also, since clacker balls came in a wide variety of colors, kids would trade off with each other so they could have the balls in many colors. They were also quite noisy, and the Wisconsin clacker ball owner recalls how they were forbidden in school for that reason. Mostly, he remembered how the balls flew up and dramatically clashed together.

Clacker balls were inexpensive. You could get them for about $1, and they came with or without glitter.

But the clacker ball fad lasted only a few months, because it was soon discovered that the balls could be dangerous. When they shattered, sometimes with great force, and flew off their cords, the balls could harm the kids who were playing with them or other kids nearby. For this reason in April 1971 the Consumer Product Safety Commission issued a warning about clacker balls.

The discovery that they could be harmful played a large role in clacker balls' losing their considerable charm. But the man from Wisconsin said that he simply got tired of their repetitious effect. He did, however, use them to scare his grandmother before growing weary of them.

PEASANT LOOK (1971)

Like the 1930s poor boy look, which became popular in the 1960s (see BONNIE PARKER LOOK), the peasant look of 1971 meant precisely the opposite of its name

when it came to prices: If you want to look like a peasant, then be ready to shell out a lot of money. After all, what with the colorful fabrics, the layers of fringe and the intricate designs on the garments, it was just the "thing" to show off.

The peasant look was not based on the clothing of just any peasants, but rather was based on the way Slavic and Ukranian peasants probably dressed in rural parts of the "old country." As such, it followed the Zhivago look of just a few years back (see ZHIVAGO LOOK). Flower motifs were big, as they were big in Eastern Europe. Dr. Michael Novak, the philospher and theologian, said, "Eastern Europe triumphs in fashion this year."

That may be true, but the peasant look also had the spirit of Greenwich Village and North Beach in San Francisco, especially since girls took the peasant look to mean high boots, large earrings and oversized shoulder bags, in addition to those pretty flowered prints.

Who wore the peasant look? Why everyone from celebrities to teen-age girls. The actress Candice Bergen, for instance, sported the peasant look; but so did a typical young high school girl in New York, who wore a light-colored peasant skirt with red flowers for a week.

Everyone, of course, talked about how wealthy you sometimes had to be if you wanted to be taken for a peasant. Anthropologist Ray Birdwhistell said of the phenomenon: "We've always had rich peasants. Most rich people are former peasants."

The peasant look showed once more that fashion-conscious people were interested in bringing back earlier periods of the century. Just as the peasant look represented people's attempt to recall rural peasants of a bygone era, so the contemporaneous interest in antique American clothing (in which women carried around a shawl from the 1930s or a patent leather pocketbook from the 1940s; see ANTIQUE CLOTHING) represented people's attempt to forget they were living in the 1970s. And what was to come was even more nostalgic—the return of the Gatsby look of the 1920s as well as the return of any number of items from the 1950s. Sometimes it even seemed that 1970s people didn't live in the 1970s at all.

TWENTIES SWEATERS (1971)

When a guy wore a 1920s sweater in 1971—and a lot of guys were doing just that—he might sport either the summer or the winter look. If he wanted to look like a 1920s cad of the summer variety, he would wear a sleeveless sweater. If he wanted to look like a 1920s cad of the winter variety, he would wear a reindeer sweater. While this was usually a sweater with a reindeer motif, there could also be pine trees on it or pictures of birds on the sleeves.

A guy wore this because there was a 1920s revival going on. It was also characterized by sporting Oxford bags, two-tone shoes and bow ties. The revival was inspired by a new version of the musical *No, No, Nanette*, which originally started in London. The first *No, No, Nannette* was produced in the 1920s.

The 1920s revival really took hold in 1972, when *The Great Gatsby* was released as a movie once more (see GATSBY LOOK).

After the 1920s revival wore off, the fashionable sweater for men looked more like a poster—namely the emblazoned T-shirt (see T-SHIRTS), which might have shown you a shot of the Golden Gate Bridge, scenes of a ski village or pictures of animals.

WATER BEDS (1971)

Seasick when you awaken? In the early 1970s this definitely could happen because of the popularity of the water bed, which could give the sleeper something of a rocking motion, just like on a boat. This was said to be a particularly sexy thing, so many an apartment in which there were "swinging singles" had a water bed, but so did married couples, and so did college students. One student at Lafayette College in Pennsylvania remembers very well the year in the early 1970s when everyone wanted to get a piece of the water bed action. Just think of drifting into slumber on a bag of heavy-duty rubber filled with water, with a vinyl liner. Hugh Hefner, the tycoon who made *Playboy* magazine so big, did it; it was said to be the height of luxurious enjoyment. On the other hand, it needn't be expensive. You could get a water bed for as little as $40. And some students were able to make the water beds themselves. At the same time, a high-fashion water bed—complete with contour pillows, a bar, a stereo and a color television set—went for $2,800. But if you had so much else to do, how could you concentrate on the water bed itself?

By 1971 the water bed was considered to be big business, not merely a very unique item used by a few forward-looking people. You didn't need to go to a special bed boutique to get one, nor to a trendy department store.

Yet the water bed fad did not last that long, because the bed—even a well-made one—really had a number of potential kinks to it. A number of the heavy beds were known to have fallen through the floor, while others split a seam and left a flooded house. For such contingencies insurance was available, but it was very expensive.

Also it was generally recognized—by *Consumer's Bulletin*, for instance—that a water bed needed a heater and that an unheated one was "clammy and uncomfortable." This was also a real problem, because the heaters that came on the market were found not to be safe enough.

Consumer's Bulletin also warned that the water bag should be vinyl not more than 20/1,000 inch thick. This was the type of consideration that would never have to trouble anyone in an ordinary single bed, twin bed, or four-poster. Water beds were also said to cause back problems, because they did not give real support to the sleeper's spine and back muscles.

The above-mentioned drawbacks weren't the only problems. Consider illustrations of water bed shortcomings like the following: In 1971, a Long Beach, New York man was moving out of his apartment and needed to empty the bed. Living on the 14th floor, he decided to connect a hose to the bed and drain it off his terrace. It worked well for him, in that his water bed was empty by morning, but the whole side of the apartment house looked as if a sudden rainstorm had drenched just selected parts of the building. Or consider another man's experience in a water bed: One night his back gave out, and he couldn't get off the bed. He had to be rescued by three firemen.

Erotic and sensual, but by no means practical, the water bed had lost much of its faddish popularity by 1972, when you could get a $500 water bed for $200. Many Americans who tried the water bed out went back to sleeping on dry land. Which isn't to say they gave up being erotic and sensual, or wanting things that made them appear that way; the warming jacuzzi and the hot tub (see HOT TUBS) were just around the bend. Now *they* put water where it was supposed to be.

Yet first the water bed and later the jacuzzi and the hot tub showed that the 1970s were going to be different from the intense 1960s. The decade was going to be a time when new and private forms of sensual pleasure would be sought. Really, only two people at most could get into a water bed. It was not a place where a tribe of "heads" could gather (see PSYCHEDELIC TRIPS). Nor would you be likely to find a water bed—with its overtones of luxuriant self-indulgence—in a commune (see COMMUNES).

Relaxing on a water bed.

CHINESE LOOK (1971–72)

They didn't build the Great Wall or go on the Long March with Mao Tse-tung in the 1930s, but that didn't prevent Americans from adopting the Chinese look in the early 1970s. For the really stylish, it might have meant wearing a sleeveless jacket of black silk; for politically conscious youth it meant wearing the black Maoist jacket or the all-purpose Maoist overalls. But that wasn't all. Other people wore mandarin collars, straw coolie hats or sensual Oriental perfumes with names like China Glaze. Jade jewelry also came into fashion once more. Bloomingdale's, the trendy New York department store, even had an Oriental boutique, China Passage.

You could show an interest in Chinese items or wear Chinese garb if you wanted to spend a lot of money or even if you wanted to spend just a little money. For instance, you could get a Chineselike back scratcher for 50 cents, but high-fashion clothes would run you between $395 and $450. The most popular item, the cotton Mao jacket, ran about $25. You could also get a Chineselike cricket cage for $1.

It was President Nixon's visit to mainland China in July 1971 and the publicity leading up to it that gave rise to a general fascination with things Chinese, although many young people, disenchanted with the American political process and with the Vietnam conflict, had been admiring Mao Tse-tung from afar. As a result of Nixon's trip, there was also a rage for the ancient Chinese medical practice known as acupuncture (see ACUPUNCTURE).

The Chinese look lasted about a year. It was probably the kind of look that people would expect to sport for an evening or so. The next big fashion splash was the Gatsby look (see GATSBY LOOK); definitely made in America, it was designed to make people look rich, never revolutionary.

ACUPUNCTURE (1971–76)

What did the passing arm of Roman Gabriel, the quarterback for the Los Angeles Rams, have in common with the elbow of Mike Gravel, a senator from Alaska? What did the right hip of Willie McCovey, the slugging first baseman for the San Francisco Giants, have in common with the eyes of Mrs. Eddie Rickenbacker, the wife of the pioneer aviator? Just that in the 1970s they were all treated with acupuncture, the ancient Chinese healing art of inserting needles into sensitive areas of the body.

And Roman Gabriel, Mike Gravel, Willie McCovey and Mrs. Eddie Rickenbacker were not alone. By August 1972 *Newsweek* magazine, reacting to acupuncture's widespread usage in this country, deemed it important enough to run a cover story, "Acupuncture: Myth or Miracle?" Insurance companies received claims for acupuncture and honored them, for hadn't a distinguished American ear specialist, who had seen the Chinese practicing acupuncture, said, "I have seen the past, and it works"? This was a bit of an overstatement. Acupuncture was indeed employed in the modern China of Mao Tse-tung, but not in all cases, and a number of Chinese doctors did not support the procedure at all.

Yet it was used often in China. During one of those times, it was brought to the attention of the American public. In July 1971 things Chinese were in the national eye because of President Nixon's recent visit to mainland China. Acupuncture became prominent when *New York Times* journalist James Reston had to have an emergency appendectomy while in Peking. To soothe the pain in his elbows and legs, acupuncture was used. Soon after that in a column for the *Times*, Reston wrote about acupuncture and prophesied that Americans would become as receptive to Chinese acupuncture as they were to the Indian process of meditation known as yoga. Interest in Oriental ways was widespread.

For instance, Dr. S. I. Heller, of the New York State Board of Medicine, said that acupuncture could be in general use as a surgical anesthetic within three to five years. A lot of Americans thought it could do more than that and sought to use acupuncture for arthritis, sciatica, some types of deafness, psoriasis and impotence. Membership in the National Acupuncture Research Society increased from 20 to 5,000, and patients numbered in the many thousands were said to be waiting for acupuncture treatments.

One variation of acupuncture that was also used was staplepuncture, in which which a staple was attached to the ear to reduce hunger pains. This was employed as a dieting technique.

The first operation in the United States in which acupuncture was used successfully was a tonsillectomy in May 1972. Soon thereafter it was employed in hospitals in California, Illinois, Virginia, New York, Massachusetts and Michigan, among other places. Private practices of acupuncture, which cost between $25 and $50 per treatment, were started and attracted waiting lists of patients. And acupuncture received official sanction when W. E. Lukash, the White House physician, made it known that he would recommend this treatment for President Nixon for certain conditions. What's more, George Wallace saw an acupuncturist to determine what could be done to promote recovery from paralysis resulting from a 1972 assassination attempt.

The medical philosophy underlying Chinese acupuncture became well known. From ancient times it was believed by the Chinese that "a single needle can free a body from a thousand maladies." When there was an imbalance in the body, and its energy (called ch'i) was upset, acupuncturists could make it healthy once more. The acupuncture masters knew 900 acupuncture points throughout the body.

Acupuncture was both voguish and something very serious in its time of unusual popularity in the 1970s. It was voguish because of President Nixon's visit to mainland China in 1971—a most historic occasion in that he was the first American president to go there; it made things Chinese seem more intriguing. For instance, an interest in Oriental clothing fashions became pervasive once more. On the other hand, since acupuncture dealt essentially with health, many people turned to it for reasons that had nothing to do with the vogue. The use of acupuncture to cure weary tennis elbows, as one American did, was a bit frivolous, however.

By 1974 a medical reaction had set in against acupuncture. Doctors warned that acupuncture could do nothing for cancer, mental illness, sickle-cell anemia, diabetes or cerebral palsy. National magazines, which had touted it as a cure only three years earlier, began to conclude that acupuncture was a "placebo," that its benefits were all in the mind. One hospital reported that a patient was experiencing pain in breathing after an operation in which acupuncture was used; another reported that a patient had muscular discomfort after acupuncture.

As early as 1973, state commissions were beginning to regulate acupuncture; by 1974 some private practices started to close. Through the 1970s and into the 1980s, however, acupuncture has continued to be used. But it is no longer an esoteric type of medical remedy that grabs headlines.

SQUASH BLOSSOMS AND OTHER INDIAN JEWELRY (1968–73)

A squash blossom costing about $500 sounds like a very expensive flower. It was expensive, but it wasn't a flower. It was a very popular piece of American Indian jewelry, which was big in the early 1970s. It was a blossom made of hand-tooled silver and chunks of turquoise, and it was worn around the neck. This made for a very heavy necklace—about five or six pounds.

But it also made for giving the possessor a sense that he or she had something truly unusual, that no one else really had. It was worth the $200 to $1,000 you had to pay for it. You could get a blossom with one large turquoise in it, or you could get one with six or eight smaller turquoises. The turquoises could be as big as silver dollars or as small as nickels. There was a turquoise that was sky blue and a turquoise that was greenish.

The hand-crafted Indian jewelry was usually Navaho and made in Arizona.

But if you couldn't afford a squash blossom, you could still take part in the fad for American Indian jewelry. You could get silver bracelets for $30. You could get rings with designs of flowers and birds. You could get earrings or pins. All of these were silver and turquoise and cost about $25.

Or you could get a silver belt buckle that had a big chunk of turquoise in its center and displayed a sunburst motif. This could cost between $25 and $150.

In any event, Indian jewelry was the chic thing, as could be seen in an article featuring it in a May 1972 issue of *Harper's Bazaar*. It was a featured item also at Macy's in New York, Neiman-Marcus in Dallas and Filene's in Boston.

Sometimes the Indian jewelry was particularly ornate. There was a silver and turquoise ring in which the silver portion was fashioned into the shape of leaves, as it held the turquoise stone in its grasp.

Yet by 1973 the fad for Indian jewelry had begun to lose its hold. Some people thought that the look was just too striking to go with very much of their wardrobe. After earning $1,000 a month for stores for about a year, Indian jewelry suddenly no longer did. American Indian jewelry would become exotic once more, not the fashionable item it had been for a while.

The interest in squash blossoms and other American Indian jewelry showed to what extent the counterculture, with its many tribes of "heads" (see PSYCHEDELIC TRIPS), had lost its momentum. In the middle and late 1960s, when it was flowering, kids would gather together, often wearing American Indian-like ornamental objects, most of which were probably hand-crafted or didn't cost very much. Now American Indian jewelry had entered the realm of high fashion. When you wore a squash blossom, you shone alone—you were not just another member of the tribe, trying to be a little exotic and distance yourself from mainstream America.

GATSBY LOOK (1973)

Can't repeat the past? Why, of course you can.
—Jay Gatsby in *The Great Gatsby*

These things made up the Gatsby look: striking white pants, for looking like a "sport" by day or by night; delicate-looking crepe evening dresses that might have been worn by Daisy Buchanan, Jay Gatsby's star-crossed sweetheart; baggy trousers, which were once known in the 1920s as Oxford bags (see OXFORD BAGS); rope necklaces, which could make a lady look like a real flapper, as girls were known in that roaring time. And if white was really your thing, instead of the white pants you could opt for a complete white suit. And the Gatsby look had much more besides: wing-tip shoes, bow ties, argyle vests, pleated white skirts and all kinds of cloches. All these and more came with the revival of the Gatsby look in 1973.

The revival came about as the result of the ballyhoo attending the movie *The Great Gatsby*, based on F. Scott Fitzgerald's landmark novel. While the rage was particularly set in motion by *Women's Wear Daily*, the major newspaper of the fashion trade, articles on the return of Gatsby and the Gatsby look were featured in most major magazines and newspapers. Although this was the third movie version of *The Great Gatsby*, it was easily the most influential in inspiring fads. For instance, the cosmetics industry came up with Daisy Pink lipstick. Bill Blass, Yves St. Laurent and Ralph Lauren all brought out Gatsby wardrobes that would suit any fledgling Jay Gatsby or Daisy Buchanan. The fact that screen idols Robert Redford and Mia Farrow played these parts further fueled the hysteria.

The Gatsby rage really lasted only a short spring season. It may have been fleeting because the clothing was just too expensive. Or perhaps it was because the 1920s fashion craze resulted from the considerable hype that predated *The Great Gatsby* movie. When the film was finally released and met with some negative reviews, this could have dulled a lot of the enthusiasm.

In any event, the Gatsby look was one of the first fads to reflect the nostalgic impulse of the 1970s. To follow was a revival of things that reminded Americans of another long-lost era: the fifties. While once they might have donned fancy wing-tip shoes to affect the Gatsby look, that time had passed. Now saddle shoes were more like it!

CITIZENS BAND RADIO (CB) (1973–77)

Citizens band radio was a two-way radio that was big in the middle 1970s. No doubt, CB had a lot going for it. It was instant communication with other people, either strangers or friends, for the sake of amusement, profit or just to cure the loneliness blues. It had its own private vocabulary, which could make you feel special or exciting when you used it. And it was associated with two groups of people whose work has sometimes struck many as romantic and larger than life: truckers and police officers. Here was an attractive way to emulate them. If you were prompted by any of these motives, all you had to do was plunk down $60–$250 for a set, and only $4 to get a license from the Federal Communications Commission, and you were on your way. Or, as they would say in CB language, "10-4, good buddy." It didn't hurt if you had just purchased stock in CB manufacturing companies, either. Between 1975 and 1976 the value of various companies' stock multiplied by 300 percent to 8,000 percent.

CB consisted of the following apparatus (which was easy enough to learn but could still give a great feeling of accomplishment when you reached that other party or when you located that signal beamed on a channel): a transceiver, or a combination of a transmitter, to send messages, and a receiver, to get incoming calls; an antenna, to pick up other sets; and a microphone. All these items got more sophisticated as the years went by.

The first citizens band radios came out in 1958, ballyhooed under the name Two Way Radio for Everyone. Yet this was hardly the case. In its first 15 years, only farmers, professional radio workers and truckers used it; the closest that most people came to seeing it was when they watched a television crime show and observed police officers using a very similar apparatus.

All this changed, however, in 1973, when there was both an oil embargo and a truckers' strike. On a television show, some truckers explained how, with CB radios, they kept in contact with each other to find out where gas was available, and also how CB made it possible for them to keep their strike organized. At this point CB became quite the thing to have. In the first 11 months of 1974, 2 million people filed their CB licenses. It had taken 15 years for the first million people to file licenses. What was called a "simpler, cheaper version of police radio" had really caught on.

People used CB not only on the highways but also on the waterways, and it was often said that CB communication among people in distant boats was a lot clearer than CB communication among people in distant cars. Hunters used CB to keep in touch with other hunters. So did fishermen. As one sea angler put it, "The best thing [about CB] is talking with the other guys out there . . . we talk about where the schools are, if we spotted any bluefish, that sort of thing." In Texas, college sports recruiters used CB to gain an advantage in trying to find prospects.

Oftentimes, CB was used much more frivolously. A family vacationing in Maine used CB in order to find out where they could locate a tasty lobster thermidor. A bunch of high school boys and girls would get together in Mobile, Alabama to play a game that might be called CB hide-and-seek. Some 20–30 people in 10 cars would try to track a signal coming from a short distance away as the cars sat in the middle of the parking lot. The first person to locate the signal precisely would win a little money. One young woman, whose handle (CB for name) was Merlin, did this three or four times before she went away to college. She was introduced to CB by another young woman, whose handle was Small Winner. For a while, Merlin said, CB hide-and-seek was a big activity on Saturday nights.

There is no way of getting around the fact that one of the basic uses of CB was to avoid the police and learn where the speed traps were. These activities also spawned a great part of CB's special vocabulary. "Smokey the Bear" was the state police. "Bears in the air" was a radar helicopter. "Feed the bears" was to get a ticket. There were, however, a lot of other CB slang phrases that you would easily pick up once you got used to your radio. Among them were "Green Stamp road" for toll road or "pregnant roller skate" for a VW.

The use of CB sometimes led to other abuses that were more antisocial than merely avoiding speed traps. There were incidents in which both drug smuggling and prostitution were abetted by CB. Also, there was a case in 1973 in the Southwest in which, following the kidnapping of a child, the police were tipped off by CB as to its possible whereabouts and searched there for about a week. The tip turned out to be a hoax.

Yet, on the whole, at the time when CB was at its most faddish, it was also very helpful—a fact testified

CB radio was used all over, even among the Amish in Pennsylvania

PUKA SHELL NECKLACES (1974)

In a Hawaiian dialect the word *puka* means hole, but a bunch of puka shells strung together into a necklace in 1974 meant quite another thing: money. These little adornments, which used to cost $6 in Hawaii in 1973, now cost as much as $150 in 1974 at the most chic boutiques on the mainland.

Historically, puka shell necklaces may have become popular because, in their novelty, they reminded people of all those items of American Indian jewelry, which were just the thing to have in 1972 and 1973 (see SQUASH BLOSSOMS AND OTHER INDIAN JEWELRY).

More than this, however, puka shell necklaces may have become popular because none other than siren and movie actress Elizabeth Taylor, who had been "wowing" them since she was a pre-teen-ager in *National Velvet*, a horsey movie, wore them first. Her brother Howard Taylor, a landowner on the Hawaiian island of Kauai, had given them to her as a gift.

What Elizabeth was wearing on her neck—as they say solemnly in fashion shows about any new item—was a necklace consisting of a strand going through a number of shells, the pukas, all of which have holes in them. A columnist for *Newsweek* said that the shell looked like a "small doughnut-shaped object."

Now many a woman has hopes of becoming a siren, and so the traffic in puka necklaces became big. That is, the dough began to roll in for this small, doughnut-shaped object.

People began to flock to Hawaii to get the pukas. And throughout the islands, any number of concerns like banks, barber shops, liquor shops and surfwear shops all began to act like a bunch of competitive Dunkin' Pukas establishments, enticing people to buy the strands of shells there, for they were much cheaper than in Honolulu.

Puka shell necklaces became a conversation piece. They even appeared on an installment of the detective television thriller set in Hawaii, "Hawaii Five-O." In this little segment, a girl who was the victim of foul play was found on a Hawaiian beach. Among other things, she was wearing a puka shell necklace.

The story has it that the first person who made the puka shell necklaces, an old gentleman named Albert Kalad (who got the idea quite by accident, when he saw the pukas while walking on the beach one fine Hawaiian day), never made any money from them. He died first.

Puka shell necklaces themselves experienced their own demise as a fad by 1975. The new item of jewelry that replaced it was much different from the exotic

to by both private citizens and police officers. People could not only be directed away from accidents but could report them. Crime, too, could be reported. There was and still is a CB channel devoted exclusively to reporting emergencies, Channel 9. A Kansas police sergeant said, "If you want to travel safely, the only way to go is by CB."

CB was also a way that people might be able to put an end to loneliness. People tried to make dates using CB—a process that, of course, also gave rise to its own vocabulary. To say "88-10" meant love and kisses.

After 1976 the CB craze began to abate somewhat, with the CB becoming more of an accepted instrument of communication than a feverish obsession. Manufacturers said that people's interest began to move to other things, like video games. But it was also true that CBs began to cost as much as $100 more because you could get 40 channels on a set instead of 23.

Still, CB has become a part of us. On any given day or night, you can probably still hear any number of handles: like Popper Stopper, Silver Fox or Mule Skinner. Or you might hear someone talking about a "Kojak with a Kodak," a police car with radar. CB did indeed become two-way radio for everyone.

bauble of the remote Hawaiian islands; it was the mood ring, which was supposed to reveal your temperament at any given instant (see MOOD RINGS), not make you look like a double of Elizabeth Taylor (at least not around the neck).

STREAKING (1974)

It's like playing bank robber. A guy jumps from the men's room without his clothes, runs across the campus and vanishes into a getaway car—just to see if he can get away with it; it's a challenge.

—Florida State coed

Streaking was nothing new. A 75-year-old California judge remembered doing the same thing when he was an undergraduate at Stanford University in 1921. He said of the streakers: "They're just a bunch of foolish kids. I was a foolish kid once, too." But these foolish kids weren't just in California this time, but everywhere in the country, precipitating hastily called student government meetings in Maine, legislative prohibitions in Montana and protests by nudist colonies in Florida, to name just a few examples of the uproar that streakers brought about. The mayor of Dover Township, New Jersey threatened to fine streakers one dollar for every pound of flesh they exposed. And in Hawaii a man ran naked through a Honolulu official assembly, calling himself "The Streaker of the House."

As a national phenomenon, streaking broke out in late January 1974. It was the first big fad to hit the nation's campuses after many years in which political protest was the students' chief organized extracurricular activity. Every streaker probably had his or her own motivation, but the reason most often given was the desire to do something exciting. One high-school senior in Texas said of streaking, "It beats sitting at the Dairy Queen." If you lived in northern climes, you and your compatriot streakers could show how you could take the cold. You think you accomplished quite a feat by standing naked when it was minus 8 degrees at the University of Alaska? Well there were people at Purdue University who could take it when it was minus 20.

Streakers also looked for the most original ways to bare it all. Streakers from the University of Georgia parachuted out of planes, although some, unfortunately, landed in a cesspool. A little further north, streakers from the University of South Carolina biked through the college town of Columbia. At Harvard streakers wearing only surgical masks dashed through a room where their classmates were taking an anatomy examination.

It thus came as no surprise that a Connecticut merchandising company put out silver-plated and gold-plated streaking medallions priced at $5.95 to $6.95, for the "free spirit shedding his inhibitions." Not all commercial ventures were so courageous, though. J.C. Penney shelved a long-standing plan to market a shoe called the "streaker," because to many streaking had come to have a bad name.

One never knew where or when a streaker would appear. This uncertainty was of great concern to many. Television officials of NBC Sports sent scouts around to make sure that no streaker could jump out of the bushes at a golf tourney that was being shown. On another NBC production, the "Johnny Carson Show," a streaker ran across the stage. Since the program was videotaped, this was cut out, and viewers saw instead a blank screen for a minute.

In a time of political chaos in America, there was also a streak for impeachment carried out in Washington, D.C. by one young man.

Streaking also became a part of the cultural world. In Florida a streaker appeared when Van Cliburn was playing Chopin's "Polonaise" and in Wisconsin when Rudolf Nureyev was dancing ballet.

Every day seemed to have its own streaking story. A naked bank employee streaked along Wall Street in New York. Two streakers collided in a Detroit restaurant, reminding one of the old story about when automobiles were new: There were only two "horseless carriages" registered in the whole state of Missouri, and the drivers still managed to have a head-on collision. A young girl streaked through a train in Huntington, Long Island, causing a five-minute delay on the 8:01. It was no wonder that a Los Angeles radio station gave "streaker reports."

The record for the most streakers to appear in one place at one time kept changing. First, it was 520 at the University of South Carolina, then 550 at the University of Maryland, followed by 1,000 at the University of Georgia and 1,200 at the University of Colorado. The longest streak was said to be 5 hours at Texas Tech.

The general rule, however, was that streakers got out of the way fast. There were exceptions, though. In

A streaker on roller skates

A cycling streaker

178

Ohio a naked man and woman in their sixties did a slow stroll and were promptly arrested. Due to their deliberate speed, they were charged not with streaking but with "snailing."

Streaking also went worldwide. They streaked at the Eiffel Tower in Paris, at St. Peter's Square in Rome, and in South Korea, Taiwan, Brazil and Kenya.

Yet by May 1974 the streaking rage had about run its course. Regarding its demise, one Princeton undergraduate said, "I never really understood why we did in the first place, and I couldn't say why we're not doing it now." Syndicated psychologist Joyce Brothers could offer no reason for the decline, either.

Perhaps it was just a case of this being a thing that was only fun to do once, and nearly everybody had tried it. That and the fact that exams were coming up as the academic year was drawing to a close.

STRING BIKINI AND THONG (1974)

This is the smallest, sexiest thing I've ever seen.
—Young guy on a California beach,
after ogling the girls in their string bikinis

The string bikini was the sensation of 1974; many of the most chic girls wore them, while other souls—male and female—simply observed this latest thing. The string bikini was to the typical female bathing suit what hot pants (see HOT PANTS) were to slacks—very little garment, a lot of flesh, while, at the same time selling for high prices and exciting great controversy. A lot of gals thought that the string bikini was the greatest thing ever to come along, but others said things like this: "You've got to be kidding!" (San Francisco public relations woman), or "Good heavens, what if I get sunburnt!" (Washington, D.C. reporter).

What manner of thing was this garment called the string bikini? It was a bikini shaped by two triangles held by cords. One triangle could be seen high up on a woman's body, covering the upper erogenous zones, while the other was lower down, covering the lower erogenous zones. The rest of the body was bare. In early 1974 string bikinis were first worn by women on Ipanema Beach in Rio de Janiero. They were so suggestive that the Brazilian military government tried to suppress the wearing of them. The work of no great fashion designer, the string bikini was said to have been patterned after the loincloth that coastal Indians of Brazil used to wear in bygone days. It came in all kinds of fabrics, like chiffon, matte and cotton.

From Rio de Janiero the string bikini—or the tanga, as it was known in Brazil, after the ancient Indian word for loincloth—spread to Rome. And from Rome the string bikini came to America, where, by the spring of 1974, it was *the* purchase to make. A string bikini cost between $35 and $45; in Rio the same tanga went for $6 to $10. No matter; they sold out in Bloomingdale's in New York City in two weeks, for instance.

Yet the string bikini did not scale the heights of high fashion, because, as many in the garment trade agreed, it was easy to make. All you needed to do was to shape and sew a little material. *People* magazine was pretty explicit about this: "Anyone could knock it off."

This may have been one reason why, in early 1974, the string bikini didn't have the slight swimwear territory all to itself: There was also something called the monokini, which meant that it had only one triangular patch, which sort of curved from the lower part of the body to the upper part, and was also topless. The monokini had its supporters, but by July it was the string bikini that held undisputed sway in the semi-skin realm.

So why did the string bikini last only one summer as a fad? Probably because it was just kind of an outrageous novelty, and who could say when the next novelty would come along? In this case, in the area of swimwear, it came along in the fall of the same year and it was known as the *thong*. Created by the designer Rudi Gernreich, it was sort of a spoof on the provocative string bikini and was explicitly bottomless; it also could be worn by men or women alike, according to Gernreich. The thong—which went for $30 to $36—also became popular, though not as popular as the string bikini, probably because anyone who wore it knew that it was merely a joking gesture, whereas string bikinis were part of the great tradition of revealing all. By 1975 hardly anybody wore the thong, either.

Yet the string bikini, the thong and, of course, the monokini all showed one thing—how much things had changed as far as women's bathing costumes were concerned. In the early 1900s, if a woman wanted to go into the water, she had to wear a dress (known as the sailor dress) and hose; in 1910, with a garment called the Annette Kellerman diving suit, she could show her neck (this was still considered an outrage); it wasn't until 1930 that there appeared the first one-piece which allowed her legs to move freely in the water and to feel whatever—ocean, lake, pond, stream. As for the bikini, this didn't appear until after the Second World War. In the 1960s came something called a vinyl see-through swimsuit, and by the 1970s, at chic places in France and California, there were selected nude beaches. Values, indeed, had changed.

So the fad for the string bikini in 1974 came and

went like so many other fads of that era, with some people becoming personally enthused and others showing outrage. Neither the police nor city hall got involved, though—far different from the response to animal dances in the second decade of the 20th century or even to long-haired youth in the 1960s. Maybe America had mellowed.

the original *Nothing Book*, may have only a simple cover that does not trumpet their message (*Nothing Book*) on it, but *The Nothing Book* phenomenon showed that when we entered a bookstore, we didn't have to render homage to its gathered authors. We had the choice of becoming authors ourselves.

Nothing Books (1974–75)

Until 1974, when someone asked for a book in a bookstore, it was assumed that what was desired was a book with words in it. But then *The Nothing Book* came along—blank pages from cover to cover, which could be filled with anything you wished, from doodles to charcoal drawings to what it was supposedly intended for: letting its possessor write his or her own book. This was sort of a highfalutin form of the blank diary, which has been around for centuries and centuries, but did it ever sell! For a while in 1974, *The Nothing Book* was high on the list when it came to best-sellers. The cloth-bound *Nothing Book* went for about $5.95 and was put out by Crown Publishers.

One suburban mall bookstore remembers the coming of *The Nothing Book* this way: "When we first received a shipment of *The Nothing Book*s, we didn't know where to put them. So we made a display in the middle of the store and left some on the counter. One of our staff thought it should go with the self-help books, for those who didn't need any help."

The Nothing Book caught on big because it was not only a fancy place to put your thoughts (as was advertised) but was also an amusing spoof of books themselves at a time when people were really interested in buying spoofy items: consider the pet rock (see PET ROCKS) and bottled money (see BOTTLED MONEY), which would soon follow. This was no longer the 1960s, when people were almost always showing what their commitment was—how they were "involved." A *Nothing Book*, which sounded like a book on a new school of philosophical thought while being just a volume of blank pages, fit into this kind of joking easily.

As a conversational item, *The Nothing Book* lost its appeal after a couple of years, but by that time, it had become something useful that has lasted to the present day: a nice place to keep a journal, or a book, already bound, that you can keep for yourself or give to a friend. Such blank volumes no longer look like

Tattoos, Particularly for Women (Mid-1970s)

When you think of tattoos, you probably conjure up some kind of macho image: a sailor with a battleship tattooed on his chest. Or you might think of that most famous of all tattoos—MOM, which could be found on many a man's body. Or you might think of Popeye, with his spinach, his pipe, his bulging muscles—and his tattoo. Now *there* was a he-man. So it was really something that tattooing not only came back as a fad in the 1970s but that it was done particularly on women's bodies—on legs, wrists, thighs, just above the waist, etc. Although done principally in California, it spread nationwide and really wasn't just a localized fad.

It wasn't limited to a few images, either: There were butterflies, which may have been the most common, but there were also flowers, birds, stars, turtles, snakes, horses, half-moons, little bolts of lightning, rainbows, Snoopy or sea gulls. Nor was it done only on the bodies of bizarre women or "crazies." No, this was just your average gal who had a tattoo for an ornament rather than another bracelet, perhaps. In California, where the revival of tattooing started, typical tattooed women included an attorney, a banker, a writer and a junior executive for a research firm; there were also doctors' wives, teachers, secretaries and stewardesses. One gal said of it proudly, "It's a statement of eccentricity," and she meant just a harmless eccentricity, to show that she was different from other blondes.

Other tattooed ladies had these perspectives: A Connecticut waitress thought she needed a red star on her shoulder to make her look distinctive, while a Texas woman stopped in a tattoo shop to get one tattoo, then got another and another, saying, "I just couldn't stop."

This is not to say that most women in America got tattooed; but enough did to keep tattooing shops in business, for it was an operation that could cost $10 to $25 for a typical tattoo or $50 an hour for the work of a good tattooist for a more complex design.

One consideration that gave impetus to the popularity of tattooing for women in the middle 1970s was that it wasn't so revolutionary as to be something frightening. Between 1966 and 1968 women had used a lot of leg decoration, consisting of flowers, birds and other symbols (see LEG DECORATION)—a cosmetic trend that probably served as a precedent.

Nor is it to suggest that in the 1970s there wasn't a revival of tattooing men's bodies, too. And now tattooed men were no longer necessarily sailor or weightlifter types. The 1970s were a time of heightened personal sensory awareness—proved by everything from water beds to hot tubs—and having a tattoo could make any kind of man feel good. You didn't have to be a sailor; you could be an attorney or an accountant or a teacher or a student. Tattooing became so prominent that it was featured on the cover of the June 1976 issue of *Esquire* magazine, which also showed how widespread tattoos had become—sometimes covering the whole body, or arms, breasts, chests, backs or legs. There were tattoo parlors from San Francisco to New London. If a national convention of tattooers was held, it was widely reported. The name Lyle Tuttle, the best-known tattooist in San Francisco, was about as widely known as the names of any number of media personalities.

Yet after 1976 tattooing began to fade as something that people just had to have. Perhaps it was that people really weren't all that happy with establishing their identity in this way, or perhaps it was that more people were realizing that a tattoo was almost impossible to remove. In any event, tattoos began to be less popular. Within a year it became hard to find a tattoo shop to decorate one's body with a favorite image, astrological sign, constellation or whatever.

T-SHIRTS—EMBLAZONED AND OTHERWISE (Mid-1970s)

When the American GIs went to fight in France during World War I, they discovered that men wore something there that was still unseen on American shores—the T-shirt. It took more than a half century, however, for the humble T-shirt to become the latest vogue in the States. But then, did it ever take off! Jacqueline Onassis and her luminary sister, Lee Radziwill, bought them, but so did nearly everybody else.

There were two kinds of chic T-shirts created by leading designers like Calvin Klein or Yves St. Laurent, and T-shirts emblazoned with some kind of state-

ment or picture. There were days in the summer when you could walk down the street and see just about one person after another wearing emblazoned T-shirts.

For instance: After the Washington, D.C. zoo received two giant pandas as a gift from Communist China, the panda T-shirt hit the streets. Other T-shirts featured the names of rock groups; one proclaiming HOT TUNA was such a number. Others recalled the pop art scene of the 1960s; painter Andy Warhol paraded around in a T-shirt that showed a Good and Plenty box. Corporations wanted to be with it, too; there were T-shirts inscribed with BUDWEISER BEER, VEGA, MERRILL LYNCH or HEINZ, to name just a very few.

In 1975 T-shirts even went one step further: They not only had an appealing picture on them but gave off an appropriate smell, too. PIZZA T-shirt smelled like pizza; CHOCOLATE T-shirt smelled like chocolate; BANANA T-shirt smelled like banana.

T-shirts were an attractive item for a number of reasons. It was kind of relaxing to wear them, and they were funny, too. Also, the way they tightly hugged the skin was enticing. And they went with everything: jeans, tank suits, short skirts—you name it.

A close relative of the T-shirt was the emblematic animal shirt. First there was the alligator shirt, then the tiger, and the golden fleece.

You could get a T-shirt for $6, or you could spend as much as $42.

After the great flowering of the T-shirt in the 1970s, it really settled down to become a familiar part of the American scene. Long gone were the days when the most frequent T-shirt to be seen was that little white shirt (which could also serve as an undershirt) worn by children.

MOOD RINGS (1975)

Mood rings got their name because they were a special kind of bauble: When you wore them, they were supposed to reflect your moods through their ever-changing colors. Blue was said to show inner tranquility; black was said to show tension; green was said to show stability; and purple was said to show a state of extreme happiness. This was all thought to be determined by the rise and fall of the body's temperature.

But if the mood ring wearer's temperature could go up and down, for a while in 1975 the mood ring itself seemed to go in only one direction—*up*—according to the merchandisers. Or as one manager of a store that stocked the mood rings reported, "We barely have time to put them in the display case, and they are already sold out." People liked to show how they were feeling with this neat piece of jewelry; your husband, wife, mother, father, friend, could say to you, for instance: "What's wrong with you today? Your ring is black. It was purple yesterday."

Celebrities must have had the same fascination, too: Football quarterback Joe Namath wore the mood ring, and so did movie actress Polly Bergen and heavyweight champion Muhammad Ali. Basketball star guard Walt Frazier gave mood rings to his friends, while Italian movie actress Sophia Loren took her mood ring off at a press conference after it turned black, because she didn't want to reveal how she was feeling to a bunch of reporters.

You can be sure that Sophia wasn't wearing the inexpensive $2.98 mood ring, either. You could pay up to $250 for a mood ring, the deluxe model coming in 14-karat gold. It was projected that 20 million mood rings were sold in 1975.

Mood rings first appeared in the summer of 1974, when they were invented by a young man in his thirties, Joshua Reynolds, who had studied meditation and biofeedback in New York City. There had been prototypes of the ring in Tokyo and in Pittsburgh earlier, but they had not caught on. They didn't catch on immediately in New York City, either, but by 1975 they were the hottest of items, not only in New York City but also nationwide. What really got them going was the interest shown in the gossip page of a newspaper: *New York Post* columnist Eugenia Shepherd thought that mood rings were great.

Just in Bonwit Teller, a New York City department store, 1,800 mood rings were sold in a week.

Surely the mood ring was a novelty, but it also picked up on the introspectiveness that was predominant at that time. Meditation was an important thing to do in the 1970s, and it is not surprising that mood rings were advertised as "first and foremost, a functional device, a mirror of one's inner world." Yet the mid-1970s were also a time of popular gimmicky items, and mood rings fit right in with the *Nothing Book* (see NOTHING BOOK) and its blank pages and the pet rock, just a stone for your mantelpiece (see PET ROCKS). All these seemed light years away from the faddish items of the 1960s, which always had an air of protest about them. Consider, for example, the business coloring book of the middle 1960s, which poked fun at the ladder of success (see BUSINESS COLORING BOOKS).

Yet these mood rings, with their liquid crystals that reflected body temperature, passed in their time, too. The idea that mood rings could actually reflect inner feelings turned out to be sort of a pseudo-scientific assumption, which should surprise no one. In a hot place,

like around the stove, the mood ring always turned blue, while in a cold place, such as when its owner reached into a refrigerator, the ring always turned black. In other words, the most lighthearted soul in the world would have a black mood ring on a chilly day, while the most nervous soul would have a blue mood ring during a sweltering spell. This had to detract from the romantic mysticism of the thing.

It was also revealed that after a maximum of two years, your mood ring's color-changing capability would wear out, and the ring would wind up black. This would have brought most mood ring wearers to around the year 1977. People wanted to get a jump on the passing of their dear mood rings, however, so they shelved the rings themselves in 1976. Mood rings ceased being big.

PET ROCKS (1975)

A pet rock was the extraordinary novelty item of 1975. The idea behind it was to give someone their very own rock as a present, which is considerably different from your typical pet dog, cat, canary or goldfish. It was neatly packaged in a box, on which the name "Pet Rock" was clearly stenciled. How did they sell? A merchandising staffer at Brentano's in New York City remembered that they sold, in their six months in the faddish sun, fantastically. Nor was Brentano's alone by any means: Pet rocks were big at the Hallmark card shops, at Bloomingdale's and Macy's in New York, at Filene's in Boston and in many another department or novelty store besides. All you needed was $5 and the pet rock was yours. In their first few months, pet rocks sold 250,000 strong—enough to populate a medium-sized city.

Why would anyone buy a pet rock? As a gag, obviously. Just like the *Executive Coloring Book* (see BUSINESS COLORING BOOKS) of the 1960s, which made fun of corporate management, the pet rock was a unique kind of spoof. It was a good gift to leave on your boss's desk if he or she were good-natured, to give to your wife or husband, or to surprise your teacher with. It was the big item for Christmas 1975.

The original pet rock was just a plain rock, but it proved so popular that soon enough there was a variation on it, also quite well received. The new twist was rocks with faces on them. Packaged in fancy boxes, often with elaborate cellophane windows so you could see the visages inside, there they were—with brightly painted wide smiles, impish grins and devilish grimaces.

183

Gary Dahl, creator of the Pet rock

These visaged rocks first appeared in San Francisco, probably thanks to the large numbers of craft-oriented residents in California. The little critters ranged from the size of an adult's thumb to that of a large hand. The box beckoned the consumer with a rather heartwarming message: "The Whole Gang Misses You." Inside was the menagerie of rocks—or perhaps only pebbles—with varying faces and in an assortment of sizes. A shopper at Filene's in Boston was so moved by them that she bought six, saying, "They're just so cute, I'm buying one for all my grandchildren."

Pet rocks, which were created by Gary Dahl, were a great conversation piece. You probably wouldn't go far without hearing the comment that they were good to have around because "you don't have to feed them anything." They used to say the same thing about the bicycle and then the automobile, in contrast with the horse. Which perhaps just goes to show that pet rocks—with or without faces—were on the side of progress.

As a crazy novelty—and the 1970s were big on crazy novelties—pet rocks took over from the *Nothing Book* (see NOTHING BOOK), with its blank pages ready to record any flight of fancy, and were then replaced by bottled money (see BOTTLED MONEY), which, sadly, turned absolutely nobody into a millionaire.

The fad lasted for about six months. Why did it end? Impossible to positively say; but it really was the type of thing that people just wanted to do for one buying season. In any event, nothing along those exact lines has replaced the pet rock. No one, as yet, has come up with the idea of adopting a glacier.

PIE KILLING (1975)

Smashing a pie in a person's face has long been a part of farce. The victim always looked very embarrassed, and who wouldn't be with custard dripping down his or her face? What could be a greater lark in the community at large than pie smashing, which could happen at any time in any place? In the spring of 1975 pie smashing became the thing to take part in. It even earned the distinguished name of pie killing.

You could find pie killing going on all over America. In a town meeting a politician might suddenly be splattered by a custard. Or a professor in a university classroom. Birthday and anniversary celebrations were spiced up with unexpected pie mayhem.

Pie killing got its start by professionals, who knew the fine art of the sudden custard heave, and how and when to insinuate themselves into the merry gathering where a victim had been pointed out. These pie killers were just like gangland hit men, on whom they were perhaps based, as a spoof of the great interest in Mafiosolike figures in the early 1970s. You could get yourself a contract to have someone pie-killed for anywhere from $20 to $300. Organizations like Pie Face International, Pie Kill, Pie Kill Ltd. and Pies Unlimited abounded. In particular, pie murder was known to be very popular in Chicago, Minneapolis, Los Angeles and Detroit.

The aim of pie killing was to be around when the splatter happened, particularly if you were responsible for setting it up. For that matter, why hire someone else to throw a custard pie when you could pick one up at your local bakery yourself? Save a few bucks, for Pete's sake! This turned out to be the reasoning of many college kids, who engaged in pie killing without hired executioners.

While 1975 may have been the first time that pie killing was done in an organized manner, pie killing itself is of course nothing new. A random poll of 18-year-old girls in the early 1980s showed that the great majority of them had been custard-pie killers sometime in their youth. And they had been victims, too.

Pie killing also went worldwide. In England there was a woman's custard-pie-killing competition. But this kind of tournament never came over to the United States.

It is not clear why the 1975 vogue for pie murder faded. Perhaps it was due to the declining publicity value of a sudden custard splatter. Perhaps it just didn't seem exciting enough. In any case, the pie-killing organizations began to go out of business.

Peculiarly enough, custard-pie killing was the only type generally done. There was no common desire to splatter anyone with blueberry, apple or peach pie.

Which only goes to show that a new fad may be just around the corner.

MOPEDS (1975–78; High Point 1977–78)

Mopeds are selling like hot buttered popcorn at the Saturday night drive-in.

—A Connecticut moped dealer

In the middle 1970s cars almost had to seem like a burden. Gas had just started to become very expensive—when you could get it at all. Sometimes you had to sit in your car in long, long, long, lines at the filling station, and just when you got there, sometimes the station closed. How nice it would be to own a vehicle that would get 130 to 220 miles on a gallon of gas. And voilà: The moped, which Europe had known for three decades, came along. The moped got this 130 to 220 miles per gallon. It was exciting. A craze was born.

Mopeds are motorized bicycles with about half the power of a lawn mower. Or as *Sports Illustrated* put it, the moped was something more than a bicycle and something less than a motorcycle. But in fashion value for a short time in the 1970s, it outstripped both. It was more glamorous than a 10-speed bicycle—which only as recently as 1970 had come to the attention of the large American public—and was also a faster seller than the motorcycle at many a bike shop.

It was predicted that the moped would take the place of the second car in the American household. Articles in national magazines all showed how the moped could be used for an amusing Sunday spin or to take a commuter to work. An organization of women in Walnut Creek, California called itself the Moped Mamas, for their frequent trips together on the bikes. A Buffalo, New York moped salesman said that most mopeds were being sold to people like parents who wanted to buy their children a moped with which to tootle around a college campus, but statistics showed that many a moped was being sold to older folks. Mopeds were often attached to the backs of cars when people took long trips; they used the car to get there but then brought out the moped to do some discovering once they arrived at their vacation spot. The Italians came up with a moped you could fold up and carry around on your shoulder. A *Popular Mechanics* article taught how you could turn a 10-speed bicycle into a friction-driven moped for an investment of $120 to $240.

Yet every now and again, you could hear a voice of warning that all was not perfect with the moped. A Florida moped dealer said, for instance: "It's not a bicycle. It has a motor that will go fast enough to get you into trouble, but not fast enough to get you out." This was a fair enough estimation, for mopeds could travel no faster than 30 miles per hour, and sometimes no faster than 20.

Mopeds became voguish because of the energy crisis, and also because of the energy crisis perhaps, the government relaxed some of its restrictions on them; mopeds in 1975 did not face the stringent safety standards as motorcycles did. Standards were not as rigorous when it came to the types of lights that were required or when it came to the types of braking mechanisms. In most states they did not have to be licensed. All these factors were a great boon to their sales.

Yet by 1979 the vogue for mopeds began to wear off. More and more doubts were raised about their safety; also a lot of people began to be aware that mopeds just did not have a lot of power and could not replace a car. The prices for mopeds had gone up, too. It used to be that you could get one for $295, but now you had to count on spending at least $400.

Mopeds have always been principally a European vehicle. There have been millions on European roads since the end of World War II. Even when mopeds were a most intriguing item in America, they were still for the most part Batavia mopeds, Puch mopeds and Motobecane mopeds (among others)—all European makes.

Mopeds are by no means a thing of the past today. Yet the conveyance no longer cuts the romantic figure it did just a half a dozen years ago.

BOTTLED MONEY (1976)

Buying $10,000 in bills for the sum of $2.50 to $5.00 seems just too good to believe. Yet there was all the cash—right in a little bottle. Unfortunately, there was one small disadvantage: The money was shredded almost beyond recognition. More's the pity, for money as crushed as this is not negotiable.

Bottled money was another of the highly popular crazy merchandising items of the middle 1970s. There was the *Nothing Book*, a collection of blank pages nicely bound; there was the Pet Rock, which was merely a stone that could be put on a mantelpiece and was the perfect gift for a time; and then there was the mood

ring, which was said to change colors according to your daily temperament (see NOTHING BOOKS, PET ROCKS, MOOD RINGS). To get a hold of just one of these 56 tons of shredded bills from the Minneapolis Federal Reserve Bank, amounting to $13 million, represented yet another dimension in owning zany goods.

The small bottle of devastated currency, about 6 inches in height and 8 ounces in weight, was the brainchild of Bud Koppang, who somehow dreamed up the idea in the summer of 1976. This entrepreneur, who owned three small corporations at the time, first bought 20 tons of bills from the Federal Reserve and used college kids who were on their summer vacations to stuff the bottles. He ran into some problems immediately. For a while he couldn't get enough bottles. Then when he had the bottles, summer was over, and the kids had gone back to college. He met this challenge, too. In fact, he did so well that he had to go back to the Federal Reserve to buy more shredded cash.

Yet despite these initial hitches, bottled money was fascinating and became something of a hot item. By November 1976, 150,000 money jars, as they were also known, had been sold and, by Christmas, perhaps 50,000 more. No wonder Koppang said, in a twist on the old cliche, "Since I was a little boy, I've always believed it takes money to make money."

Bottled money became an object of much meditation. A psychologist from Brooklyn College commented:

Though the idea of a jar full of money is most intriguing, it is just too frustrating to be that close to all that cash and have it do the owner no good whatsoever. . . . It could even start an angry response if the frustration built up to any large extent.

Of course, there were accounts of people smashing the jars to get at the money because they couldn't stand fantasizing anymore about all that currency floating around in that little bottle (never mind that even if you were able to reassemble the bills, you would still not get whole bills, because they had miscellaneous, unconnected serial numbers). At Fairfield University in Connecticut, students bought a number of bottles, broke them and tried to match up the shredded fortune. It didn't work, and probably no one could say he or she was surprised.

Yet interest in the smashed cash really waned after Christmas 1976. Perhaps this was the kind of gag that people tired of quickly. In any event, stores carrying the currency jars were left with a large supply sitting prettily on their shelves. Now it was the merchandisers' turn to want to break them! Like everybody else, they just had to conclude that attainable dollar bills were a whole lot better.

DOROTHY HAMILL HAIRDO (1976)

The Dorothy Hamill was named after this young figure skater who won Olympic gold medals in Innsbruck, Austria in 1976 while wearing this short hairstyle. And did it ever attract attention and imitation! Her stylist, the Japanese hairdresser Suga, was astounded by the rage for the hairdo, also called the wedge (for the shape the hair formed in the sides and back), as was Dorothy Hamill herself, probably.

Supposedly the attraction of the Dorothy Hamill hairdo was that it was said to be easy to manage, but there was nothing wrong with looking like Dorothy Hamill, either. It was just like in the early years of the century when women wanted to look like the dancer Irene Castle and bobbed their hair (see BOBBED HAIR). Dancer Twyla Tharp affected the Hamill look, as did newscaster Pia Lindstrom. So did college girls and high school girls. Older women said it made them look younger.

With the decline of the wedge, long hair on women became prominent once again. One really significant fad the following year was the Farrah Fawcett look, which featured thick, curly hair (see FARRAH FAWCETT LOOK). Television, not sports events, had once again come to set the fashion pace.

INDOOR PLANTS (1976)

Instead of curtains going down on stage, they were coming down from the windows in 1976, to be replaced by luscious, exotic indoor plants. Suddenly, city folk decided to bring nature indoors. Plant sales flourished, with plant shops blossoming all over shopping malls and city streets and plants even being sold from the backs of trucks parked off highways. Everybody was buying indoor plants.

A New Yorker cares for her indoor plants

Books for the indoor gardener popped out at an incredible rate, all giving expert advice on raising healthy and happy plants. From *The New York Times Book of Houseplants* to the *Plant Doctor* and the *Woman's Day Book of Houseplants*, *The Complete Indoor Gardener* and even *The Secret Life of Plants* (which discussed the inner worship and the nature of plant life), one book after another explained in varying ways the needs, nature and best possible care for a host of indoor plants.

As for favorites, the spider plant, a green-and-white-striped hanging variety, was one of the more popular indoor plants. It was easy to maintain, and its plantlets could be cut from their stems and used to start new plants. Also really popular were begonias, Boston ferns, jade plants, coleus, dracaena marginata and ficus trees—all easily grown.

Discount chain stores sold plants priced from about $2 up to about $15. Chic plant shops carried more exotic varieties that cost over $100, such as clivia, from South Africa; genista, from England, whose broomlike branches intrigued medieval royalty; and cyperus papyrus, from Syria, which can grow up to eight feet tall in a city apartment. But the average price ranged from $15 to $35 for large plants in hanging baskets and others that stood tall enough to be placed on the floor.

Talk at parties often revolved around indoor plants—the best care hints, the better buys and the music that was the most soothing. It was often said that experts advised plant owners to talk to their greenery and to play music to make it happy. It didn't matter what you said to the plants—anything from "What do you think of the world situation?" to "Would you be happier with another family?" would be fine, as long as it sounded sweet. Likewise, it didn't matter what music you played to the plants—Brahms' German Lullaby or Elvis Presley's Love Me Tender would do, as long as it sounded sweet. Both the sweet talk and the sweet music were said to keep the plants' carbon dioxide flowing.

Another facet of the plant craze involved the supplies needed. Miniature plant care kits containing fork, shovel and pick were sold. Bottles with spray attachments were very important for misting each plant, as were indoor hoses. These latter, which ran as long as 60 feet, were attached to a kitchen faucet and used to water a houseful of plants.

More energetic plant owners carried, dragged and pulled their plants into the bathtub and gave them showers, a technique that both freshened the leaves and watered the plants.

The sale of plants, pots and plant care books dropped suddenly at the end of 1976, according to reports of plant store onwers. A corresponding drop was doubtless experienced in record store sales of plant-soothing music.

THE FONZ (1976–77)

BRETT, 8: I don't want to eat my vegetables.
SHANNON, 10: Then you won't grow up to like the Fonz.

—Conversation reported by Lee Margulies, newspaper reporter, about the television character Arthur Fonzarelli

When the Fonz arrived, people paid heed. The man had a black leather jacket and skinny-legged jeans, all the better to zoom on his motorcycle with. And what a style, what a style. No wonder there were Fonzie (Fonzarelli is interchangeably the Fonz and Fonzie) dolls, miniature plastic imitations of Fonzie's motorcycle, buttons proclaiming one's love for Fonzie, Fonzie posters, Fonzie buttons, Fonzie beanbags, Fonzie pillowcases and sheets, Fonzie knee socks and Fonzie paint-by-number sets. Finally, there was the Fonzie T-shirt, to remind everyone of Fonzie's best-known gesture: The shirt bears Fonzarelli's nickname, along with a large representation of a thumb, jauntily sticking up. Now this TV character, who was supposed to be sort of a 1950s high school thug, actually turned out to be a nice tough guy. And in 1976–77 it's hard to think of anybody who was having it tough with Fonzie. Not the television people, who basked in the high ratings of "Happy Days," the TV show in which Arthur was featured; nor the merchandising people, who were raking in all the money; nor the viewers who watched "Happy Days" or the people who bought the Fonzie stuff—they all just loved Fonzie. Their response to the "tough guy" was to demand lots more of him.

The Fonz, as portrayed by Henry Winkler (who had never ridden a motorcycle in his life before the series, according to the actor), was the tough guy in "Happy Days," a situation comedy that began in January 1974 but was set in the 1950s, as has already been noted. More important, Fonzie was really just the opposite of teenager Richie Cunningham, played by Ron Howard. Much more wholesome than the Fonz, Richie didn't know any of the ropes of life and had a teenager's problem with . . . with . . . (are you ready?)—girls! This was one problem Fonzie did not have, since almost with a mere snap of the Fonz's fingers, a flock of pretty teen-age girls would appear from nowhere and lovingly surround their hero. Hence, Richie looked up to the Fonz. Hence, a situation comedy was made. Hence, a fad was born.

Well, perhaps it wasn't quite that simple. In the beginning the Fonz was important enough in the show, but he was still an outcast—not as tough as the 1950s kids known as juvenile delinquents actually were, but certainly no one to be welcomed into the Cunningham home. Richie was in some fear of him, and when Arthur F. wanted Richie, he barked commandingly, "Cunningham" (as in "Cunningham, get over here. I want to talk to you"). What's more, one time the Fonz asked Cunningham to help him cheat on an exam; Richie refused and was afraid the Fonz would beat him up or something. Well, this early Fonz was intriguing but not the stuff of which buttons or pillowcases are made. And one day in 1975 Fred Silverman, head of programming for ABC, the network on which "Happy Days" was aired, realized it, too, saying, "Give that crazy biker more to do."

Thus was born the Fonz that many a person grew to know and love: the Fonz with all the warmth and sincerity, the Fonz who was really a good fellow, the black-leather-jacketed tough guy with a heart. This was in 1976. After that time the Fonz was accepted—perhaps embraced—by the Cunningham household. As for Richie himself, he need no longer have worried about being ordered around with a curt "Cunningham"; the Fonz now called him "Red" (Richie had red hair). Young Mr. Cunningham could now get all the lessons he wanted on girls without worrying about having to deal with some gangster type.

And so the Fonz—just after the halfway mark of the 1970s—became faddish table talk. People discussed the Fonz and Richie's escapades at Arnold's, the burger place where they hung out. Or they recounted how the Fonz, with a gentle, well-placed tap of his fist, started a dead engine. Or they displayed the great Fonz gesture—holding both thumbs up with the rest of the hand clenched into a fist—while intoning Fonzie's favorite phrase—"E-E-E-A-Y." Fonzie became a national institution. In 1980 he (Henry Winkler, actually) gave his famous leather jacket to the Smithsonian Institution.

Even the television critics were won over. In the beginning "Happy Days" was looked down upon as being too syrupy. But by 1977 many a national publication—not only *TV Guide* but *Newsweek*, *Seventeen*, *McCall's* and *Playboy* as well—went out of its way to interview Henry Winkler. These journals actually had only one question: Was Henry Winkler really like the Fonz? People just couldn't get the Fonz out of their minds.

At the end of the 1970s, the great interest in the Fonz began to wane. He was replaced in large part because of the rise of disco and disco's hero, John Travolta (see DISCO). But it was also true that the Fonz had sort of run his course. Yet Arthur Fonzarelli had nevertheless gained a secure niche in the national consciousness. "E-E-E-A-Y" will never again be the same. Nor will black leather jackets. And having a way with the girls has come to be synonymous with being like the Fonz.

FARRAH FAWCETT LOOK (1977)

A year earlier, in 1976, a lot of girls had trooped into hairstylists' shops to get a short Dorothy Hamill (see DOROTHY HAMILL HAIRDO), making them almost resemble the flappers of the Roaring Twenties. A year later, however, longer hair (beyond shoulder-length) was back, and—in complete contrast to the Dorothy Hamill look—it was thick, layered and fluffy. It was also usually blonde, for the young lady who sparked the longer-hair revival was Farrah Fawcett, a blonde Texan and one of the heroines in the TV show "Charlie's Angels." In fact, gals who wanted to affect the Farrah look were known to have squeezed lemons into their hair or added peroxide to get just the right color.

Farrah was really big. There was not only the Farrah hairdo but Farrah T-shirts and Farrah posters. It was the Farrah hairdo, however, that was particularly prominent.

However, the look was not that easy to create. One hairdresser described it this way:

Volume blowing, we call it. First, with her [the client's] head held down, I blow it out from the back with my hands going forward, lifting up the base for volume. When it's 85 percent dry, I put all the ends into pincurls and attach them to the head so the ends have that feathery look.

Farrah Fawcett, of course, declared that it wasn't all that hard. She said she arranged the billowing tresses herself and only twice a year did she go to a hairstylist to have it cut and streaked. Still, one must keep in mind that it was Fawcett's hair, and a lady should be able to find her own hair easy to manage.

Scholastic Magazine named Farrah Fawcett the number one teen-age hero of 1977, and many young girls from coast to coast sought to emulate her. For instance, at a Roslyn, Long Island hair school in 1977, the Farrah Fawcett hairstyle was the most voguish thing.

The Farrah Fawcett look remained the rage for only about a year, although girls continued to wear it beyond 1978. Perhaps a great number of girls began to agree with one hairdresser's assessment of Farrah: "She has a nice face and all her hair covers it."

In any event, the flamboyant Farrah Fawcett look was kind of a return to glamor after the austere Dorothy Hamill look.

"MAY THE FORCE BE WITH YOU" (1977)

The expression from *Star Wars* "May the force be with you" rescued from oblivion a much-neglected English verb tense—the subjunctive. But *may* is no word for describing the influence that *Star Wars* had on American life; the word is *did*—without a doubt *did*, indubitably *did*. Starting in July, *Star Wars* was the talk of 1977. It was science fiction with a fascination that was carried to extremes—bigger than Flash Gordon, bigger than Buck Rogers, bigger even than "Star Trek," with its First Officer Spock, its Captain Kirk, its Starship Enterprise and its very devoted following, known as "trekkies."

Star Wars was bigger than all that, and even as early as the movie was being made, there were indications of exactly what was going to come to pass. Consider this: One character in *Star Wars* was a tall robot named C3PO, constructed of aluminum, steel and vulcanized rubber, and played by Englishman Anthony Daniels. Daniels related to the *Los Angeles Times* what happened when he first appeared on the set in his full futuristic garb. The rest of the cast stared at him, giving Daniels this impression: "I felt totally alone. . . . It was like they had all seen God for the first time."

"May the force be with you" was the phrase that the heroes of this movie like Luke Skywalker used to give themselves the spirit to overcome the villains, known as the Empire, which was led by one black-caped Darth Vader, who had a deadly laser sword. And soon enough, there were millions of buttons, each selling for $1, inscribed with "May the Force Be with You." The bonanza in merchandising even began a week before the movie was officially released and, of course, gathered incredible strength. These items included posters, T-shirts, toys, lunch boxes, digital watches, nightgowns and jewelry. Also there were costumes aplenty: like those of Darth Vader; Luke Skywalker; either of the two robots, R2D2 or C3P0; or Chewbacca, the "wookie" (a gorillalike alien) who was a sidekick of the heroes. They went for $40.00. Posters of Darth Vader in a San Francisco novelty shop outsold posters of long-haired Farrah Fawcett-Majors, just recently a faddish darling of the public, more than two to one. You could also get *Star Wars* keychains for $1.50, *Star Wars* tote bags for $5.00 and *Star Wars* chain necklaces for $1.00.

The movie *Star Wars* had been germinating in director George Lucas's mind since 1973. When he finally got around to doing it in 1976, a whole city in California was built so that the extraordinary science fiction special effects could be created. These would give the impression of something that took place on a faraway galaxy long, long ago (as the opening line of *Star Wars* has it), though everything looked futuristic.

And in 1977—well into the 20th century (almost into the 21st century, in fact)—this is what people wanted to see; indeed, they wanted to be swept away by it. It was an exaggeration of their lives that had become so absorbed by gadgetry, but a recognizable exaggeration; and also its heroes came out on top. By February 1978 the movie had grossed $207 million in ticket receipts alone.

However, statistics did not tell the entire story by a long shot. People were just obsessed, stood in long lines in every city in the nation to see it, clapped and jeered like they did for old-fashioned Western movies and really even got kind of a fixation about it. The *San Francisco Chronicle*, for instance, told of two young girls who went to see *Star Wars* 41 times. One girl called *Star Wars* "a way of life," while the other girl said, "I get really nervous when I haven't seen it for three days." Also, in San Francisco, a *Star Wars* drink began to sell well. It consisted of rum, brandy, sloe gin, amaretto, passion fruit and soda water and sold for $2.50.

Yet *Star Wars* did not intrigue everybody; on the contrary, sometimes it inspired intense hostility. A San Francisco merchant who saw people lined up for the midnight show of *Star Wars* and noticed the way they messed up the rest rooms in his gas station and also spat on the windows of a photography shop nearby said, "These people are the greatest conglomeration of pigs I've ever seen." In a Washington, D.C. suburb, a housewife speaking to the *Washington Post* commented along much the same lines, as she observed how all the cars belonging to people who had come to see *Star Wars* had blocked the street and created a fire hazard: "I just wanted to scream and beat up the cars."

These were the voices of the few, however. Most people were captivated by the movie and everything about it.

And the interest in *Star Wars* and *Star Wars*'s "force" has outlived the picture, which has had two popular sequels, *The Empire Strikes Back* and *Return of the Jedi*. Moreover, it is probably anything but coincidental that video games made their first big national "splash" in 1978, with games like "Space Invaders" and later "Asteroids" (see VIDEO GAMES AND PAC-MAN). At the video screen you could now control interstellar gadgetry and be like one of the heroes of *Star Wars*. In many an arcade, from an ice cream parlor to a bar, you could recreate their world. You were capable of handling the 21st century; *Star Wars* had told us this. So why not get into practice?

DISCO (1977–83; High Point, 1978–80)

It's how you look and move and who you're with, not the bucks you have.
        —A Pasadena fellow, on the attraction of disco

In the middle 1970s young Frenchmen and Frenchwomen started gathering at clubs where they could dance not to live bands, but to heavily amplified records, while moving in the midst of colored floodlights and flashing strobes. This kind of club, which became known as *le disco* (after discotheque, or nightclub), spread throughout Europe and, from the beginning, was a place where dancing was done into the very early hours of the morning. When discomania became really prominent in the United States between 1977 and 1980 as a result of the movie *Saturday Night Fever* with John Travolta, when the goings-on at Manhattan's Studio 54 were reported daily, when the department stores were scrambling to take advantage of the elegant disco clothes trade and when memberships in disco clubs sometimes went for $275 to $350 (this only guaranteed you entrance to the club and a slightly reduced admission fee), it was really easy to see how far the disco craze had gone. One Los Angeles attorney told *Business Week*, "The profit at a good disco is so incredible that when you talk about it to a person sophisticated in finance, they think you're dreaming."

Disco is still an intense experience, where your senses are really almost battered by any number of impressions. On a slightly sunken floor, many couples dance, leaving very little empty space between them, while a light as direct and as strong as a police searchlight may shine in your face; since it only does so intermittently, it can cause you a distinct feeling of vertigo. There really is no interval between the songs, nor do they vary between fast pieces and slow pieces—to do a waltz would definitely be out of place (though to do any of the animal dances of the early 20th century, like the turkey trot, the grizzly bear, or the chicken scratch—see TURKEY TROT AND OTHER ANIMAL DANCES—definitely wouldn't be, if anyone knew how anymore). While the amplification is not so loud as to crack your eardrum, it is loud enough to effectively drown out conversation.

At the same time, people who are not dancing—easily the great majority—are drawn into the "disco experience" also. By the bar there is a large movie screen on which the song being danced to (say the BeeGees' Staying Alive or More Than a Woman, both of which were featured as part of the sound track for *Saturday Night Fever*) is turned into story form, with imagery of sexuality and seduction, which is titillating but not terribly explicit; this is all in a very vivid technicolor. And then there are the many mirrors.

All this takes place in a disco in the Bay Ridge section of Brooklyn, New York, not far from the club where many of the scenes for *Saturday Night Fever* were shot. The movie was based on an article in *New York* magazine—Nik Cohn's "Tribal Rites of the New Saturday Night" (June 7, 1976). And as far as disco and its extraordinary popularity is concerned, the movie is what made all the difference.

Saturday night fever is the rage for dancing continuously in these places of heavy noise and illusion—or disco. This is not meant sarcastically, for the movie was all about a character, Tony Manero (Travolta), who escaped the tedium of his job and daily life by going to the disco, as did many of his friends. Certainly it was only celluloid, but what Tony was doing cut deep and caused many young guys to try to look and act like him and many young girls to try to look and act the way his girls did. It was like the rage for movie actor James Dean in the fifties (see MOTORCYCLE JACKETS) or the rage to look like the ballroom dancer Irene Castle a little after 1910 (see TANGO AND DANCES OF IRENE AND VERNON CASTLE).

This meant a whole host of white suits, gold chains, stiletto heels and tight pants were worn because it was now the thing to look fancy. Within a short time, this evolved into the dancers' looking really unusual: There was the thrift-shop disco look, consisting perhaps of 1920s-like flannels for the men and cloches and fake pearls for the women; there was the bodywear disco look, consisting of spandex; and the futuristic disco look, consisting of aluminum lame jump suits and plastic jeans. Disco went big time, the gig now not only of young kids who had to work for a living but also of the rich and celebrated. It was statusy to go disco.

In New York City, for instance, disco raged everywhere, and some prominent old dancing places like the Empire Room at the Waldorf-Astoria and the Persian Room at the Plaza Hotel were forced to close, while the old-time dance hall Roseland, where the Charleston had flourished, turned itself largely into a disco parlor.

At the same time, many disco clubs became most selective about who would get to move to their amplified music and startling lights: There were always long lines outside many discos. Then, a few people, chosen at random, who looked the most unusual and who looked as if they would mesh with the wild crowd inside would be asked to come in. One disco manager freely admitted that men in two-piece suits were not likely to be chosen, nor were couples who appeared to be very much interested in each other—they would just hang around, hold hands, look into each others'

eyes and not be the least bit wild. He continued, "I let a lot of dancers and Broadway actors in for nothing. . . . If people are dressed to have fun—the crazier, the better—they get in." It went without saying that sometimes you would have to work all day on your getup. (Well, you could always take a sick day, right?)

Department stores picked up on the obsession with disco. At Charles A. Stevens in Chicago, there were mannequins of disco dancers in the window, while amplifiers blared the disco sound out into State Street; dance instructors taught disco, while people could dance disco in the store from noon to 2 p.m.; this went on for one week. Wanamaker's store in Philadelphia had a disco dance contest, and the winner won a trip to Hollywood. There were also disco promotions at Macy's in San Francisco, Joske's in Houston, Davison's in Atlanta, Shillito's in Cincinnati and Nordstorm's in Portland (Oregon). Of course, these department stores were doing more than good-heartedly showing that they had caught the pulse of the times. It was their opportunity to sell fancy disco clothes items that people wanted to buy—to show off the sensual leotards, tight pants, bodysuits, corduroy and plastic jeans.

In the beginning, if you went out to a disco, you went out to dance elegantly, just as you went out dressed elegantly. Among the disco dance steps you would see on the floor were the freak, the bus stop, the hustle and the tango hustle. (This was in marked contrast to the amorphous twist of the 1960s, in which all you had to do was "twist around"—the 1960s not being a time that saw itself as regulated in any form, including dance.) There was also real enthusiasm in disco: John Travolta said himself in filming *Saturday Night Fever*, "I really get off on dancing, it's a high." Medical specialists said, too, that disco was good for "cardio-respiratory fitness and leg endurance."

Yet as was the case with activities as diverse as skateboarding (see SKATEBOARDING) and ping-pong (see PING-PONG), disco found itself in some medical disfavor. One physician said that a person who stayed too long at a disco and sat too close to an amplifier risked permanent ear injury and added that if "a laser beam of a mirrored globe entered your eye, you could get a burn in the retina and a permanent blind spot."

This was, however, not the reason why disco began to decline as an obsession in the late 1970s. Many people had just begun to discover that discos often turned out to be really tense places and that too much emphasis was put on the way your clothes looked. *New York Magazine* suggested, for instance, that the basic dictates of disco constituted the following feelings: "I am great looking. I have great clothes on. People less than great than I will surely be staring at me." This was found troubling, and in 1980, while disco remained, people were becoming more interested in being urban cowboys at dance gathering places (see URBAN COWBOYS). Somehow, this was regarded as less threatening.

Also, there were items like T-shirts reading "Disco s----." And then many people were turned off by the indulgent stunts played at the celebrated disco joints—like at artist Andy Warhol's birthday celebration at Studio 54, when $800 in $1 bills was dumped from a trash can onto his head. This would be hard to explain to all those Manero look-alikes, who worked week in and week out just for survival wages.

This is not to say that disco is about to perish. Far from it. That disco joint in the Bay Ridge section spoken about earlier still had girls wrestling in the mud one night and girls wearing sexy wet T-shirts another night; it still is crowded. Yet it doesn't have an "I'm glad to be with it" frenzy. One girl, when asked what she liked about the place, replied, "the drinks." When it was suggested to her that she could get those anywhere and didn't have to go to a disco for them, she just shrugged.

TOGA PARTIES (1978)

All you had to do was drape a sheet over yourself and you could be a part of the biggest collegiate party-going fad of the late 1970s—toga parties. You could be Brutus, Julius Caesar or the cunning Livia. This is not to say that you had to stick around in the forum. In New York City, for instance, toga wearers went to the movies.

This blast from ancient Rome came about as a result of the toga party that was featured in the movie *Animal House*, in which the frolickers of Delta House at Faber College threw the gathering. Kids took naturally to this bacchanalia, which was helped in no small way by the movie's own promotional campaign. At some of the toga parties, John Belushi (who died in March 1982) and some other actors from the film would appear.

The toga-wearing parties were like rock concerts, those extraordinary gatherings in the 1960s, but without the political involvement. They took hold everywhere, both in private fraternity houses and at college unions. The best-known toga party was at the Univer-

Disco dancing at Regine's, New York City

Three fellows at the biggest toga party of 1978, held at the University of Wisconsin and attended by more than 10,000 toga wearers

sity of Wisconsin, where more than 10,000 toga wearers—many with garlands in their hair—appeared at a celebration that started at 10 p.m. and lasted until the wee hours of the morning.

This was nothing like a toga party that took place in the early 1930s. That earlier bash was thrown by first lady Eleanor Roosevelt, who was trying to spoof all the politicians and newswriters who looked on FDR as another Caesar.

The toga party was the rage of the 1978 spring season, just as *Animal House* was the fashionable movie. After the film's popularity passed, toga parties were no longer such a hot item.

HOT TUBS (Late 1970s; PARTICULARLY 1978–79)

When the fog comes rushing in and you're sitting in your tub, nothing is more fabulous.
—San Francisco man, commenting on his hot tub

Hot tubs originated in California in the mid-1970s (the first were made in Santa Barbara) and remained popular in that region even into the 1980s. The craze enjoyed national popularity in the late seventies, since these hot tubs were something new; since the hot jet streams in the tubs were seen as therapeutic; since they

resembled very handsome wooden barrels; and since their warmth brought people together in the same outdoor wooden tub—not only couples but families, too. The fad was not sustained throughout the country as it was on the West Coast, however. The reasons for the long-lasting popularity of hot tubs in California are rather obvious: The weather is ideal year round, and the sometimes very casual West Coast life-styles lend themselves well to the pleasures of the hot tub.

What were, or are, the pleasures of the hot tub? That it was perceived to be relaxing—so relaxing that some people took three baths a day in it. And that it was so warm. It was like swimming in the Mediterranean Sea, and then some. In the 1970s people had got into different kinds of water pleasures, and to many the hot tub proved a lot less clammy than the water bed (which was really never warm enough, it seemed; see WATER BEDS).

An outdoor tub that looked like half a wooden barrel, the hot tub was most famously made of redwood (talk was of the sensual redwood hot tub) but it could also be made of cedar, oak, teak or any other wood that was rot-resistant. The right water temperature was about 105 degrees. This was true of all the luxuriant hot tubs, whether they were found at a home on San Francisco Bay; on a porch in Boulder, Colorado; or on a ledge overlooking the mountains in Golden, Colorado. It was true of the hot tubs that the movie stars swam in (movie stars were big for hot tubs; Sissy Spacek spoke particularly warmly of them) or the hot tub in a New York City one-bedroom apartment.

Wherever the hot tub was, people had to take precautions. A chemical balance had to be maintained, or bacteria would grow in the heated water and infect the bathers.

In the beginning this seemed a small enough thing to worry about. The hot tub was an experience, a bringer of personal intimacy. Couples and families told how it brought them closer together, and people discovered how intimate they could be with their neighbors, too. Hot tubs could take the interpersonal anxiety out of life.

Thus, it is not surprising that advertisements for hot tubs inevitably showed a picture of happy young people, all with cocktails in hand, submerged chest-deep in a redwood tub. Drinking is, in fact, not healthy for those partaking of the pleasures of the hot tub. The human body cannot adjust its temperature properly when liquor is consumed while the body is in hot water. The blood vessels become too overheated.

In June 1979, about two years after the heyday of the hot tub started, the perils of hot tub bathing became nationally known. *Time* magazine featured a story about a California couple found dead because they had stayed in an overheated hot tub. Doctors began to point out that dallying in a hot tub was particularly a health hazard to people with weak hearts.

This sort of diminished the interest in hot tubs. Sure, they were pleasant, relaxing, intimate—but there were hidden dangers. Hot tubs no longer were the wave of the future; in April 1980 *Newsweek* observed how people were beginning to enjoy something called an extrasoft bathtub, lined with polyurethene foam.

Yet in its own time, the hot tub was quite the thing. Hundreds of thousands were sold, at prices ranging from $1,000 to $3,500. Soaking in that tub 6 feet in diameter and 4 feet deep was a real pleasure. *Popular Mechanics* ran a story on how you could build your own tub: what kind of wood to choose, how to assemble the boards and how to sink the tub into the ground.

Many people may have lost interest because of the hot tubs' perils, but it is also true that an overdose of intimacy may have discouraged other hot tubbers. For instance, consider the California couple who owned a hot tub for two years before they realized that they were never alone. The husband observed that at least four times a week someone would appear at their door, towel in hand, ready to enjoy the pleasures of hot tubbing. The couple thereupon decided to give up the hot tub, the husband remarking, "It just wasn't worth running a resort for fun-loving friends."

Perhaps it wasn't worth it to run a hot tub spa for friends, but in the summer of 1982, at least one distinguished law firm—Ropes and Gray in Boston—thought a hot tub was the ideal place to discuss an important matter with one of its clients. So there, in a hot tub, sat the attorneys and the representatives for the client, perhaps working out a big deal, according to *The American Lawyer*.

Now here's a trend that bears watching.

A couple enjoys their hot tub

ROLLER SKATING AND ROLLER DISCO SKATING (1978–79)

Palm Springs Avenue is to roller skaters what filet mignon is to steak lovers, and you want to take our mignon away.

—A habitual Palm Springs, California roller skater

If I was wearing a $60 pair of fancy pants, I would feel horrid if I fell and ripped them.

—Observation of one San Francisco roller disco skater

Neither roller skating nor roller disco skating are new to the American scene; there was a roller skating craze as early as a decade or so before 1890 and an interest in dancing on roller skates in the 1940s. The author remembers kids getting roller skates as presents in the 1950s and once roller skating in an arena to organ music. Yet such things were "small potatoes" compared to the fascination with roller skating and roller disco skating in the late 1970s. Then, a San Francisco judge would roller skate through his august chambers. A Washington, D.C. man would roller skate to the supermarket and only then take the skates off in deference to the store manager's order that there would be no roller skating in the aisles. As for roller disco skating—an offshoot of disco, with its continuous movement and its unusual apparel (see DISCO)—this was also picked up by celebrity and commoner alike. The singer Cher, who was a real star of the roller disco scene, made plans to start a roller disco club, to be called Hell on Wheels. Stewardesses who were on strike against their airlines took up roller disco skating, and so did truck drivers, for instance.

You just couldn't get away from roller skating then. If you went to a fashionable restaurant, you might well have been asked what your eating pleasure was by a waiter wearing roller skates. This happened in New York City, for instance.

Roller disco skating caught on big almost precisely in the year 1978, as could be seen from an article in the California publication *Sunset* in late 1977; it said that dancing in roller skating arenas was once more beginning to get popular. The same may be said of just plain outdoor roller skating. In 1978 things revved up, people laced up their skates and just merrily took off. Or as an executive for the Chicago Roller Skating Company said to *Business Week* of the extraordinary business his firm was experiencing, "Our business is exploding with the crocuses and tulips of spring."

This new roller skating boom is often attributed to the new and ultrasleek look of the modern roller skates themselves: Like the skateboards of the 1970s, roller skates no longer had those rather noisy and clumsy steel wheels; instead, they had polyurethane wheels. This enabled the roller skater to have more flexibility on the skates and turn more gracefully, and it also meant he or she had a much quieter ride, which may have been rewarding if you were roller disco skating and wanted to pay attention to the "beat." Yet this explanation seems perhaps just a little bit off the mark. The difference between the old steel roller skates and the new polyurethane roller skates lies in the smoothness of the ride, certainly, but compared to the difference between the high-front-wheeled velocipede of the 1880s and the "safety" bicycle in the 1890s (see BICYCLING), the differences among roller skates were not that great.

People liked the sleek, colorful look of these new roller skates, which could cost between $60 and $1,000; it was a chance to look stylish, like wearing those high, cowboy boot roller skates. Also, the rage for roller skating also came about because it was found to be really great exercise that burned just the right amount of calories. And many people had found for years that going on a Sunday ride in a big, gas-guzzling car—or in any kind of car, for that matter—was just too commonplace. People wanted to feel the breezes, and they turned first to the 10-speed bicycle, (see BICYCLING) then to the moped, (see MOPEDS) and now, as something even more exotic, to roller skates. They either bought the skates, or for about $1.50 to $3.00 an hour, they could rent them. The owner of the roller skating concession at Manhattan's Central Park was particularly effusive, as she said "I firmly believe that roller skating is going to change humanity."

As a national craze in the 1970s, roller skating started in California, or one coast away from Newport, Rhode Island, where it had flourished in the late 19th century as something the really rich were the first to enjoy doing. More particularly, it probably started in Los Angeles, where young movie stars and pop singers were among the first to lace on the skates; pictures of Cher, Lily Tomlin, Olivia Newton-John, Robin Williams and Linda Ronstadt roller skating were soon appearing in national magazines.

And so the Golden State landscape began to be dotted with roller skaters. In the Los Angeles environs, a Beverly Hills lawyer could be seen roller skating at work, while in nearby Venice roller skaters and cyclists waged an in no way friendly battle for the use of the boardwalk overlooking the Pacific. In San Francisco roller skaters took their gear to Golden Gate Park; again, however, there were problems, since the city of San Francisco restricted the skaters to certain areas, and

skaters were prohibited from going near places where there was a profusion of flowers. They were also restricted from using the Golden Gate Bridge after they had become accustomed to making that part of their roller skating itinerary. In Milpitas, California there were roller skating lessons for the blind. At San Diego harbor there was a roller skating marathon. A 16-year-old guy and two older buddies roller skated from San Francisco to Los Angeles in a record six days. The 16-year-old, Anthony Caravas, was not terribly overwhelmed by the accomplishment and would only say, "We slept until 11 a.m., and skated from 1 p.m. to 7 p.m.; we could've made better time."

Yet there were no roller skating discos in the heart of San Francisco even by June 1979, although those who wanted to dance while roller skating could go to south San Francisco. The reason for this was not particularly strange: Roller disco was a New York City craze that traveled westward, just like disco itself. It was here in chic clubs like Xenon in Manhattan every Tuesday night, as well as in old-time roller skating arenas that had been transformed to look like real disco spots in Brooklyn, Queens and the Bronx, that roller disco caught on. Here were the first flashing lights, the first booming amplifiers, the first globes hanging from the ceiling, which items are so prominent in disco. And here were the first exotic clothing items—also found in regular disco—like flashy short pants, spandex, jump suits and strapless dresses. Why its bizarreness—the wheels, the clothes, the futuristic lighting, the gyrations of the skaters—just made you think of platform go-go dancing from the 1960s (see PLATFORM GO-GO DANCING).

Not that roller disco stayed in New York. It spread nationwide. There was a day for roller discoing at DuPont Circle in Washington, D.C. And when it hit California, it hit big—and sometimes strangely. At the Aloha Roller Palace in south San Francisco, not only were there the usual amplifiers, lights and mirrors, but overlooking it all was a giant figurehead of a Hawaiian god. One frequent roller disco skater said of it all, "Everybody should roller-disco; everybody's got some goochy-goochy in them, and this brings it out." In New Orleans and Chicago, roller disco skating was also big. A Chicago newspaper columnist really disapproved of it, but to no avail. The roller disco life in New Orleans was so intense that all the locals agreed that it didn't have to take second place to New York City, in dancing or clothes or anything. This may well have been true, but it is hard to think that anyone anywhere besides New York would buy up fashionable Gucci shoes and turn them into roller skates.

Yet by 1980 roller disco began to be a little bit unfashionable, and the new futuristic arenas were no longer the place above all others to be seen. A number of people also lost interest because they fell down a lot. As a typical example of this loss of interest, an active roller disco club in the Bensonhurst section of Brooklyn closed down and became a "flea market."

As for roller skating itself that, too, lost some of its vogue by 1980. Typically, the concession The Good Skate in Central Park in Manhattan, which was so big in the late 1970s, was no longer so big in the early 1980s. Roller skating, which was predicted in the heady days to be "the sport of the 1980s," turned out to be only one nice, active diversion among many.

Yet roller skating or dancing on skates in arenas is cyclical. It was big in the 1880s and again in the 1930s and again in the 1940s, and it will surely become big in the future. More than one analyst of the roller skating scene has said that it happens when the nation is in some kind of recession. But it may simply happen when many people only want to feel a lot of motion under their feet—metal wheels one time, polyurethane another time and who knows what the coming time?

VIDEO GAMES (1978–) AND PAC-MAN (1981–)

You could walk around and look at girls all day, but sometimes you need a diversion.
—A comment heard on why people play video games

You don't have to be a macho six-footer who's trying to save the universe every time you play.
—Stanley Jarocki, vice president of marketing for Bally Manufacturing on why people play Pac-Man

The obsession with a video game—which turned out to be one called Pac-Man—was an event that just had to happen. Ever since Pong, the first such game, came along in 1972, video games had attracted more and more interest; what had started as a small group of followers had become almost an army. In the Pac-Man® video game, the object is to guide the pie-shaped Pac-Man through a maze eating up all the dots which line the paths of the maze, while avoiding being eaten by the four colored circles which are chasing you. Now, this game has become a faddish bonanza. According to the New York *Daily News*, you could wear a Pac-Man hat, go to sleep with Pac-Man pajamas, go to the beach and dry off with Pac-Man towels, solve Pac-Man puzzles, write with Pac-Man ball-point pens, play with Pac-Man toys or eat Pac-Man cookies, not to mention any number of other Pac-Man-inspired things that you could call your own. This was in the spring and summer of 1982.

Not everyone wanted to wear Pac-Man or eat Pac-Man, though; it was enough for some just to play the game, which they often did unceasingly. One game cost only 25 cents, but many people had to keep feeding the machine in order to keep playing for hours. The game's duration depended on your Pac-Man skill. You could play play one game (while scoring points all the time) as long as Pac-Man wasn't eaten by dots that looked like ghosts; once he was consumed, the game was over. A beginner would be finished in a matter of seconds, but a master could play one game for hours, not only showing good hand-eye coordination but also making use of his or her knowledge of patterns. This could be addictive, and there was also a song, called Pac-Man Fever, about the obsession, composed by two Atlantans, Jerry Buckner and Gary Garcia, near the end of 1981. Buckner played for hours at a time; no wonder he and Garcia would come up with lyrics like "I've got Pac-Man fever." The record was a big seller as a 45 RPM but also did well as a long-playing disc.

Pac-Man was the first video game to really catch on that did not make use of outer space themes, which were very common in the late 1970s. It was also the first video game to catch on among women; in fact, the "female market"—as the researchers put it—became so much of a factor that the Ms. Pac-Man video game was introduced in the spring of 1982. Ms. Pac-Man acts very much like Pac-Man and faces the same obstacles from menacing ghosts, but she looks different, with her yellow face, lipstick and Marilyn Monroe-like beauty mark. Both Pac-Man and Ms. Pac-Man are comely video creatures—something you might want to bring home to play with the kids—and this also accounts for their faddish popularity, which had gone far beyond inserting a quarter into a slot.

The first Pac-Man machines were produced in November 1980 by Midway Manufacturing, a firm that at one time specialized in pinball machines and came up with some of the most popular ones in the 1930s. The name *Pac-Man*, which is Japanese in origin, means "eating (pac) man." For Pac-Man, it is indeed eat or be eaten.

You could play Pac-Man or Ms. Pac-Man at probably as many as 180,000 locations throughout America. Also, you could get a home Pac-Man video game for $39.95. Whether you played it at home or in an arcade or at a diner or at a beauty salon (video games were all over the place), you could get better at it—perhaps—if you had mastered the books about Pac-Man, which abounded, like *Mastering* or *How to Win at Pac-Man*. Sometimes it semed that everyone wanted to know how to handle the Pac video display, with its 240 dots, its mazelike paths and its ghostly looking monsters.

One distributor called Pac-Man "the Mickey Mouse of the 80's." That remains to be seen.

Pac-Man, like all video games, makes use of computer technology. In all these games a microcomputer makes it possible for items like dots, stars, representations of animals, spaceships and others to move across the screen. By comparison with pinball machines, with their big marble balls, relay banks and holes, video games have been seen by many as more exciting, more attuned to the present. Or as one 29-year-old fellow put it: "I'm not crazy about pinball. But I love these electronic gadgets. There's more action." And the video game makers quickly learned that people wanted more than the sound of electronic blip-blips on the screen; soon there were simulated explosions to go along with flashing colors.

Pong, the first video game (made by Atari), was like ping-pong, except the ping-pong ball (or something that looked very much like it) was on the screen and was controlled by a player who used a knob. This became something of a fad, just like the game ping-pong itself, with its crazy celluloid ball, was a fad in the early 20th century (see PING-PONG). The knob controlling the video game came to stay.

Throughout the 1970s video games became more and more important, but no single video game became extraordinarily voguish. Then in 1978 along came Space Invaders, which not only tapped the popular outer space theme but also was somewhat more challenging than the video games that preceded it. With Space Invaders came the great interest in video games, which may have resulted in part because of the fascination with the 1977 movie *Star Wars* (see "MAY THE FORCE BE WITH YOU"). Space Invaders was, after all, sort of a *Star Wars* set that you could manipulate yourself so as to be in control of your very own galaxy. Two years later Asteroids came along, and this was so popular that a special feature article was written about it in *Esquire* magazine in 1981. Or as one 16-year-old Hoboken, New Jersey boy said of video games in 1980, "We [he and his friends] spend our earnings in here" (an arcade housing video games).

Which has raised something of a problem. Just as in times past—when civic authorities tried to stop dances like the tango and the Charleston and the twist, and other activities like skateboarding (see TANGO AND DANCES OF IRENE AND VERNON CASTLE, TWIST, SKATEBOARDING)—they tried to stop video games. In Chicago, for instance, a city councilman proposed that video games be banned, and town leaders in the suburbs of Detroit did the same thing. Proposals for prohibiting video games in some way have also been made in New Jersey, California, New York and Maryland in recent months. The reason? Just as it was with the offending dances and other activities: It encourages the young to waste their time (and their money).

Yet there doesn't seem to be any stopping of the video games. If it isn't Pac-Man or Space Invaders or Asteroids being played, it may be the very popular Donkey Kong, with its King Kong-like gorilla, endangered maiden and hero. Or Frogger, in which you try to get the frog across the street before it's run down by a car, and in which it has to face deadly snakes, otters and crocodiles. Or Zaxxon, in which you try to invade an enemy fortress; your daring attempt is over once your fuel tank gets depleted and your plane crashes. There is a video game for nearly every temperament.

There are not only video games in arcades but many home video games as well. There is Blast It, where you try to chip away at a wall; Bank Shot, which looks like a pool table; Le Boom, which is a race against time; Wildfire, which looks like a pinball game; not to mention the numerous football, baseball, boxing and hockey video games. You can play any of these at your leisure. Video games have become one of the most significant diversions of the 1980s.

Yet will video games last indefinitely as a most favored item? One New York City distributor, who used to sell mostly pinball machines, thinks so. He says, "Pinball machines are being phased out." This outcome is far from certain, though. Perhaps because people can be very nostalgic, they might get a hankering again for the marble balls, the tilt mechanism, the open and closed gates, and the flippers of the pinball machine. Perhaps they will get tired of moving objects around on a screen. Perhaps, perhaps not. In 1983 you can't really say.

There have been a number of financial articles showing how the interest in video games has leveled off. Also, in 1983 there is a really large market for home video computers, which might include plug-in cassettes for video games. But at the same time, people just might prefer figuring out a calculus problem or working out a chess game and want no part of the old-fashioned, slam-bang video games. Then again, places like bars, doughnut shops and arcades have remained as busy as ever with boys and girls playing video games.

There is no doubting, however, that Pac-Man is still a big fad. You can take keys from a Pac-Man key holder to open your door, wear a Pac-Man pin or throw all the stuff you don't want into a Pac-Man wastebasket. What's more, the physicians have gotten up in arms against Pac-Man, as they often do with fads. If you play Pac-Man too much they say, you will be subject to neuralgic pain in the fingers, wrists, palms or arms, or to a temporary condition known as "arcade arthritis." This means that Pac-Man is right up there with ping-pong, which could cause foot sprains; hula hoops, which could cause muscular dislocations; and even postcards, which caused "faddy degeneration of the brain," because people were not challenged to write. Pac-Man has made it!

MUPPETS: STARRING KERMIT THE FROG AND MISS PIGGY (Late 1970s)

Muppets are puppets with names like Kermit the Frog; Miss Piggy, a pig; Rowlf, a piano-playing dog; and Sam, an American eagle. There were also the old creatures like Statler and Waldorf and the Great Gonzo. The Muppets were so popular in December 1979 that the group was featured on the cover of *Time* magazine. They were, of course, also a merchandising gold mine, with all the Muppet coffee mugs, Muppet T-shirts, Muppet pillowcases and Muppet calendars around. In fact, if you owned a Mupper calendar, you knew for sure that you were in the late 1970s. Nearly everyone liked the Muppets: kids like the Muppets, and social critics such as writers liked the Muppets.

The Muppets first appeared on the children's educational television show "Sesame Street," but later they got their own program, "The Muppet Show." Kermit the Frog was the first Muppet created by Muppet mastermind Jim Henson, back in 1957. For many years after that, Kermit remained the Muppet favorite. Then in the 1970s a female pig who wore low-cut clothing and was always very elegant came along: Miss Piggy. She became as popular as Kermit the Frog and was a favorite topic of conversation.

Miss Piggy was even nominated for an Academy Award as best actress in 1979. Some 20,000 men and women wrote in to suggest that what Faye Dunaway, Joan Crawford or Katherine Hepburn was deserving of, so was Miss Piggy. This was because Miss Piggy was preparing to act in the Muppet's first film, *The Muppet Movie*.

Miss Piggy did not get the Academy Award, and when the Muppets went from television to movies, a lot of the steam went out of their vogue. In 1980 strawberry-scented Strawberry Shortcake (see STRAWBERRY SHORTCAKE) came along, and she was a real faddish bonanza. The social critics didn't like Strawberry Shortcake quite as much as the Muppets, but she really sold better. Which isn't to say that the Muppets were no longer a fad—just that they had become maybe a little bit more of a conversation piece than a merchandising phenomenon.

Muppet puppets and other items, however, are still around. And given the fact that big-selling department store items, like Muppets, Strawberry Shortcake or those all-blue smurfs (see SMURFS), have an intense life of about a year, you might see a rage for Muppets once more. A sudden, overwhelming TV special, a bizarre book—anything like this could bring the Muppets back strong, for anything can happen in the fad world. And *then* just try to get a date with Miss Piggy. She'll be booked solid.

BED TUCKING (1980)

In the spring of 1980 students in the Middle Atlantic states kind of forgot the upheaval of the past decade and a half: forgot that the sexual revolution often wiped out inhibitions between man and woman; forgot the generation gap and the alienation between parent and child; even forgot how the 1970s (with their slogan about the "me generation" and their all-important cliche about "getting your act together") seemed to teach that you should really look out for yourself first. No, in May in the Middle Atlantic states, such as Pennsylvania and Maryland, students wanted to be tucked warmly into bed (and with a teddy bear, no less); they wanted to be told a bedtime story—just like Mother used to do years ago.

The college fads of bed tucking and bedtime reading started either at Penn State University or at the University of Maryland. In any event, it was girls who were first tucked in. If a girl wanted to be tucked in by three guy students, two of them would get the sheets of her bed cozy. Both of them would give her a kiss on the cheek. The girl would be presented with a teddy bear, and the third guy, clad in pajamas, would then read her a bedtime story.

For all this, a young lady would have to pay only 99 cents.

If you think that this was a good deal, consider what a guy could get for only a quarter: five girls tucking him into bed. Guy-tucking in came along somewhat later than gal-tucking in. No reason was given why it was so much less expensive. Maybe it was the teddy bear. The gals seemed to have skimped on the teddy bear when they tucked in the guys.

This fad was fairly silly, which probably explained why it passed so quickly. Another reason for its rapid demise was that the fad came about at the end of the spring semester, only a short time before summer vacations. When college students return in the fall, nearly anything that happened only a few months before is typically regarded as being in the ancient past.

But the fad was also a little bit sad, being so obviously a kind of "put-on." Participating undergraduates knew there was no such innocence, and they probably knew it when they were 5 years old too.

"DALLAS" FAD MANIFESTATIONS (1980)

In the not-so-distant future, the initials J.R.—as in J.R. Ewing—will probably be mostly forgotten; then, maybe in a couple of decades after that, during another surge of American nostalgia (like the one in the 1950s about the 1920s or the one in the 1970s about the 1950s), people might be saying things like "You remember J.R. Ewing"; "Why I have a J.R. doll"; "That's nothing. I have a Sue Ellen doll"; "Well, I have a dozen pictures of Southfork." They will all be recounting a time in 1980 when the public's most obsessive interest was the televised goings-on of the oil-rich Ewing family of "Dallas"—their rivals, their lovers and their victims. People hung in suspense on every twist of the narrative of the Friday night CBS show.

Not only that, they played DALLAS: A GAME OF THE EWING FAMILY, or they were invited to costume parties where people were supposed to dress up as one of the show's characters, or they drank J.R. beer (not that the archvillain himself was into anything so common; he knew all about the finest wines, when he wasn't slickly pouring himself some hard whiskey), or they were wearing black cowboy hats just like J.R. does, or they were simply cutting short their dinner engagements to get back to see "Dallas" on time. The fourth estate took note of "Dallas" too: In the space of eight months in 1980—March to November—there were articles on "Dallas" in *Time*, *The New Yorker*, *Newsweek*, *People*, *The Wall Street Journal*, *Vogue*, *Advertising Age* and the *New York Times*.

This contemporary soap opera—or saga, if you prefer—received its most frenzied reception on March 21, 1980, when the guileful J.R. (played by Larry Hagman) was found shot near his office. Both new viewers and old viewers who had been watching his machinations since the show first aired in April 1978 were really hooked by this, some of them no doubt reasoning "If I knew a charming snake like that, I'd love to do him in, too." At a time when the national pastime—baseball—was about to close up shop on spring training and head for the diamonds where the runs counted, it found that it was no longer the national pastime after all; figuring out who had tried to dispatch J.R. Ewing was. Was it Sue Ellen, the exploited wife; or was it Bobby, the really good brother who must have had it up to here with J.R., or was it Cliff Barnes, the long-time business rival; or was it Kristen, the sensual, gold-digging sister-in-law; or was it big Jock, who decided that this was one son he could easily do without? Questions, questions, questions. There were not only very serious conversations about this at cocktail parties and in offices, but it also challenged many a merchandising mind. The merchandisers decided to show their bewilderment publicly by coming up, for instance, with T-shirts like "Sue Ellen is innocent" or buttons proclaiming "I shot J.R."

Not that the curiosity was limited to America. In Great Britain wagering booths took bets on who shot Mr. J.R. Ewing; the book had Dusty Furlow, the overseer of the Southfork property, who also turned out to be the bastard son of Jock Ewing, at 6-4, Kristin at 4-1 and Sue Ellen at 25-1, among other odds. The equivalent in British sterling of $235,000 was wagered. In France, also, nearly everyone was asking "*qui a tiré sur J.R.?*" ("Who shot J.R.?") *Time* magazine pondered the question in a lengthy article and also had "Dallas" personalities on the cover; this was for those who thought that one picture was worth a thousand words.

Well, the nation had to wait in suspense until November 24, 1980 to find out; for after the March 21 dastardly deed, the reruns began once more on the tube. During this finger-biting time, many a peson sought to comfort himself or herself with "Dallas" novelties. Some bought buttons saying "J.R. for President" (this was, of course, assuming that the poor gent recovered). Others took part in a J.R. look-alike contest at Higbee's Department Store in Cleveland (three decades earlier, there was a Howdy Doody look-alike contest, which just goes to show that everybody wants to be a cowboy, whether the cowboy is a puppet or a flesh-and-blood sneak), with the winner receiving a day's interest on a billion dollars, or $187. Rock fans could buy a record with the song I Love J.R. on one side and the song I Hate J.R. on the flip side.

Other examples of the concern about J.R. and the rest of the Ewings were that there were considerably fewer traffic accidents than usual on a British bank holiday because people wanted to get home to see "Dallas"; also the Turkish government said of "Dallas" and the whole Ewing bunch that the show was "degrading" and aimed to destroy "Turkish family life."

On November 24 it turned out that it was Kristin, the sister-in-law, who had tried to kill J.R. J.R. himself was beginning to make a slow recovery (he was still as

guileful as ever, but his mobility had been greatly impaired).

By 1981 the obsessive interest in "Dallas" had passed, and it was just a plain, popular television show. As for its characters in the following seasons, J.R. remarried Sue Ellen; Kristin was murdered; Jock was lost when he had trouble with his private plane flying the skies of South America; and Bobby remained his good old self. J.R., of course, continued to pile up money by scheming. Rumor has it that he plans to use a lot of it to buy up all the remaining J.R. buttons and records and board games.

DUNGEONS AND DRAGONS (1980)

Dungeons and Dragons® is a complicated board game in which almost anything can happen, which intrigued people so much that it became a big rage in 1980. Not only did the board conjure up a fanciful medieval atmosphere (with places like the Vault of the Drow and the Glacial Rift of the Forest Giant Jarl), but winning depended on how skilled you were in thinking on your feet when facing dragons and required that you put yourself into many unusual roles, like that of elves, sorcerers or dwarves. College kids were the first to pick up on the fascination of the game. One Rice University student told the *Houston Post* that he remembers his first Dungeons and Dragons experience like this: "One day a few years ago I was walking through the commons at Rice, and I saw about 20 people sitting around tables throwing dice and just having a helluva good time. I've been playing ever since."

Dungeons and Dragons was unusual in many ways, but for one thing, just consider the dice. Most board games that use dice at all use two 6-sided dice. Not Dungeons and Dragons; it uses a number of dice, with 12 to 20 sides. In most board games, the dice determine how many squares you can move; in Dungeons and Dragons they determine the personal characteristics of the roles you play: your constitution and whether you have more intelligence, wisdom, strength, dexterity or charisma. This is important, because Dungeons and Dragons always has a person overseeing the game and determining what trials the players have to face; he or she is the Dungeonmaster. After you roll the dice, you have to figure out how best to accomplish the trials.

Dungeons and Dragons was created in 1974 by Gary Gygax, a Wisconsin insurance man who was obsessed by games in his spare time. It might have remained just an avocation, but for the fact that Gygax suddenly found himself without a job. Deciding that this medieval game he was working on would take his full attention, he went and got himself $1,000 seed money to get the project going. By 1975 the game, which was now known as Dungeons and Dragons, was paying its own way, and by the end of the 1970s, it was raking in enough cash to keep an army of trolls, elves, dragons and sorcerers living in the style to which they were accustomed. Both the *New York Times* and *Forbes* magazine, noting the fad for D&D (as the game was familiarly known), titled articles on it "Dungeons and Dollars."

When Dungeons and Dragons first came out, it was mostly college kids who bought the game. Many have said that it was the science and mathematics majors who were particularly enamored. Yet by 1980 the 10- to 14-year-old market for Dungeons and Dragons was just as big.

The game cost $9.98, but for the thousands upon thousands of Dungeons and Dragons mavens, this was only the beginning. The game was so complicated that it required separate rule manuals for special variations in its action; these books were known as modules, in keeping with the vocabulary of the computer age. There were modules about Dungeons and Dragons locations such as "The Isle of Dread" and "The Keep on the Borderlands." You could also buy additional special dice, a monthly magazine on the game or something known as hex pads, which start out as pieces of paper with many hexagons (also the dominant shape on the board, just as squares are in checkers) but are then used by players to form "probability distribution charts" (which identify the possible occurrences that can befall them in any given situation), according to one Dungeons and Dragons player. Additional expenses could amount to $60: Typically, dice went for $2 to $7; advanced modules went from $12 to $18, and hex pads went for $1 for five of them. And the modules kept coming. The variations in Dungeons and Dragons are endless.

This, of course, sparked controversy. A youth from Stony Brook, New York, in writing to the *New York Times*, claimed that in Dungeons and Dragons, "if you get killed, you can come back alive," while another teen-ager an hour's drive west in Queens differed, saying that not all characters can come back to life—only those with the proper capabilities. At any given Dungeons and Dragons board, as many as 18 people could play, and disagreements about ways to escape and about the nature of trials were common. Dungeons and Dragons players had to know a lot, or as one youth recounted to a newspaper reporter, at given times a player had to know how many defenders to use per linear foot at a castle wall or the moment daylight is lost in a quest. Not all Dungeons and Dragons players would come up with the same solution to such problems.

Dungeons and Dragons inspired some disagreement not only among its players but also among the general public. A number of schoolteachers who used D&D claimed that it taught problem solving, survival and how to lead; other teachers, however, thought it was much too distracting and took kids away from their studies. A community in Utah tried to prohibit Dungeons and Dragons because it was overly antisocial and was marked by too much witchcraft and demonology. Other people claimed that Dungeons and Dragons was too violent.

By 1981 the great vogue for the game had passed, though it is not clear that such objections were the reason for the decline in interest. It used to be that at a game club in lower Manhattan kids could go play Dungeons and Dragons but the game has now been put away. A manager there speculated about the reasons. He didn't know for sure but said maybe it was because video games had taken hold. Kids were more interested in moving dots electronically with a lever than with figuring out how to combat a fiery brass dragon. Perhaps. But it has only been a couple of years since the rage. There could be a boom again at any time. Who knows? A sports figure or a movie star in the 1980s might confide that he or she plays Dungeons and Dragons all the time.

Well, then something would have to give! Because as of now (1983), of 15 people asked at random whether they had ever played Dungeons and Dragons, not a one said yes. Dungeons and Dragons (with its underground chambers, fiery serpents and all) seems to have definitively passed out of fad country.

URBAN COWBOYS (1980)

There was once a hangout in Fort Lauderdale, Florida for dancing and gathering known as Bachelors. This was way back in the 1970s, when the big fancy was for the glitter and the intricate steps of disco (see DISCO), which made people think of wild life in New York City. But the wild life caught on not only at Bachelors, and at New York City's fashionable Studio 54, but at places where people could dance and talk from coast to coast.

Then 1980 came along, and disco gave way to people wanting to have a good old time cowboy style. It was big to ride something called a mechanical bull;

to wear cowboy boots, black 10-gallon hats, string ties and belts with your initials on them; and to dance Texas-style dances. In Fort Lauderdale, Bachelors was renamed The Silver Saddle, because it sounded a lot more Western. Cowboy boots, which used to go for $25 to $50, now went for $100 to $150. People wanted to look just as good and enticing in their cowboy togs as they had in their white suits for discoing. What's more, the atmosphere was new, or as the manager of Cody's, a new Western-style bar in New York City, would say about why many people wanted something different from disco, "It was a super-cool uptight atmosphere—people wearing three-piece suits, and gold chains, and a lot of noise."

Consider the mechanical bull. This was not something that you would find in a typical disco club. It was nothing more than a big saddle (unlike a real bull, it had neither a head nor a body) planted on the floor with a motor in its base and a remote control mechanism. When people got on it, they could get the ride of their lives, as the mechanical bull would buck repeatedly when an operator or a bartender (at another location in the bar) moved a dial; all types of ride from peaceful to really scary were possible.

Or as an excited, young Anaheim, California girl said of her growing success as a rider and the thrill it gave her: "I've worked my way up to a 7 from a 3 [10 is the hardest ride]. It's fun, it's an escape, a fantasy. You can be what you want to be." And she was hardly the only rider on the mechanical bull. A tourist in New Orleans could see mechanical bull riding done in a bar on Bourbon Street. To take a few other examples, there were also mechanical bull riders in Nashua, New Hampshire; New Paltz, New York; Chicago; Detroit; Los Angeles; Columbus, Ohio; and in Manhattan.

It cost $1 or $2 to mount and ride a mechanical bull, and if you rode one, you were usually required to sign a waiver beforehand, taking all responsibility for any fall that could lead to broken limbs. Broken arms and legs were not infrequent, but the mechanical bull was a dare, a kick. Also, the operator could control the beast for the greenhorns.

The fascination with wearing Western clothing, taming mechanical bulls and acting like a cowpoke all stemmed from the 1980 movie Urban Cowboy, a lot of which took place in a bar just outside Houston, Texas (in Pasadena) named Gilley's. There, they had been riding mechanical bulls and wearing Western apparel for years. And the mechanical bulls were ridden not only as a dare but also to train rodeo riders. But for sport or for experience, anyone who went into Gilley's couldn't miss the sign, "Try Your Luck at Riding Our Bucking Bull."

But it wasn't John Travolta who rode it there on the big Saturday nights or any other night of the week—

at least not until 1980. Then John Travolta—who played the hero, Bud, in Urban Cowboy—stimulated an obsession with riding mechanical bulls, just as he had stimulated the craze for disco a few years earlier with Saturday Night Fever. Bud wanted to ride the bull, just as his girl friend Sissy (played by Debra Winger) did. And so riding the bull became voguish, as did cowboy-style wear. Derisively, these urban cowpokes were called drugstore cowboys, barroom cowboys and disco cowboys. But this really wasn't the whole truth. Riding a mechanical bull was a challenge, just like hang gliding or going on a terrifying roller coaster ride. Wearing Western fashions made people feel good. Doing Western dances with names like cotton-eyed Joe and the crow's step was a new thing and therefore exciting. Nor was it necessary to spend a lot of money if you were going to be an urban cowboy. For a few dollars, you could get Gilley's Club T-shirts, ladies' panties, suspenders and belt buckles. Of course, if you wanted to, you could also spend $400 for Western boaskin boots.

The urban cowboy phenomenon became so big that in 1980, for the first time in five years, a rodeo came to New York City.

Yet urban cowboys had not come to stay. Interest in riding a mechanical bull waned because there continued to be a number of falls and injuries. Also the mechanical bull sometimes took up so much space on a club's dance floor that there was no room for dancing. Nor was it only the mechanical bull that took up space. A few mattresses were needed on the floor to break the impact of the inevitable falls. All this ultimately got in the way of relaxed conversation and dancing, and both the mechanical bulls and the mattresses were put away.

As for the boots, black 10-gallon hats, string ties and Western-style belts—these, too, ceased being faddish items. Coming along in their place were jump suits, metallic pants, spandex and leather jackets.

PREPPY, PREPPIER, PREPPIEST (1980–81)

I was wearing preppy clothes when I was 11 years old, and I didn't even know I was preppy.
—Manager, Charivari, clothing store in New York City

Way back in the 1960s and the 1970s, it was voguish to stand out, to avoid looking or acting like any part of mainstream America. Hot pants, bell bottoms, long hair on men, miniskirts, Mao jackets—they all seemed somewhat bizarre at one time or another, and they all caught on. As far as behavior was concerned, this, too, had a considerable "against the wall, establishment" flavor to it: the Hippies, followed by the Yippies and then by the Zippies, streaking, even doing the twist—all a bit defiant. Which takes us to the year 1980. What type of bizarreness would usher in the new decade? Why none other than looking and acting like a preparatory school student, a pillar of the establishment if ever there was one, and a rich young pillar, to be sure. A *preppy*?? Where had all the day-glo and long hair gone? Gone to alligator shirts, every one. To alligator shirts, top-sider shoes, Shetland sweaters, blue blazers, madras jackets and khaki—preppy looks, all.

A vice president of Brooks Brothers, the elegant clothing house, said of this craze to emulate preppy: "It's all part of a growing trend to conservatism in the country . . . it also repudiates the values and extreme looks of the late 1960s." Now, that's laying it on the line, and who is to say he was wrong? Consider the preppy top-sider shoe. One manufacturer said of these moccasin-topped, white-soled boat shoes, "We can't make them fast enough," while another said, "It's becoming the status shoe. You look like you're rubbing shoulders with wealthy people." Although that might not have been so bad, there was a time not so far back when who would have wanted to admit it? Needless to say, most of the boat shoes were not worn on boats. They were worn on the streets, to impress other pedestrians; then they arrived at the office, to impress other workers.

The boat shoe and its fascination is what is called a working example. The same preppy status applied to alligator shirts, Shetland sweaters and blue blazers, and when more than one of them was worn at a time, admiration multiplied, too. Being thought of as preppie—ay, there's the rub. In a time of much discoing (see DISCO), there was also a look for preppy discoers, consisting of corduroy, khaki shorts, buckskin shoes and alligator shirts, among other things. This made many a dance floor look like . . . well . . . like Groton.

The great interest in the preppy look started in early 1980, but it only really began to gather steam after the appearance of a manual on preppiness, *The Official Preppy Handbook*, published later in the year, and written by Lisa Birnbaum and collaborators. Now this book was indeed something of a spoof (who could take seriously a statement like this on the right kind of men's jewelry: "One signet ring is allowed, either a family or a school crest"?), but it was also a how-to, which, taken literally, would teach you how to be a preppie: what the right clothes were, what the right schools were, what the right sports were, even what the right romantic gestures were—all available for $4.95.

Ms. Birnbaum and associates called it a "self-help" book and said that "Looking, acting, and ultimately being Prep is not restricted to an elite minority lucky enough to attend private schools." Maybe, in fact, they were trying to start a social revolution.

Anyway, the book became a runaway best-seller, and all the talk was of how to become a preppie. People sitting down to a meal at Mount Washington Tavern in Baltimore (that's where all the preppies went) could feel very proud, as could patrons of D'Poos in Cleveland or Clyde's in Washington. And what about wearing a down jacket? That was certainly being on the right track. And what about carrying a Swiss army knife? Better and better. And what about monogramming your possessions? Now here was a dilemma. Guest towels were OK, but cashmere sweaters—they were not monogram material. What about men's shirts? Best to do it on the left-hand side, near the breast pocket—and use initials, not full nicknames like Duke. But always remember, no matter what you wear and what you do, if you want to be a good preppy, "understatement is key."

Well, it wasn't so very long before there was a hue and cry about all of this. Some old-line preppy types couldn't stand all these interlopers who had so easily learned the formula for preppiness without years of trying and generations of family tradition. One Harvard man said, "I have a bit of casual contempt for all these people," while a Princeton man showed a trifle more understanding: "You can tell when people are faking it. They try too hard."

But it wasn't only the old-line preppies who felt offended by all this newfangled preppiness; there were others who claimed that emphasis like this on what you wear and who you hang out with was just plain undemocratic, which perhaps only went to show that the spirit of the 1960s could live again. A senior at Princeton, Michael Katz, was particularly alarmed. First, he came up with a button showing an alligator (for Izod-LaCoste's emblem—the preppy favorite) with a red slash through it and bearing the statement, "I am for saving alligators and killing preppies." People began to wear these buttons. Then, in an interview with *People* magazine, held jointly with Lisa Birnbaum, Katz said of her and preppiness, "I thought you were some kind of archaic British institution" (many prep schools being based on British models). What Katz wanted was for "people . . . [not to] have to worry [about] what they wear or say, or who they were with." This debate was truly serious business, not just a matter of wearing or not wearing alligator shirts.

But no sooner had Katz taken his stand than another perspective on preppiness asserted itself: making preppies into a laughing matter of the belly laugh variety. Never mind if people should contrive to become part of some artificial elite, just turn the whole matter into a cartoon. And so cartoon books of the I-hate-preppies variety became big. Everyone was talking about books like *The Joy of Stuffed Preppies* and *101 Uses for a Dead Preppie*. In *The Joy of Stuffed Preppies*, there were pictures of stuffed preppies used as cocktail drink trays, lamp shades, TV antennae, scarecrows or weather vanes. In *101 Uses for a Dead Preppie*, defunct preppies served as ironing boards; figureheads on a boat, the S.S. Muffie (Muffie being an important preppy name); armless fire hydrants; tinders for dynamite; and bobsleds. Often you would see the remains of alligator shirts, topsider shoes, madras jackets. You couldn't miss the point—could you? Was it a reaction against a silly, faddish fashion trend, or was it just easy laughs?

In an event, the preppy fad—both enthusiastically propreppie and enthusiastically antipreppie—lasted through 1980 and 1981. What finally took its place was an interest in cartoon cat books, which had been gathering for years but had now found Garfield the cat, who would put felines over the faddish top. Dyed-in-the-wool preppies probably couldn't have resisted a disapproving smirk about this. As any aspiring elitist knows from consulting the preppy self-help book, when preppies have pets, they have dogs.

As for the preppy look itself, people continued to wear their blue blazers, madras jackets and topsiders, and they continued to carry their Swiss army knives if they wanted to. After all, preppy fashion started long before 1980—students had been wearing it in real prep schools for years. But no longer would anyone look down on you if you sported tie shoes or, by some strange happenstance, monogrammed your shirts on the right-hand side.

RUBIK'S CUBE (1980–81)

Rubik's Cube™ was the puzzle fascination of 1981. It was the only 3-inch high cube around that could be moved into a cool 43,252,003,274,489,856,000 positions (or 43 quintillion, 252 quadrillion, 3 trillion, 274 billion, 480 million, 856 thousand). No wonder unusual stories abounded about how people were fixated on it. There was the Brooklyn, New York toy entrepreneur who got so fascinated by Rubik's Cube while he was taking a bath he didn't notice that the tub was about to overflow. There was the Connecticut high school football player who was supposed to be on the gridiron as the third quarter was beginning and had to be rounded up in the locker room, where he

was struggling to master his Rubik's Cube. There was the computer analyst who was so much in need of a Rubik's Cube one day that he tried to form one out of clay, because he could not find a toy store open.

Not that Rubik's Cube was a craze only in the United States; it was a craze worldwide. In Japan, for instance, people used to line up for hours at the docks to buy them when a shipment was expected. In West Germany a woman sued for divorce because her husband paid too much attention to his Rubik's Cube and too little to her. Insult was added to injury: She had given her husband the Rubik's Cube as his last Christmas present.

Of course, the challenge of Rubik's Cube lay in finding the one solution to the puzzle, not in manipulating it into millions of positions, though this might very well happen to you as you sought that solution. Consider the Rubik's Cube itself, just as so many have in the very recent past.

Upon buying a Rubik's Cube, you have before you a six-sided object with a distinct color on each side. But this isn't quite the cube that you have known about since the days when you took geometry or before. Compared to that simple cube, Rubik's Cube is a monster.

Here is what you do when you have your cube. First, scramble the initial orderly arrangement of colors by randomly rotating the sections of the cube (in other words, just twist it around like mad). After a few turns, there will be squares of different colors on each face. To solve it, you have to rotate the sections in such a way that the cube goes back to its original arrangement, in which there was only one color on each face. And this is very, very, very hard. Really smart children have been known to do it in 10 minutes, but serious mathematicians have said that it could take a person up to a year to do. This, of course, includes time out for eating.

And did Rubik's Cube ever become a fascination! One British mayor who played it all the time had to have surgery on her thumb because she contracted tendinitis while being obsessed with Rubik's Cube and rotating the sections with that poor finger. And of course, every person would work on the Rubik's Cube to his or her own level of frustration. One easily frustrated man threw his cube out of a Fifth Avenue bus in New York City, while another individual got so incensed about his inability to solve it that he placed the cube in the middle of his driveway and ran over it with his truck. A California organization came up with a plastic paddle that was guaranteed to smash the Rubik's Cube to smithereens. About 100,000 of these were sold. As was the case with other and much different fads (cats and being preppy), hostility was on its commercial way: There was a book entitled *101 Uses for a Dead Cube*.

Rubik's Cube™

A young girl ponders how to solve Rubik's Cube™

These cubes had caused quite a stir, selling many millions before March of the year 1981 alone, at prices ranging from $4.95 to $13.00. An executive at F.A.O. Schwarz, the big toy store in New York City, called it "the world's most asked for plaything." There were constant comparisons of the Rubik's Cube craze with crazes for hula hoops and frisbees. Now this was big stuff.

It wasn't always this way with the cube, though. The inventor of it, the Hungarian Erno Rubik, came up with the cube as a teaching device for his students at the Budapest School of Commercial Art in 1974; he wanted to show them ways "to visualize in three dimensions." He absolutely did not aspire at that point to create a universal plaything; nonetheless, the cube became well known in Hungary, and in 1975 Rubik received a patent for the cube. (It has been maintained that there were a number of early variations of the cube in Istanbul and Marseilles, and that a Japanese engineer, Terotoshi Ishige, independently came

up with almost the same idea about the same time as Rubik.)

And Hungarians—who called the cube *Buvos Kocka*—were the only ones to scramble the colors and try to get them back to their original arrangement for a few years even though Rubik was trying to get other Europeans interested in the puzzle. Then in 1979 the cube earned a lot of praise at the German Toy Fair in Nuremberg, and more cubes began to sell in Europe; at the following year's German Toy Fair, it became even more prominent. Then the American corporation Ideal Toys entered into a contract with Rubik to be the cube's producer in the States and brought it to the public's attention by means of television spots. Ideal also used the Hungarian movie actress Zsa Zsa Gabor for a short time to promote the cube.

It may have been the television spots, or it may have been Zsa Zsa Gabor, but chances are that it was the fascination with the cube itself that caused it to become a rage in 1980. By the end of the year, 4½ million had been sold. And that was only the beginning: 1981 was much, much bigger. There were Rubik Cube necklaces and keyrings, as well as best-sellers that instructed people how to solve it. One of the best-known of these in America was James Nourse's *The Simple Solution to Rubik's Cube*. On any given day when the weather was warm, you would be likely to come across someone wearing a T-shirt bearing the message RUBIK'S CUBE CURES SANITY. Over in London the celebration of the marriage between Prince Charles and Lady Diana Spencer was commemorated with a Rubik's Cube bearing the likenesses of Charles and Diana on two sides and the Union Jack on the other four.

The interest in Rubik's Cube continues today, but it did fall off in 1982. This was the year of those all-blue darling little creatures known as Smurfs; the year of that attractive and intelligent movie alien, E.T., and also the year of the most obsessively popular of all video games, Pac-Man. At the same time, a number of puzzles based on Rubik's Cube have been introduced on the market and have done well: There is Snake, another three-dimensional object that, after manipulation, can look like a swan, a saxophone or a steamroller; and there is Rubik's Revenge, which has even more sides than Rubik's Cube. The 1980s may prove to be a time when different types of complicated puzzles are the rage, just as the 1970s proved to be a time when things that offered sensual gratification— like hot tubs, water beds and jacuzzis—were the rage. What's more, giving people a gift like Rubik's Cube or one of its variants is a lot different from giving them "put-ons" like a pet rock, bottled money or a *Nothing Book*, which were common in the 1970s. Using the brain may once again become voguish.

207

STRAWBERRY SHORTCAKE (1981)

Strawberry Shortcake™ is a doll with a bonnet, freckles on her face and a dress with strawberries on it. When she was a big item in 1981, a young mother said of her, "It's one of those cuddly kinds of things your 5-year-old can have tea with." This was not the first time that tea and children and playthings were thought of together: When the teddy bear (known as the Roosevelt bear then) was first introduced in the opening decade of the 20th century, one magazine featured teddy bears having tea parties with little girls. History was definitely on Strawberry Shortcake's side if this little doll was going to have any chance of being as big a children's item as the sawdust-stuffed, button-eyed bear. Strawberry Shortcake was a warm-looking creature and easy to be fond of. She also appeared on a float in the Macy's Thanksgiving Day parade in New York City in 1980. She was so popular that she went beyond being a simple doll: There were Strawberry Shortcake boots, tricycles, blankets and clothes like dresses, blouses and skirts, which might fill up an entire miniature wardrobe. Strawberry Shortcake was very much part of the scene.

She was also a bit of an accident. When she was first introduced in the late 1970s by a Cleveland greeting card company, American Greetings, she was only meant to take the place of a fading young lass found on letter paper, known as Holly Hobbie. How did it happen that it was Strawberry Shortcake? A research organization came to the conclusion that "females were wild about strawberries," that a strawberry figure on paper had the most pleasant associations. No one really had any idea of turning Strawberry Shortcake into a doll, though—not until they found out how Strawberry Shortcake on letter paper caught on.

So in March 1980 the Strawberry Shortcake doll was created, at 5½ inches high. There was nothing really special about her, but in keeping with her fruit theme she was scented with the aroma of strawberries, or as the doll's box put it, she gave a "scented kiss." This was the first scented doll there was. The result: Bonanza. At K-Mart, a department store chain, a buyer said, "Strawberry Shortcake dolls are flying off the shelves." Other stores added special Strawberry Shortcake boutiques. Toy stores included other Strawberry Shortcake items of great interest. For instance, there was something called the Big Berry Trolley Car, which went for $15. There was also a cart drawn by a snail, who carried a big strawberry; this went for $25. Strawberry Shortcake—or Baby Strawberry Shortcake—went for about $20. What did merchandisers say about Baby Strawberry Shortcake? That her popularity was "nip and tuck with the Barbie Doll," which had been popular for quite some time (see BARBIE DOLL).

Scented Strawberry Shortcake was a novel idea, and it caused American Greetings to pause for thought and then create a whole family of scented dolls. There was Baby Lemon Meringue, which smelled of lemon; Baby Apricot, which smelled of apricot; Baby Apple Dumplin', which smelled of apple, and Baby Blueberry Muffin, which smelled of blueberries. Not enough to overpower you, just enough to give you a "scented kiss." They wore apparel that reminded you of the chosen fruit, too.

During Strawberry Shortcake's heyday, there were also television specials about the doll. Expressions with "berry" in them—like I'm feeling "berry fine"—became quite popular as well. Altogether, Strawberry Shortcake was a $500 million industry in 1981.

Yet Strawberry Shortcake began to "die," as a New York City novelty store manager put it, in 1982. What happened? Some all-blue cartoon characters who lived in mushroom houses and who were called smurfs came along and everyone wanted something smurfy (see SMURFS). You could get a Strawberry Shortcake game consisting of Lemon Meringue Lotto and Berry Picking Bingo for $5.00 instead of $6.50. You could still have tea with Strawberry Shortcake, although she hadn't turned out to be as popular as a Roosevelt bear. But she might yet—you never know.

BICYCLE MOTOCROSS AND BMX BICYCLES (1982–   )

The stubby little bicycles with the stubby little tires that people now see so often on the streets are BMX bikes, and riding them is the latest cycling obsession. The shape is no accident; the bikes are built like that so they can compete in the BMX sport—or bicycle motocross—which consists of going over jumps and bumps in out-of-the-way places full of dirt. (The normal, sleek bike just doesn't stand up as well under such abuse, and the BMX bikes are in fact also known as dirt bikes.)

Both BMX bikes and the sport of bicycle motocross started in California in 1972, but by 1982 both were going strong throughout the nation. To take but one example, *The Wall Street Journal* reported on one mother who traveled with her 13-year-old son, an accomplished bicycle motocross rider, from their home near Pittsburgh to BMX tournaments in Missouri, Tennessee, Ohio, New York and Indiana. Parents of bi-

208

cycle motocross kids are as into the sport as little league parents used to be in the 1950s with their baseball-playing offspring.

Bicycle motocross, which is much different than peddling along or even racing on a streamlined and lightweight bicycle with 10 or more speeds, responded to the need of every child (and even every man or woman) to project a "tough guy" or "tough gal" image. It meant riding the bike over nasty knolls and other kinds of humps, almost like ski jumping, and there is absolutely nothing terribly genteel about this. Indeed, bicycle motocross was a variation on motorcycle motocross, and the motorcycle was a he-man machine if there ever was one. Just think of its image, particularly in the 1950s (see MOTORCYCLE JACKETS).

Yet the BMXs were ridden by a lot more people than those who competed on these dirt tracks. Many a young lad or lass would buy them—or have their parents buy the bikes for them—in 1982 just because they were different from a regular bicycle, just because they wanted a tough-*looking* bike. This growing cycling fad was intensified by the fact that the kids in the most popular movie of 1982, *E.T.: The Extra-Terrestrial* (see E. T. DOLLS), rode BMX bikes. Moreover, in older cities the BMX is practical: It takes potholes a lot better. This was not the usual motivation for an average city kid who wanted a BMX, however; he or she didn't tease, "Hey, Ma, hey, Dad, I want a BMX. They take potholes better." The kid just wanted that strange stubby device because it was the newest item.

Now in 1983 BMX bikes are still the latest thing when it comes to cycling, which has been popular in some form or other since the 1890s, when the "safety bicycle" (see BICYCLING) was introduced on a large scale. There is no telling when it all will end—when the last BMX bike will be ridden through its final obstacle course into oblivion, leaving the dust of the Earth itself less disturbed.

DEELY BOBBERS (1982)

Deely bobbers were nothing more than toy antennae, which you could wear on top of your head. You could find affixed to these antennae almost anything: balls, stars, pinwheels or other assorted items (which adornments were held on by coils). And in the summer of 1982, deely bobbers were big. You would see people in this carnivalesque, sci-fi-like headgear on the streets, in the parks, carrying out transactions at the bank or just sitting on the stoop talking—one deelybobbed person to another. It was all in good fun to wear these gewgaws, which were often known as Martian ears.

You could get deely bobbers for anywhere from $1 to $5—$1 if you bought imitation deely bobbers on the street or $5 if you got the genuine, original McCoy Deelybobber article in department stores.

Deely bobbers weighed in with an estimated $15 million in sales in 1982. People were just enamored of the little things. Why? Perhaps because they were so obviously amusing. And also perhaps because people wanted to spoof the great rage for science fiction that had become prominent, particularly since the 1977 movie *Star Wars*, with its little robot R2D2—a rage that gained even more momentum with *ET* in 1982.

The first deely bobbers were sold to a few department stores and amusement parks in February 1981. Produced by one Stephen Askin, a Los Angeles creator of novelty items, they were modeled after the insect headgear worn by John Belushi in the comedy spoof "Saturday Night Live" and also on the mock arrows that comedian Steve Martin used to hold to his head.

People were immediately intrigued by deely bobbers, but by the summer of 1982, their allure had reached such proportions that millions bought them. With passers-by decked out in a bedazzling array of stars, pinwheels and balls—all bobbing ceaselessly— just walking down the street became a real experience.

Yet, by 1983, deely bobbers were a thing of the past.

E.T. DOLLS (1982)

"We wanted him to be ugly so that you learn to love him despite what he looks like. So that in the end you think he's wonderful-looking even though in the beginning you thought he was somewhat hideous."
—screenwriter Melissa Mathison (to the newspaper, *The Aquarian*) on her character E.T. of *E.T. The Extra Terrestrial*

There was no way of knowing what an extraordinary alien E.T. was going to turn out to be when moviemaker Stephen Spielberg began to make a clay model of the figure in the 1970's. He worked in solitude; then later, Carlo Rambaldi, an Italian designer and sculptor whom Spielberg hired to make E.T. a more substantial reality labored in solitude giving the clay model an aluminum and steel skeleton, and then a musculature of fiberglass, polyurethane, foam, and rubber. And here ended the solitude. When E.T. appeared before a nationwide movie audience in June 1982, this affable being—accidently abandoned by his mates in the environs of Los Angeles— with the lumpy skull became an obsession from coast to coast. *E.T.: The Extra-*

Terrestrial was more than an extraordinary film bonanza; it was a mysterious tale full of intimacy, love of childhood, and the constant lurking of danger. One movie executive said of him, "E.T. has become more popular than the flag, as American as apple pie." And Astrid Kamar, a major supplier of E.T.™ dolls, incredulously said of her customers, the buyers, usually a very cool bunch, "I have never received flowers or been taken to dinner by customers; usually, I take them."

The E.T. craze involved more than E.T. dolls; BMX bicycles became more popular because the kids in *E.T.* rode them, but there were also E.T. bed sheets, alarm clocks, T-shirts, key chains, mirrors, and even a phonograph record, *I Had Sex with E.T.* Yet, think about the E.T. doll itself, for it says something about the nature of fads.

SMURFS (1982–)

Every smurf must pull his own weight.

—Papa Smurf

Smurfs© started out as simple, all-blue cartoon characters—which looked something like dwarfs—in Belgium in the late 1950s, but they wound up being a great rage in the United States in 1982. It was a rage great enough to change the fortunes of a mighty television network. But it was also a rage that offered simple pleasures: something cute to look at or play with or own—in other words, not so very much different from the kewpie dolls of the early 20th century (see KEWPIES). But there were not only smurf stuffed figures but also smurf puzzles, smurf lunch boxes, smurf watches, smurf calendars, smurf buttons, smurf balloons, smurf nightlights and smurf tricycles. Or as one of the first distributors of smurf items, Wallace Berrie of California, said of this cute little blue explosion: "It's Smurfee's law: Whatever can go right, will." (a spoof on Murphy's Law, very popular to cite in the 1970s, that whatever could go wrong, would).

A typical smurf lived in a mushroom house and dwelt in an area very much like a forest. Among themselves the smurfs got along fine and were watched over by a whiskered old fellow, Papa Smurf, who somehow kept all the other little creatures busy and happy, though he slept a lot of the time himself. But the smurfs had enemies, like Gargamel, who was much more human-looking (although sometimes he also looked like a wolf), and his sidekick, the cat Azrael. Gargamel and Azrael would plot and say things like "Here's my foolproof plan to catch the smurfs." This would cause the frightened smurfs to say things like "Smurf for your life." Smurfs came on for an hour every Saturday morning on television, and the nonstop action, with all those kindly looking blue folk, was very engaging for young kids.

Smurfs were not only for young kids, though. Teenagers, who only a few years back would likely have been collecting rock records or stringing up psychedelic lighting in their rooms, now sought to get little smurf statuettes—smurfs in an orchestra, smurfs chopping wood, smurfs in a boat or other smurfy activities. Young secretaries might be seen carrying a smurf that was almost adult-size to the office.

This was all a long way from the smurf's humble beginnings in 1958 in Belgium. There, an illustrator named Pierre Culliford, who went by the pen name of Peyo, began to write and draw books about smurfs. In continental Europe, Peyo's books gained something of a following in the next two decades. But the smurfs had to cross the channel to England to make their first big splash, which they did in 1978. There, in Britain, smurfs really caught on after they were given as T-shirt premiums and poster premiums by the National Benzole Company when motorists filled up their cars' gas tanks. There was also a smurf song, which almost reached the top of the pop charts.

The English fascination with smurfs came to the attention of Californian Wallace Berrie, whose company began to distribute two-inch figurines of them on the West Coast for $1.50 apiece; they sold out very quickly. An then came the smurf breakthrough into television, when Fred Silverman, then president of the NBC television network, saw his children playing with them. This was just the type of character NBC needed, Silverman reasoned. He put smurfs on the air, settling them on Saturday morning. An official of a competing network would soon have this to say about the whole picture—smurfs, ratings and all: "A year ago they [NBC] were no place, but then along came the smurfs and took Saturday morning by storm." Obviously, it wasn't only Gargamel and Azrael who found the smurfs too great a power to control.

Smurfs are still an overwhelmingly popular item, perhaps because they are such an intimate community of creatures. There is Brady Smurf, with the glasses; there is Grumpy Smurf; there are Clumsy Smurf and Greedy Smurf; there are smurfs with southern accents and smurfs with German accents; there are smurfettes. This is "what the smurf is going on" now, as a smurf himself or herself would say.

There is no guarantee, however, that this is what will be going on for a long time. Strawberry Shortcake (see STRAWBERRY SHORTCAKE), the little girl with the strawberry mannerisms, and the Muppets (see MUPPETS), a gathering of puppets starring a frog (Kermit the Frog) and a pig (Miss Piggy), were big in the 1970s and 1980s—but only while they were on television. Moreover, in New York City, for example, a number of novelty store managers agreed that though smurfs were still big in the fall of 1982, they were a little bit weaker than they had been in the spring. Yet in early 1983, smurfs were still riding strong or, as they would probably say among themselves, still smurfing strong. The winner of Super Bowl XVII in 1983, the Washington Redskins, called their wide receivers the smurfs. And the Ice Capades includes a gang of skating smurfs.

It could be that the smurfs will be like Mickey Mouse or Charlie Brown—perennial cartoon favorites—but it is also possible that they will not. In a few years a puzzled young child may well be asking his or her slightly older brother or sister what all those strange-looking blue animals are. In any event, the time has not yet come to get blue because of the passing of these blue creatures.

SLAM DANCING (1983)

Slam dancing is not yet a fad, but it's being practiced in some nightclubs in Los Angeles and in New York City, and you never know what's going to happen. Just think of the animal dances (see TURKEY TROT AND OTHER ANIMAL DANCES) of the early 20th century: The Turkey trot just started in a few clubs in a section of San Francisco. And there was also a time when disco was only being done by a few people.

Slam dancing is something really new on the American scene; in it men slam and pile into each other in time to loud music; there is nothing about the dance that says it has to be restricted to men alone, but the violence of it all rather discourages women from joining in. Yet its violence has limits; the men impose limits so that no one gets hurt and even help others who perhaps had a bad fall.

Right now, slam dancing in New York city, for instance, is something done by teen-agers who seem to wear the same kind of outfit, consisting of "black combat boots, old Levis, black belts, and almost white T-shirts," as Manhattan's *Village Voice* put it.

Like disco, slam dancing, as the teen-agers see it and relate it, is an escape from the tedium of everyday activities during the week and is a way of letting off steam. They look forward to having their bodies "hunkered over" and their arms "flailing" while "slamming into each other," according to the *Voice*.

In the 1950s there was a term *JD*, or juvenile delinquent. Slam dancers, though they wear some of the "tough-guy" apparel of the 1950s, do not seem to be

JDs. In fact, a Queens, New York fellow related how he would try to get good grades all week so that his parents would allow him to slam dance on the weekends.

Slam dancing is still a minor phenomenon, but in terms of faddery, it has one thing going for it: It's out of the ordinary. Let it get tamer or let it get slickened up a bit at an established nightclub, and you might just see it around for a while. It would help to make it easier for women to participate.

CATS (Timeless, but Very Big in Recent Years)

Everyone knows what a cat is, so there is nothing to be gained by classifying it as a four-legged beast. What's important is that cats are now bigger than they ever were, except maybe when they were venerated as deities in ancient Egypt. In 1981, 250 books were published about cats. There were two best-selling cartoon cats—the mighty seller Heathcliff and the out-of-this-world seller Garfield—both of whom were inspired in large part by the cartoon cats of P. Kliban, which are still prominent. *Time* magazine, a couple of weeks before Christmas in 1981, ran a cover story all about cats. There was a recent board game with cat-tastrophe cards. Its players could take time out to drink from cat coffee mugs, and if perchance the game was a gift from friends in a distant city, you could send them a warm thank-you note on cat stationery. One Manhattan store manager, in observing all the cat items being sold (like the cat coffee mugs, cat posters, cat buttons, cat neckties, cat pajamas, cat potholders and cat stationery), said of it, "I haven't seen anything like this since Peanuts in the late 1960s."

What has inspired all this fascination with cats? At one time, when the author was young, cats were far from unknown, but they were classed in the same league as dogs—as in dogs and cats are the basic household pets or as in dogs and cats always hate and fight each other. Then he reached graduate school age (this was in 1965), spent a lot of time with his friends in New York City, and found that for the most part (like in about two out of every three cases), they kept cats—usually two of them together. In graduate school towns like Bloomington, Indiana he found the same thing to be the case. Yet this was far from the time when cats were media personalities or figured as the subject of many a story, or when their features were copied by the makers of a thousand novelty items.

Yet the very popular and sometimes strange feline was beginning to assert itself, even if the commentators on the national television networks didn't know it yet. Already, the cat had distanced itself from the dog, which had retained the rather unexciting image of being old and faithful. The 1960s really were a time when people lost many of their moorings and talked a lot about alienation, loneliness, being exploited by society as an object. What could give meaning to life, save it from some of its sterility (another sad, bleak word that often cropped up in conversation)? One thing that could turned out to be the cat. Cats had personality. When cats slept, you could see that they were revealing things about themselves. When cats ate, they were revealing other things about themselves. Cats were cunning in the most intriguing ways. Cats knew how to be independent. Cats knew how to manipulate other creatures—like the people with whom they lived. Cats were . . . well, cats were like us.

If someone came to visit, the first news he or she would learn was the latest thing the cat was doing. People who you thought didn't care about pets at all, who threw their lifeblood into existentialism or Marxism-Leninism, were going crazy about the right kinds of cat litter, the right kinds of cat biscuits and whether Morris (the cat on television advertisements) was typical of cats in general.

This was way back in the late 1960s or the early 1970s, long before cats appeared in books and novelty items, and even longer before 1982, when the Broadway smash of the year was *Cats*, a musical based on T.S. Eliot's group of poems *Old Possum's Book of Practical Cats*.

Yet people who owned cats, who lived in cities or in graduate shool towns, made no secret of their admiration, and by 1975 the whole nation was tuned in to cats, the idea of the feline's unique personality having really taken hold. In that year Kliban cats, created by cartoonist P. Kliban of Marin County, California, came along. Soon enough, there were Kliban cat T-shirts, Kliban cat toaster covers, Kliban cat calendars, Kliban cat shower curtains and Kliban cat ice buckets. Now this was a great change, indeed. Just a few years earlier, cats had been a private pleasure, though one that cat cultists loved to talk about. Now cats were really in the public eye. In New York City alone, Kliban's cats were compared to Mayor Edward Koch, President Jimmy Carter and baseball slugger Reggie Jackson, as far as personality was concerned. Now that was quite a bit different than being compared to a phlegmatic philosophy professor or to somebody's cousin who won't give you a straight answer. Cats had reached the big league.

So soon enough all kinds of cat things abounded. A motel in Illinois had cat apartments, cat roomettes, and cat imperial suites. There was a cat dating service in California and an annual contest to judge the quality of cats' meows. The director of a Chicago organization, Pets Are Wonderful, said, "We project the cat as the pet of the 1980s." In the bookstalls there were not only the cartoon cats but also spoofy books like *The Cinematic Cat*, with Joan Clawford and Tony Purrkins and *The Social Climbing Cat*.

Cats were obviously something that people latched onto as the conversational item *par excellence*. Sometimes things featuring cats were imaginative, and sometimes they weren't. One of the more unimaginative—but still extremely popular—things was a whole series of *I Hate Cats* books, which were an imitation of the popular *I Hate Preppies* books of the early 1980s (see PREPPY, PREPPIER, PREPPIEST), in which self-conscious dead preppies in their proper shoes and their proper blazers were used for bobsleds, hammocks or ironing boards. Dear old feline was about to get the same treatment. Defunct cats were shown stuffed in a big symphonic horn and used as a bookmark, a pool cue or a punching bag, to give but four of many, many examples. This spoofery peaked in December 1981, according to one salesman on the floor of a New York city bookstore. By 1982 cat spoofery had really petered out. Or as he put it, the spoofs had had "their day."

The obsession with cats, though, has not as yet had its day. One of the hottest tickets in New York City as this book goes to press is to the musical *Cats*, and the only reason this isn't happening in other cities is probably because *Cats* isn't playing there. Garfield, the cunning and corpulent, remains number one or close to it on the best-seller list. You still go to an urban apartment to talk to friends and find them there with their two cats. The cats, of course, are more personalities than they are pets.

What's more, a very well known editor writes a book on how to please a man, and one of the things she says is not to get angry with him, and if you feel frustrated, talk to your cats. Dancers note with pride that they always bring their cats with them on their tours. Cats, cats, cats—the interest in felines still seems unabated.

It may be so next year as well. And the year after that. Or it may not. Someone may well note that canaries have personalities that are reflected by how they fly around in their cages, and that tropical fish have personalities that you can distinguish by how they swim. Or maybe dogs (there are still more dogs than cats in the United States as pets) will get a jazzier image than "old and faithful." But some other author will see this happening. Whether he or she notes it first happening in walk-up apartments in big cities, in college towns or perhaps in suburbia near shopping centers or out on farms on the prairie is anybody's guess. That's the way fads are, and that's the way they will always be.

SELECTED BIBLIOGRAPHY

Arts of Woodcarving and Pyrography. London: Butterick Publishing Company, 1893.

Birnbach, Lisa, ed. *The Official Preppy Handbook.* New York: Workmen, 1980.

Butler, Albert and Josephine. *Encyclopedia of Social Dance.* New York: n.p., 1967.

Castle, Vernon and Irene. *Modern Dancing.* New York: Harper & Bros., 1914.

Cohn, David L. *The Good Old Days.* New York: Simon and Schuster, 1940.

Combs, Ralph C. *Who Called Me a Canastard?* Seattle: Superior Publishing Company, 1950.

Doody, Andrew. *The Films of the Fifties: The American State of Mind.* New York: Morrow, 1973.

Douglas, Randall. *The Joy of Stuffed Preppies.* New York: Holt, Rinehart & Winston, 1982.

Eaton, Seymour. *The Roosevelt Bears: Their Travels and Adventures.* New York: 1905.

F.F.C. *A Guide to Pyrography.* Philadelphia: F. Weber & Co., 1900.

Gibson, Charles Dana. *Education of Mr. Pipp.* New York: R. H. Russell, 1899.

———. *Pictures of People.* New York: R. H. Russell, 1896.

———. *Sketches and Cartoons.* New York: R. H. Russell, 1898.

Glassner, Lester, and Harris, Brownie. *Dime Store Days.* New York: Viking, 1981.

Gold, Annalee. *75 Years of Fashion.* New York: Fairchild Publications, 1975.

Goldsmith, Barbara. *Little Gloria . . . Happy at Last.* New York: Knopf, 1980.

Heide, Robert, and Gilman, John. *Dime Store Dream Parade.* New York: Dutton, 1979.

Keller, Keith. *The Mickey Mouse Scrapbook.* New York: Grosset & Dunlap, 1975.

A Little Book of Pingpong Verse. Boston: D. Ester & Co., 1902.

Morrow, Skip. *The Official I Hate Cats Book.* New York: Holt, Rinehart & Winston, 1980.

Nash, Jay Robert. *Bloodletters and Bad Men.* New York: Evans, 1973.

Nicholls, C. W. De Lyon. *The Ultra-Fashionables of America.* New York: Harjes, 1904.

One Hundred More Uses for a Dead Cat. New York: Crown, 1981.

One Hundred One Uses for a Dead Preppie. Berkeley: Ten Speed Press, 1981.

Parker, Arnold. *Ping-Pong—The Game and How to Play It.* New York: G. P. Putnam, 1902.

Price List of Articles for Carving on Wood with a Pyrographic Pencil. N.p. [circa 1890s].

Ruggles, Rowena Fay. *The One Rose, Mother of the Immortal Kewpies.* Oakland: n.p., 1964.

Sann, Paul. *Fads, Follies and Delusions of the American People.* New York: Crown, 1967.

Sears Roebuck and Co. Mail Order Catalogues. 1902–1908.

Shaw, Lloyd. *Cowboy Dances.* Caldwell, Idaho: Caxton Printers, 1939.

Sherwood, M. E. W. *The Art of Entertaining.* New York: Dodd & Mead, 1893.

Skolnik, Peter L. *FADS: America's Crazes, Fevers and Fancies.* New York: Crowell, 1972.

Stearns, Marshall. *Jazz Dance.* New York: Macmillan, 1968.

This Fabulous Century: 1900–1910, 1910–1920, 1920–1930. New York: Time-Life Books, 1969.

Wolfe, Tom. *The Electric Kool-Aid Acid Test.* New York: Farrar, Straus & Giroux, 1968.

Youmans, John G. *Social Dance.* Santa Monica: Goodyear Publishing Company, 1969.

A

B

C

D

E

E.T. dolls—209-210
E.T.: The Extra-Terrestrial—209-210
Eugenie hat—61-62
Executive Coloring Book—119, 120

F

Facial hair, fake—157
Farrah Fawcett look—189
"Father Knows Best"—96
Fawcett, Farrah—189
Feathers, tell-all—127
Fitzgerald, F. Scott—40, 175
Flagpole sitting—42-43
Flappers—40
Floradora girls—19
Floradora—19-20
Floral parades—16-18
Folk music—127
Fonz, the—188-189
Fool There Was, A—36
Frank Merriwell—15-16
Frisbees—101-102
Frug—137-138
Fur coats, tots'—158

G

Garrison belts—95
Gatsby look—175-176
Gernreich, Rudi—158, 180
Gibson, Charles Dana—7, 8
Gibson Girl—7-8
Gibson Man—8
Glassless glasses—138
Gloves, lavender—15
Givenchy, Huber de—106
Glasses, glassless—*See* Glassless glasses
Go-go dancing, platform—140
Going steady, manifestations of—157 *See also* Feathers, tell-all; Ankle bracelets
Goldfish swallowing—67-68
Golf, miniature—*See* Miniature golf
Golfball bouncers—56, 57
Goodman, Theodosia—*See* Bara, Theda
"Good Ship Lollipop, The"—62

Granny dresses—140
Granny glasses—152
Great Gatsby, The—172, 175
Grey, Sylvia—11
Grizzly bear—31
Gronking—138-139
Gunfights, fast—106-107

H

Haight-Ashbury—135, 136
Hair
    ironing—139
    long—133-137
    two-tone—84
    waxing—95-96
    See also Ape hair style; Bobbed hair; Bouffant hairdo; Crew cut; Dodgson Elvis hairdo; Dorothy Hamill hairdo; Marienbad cut; Sideburns; Wigs
Hair (musical)—136
Hamill, Dorothy—187
"Happy Days"—188, 189
Harem skirt—30-31
Hats—*See* Beach hats; Bowler hats; Eugenie hats; Pillbox hats
Head shops—135
Hippies—135, 136
Hobble skirts—30
Hog Farm commune—131
Hootchy-kootchy ties—*See* Neckties
Hopalong Cassidy—83-84
Horn and Hardart necklaces—*See* Necklaces
Hornby, Leslie—*See* Twiggy
Hot pants—169-171
Hot tubs—194-195
House of Wax—88
Howdy Doody (puppet)—66, 75-77
Hula hoops—104-105
Hunkerin'—107
Hunter and victims—145

I

Ink-kissed kisses—26
Iron cross—145
"It" look—41

J

Jewelry, Indian—175-177
Jewelry, snakelike—22
Jerk—123
JFK Coloring Book—120
Johnson, Lyndon Baines—127, 128
Jug bands—127
Jungle jackets—90-91
Juvenile delinquency—95

K

Kane, Helen—59
Kangaroo dip—31
Kennedy, Jaquelin—116
Kermit the Frog (puppet)—200
Kewpie dolls—32-34
King Tut—47-48
Kiss Me Kate (film)—89
Kliban, P.—211
Klova—86
Knee watches—152
Kookie—107-108

L

Lambeth Walk—66-67
Last Year at Marienbad—122
Leary, Timothy—133, 134
Leg decoration—149
Light shows—135
L'il Abner—78
Lipstick, white—110
Locks, old—26
LSD (lysergic acid diethylamide)—133, 134, 135

M

Magic lantern—18-19
Mah-Jongg—43-44